Artificial Intelligence for Risk Mitigation in the Financial Industry

Scrivener Publishing
100 Cummings Center, Suite 541J
Beverly, MA 01915-6106

Publishers at Scrivener
Martin Scrivener (martin@scrivenerpublishing.com)
Phillip Carmical (pcarmical@scrivenerpublishing.com)

Artificial Intelligence for Risk Mitigation in the Financial Industry

Edited by

Ambrish Kumar Mishra
School of Management, Gautam Buddha University, Greater Noida, Uttar Pradesh, India

Shweta Anand
School of Management, Gautam Buddha University, Greater Noida, Uttar Pradesh, India

Narayan C. Debnath
Department of Software Engineering, Eastern International University, Vietnam

Purvi Pokhariyal
National Forensic Sciences University, Delhi

and

Archana Patel
National Forensic Sciences University, Gujarat, India

Scrivener
Publishing

This edition first published 2024 by John Wiley & Sons, Inc., 111 River Street, Hoboken, NJ 07030, USA and Scrivener Publishing LLC, 100 Cummings Center, Suite 541J, Beverly, MA 01915, USA
© 2024 Scrivener Publishing LLC
For more information about Scrivener publications please visit www.scrivenerpublishing.com.

Wiley Global Headquarters
111 River Street, Hoboken, NJ 07030, USA

For details of our global editorial offices, customer services, and more information about Wiley products visit us at www.wiley.com.

Limit of Liability/Disclaimer of Warranty
While the publisher and authors have used their best efforts in preparing this work, they make no representations or warranties with respect to the accuracy or completeness of the contents of this work and specifically disclaim all warranties, including without limitation any implied warranties of merchantability or fitness for a particular purpose. No warranty may be created or extended by sales representatives, written sales materials, or promotional statements for this work. The fact that an organization, website, or product is referred to in this work as a citation and/or potential source of further information does not mean that the publisher and authors endorse the information or services the organization, website, or product may provide or recommendations it may make. This work is sold with the understanding that the publisher is not engaged in rendering professional services. The advice and strategies contained herein may not be suitable for your situation. You should consult with a specialist where appropriate. Neither the publisher nor authors shall be liable for any loss of profit or any other commercial damages, including but not limited to special, incidental, consequential, or other damages. Further, readers should be aware that websites listed in this work may have changed or disappeared between when this work was written and when it is read.

Library of Congress Cataloging-in-Publication Data

ISBN 978-1-394-17471-3

Cover image: Pixabay.Com
Cover design by Russell Richardson

Set in size of 11pt and Minion Pro by Manila Typesetting Company, Makati, Philippines

Printed in the USA

10 9 8 7 6 5 4 3 2 1

Contents

Preface

The financial industry plays a vital role in the social and economic development of any country. Economic growth lends complexity to operations, and the leveraging of technology-based decision tools is becoming prominent in today's world. Consequently, risk mitigation in the financial industry is tuning into this change with the integration of artificial intelligence (AI) systems. The audit process recognizes associated risks and suggests possible transformations to mitigate them. The idea of using AI technology in risk mitigation is not entirely new, because it has been used as a decision-support model for the auditors in past. Since the 1950s, researchers have tried to find opportunities to make machines act with human intelligence, and this started to happen at the beginning of the 21st century when machines became able to work on advanced algorithms and perform the analysis and decision-making more intelligently. Due to continuous advancement in technology, availability of enormous big data, and processing capacity, there is reason to believe that it will continue to make a significant impact in risk mitigation in the financial industry.

The applications of the financial industry incorporate vast volumes of structured and unstructured data to gain insight into the financial and non-financial performance of companies. As a result of exponentially increasing data, auditors and management professionals need to enhance processing capabilities while maintaining the effectiveness and reliability of the risk mitigation process. The risk mitigation and audit procedures are processes involving the progression of activities to "transform inputs into output." As AI systems continue to grow mainstream, it is difficult to imagine an aspect of risk mitigation in the financial industry that will not require AI-related assurance or AI-assisted advisory services. AI can be used as a strong tool in many ways, like the prevention of fraud, money laundering, and cybercrime, detection of risks and probability of NPAs at early stages, sound lending, etc. There is no closely related study, or a smaller number of studies, being published to help mitigate the risk in the financial industry with AI. Hence, there is a gap that inspires researchers to develop a strong foundation for prospective research that will benefit industries across the globe.

This is an introductory book that provides insights on the advantages of risk mitigation by the adoption of AI in the financial industry. The subject is not only restricted to individuals like researchers, auditors, and management professionals, but also includes decision-making authorities like government. By extensively exploring the implementation of AI in the risk mitigation process enhances the effectiveness and reliability of the process. This book is a valuable guide to the utilization of AI for risk mitigation and will serve as an important standalone reference for years to come.

We are deeply grateful to everyone who helped with this book and greatly appreciate the dedicated support and valuable assistance rendered by Martin Scrivener and the Scrivener Publishing team during its publication.

The Editors

Artificial Intelligence in Risk Management

Pankaj Yadav, Priya Gupta, Rajeev Sijariya and Yogesh Sharma*

*Atal Bihari Vajpayee School of Management and Entrepreneurship,
Jawaharlal Nehru University, New Delhi, India*

Abstract

The financial industry is well known for a high level of complexity in addition to a rapid rate of change; hence, it is important that effective risk management practices should be put into place. Traditional methods of risk management have many limitations, such as their inability to manage huge amounts of data, their inability to react quickly to swings in the market, and their inability to give real-time monitoring of market trends. Artificial intelligence (AI) can enhance the efficiency and effectiveness of risk management in the financial sector using deep learning, machine learning algorithms, and natural language processing. These methods can be used to ascertain the existence of potential threats, unearth fraudulent activities, and provide predictive analytics that are helpful in making decisions. The application of artificial intelligence to risk management has the potential to significantly improve decision-making and to reduce risks and raise overall financial stability. These benefits could be achieved through the use of artificial intelligence. The chapter presents an in-depth review of the potential ways in which AI could improve risk management methods in the financial industry. The chapter includes types of risks in the financial industry with the light on the various advantages that artificial intelligence could bring to mitigate this risk. These advantages include the capacity to analyze huge volumes of data and the flexibility to respond to altering market conditions. The chapter will also discuss real-time monitoring of market trends as well as alerts for potential risks, different tools of artificial intelligence make it possible for businesses to proactively manage the risks to which they are exposed. This chapter will provide an insight into the opportunities and limitations and ethical challenges of this technology by providing the tools and methodologies that are used in AI-based risk management.

Corresponding author: yogesh.ysharma93@gmail.com

Ambrish Kumar Mishra, Shweta Anand, Narayan C. Debnath, Purvi Pokhariyal and Archana Patel (eds.) Artificial Intelligence for Risk Mitigation in the Financial Industry, (1–26) © 2024 Scrivener Publishing LLC

Keywords: Artificial intelligence, machine learning, risk management, sentiment analysis, predictive analysis

1.1   Introduction

The financial industry operates within a dynamic and intricate environment that is characterized by complicated transactions, volatile markets, and regulatory limits. This environment is necessary for the sector to function effectively. In recent years, there have been significant shifts in the global economy as a result of technology upheavals, economic uncertainties, and evolving geopolitical landscapes. These factors have shaped these changes. It is essential to be aware that the financial sector makes a considerable contribution to the economy of the entire world, accounting for approximately 7%–8% of the total gross domestic product (GDP) of the entire world[1]. The contribution of India's financial sector to the country's GDP has been gradually expanding in recent years, reaching approximately 7.5% of the total[2].

The overall market capitalization of the global financial markets is measured in the trillions of dollars. These markets are enormous. For illustration, the New York Stock Exchange alone had a market capitalization of more than $19 trillion[3]. On the other hand, throughout the course of the past few years, the stock market in India has experienced a substantial amount of expansion. The overall market capitalization of the Bombay Stock Exchange (BSE) was close to $3 trillion [1].

The global banking industry is controlled by significant businesses based in a variety of geographic locations. To give just one illustration, the 10 largest banks in the world collectively have assets that are worth trillions of dollars. According to S&P Global Market Intelligence, the banking industry in India is made up of a combination of public sector, private sector, and international banks. The State Bank of India (SBI), which is India's most prominent financial institution, has assets worth more than 600 billion dollars in total (Information obtained from the State Bank of India).

---

[1]https://www.investopedia.com/ask/answers/030515/what-percentage-global-economy-comprised-financial-services-sector.asp, extracted on May 10, 2023.

[2]https://static.pib.gov.in/WriteReadData/userfiles/file/EconomicSurvey2023Q44O.pdf (Accessed on May 10, 2023).

[3]https://www.forbes.com/advisor/investing/nyse-new-york-stock-exchange (Data extracted on May 10, 2023).

When the economy of India is compared to the economy of the world as a whole, it becomes abundantly evident that both must contend with the presence of a unique set of challenges. Following the global economic crisis of 2008, governments and financial institutions in every region of the world came to the realization that they needed to do a better job of risk management.

As a direct consequence of this, artificial intelligence (AI) is being applied in an increasing number of risk assessment methodologies, leading to the creation of risk models that are more accurate. The major global financial centers of New York, London, and Hong Kong have been at the forefront of the use of artificial intelligence for risk management. These major global financial centers have been utilizing AI's capabilities to minimize systemic risks, handle credit and market risks, and combat financial crime. The way risk management is carried out in these spheres has been revolutionized by AI, which has enabled financial institutions to better keep up with the rapid shifts that are occurring in the market and in the rules.

It has become essential for financial institutions all over the world to include AI into their risk management processes. This gives these institutions the ability to negotiate the intricacies and difficulties connected with modern banking. Real-time monitoring, predictive analytics, and the ability to automate decision-making are just a few of the benefits offered by risk management systems that are powered by artificial intelligence. These technologies give financial institutions the ability to recognize possible hazards, spot irregularities, and react quickly to newly emerging dangers, thereby boosting their capacity to protect investments and keep operations steady.

1.1.1 Context and the Driving Force Behind It

For the purpose of guaranteeing financial stability, protecting investments, and defending the interests of stakeholders, effective risk management is an absolute necessity. Traditional techniques of risk management, on the other hand, have a difficult time keeping up with the volumes of data that need to be managed, responding quickly to fluctuations in the market, and providing real-time monitoring of market trends. In this chapter, these constraints are discussed, and an investigation of the potential of artificial intelligence to improve risk management in the financial sector is conducted.

1.1.2   Aim of This Chapter

To provide an in-depth understanding of how AI can improve risk management practices in the financial industry is the primary purpose of this chapter. The goals of this chapter are to:

a) Explain what artificial intelligence is and how it relates to risk management.
b) Engage in a discussion on the shortcomings of conventional approaches to risk management.
c) Investigate the potential applications of a variety of AI-based methodologies, including deep learning, machine learning algorithms, and natural language processing, in the context of risk management.
d) Discuss the difficulties and factors to consider when putting artificial intelligence into risk management systems.
e) Explain the benefits of artificial intelligence, such as its capacity to process large amounts of data and adapt quickly to shifting market conditions.
f) Give some background information on the approaches and tools that are utilized in AI-based risk management.
g) Discuss the restrictions, obstacles, and ethical concerns that are involved with the use of AI in risk management.
h) As a last step, provide a high-level summary of the potential effects that AI could have on decision-making, risk reduction, and overall financial stability.

1.1.3   Outline of This Chapter

This chapter is structured as follows: Section 1.2 provides an overview of risk management in the financial sector. Section 1.3 discusses the role of artificial intelligence in risk management. Section 1.4 addresses the issues that arise when implementing AI-based risk management systems. Section 1.5 highlights the advantages of utilizing artificial intelligence in risk management. Section 1.6 delves into the methodologies and tools available for AI-based risk management. Section 1.7 examines the limitations and key considerations associated with AI-based risk management. Finally, Section 1.8 concludes the chapter, summarizing the main points discussed throughout.

1.2   The Role of AI in Risk Management

1.2.1   The Significance of Risk Management

Risk management is very important in the financial industry, which is subject to numerous different sorts of risks, such as market risk, credit risk, liquidity risk, operational risk, and regulatory compliance risk [2]. Institutions in this industry are susceptible to all of these types of risks. It is possible for financial institutions to identify, evaluate, and mitigate risks through effective risk management, which in turn ensures the stability and resilience of the institutions' operational processes. It entails the formulation and execution of plans, policies, and procedures with the purpose of proactively managing risks while simultaneously optimizing returns on investments [3].

In a nutshell, risk management is important because it enables businesses to foresee the occurrence of prospective risks and take preventative measures before the dangers actually materialize. It secures an organization's reputation, prevents financial losses, helps with decision-making, guarantees compliance, provides operational continuity, and cultivates confidence and trust among stakeholders. In today's increasingly volatile economic climate, businesses can improve their resiliency, adaptability, and long-term success by putting in place effective risk management practices.

1.2.2   Deficiencies in Conventional Methods of Risk Management

Methods of risk management that have been around for a long time have a number of drawbacks that reduce their efficiency in today's fast shifting financial world. These restrictions include the following:

a) An inability to manage big quantities of data: Financial organizations produce enormous volumes of data from a variety of sources, including trading operations, customer information, market data, and regulatory reports. These institutions face a challenge when it comes to managing these data. When dealing with datasets of this size, traditional approaches frequently struggle to perform an effective processing and analysis [4].

b) An absence of real-time monitoring: Conventional risk management systems often rely on monthly reports and assessments, which may not provide real-time insights into newly developing risks and market trends. This lag in knowledge makes it more difficult to make decisions in a timely manner and raises exposure to the possibility of risks [5].

c) A limited capacity to adjust to changes in market conditions: The financial markets are notorious for their volatility and their constantly shifting conditions. Traditional techniques of risk management may be unable to respond rapidly enough to these market movements, which may result in delayed risk mitigation steps and possible financial losses [6].

d) Traditional methods of risk management frequently rely on historical data and statistical models to evaluate risks, which can limit their ability to make accurate predictions. Although these strategies are useful, it is possible that they might not properly capture complicated patterns, developing risks, or changing market dynamics. It is possible that they do not have the predictive skills necessary to foresee and avert future risks [7].

In order for organizations to address these shortcomings, they need to adopt risk management strategies that are more comprehensive and look further into the future. This involves the adoption of integrated risk management frameworks, the promotion of a culture that is risk-aware, the use of advanced analytics and data-driven insights, the improvement of risk communication practices, and the encouragement of cross-functional collaboration. The ability of organizations to successfully traverse uncertainty and create long-term resilience can be improved via the remediation of these weaknesses.

1.2.3 The Requirement for Advanced Methods

The dynamic and complicated nature of today's business environments necessitates the use of more advanced risk management techniques. Traditional risk management approaches may fail to address emerging hazards and constantly changing risk landscapes effectively. Because of the constraints of more conventional approaches to risk management, there is an urgent requirement for the development of more sophisticated strategies to improve risk management in the financial industry [8]. The use of data analysis, pattern recognition, and real-time processing are all areas in which artificial intelligence excels, making it a promising tool for developing potential solutions [4]. Artificial intelligence-based risk management has the potential to transcend the limits of traditional methods and create risk management tactics that are more accurate, efficient, and proactive [2]. Organizations can improve their ability to identify, assess, and mitigate risks in a business environment that is continually evolving by adopting more advanced ways of risk management and putting those approaches into practice. These techniques make use of cutting-edge technologies, analytics, and data integration so that real-time risk monitoring, predictive insights, scenario analysis, and dynamic risk assessments may be carried out. The implementation of sophisticated risk management strategies helps organizations to make decisions that are both proactive and well-informed in order to effectively minimize risks.

1.3   Role of Artificial Intelligence in Risk Management

1.3.1   An Overview of Artificial Intelligence and Its Applications

Artificial intelligence is a branch of computer science that works on making machines smart enough to do tasks that usually require a smart person. AI includes machine learning, natural language processing, computer vision, robotics, recommendation systems, autonomous cars, healthcare applications, banking services, virtual assistants, and cybersecurity. AI lets machines learn from data, understand language, read visual information, automate processes, make predictions, and solve hard problems. It can be used in many different fields, changing how we deal with technology, making us more efficient, and giving us better ways to make decisions. Organizations can improve their risk identification, assessment, and mitigation capabilities by using AI in this area. Thanks to AI, we can now perform tasks like real-time monitoring, fraud detection, scenario analysis, risk communication, and informed decision-making. To guarantee competent and ethical risk management, however, AI must be utilized in tandem with human skill and judgment.

The goal of the field of study and technology known as artificial intelligence is to develop intelligent computer systems that are capable of emulating human-like intelligence and decision-making capabilities. The algorithms that power AI are able to process large volumes of data, recognize patterns, gain knowledge from previous experiences, and then either make predictions or perform actions based on that information. In the context of risk management, artificial intelligence presents a significant opportunity to improve the speed and accuracy of risk assessment, fraud detection, and decision-making procedures.

1.3.2   Applications of AI-Based Methods in Risk Management

AI-based methods have changed risk management in a lot of different areas by giving people better ways to measure and deal with risks. These methods can be used in a number of important ways. First, AI algorithms use historical data, market trends, and outside factors to correctly evaluate risks and predict possible outcomes. This lets risk management be proactive. Second, AI is very good at finding fraud. It does this by using anomaly detection and pattern recognition to look at huge amounts of transactional data and find suspicious actions in real time. This helps organizations avoid losing money. Third, AI is an important part of cybersecurity because it helps strengthen defenses by analyzing network data, finding oddities, and finding potential cyber threats. This lets organizations keep an eye on and protect critical infrastructure, find weaknesses, and quickly react to new cybersecurity threats. AI also helps with credit risk management by looking at information about borrowers, their payment history, their financial statements, and data from the market. This gives correct assessments of credit risk and helps lenders make smart lending decisions.

This section examines a variety of AI-based strategies that might be utilized for risk management within the financial sector, including the following:

• **Deep Learning for Risk Assessment**
Deep learning is a subfield of AI that involves the processing of complicated data representations and the identification of significant patterns using artificial neural networks. Deep learning algorithms can examine past data on market conditions, financial accounts, and other information that is pertinent to the risk assessment process in order to detect potential risks. Deep learning models are able to deliver more accurate risk predictions when compared to more typical statistical models, since they can recognize more complex linkages and nonlinear correlations [9].

• **Fraud Detection Methods Employing Machine Learning Algorithms**
Detecting fraudulent actions in the financial industry using machine learning algorithms is one of the many important applications of artificial intelligence. These algorithms can learn to recognize patterns and abnormalities in behavior that are characteristic of fraudulent activity by being trained on past examples of fraud. Machine learning models are able to

analyze vast volumes of transactional data, monitor behavioral patterns, and flag questionable behaviors, all of which contribute to the early detection and prevention of fraud [10].

• Applications of Natural Language Processing to the Study of Emotion
Techniques referred to as Natural Language Processing (NLP) provide computers the ability to comprehend and make sense of human discourse. In the field of risk management, natural language processing algorithms can be used to analyze textual data taken from news stories, social media, and financial reports. This can help assess the impact of events on the financial landscape, gauge market sentiment, and identify developing risks. The use of NLP to perform sentiment analysis can give risk managers significant insights that can help them make informed decisions [11, 12].

• Other AI Techniques in Risk Management
In addition to deep learning, machine learning, and natural language processing, additional artificial intelligence methods such as reinforcement learning, expert systems, and genetic algorithms are also viable options for use in risk management [13, 14]. The optimization of risk mitigation measures is possible with the help of reinforcement learning algorithms, which continuously learn from feedback and alter actions accordingly. Expert systems are able to both capture domain expertise and make suggestions for risk management based on previously set criteria [15]. In order to generate effective investment strategies and take into account risk–return trade-offs, genetic algorithms can be of assistance in optimizing investment portfolios.

By utilizing these AI-based methodologies, financial institutions have the potential to gain considerable advantages in risk management. Some of these advantages include increased risk assessment accuracy, enhanced fraud detection capabilities, and decision-making processes that are more informed.

1.4   The Challenges of Implementing AI-Based Risk Management Systems

There are many problems that come with putting AI-based risk management systems into the finance field. These include making sure data are good and available, taking into account ethics and regulations, making sure models can be understood, integrating AI systems with existing infrastructure, filling talent gaps, managing organizational change, making sure regulations are followed and risks are managed, and keeping AI models strong and resilient. To overcome these problems, you need to put in place data governance processes, follow ethical guidelines, develop model interpretability techniques, make sure models work well with existing systems, invest in developing talent, handle change well, set up regulatory compliance frameworks, and put in place strong monitoring and validation mechanisms. Working with peers in the industry, regulators, and AI experts can give you useful insights and tips on how to handle these challenges and get the most out of AI-based risk management in the finance sector. These challenges include the following:

• **Data Quality and Availability**
In order to successfully adopt AI-based risk management systems, one of the key hurdles that must be overcome is ensuring the availability and quality of data. When it comes to training and creating correct predictions, AI algorithms significantly rely on data that are both of high quality and relevant [16]. On the other hand, problems such as missing, inconsistent, or biased data, which can have a detrimental impact on the performance and dependability of AI models, may be encountered by financial organizations. In addition, there are additional difficulties that need to be handled, such as guaranteeing data privacy and security and gaining access to important data from a variety of sources [17].

• **Bias and Fairness in Algorithmic Decisions**
The algorithms that make up AI are prone to have biases, both those that are built in and those that are learned from the training data. In the context of the management of risks, algorithmic bias can lead to unfair treatment, discrimination, or an inadequate risk assessment for particular individuals or groups [18]. In order to prevent unexpected outcomes and continue to maintain regulatory compliance, it is vital to remove algorithmic bias and ensure fairness in AI-based risk management systems. Methods such as data pretreatment, training datasets that are varied and representative, and algorithmic audits are some examples of techniques that might assist in eliminating bias and improve fairness [19].

• **Considerations with Regard to the Law and Ethics**
When putting into practice risk management systems that are powered by AI, it is necessary to give careful consideration to legislative requirements and ethical consequences [19]. Financial institutions have a responsibility to ensure that they are in conformity with all applicable legislation,

such as those pertaining to data protection, privacy, and laws that prohibit discrimination. It is very important to have AI models that are transparent and can be explained in order to satisfy regulatory requirements and earn the trust of stakeholders [20]. For the purpose of upholding ethical norms and mitigating potential risks, artificial intelligence system development and deployment must incorporate ethical considerations such as accountable and transparent AI use, responsible AI application, and transparency [21].

• **Explicability and Openness to Public Inspection**
AI models, particularly those based on deep learning and other complicated machine learning algorithms, have the potential to be interpreted as "black boxes" due to the lack of transparency that exists within their decision-making processes. When it comes to risk management, where stakeholders want explicable rationale for choices and risk assessments, this lack of explainability and openness is a barrier [22]. It is essential for risk managers, auditors, and regulators to ensure that artificial intelligence models are explainable and interpretable in order to comprehend the decision-making process and evaluate the robustness and dependability of the models [23].

To effectively address these difficulties, a comprehensive strategy is required, one that includes the participation of risk management specialists, data scientists, ethicists, and regulators in collaborative effort. The incorporation of data governance practices, the adoption of techniques for bias detection and mitigation, adherence to regulatory norms, and the development of AI models that are visible and explainable are crucial steps toward addressing the problems connected with the implementation of AI-based risk management systems [24].

1.5   The Benefits of Using Artificial Intelligence in Risk Management

Using artificial intelligence in risk management can help organizations in a number of important ways. AI makes risk assessment better by analyzing a lot of data from many different sources. This leads to more accurate and complete risk assessments. AI's ability to quickly handle large amounts of data makes real-time risk monitoring possible. This lets organizations find risks quickly and act on them right away. AI is very good at finding fraud. It does this by using anomaly detection and pattern recognition to find suspicious behaviors and stop money from being lost. Automation of physical tasks makes operations more efficient, cuts down on mistakes, and frees up people to work on more important tasks. AI's predictive analytics use past data and machine learning algorithms to predict future risks, which helps with preparing for risks and making decisions. AI's main benefits are that it can be used on a large scale and can adapt to new situations. It can also handle large and complex datasets and learn from new information all the time. Cost savings are made possible by less physical labor, fewer losses, and more efficient use of resources. AI-based risk management systems give you tools to help you make decisions based on facts and information. Overall, the benefits of AI in risk management include better risk assessment, real-time monitoring, fraud detection, automation, predictive analytics, scalability, adaptability, cost savings, and decision support. This helps organizations improve their risk management practices and get better business results. These benefits include the following:

• **Conducting Analyses on Massive Amounts of Data**

Utilizing artificial intelligence in risk management is advantageous for a number of reasons, but one of the most important is its capacity to analyze massive amounts of data quickly [25]. Trading operations, customer information, market data, and regulatory reports are just some of the sources that contribute to the massive amounts of data that are produced by financial institutions. AI algorithms, such as machine learning and deep learning models, are able to handle and analyze these huge datasets in a timely and accurate manner, thereby eliciting new insights that might improve risk assessment and decision-making procedures [22].

• **Continuous Observation of Changes in Market Trends**

Traditional methods of risk management frequently rely on periodic reports and evaluations, which can result in delayed knowledge and responses to newly developing risks and market trends [26]. The ability to provide real-time monitoring and analysis of market movements is an area in which AI-based risk management solutions thrive [5]. AI models can spot patterns, detect abnormalities, and deliver early alerts by continuously gathering and analyzing data from many sources. This enables risk managers to proactively respond to possible risks and grasp opportunities.

• **Application of Predictive Analytics to Risk Evaluation**

The application of AI algorithms, which are equipped with tremendous predictive skills, has the potential to significantly improve risk assessment in the financial industry [27]. Traditional methods of risk assessment place a heavy reliance on historical data and statistical models, both of which have their limitations and may not adequately represent more complex patterns or the continually shifting dynamics of the market. The use of machine learning techniques, which allow AI-based risk management systems to learn from historical data and recognize trends, enables more accurate risk forecasts [14]. Artificial intelligence models can provide a more comprehensive and forward-looking picture of potential risks if they take into consideration a wider range of components and their interdependencies [2].

• Robotics and Operational Effectiveness

Automating time-consuming and repetitive operations is one of the ways that AI-based risk management solutions let risk managers focus on higher-value activities. AI helps to improve overall efficiency by streamlining risk management operations, reducing the likelihood of errors caused by humans, and automating data collecting, preprocessing, and analysis [25]. This automation not only helps risk managers save time but also enables them to more effectively allocate their expertise and resources, which ultimately improves the efficiency with which risk management policies are implemented.

• Improved Capacity for Decision-Making

Artificial intelligence-based risk management solutions provide significant insights and recommendations that aid in the process of decision-making. These systems help risk managers evaluate risks, evaluate potential repercussions, and find appropriate risk mitigation measures by employing advanced analytics and machine learning algorithms. These systems also aid risk managers in identifying appropriate risk mitigation techniques. The insights that are generated by data and offered by AI models allow risk managers to make decisions that are more informed and evidence-based, which improves the accuracy and efficacy of risk management practices [28].

Incorporating AI into risk management processes has a number of potential benefits, including the ability to analyze enormous amounts of data, real-time monitoring of market trends, predictive analytics for risk assessment, proactive risk management, automation, efficiency, and improved decision-making. Other potential benefits include monitoring market trends in real-time, monitoring big volumes of data, automating decision-making, and monitoring market trends in real time. Financial institutions may increase their risk management practices and navigate the complex and dynamic financial landscape more successfully if they take advantage of these benefits and harness their potential.

1.6 Conclusions and Future Considerations of AI in Risk Management

1.6.1 A Brief Review of the Role of AI in Risk Management

The application of artificial intelligence in risk management within the financial sector has been investigated throughout this chapter. It explored how AI-based approaches may improve risk management practices and emphasized the limitations of traditional risk management methods. These limitations were highlighted, and it discussed how AI-based approaches can overcome these limitations. This chapter examined a variety of artificial intelligence techniques that, among other things, help improve risk assessment, fraud detection, and decision-making procedures [25]. Some examples of these techniques include deep learning, machine learning algorithms, and natural language processing. In addition, it addressed the difficulties that are involved with the deployment of AI, such as the quality of the data, the biases introduced by algorithms, the concerns raised by regulatory authorities, and the requirement for explainability and transparency [23]. At the end of the chapter, a discussion of the benefits of AI in risk management was presented. These benefits included the analysis of vast amounts of data, real-time monitoring of market trends, predictive analytics, proactive risk management, automation, efficiency, and improved decision-making [29].

1.6.2 Perspectives on the Future

The application of artificial intelligence in risk management is a field that is quickly advancing, and there are various future prospects that should be considered:

• **Advancements in AI Techniques**
The continued development of AI technologies will lead to the invention of novel approaches and algorithms, which will make it possible to conduct risk assessments and make predictions that are even more precise. Deep learning, reinforcement learning, and other areas of artificial intelligence that are advancing will lead to the development of risk management systems that are more sophisticated. These systems will be able to handle large datasets, recognize hidden patterns, and adapt more effectively to shifting market dynamics.

• **Application of AI in Conjunction with Other Technologies**
Integrating AI with other technologies, such as blockchain, the Internet of Things (IoT), and cloud computing, can result in additional improvements to the capabilities of AI [30]. This integration has the potential to supply extra layers of security, maintain the integrity of data, and collect data in real time, which will enable more comprehensive risk management systems. Combining AI with blockchain, for instance, can improve the accuracy of fraud detection while increasing the auditability and openness of financial transactions [31].

• **Responsible and Ethical Artificial Intelligence**
The responsible application of AI in risk management will remain an important area of concentration. Stakeholders have a responsibility to ensure that AI models and systems are built and put into production in a responsible manner, taking into account concerns such as algorithmic bias, fairness, privacy, and accountability [23]. The development and application of AI-based risk management systems will be guided by ethical principles and rules [19]. This will ensure that the systems are in line with societal values, that they do not cause harm to individuals, and that they do not perpetuate discrimination.

• **Collaboration Between Humans and Machines**
Fostering productive collaboration between humans and machines is where artificial intelligence stands to make the most progress in many fields [32]. Even if AI can automate jobs and deliver useful insights, there is still no substitute for the expertise and judgment of humans. The role of risk managers will shift in the future to place a greater emphasis on strategic decision-making, the interpretation of insights given by AI, and the verification of the outputs created by AI models [33]. The optimal results in risk management can be achieved through the collaboration of humans and machines by utilizing the strengths of each.

1.6.3   The Transformative Power of AI in Risk Management

It is possible that the application of AI in risk management may completely transform the financial industry by enabling more accurate risk assessment, proactive risk mitigation, and improved decision-making [26]. Financial institutions can analyze large volumes of data, monitor real-time market movements, and predict risks more accurately by employing AI techniques such as deep learning, machine learning, and natural language processing [25]. However, the adoption of AI-based risk management systems must address difficulties relating to data quality, algorithmic bias, transparency, and ethical considerations in order to be successful [4]. AI has the potential to revolutionize risk management practices and assist financial institutions in navigating the intricacies of a financial landscape that is always shifting. This can be accomplished with the correct strategy.

1.7   The Implications and Factors to Take Into Account While Using AI in Risk Management

a) Navigating Implications and Considerations of AI

The use of artificial intelligence in risk management brings about a variety of implications and concerns that need to be addressed before moving further. Artificial intelligence, despite the fact that it presents substantial benefits, also presents new obstacles and potential risks. Within the context of risk management in the financial industry, this chapter examines the consequences and factors to take into mind connected with AI.

b) Implications for Ethical Behavior

When it comes to risk management, the employment of AI presents certain ethical problems. AI algorithms arrive at conclusions based on the examination of patterns and data, but they do not possess the moral judgment of humans [19]. When AI systems are used to make judgements that have repercussions for persons or groups, this might give rise to ethical conundrums. The ethical consequences of entirely relying on AI for risk management need to be carefully considered by financial institutions, and these institutions must also make certain that human oversight and responsibility are maintained [16].

c) Expertise and Judgment Relating to People

Although AI algorithms are great tools, they should not be used in place of the knowledge and discretion of humans when it comes to risk management [34]. Interpreting the insights that AI has created, validating the results of models, and making decisions based on that information require human interaction and oversight. Collaboration between AI and human risk managers is essential for striking a balance between human judgment and automation in risk management [35]. This collaboration is also necessary for ensuring the ethical and effective use of AI in risk management.

d) Governance and Compliance With Regulatory Authorities

The use of AI in risk management systems necessitates the establishment of a solid governance framework in addition to the observance of regulatory norms. In order to properly integrate artificial intelligence, data governance, model validation, and risk assessment, financial organizations need to establish clear policies and procedures [26]. In addition, they need to ensure compliance with data protection, privacy, and anti-discrimination rules in order to reduce the potential legal and reputational risks that are linked with the utilization of AI [20].

e) Dangers to Physical and Digital Security

Artificial intelligence technologies that are used in risk management are vulnerable to security flaws and cyber risks. In order to prevent unauthorized access, manipulation, or security breaches, it is imperative that financial institutions employ stringent cybersecurity measures [36]. This will secure AI models, data, and communication channels. When it comes to protecting AI-based risk management systems from cyberattacks, one of the most important things that can be done is to adhere to the best practices in the industry and use advanced security measures.

f) Confidentiality of Data and Openness of Access

For both training and decision-making, artificial intelligence relies on vast volumes of data, which raises concerns about the privacy and transparency of data. Privacy of customer data should be a top priority for all financial institutions; this should be accomplished by ensuring compliance with all applicable data protection rules and putting in place practices that preserve customer confidentiality [37]. In addition, it is vital that there is openness in artificial intelligence models and the decision-making processes in order for stakeholders to understand how risk assessments are produced, which enables trust and accountability.

g) Lessening the Effects of Prejudice and Discrimination

It is possible for artificial intelligence models to unwittingly inherit biases from the data on which they are trained, which can lead to biased outcomes in risk management. Approaches such as varied and representative training datasets, bias detection and mitigation strategies, and continual monitoring and auditing of AI systems are some of the methods that financial institutions need to adopt in order to actively address and mitigate biases in artificial intelligence algorithms [38]. It is absolutely necessary, in order to keep up trust and ethical standards, to conduct risk management in a fair and nondiscriminatory manner [19].

h) Unceasing Surveillance and Evaluation
When AI is used in risk management, it is necessary to perform ongoing monitoring and evaluation in order to determine the degree to which it is useful and to pinpoint any potential limitations or deficiencies. Establishing effective monitoring tools to track the performance of artificial intelligence models, identifying drift or decrease in accuracy, and taking corrective actions when appropriate should be a priority for financial institutions [39]. It is important for AI-based risk management systems to undergo routine audits and reviews so that they can maintain their reliability, accountability, and ongoing progress [38].

i) Cooperative Efforts and the Exchange of Information
The application of artificial intelligence in risk management ought to involve cooperation and the exchange of information between various industrial stakeholders, regulatory bodies, and academic institutions. A better understanding of the benefits and risks posed by AI for risk management can be achieved through the sharing of best practices, experiences, and lessons learned [26]. The development of standards, norms, and frameworks that encourage the ethical and responsible use of artificial intelligence in the financial industry can also be made possible through collaboration [21].

j) Leveraging AI for Ethical and Secure Risk Management in Financial Institutions
The use of artificial intelligence involves careful consideration of its ethical implications, human expertise, governance, security, data protection, bias reduction, and continual monitoring. This is despite the fact that AI provides enormous potential for improving risk management in the financial sector. Financial institutions are able to reap the benefits of artificial intelligence in risk management by addressing the aforementioned factors. In doing so, they can also ensure ethical practices, regulatory compliance, and the protection of both individuals and organizations.

1.8   Overcoming Obstacles and Putting AI to Work in Risk Management

a) Overcoming Challenges and Achieving Seamless Deployment
The application of artificial intelligence in risk management involves a number of obstacles as discussed earlier, each of which needs to be conquered before the integration can be considered successful. This chapter

focuses on overcoming these problems and provides insights into effectively deploying AI-based risk management systems within the financial industry. The chapter is titled "AI-Based Risk Management Systems for the Financial Sector."

b) The Quality of the Data and Their Preparation

In order to successfully integrate AI in risk management, one of the most significant issues involves ensuring the high quality and dependability of the data that are utilized for training and analysis. The procedures of data cleansing, normalization, and validation are examples of the kind of data quality projects that financial organizations need to invest in. This requires locating discrepancies, inaccuracies, and missing values within the data and devising solutions to fix them. In addition, robust data governance practices need to be built in order to preserve the correctness, completeness, and consistency of the data over the course of time.

c) Bias and Fairness in Algorithmic Decisions

When it comes to the application of AI in risk management, one of the most serious concerns is algorithmic bias. It is possible for historical data to give rise to biases, which can then lead to biased results or the unfair treatment of persons or groups. Techniques for bias detection and mitigation should be implemented in order for financial institutions to successfully address this challenge. This requires analyzing AI models for potential biases, thinking about alternate data sources, and implementing algorithms that are aware of fairness issues. It is vital to do routine monitoring and auditing of AI systems in order to guarantee fairness and protect against any harm.

d) The Capacity for Interpretation and Explanation

It might be challenging to comprehend the logic behind the judgments made by AI algorithms because they frequently function in opaque environments. On the other hand, interpretability and explainability are absolutely necessary in risk management in order to ensure regulatory compliance, maintain transparency, and earn the trust of stakeholders. The development of interpretable artificial intelligence models that can offer financial institutions with reasons for their actions should be a primary goal. When it comes to risk management, explainable artificial intelligence can be accomplished through the use of strategies such as rule-based models, model-agnostic interpretability methodologies, and the incorporation of expert knowledge.

e) Integration with Previously Deployed Systems
The integration of artificial intelligence-based risk management systems with preexisting infrastructure and legacy systems can be a difficult task. The process of integration must be meticulously planned and designed by financial institutions in order to guarantee compatibility, data flow, and system interoperability. It is absolutely necessary for there to be close communication between risk management departments, IT teams, and AI experts in order to properly address integration difficulties. The implementation of standardized data formats and application programming interfaces (APIs), on the other hand, can make integration and the interchange of data much easier to do.

f) Talent and Skill Gap
The application of artificial intelligence in risk management necessitates the employment of trained specialists who have an in-depth knowledge of AI methods, the fundamentals of risk management, and extensive experience working in the financial sector. In order to close the talent and skill gap, financial institutions should make investments in the training and upskilling of their existing personnel. The development of specialized AI abilities that are applicable to risk management can be aided through collaborations with academic institutions, industry groups, and AI experts.

g) Things to Consider Regarding Regulations and Compliance
The application of AI in risk management must comply with all regulatory regulations and norms of compliance. In order to ensure that their AI-based risk management systems are in accordance with the relevant regulations, financial institutions should pay close attention to the applicable rules and actively participate in the relevant regulatory bodies' processes. This requires taking into consideration things like data protection and security, as well as ethics and any applicable financial restrictions. Proactive interaction with regulators can assist build a regulatory environment that is favorable and can also contribute to the formation of industry standards.

h) Tests and Validations That Are Reliable
It is vital to do exhaustive testing and validation on AI-based risk management systems prior to putting them into production in order to guarantee their precision, dependability, and efficiency. To evaluate the performance of AI models, examine their robustness against a variety of scenarios, and validate their outputs against established benchmarks or historical data, rigorous testing should be carried out. In order to guarantee that the

models are accurate when applied to real-world scenarios, validation pro-cedures need to take into account model stability, predictive power, and generalization capabilities.

i) Ongoing Observation and Efforts at Improvement

Continuous monitoring of AI-based risk management systems is neces-sary in order to identify and handle performance issues, model drift, and new risks as they emerge. Establishing monitoring frameworks that follow the performance of artificial intelligence models, assess their continuous usefulness, and identify potential for development should be a priority for financial institutions. To be able to accommodate the ever-shifting dynam-ics of the market and to ensure that AI models continue to be accurate and relevant, regular feedback loops, model recalibration, and retraining are required.

j) Cooperative Efforts and the Exchange of Information

It is vital for regulatory bodies, industry groups, technology providers, and financial institutions to work together and share their experience in order to solve hurdles and stimulate innovation in AI-based risk management. The act of sharing one's experiences, as well as one's best practices and les-sons learnt, can help to expedite the adoption of AI and jointly handle difficulties in a manner that is collaborative. In order to further push the successful deployment of AI in risk management, establishing industry standards, guidelines, and benchmarks can be helpful.

k) Overcoming Challenges for Effective AI Implementation in Risk Management

In order to successfully implement AI in risk management, it is necessary to solve difficulties relating to the quality of the data, algorithmic bias, interpretability, integration, skill gap, regulatory compliance, testing, and continuous development. If financial institutions can successfully navigate these difficulties, they will be able to leverage the potential of artificial intel-ligence to increase risk management practices, improve decision-making, and boost operational efficiency in today's changing financial world.

1.9   Conclusion

The financial sector is subject to an excess of dangers that are both intricate and dynamic, making it essential to implement efficient risk management practices. The conventional approaches to risk management have their drawbacks when it comes to managing massive volumes of data, responding rapidly to shifts in the market, and offering real-time monitoring of market tendencies. On the other hand, the implementation of artificial intelligence in the financial industry can greatly improve risk management.

Deep learning, machine learning algorithms, and natural language processing are some of the ways that artificial intelligence can be used to mitigate risks in the financial industry. AI also offers a number of other advantages. It makes it possible to identify potential dangers, detect fraudulent actions, and provide predictive analytics in order to make decision-making easier. One of the primary benefits of using AI in risk management is that it can analyze enormous amounts of data and adapt quickly to shifting market conditions.

Various AI systems enable real-time monitoring of market patterns and alerts for potential threats, giving firms the ability to proactively manage their exposures to risks. It is possible for financial institutions to improve their decision-making processes, minimize risks, and enhance overall financial stability by harnessing the power of AI.

Nevertheless, it is necessary to consider the opportunities, limitations, and ethical challenges that are linked with AI-based risk management. Artificial intelligence has the potential to deliver enormous benefits, such as enhanced efficiency and effectiveness; yet, it also necessitates careful consideration of ethical implications, data protection, and potential biases in algorithms.

Finally, the incorporation of AI into risk management procedures in the financial industry holds infinite promise for improving decision-making and reducing risk. By utilizing artificial intelligence technologies, financial institutions may improve their ability to traverse the complicated and ever-changing landscape of the financial sector, which will, in the end, encourage greater stability and resilience. Nevertheless, in order to ensure the appropriate and fruitful application of this technology in risk management, an AI deployment strategy that is intelligent and ethical is absolutely necessary.

References

1. Praveen Kumar, M. and Manoj Kumara, N.V., Market capitalization: Pre and post COVID-19 analysis. *Mater. Today Proc.*, 37, 2553–2557, 2021.
2. Leo, M., Sharma, S., Maddulety, K., Machine learning in banking risk management: A literature review. *Risks*, 7, 29, 2019.

3. Dupont, B., The cyber-resilience of financial institutions: Significance and applicability. *J. Cyber Secur.*, 5, 1, Jan. 2019.

4. Lee, I., Big data: Dimensions, evolution, impacts, and challenges. *Bus. Horiz.*, 60, 293–303, 2017.

5. Aldridge, I. and Krawciw, S., *Real-Time Risk: What Investors Should Know About Fintech, High-Frequency Trading, And Flash Crashes*, Wiley, Hoboken, NJ, USA, 2017.

6. Crotty, J., If financial market competition is intense, why are financial firm profits so high?: Reflections on the current "golden age" of finance, in: *Capitalism, Macroeconomics And Reality: Understanding Globalization, Financialization, Competition And Crisis*, Edward Elgar Publishing, Cheltenham, UK, 2017.

7. Ahmed, H. and Khan, T., Risk management in islamic banking, in: *Handbook of Islamic Banking*, M.K. Hassan and M.K. Lewis (Eds.), Edward Elgar Publishing, Cheltenham, UK, 2007.

8. Hubbard, D.W., *The Failure of Risk Management: Why It's Broken and How To Fix It*, Wiley, Hoboken, NJ, USA, 2020.

9. Heaton, J.B. and Polson, N., Deep learning for finance: Deep portfolios. *SSRN J.*, 33, 1, 3–12, 2016.

10. Ali, A., Abd Razak, S., Othman, S.H., Eisa, T.A.E., Al-Dhaqm, A., Nasser, M., Elhassan, T., Elshafie, H., Saif, A., Financial fraud detection based on machine learning: A systematic literature review. *Appl. Sci.*, 12, 9637, 2022.

11. Gao, R., Zhang, Z., Shi, Z., Xu, D., Zhang, W., Zhu, D., A review of natural language processing for financial technology, in: *International Symposium on Artificial Intelligence and Robotics 2021*, SPIE, p. 54, 2021.

12. Fisher, I.E., Garnsey, M.R., Hughes, M.E., Natural language processing in accounting, auditing and finance: A synthesis of the literature with a road-map for future research. *Intell. Syst. Account Finance Manag.*, 23, 157–214, 2016.

13. Lappas, P.Z. and Yannacopoulos, A.N., A machine learning approach combining expert knowledge with genetic algorithms in feature selection for credit risk assessment. *Appl. Soft Comput.*, 107, 107391, 2021.

14. Machado, M.R. and Karray, S., Assessing credit risk of commercial customers using hybrid machine learning algorithms. *Expert Syst. Appl.*, 200, 116889, 2022.

15. Hossain, E., Hossain, M.S., Zander, P.-O., Andersson, K., Machine learning with Belief Rule-Based Expert Systems to predict stock price movements. *Expert Syst. Appl.*, 206, 117706, 2022.

16. Enholm, I.M., Papagiannidis, E., Mikalef, P., Krogstie, J., Artificial intelligence and business value: A literature review. *Inf. Syst. Front.*, 24, 1709–1734, 2021.

17. Dwivedi, Y.K., Hughes, L., Ismagilova, E., Aarts, G., Coombs, C., Crick, T., Duan, Y., Dwivedi, R., Edwards, J., Eirug, A. *et al.*, Artificial Intelligence (AI):

Multidisciplinary perspectives on emerging challenges, opportunities, and agenda for research, practice and policy. *Int. J. Inf. Manage.*, 57, 101994, 2019.

18. Grgić-Hlača, N., Zafar, M.B., Gummadi, K.P., Weller, A., Beyond distributive fairness in algorithmic decision making: Feature selection for procedurally fair learning. *AAAI*, vol. 32, 2018.

19. Ayling, J. and Chapman, A., Putting AI ethics to work: Are the tools fit for purpose? *AI Ethics*, 2, 405–429, 2021.

20. Borgesius, F.J.Z., Strengthening legal protection against discrimination by algorithms and artificial intelligence. *Int. J. Hum. Rights*, 1–22, 2020.

21. Shneiderman, B., Bridging the gap between ethics and practice. *ACM Trans. Interact. Intell. Syst.*, 10, 1–31, 2020.

22. Fazi, M.B., Beyond human: deep learning, explainability and representation. *Theory Cult. Soc.*, 38, 7–8, 026327642096638, 2020.

23. Fritz-Morgenthal, S., Hein, B., Papenbrock, J., Financial risk management and explainable, trustworthy, responsible AI. *Front. Artif. Intell.*, 5, 779799, 2022.

24. Van Greuning, H. and Brajovic Bratanovic, S., *Analyzing Banking Risk (Fourth Edition): A Framework for Assessing Corporate Governance and Risk Management*, World Bank, Washington, DC, 2020.

25. Aziz, S. and Dowling, M.M., AI and machine learning for risk management. *SSRN J.*, 33–50, 2018.

26. O.E.C.D., *Artificial Intelligence Machine Learning and Big Data in Finance: Opportunities, Challenges,and Implications for Policy Makers*, Available at: https://www.oecd.org/finance/financial-markets/Artificial-intelligence-machine-learning-big-data-in-finance.pdf [Accessed May 23, 2023].

27. Broby, D., The use of predictive analytics in finance. *SSRN J.*, 8, 145-161, 2022.

28. Deiva Ganesh, A. and Kalpana, P., Future of artificial intelligence and its influence on supply chain risk management–a systematic review. *Comput. Ind. Eng.*, 169, 108206, 2022.

29. Bicheva, P. and Valchev, E., Methodology for implementation of intelligent risk management in the business processes of organizations, in: *Intelligent Sustainable Systems: Selected Papers of WorldS4 2022, Volume 1 Lecture Notes in Networks and Systems*, A.K. Nagar, D. Singh Jat, D.K. Mishra, A. Joshi (Eds.), pp. 127–139, Springer Nature Singapore, Singapore, 2023.

30. Gill, S.S., Tuli, S., Xu, M., Singh, I., Singh, K.V., Lindsay, D., Tuli, S., Smirnova, D., Singh, M., Jain, U. *et al.*, Transformative effects of IoT, blockchain and artificial Intelligence on cloud computing: Evolution, vision, trends and open challenges. *Internet Things*, 8, 100118, 2019.

31. Javaid, M., Haleem, A., Singh, R.P., Suman, R., Khan, S., A review of Blockchain Technology applications for financial services. *TBench*, 2, 100073, 2022.

32. Mühlhoff, R., Human-aided artificial intelligence: Or, how to run large computations in human brains? Toward a media sociology of machine learning. *New Media Soc.*, 22, 10, 146144481988533, 2019.

33. Howard, J., Artificial intelligence: Implications for the future of work. *Am. J. Ind. Med.*, 62, 917–926, 2019.

34. Busuioc, M., Accountable artificial intelligence: holding algorithms to account. *Public Adm. Rev.*, 81, 825–836, 2021.

35. Bannister, F. and Connolly, R., Administration by algorithm: A risk management framework. *Inf. Polity*, 25, 471–490, 2020.

36. Durodola, L.O., Towards a responsible use of artificial intelligence (AI) and fintech in modern banking, in: *Fintech, Artificial Intelligence And The Law: Regulation And Crime Prevention*, pp. 262–278, Routledge, London, 2021.

37. Martin, K.D., Kim, J.J., Palmatier, R.W., Steinhoff, L., Stewart, D.W., Walker, B.A., Wang, Y., Weaven, S.K., Data privacy in retail. *J. Retail.*, 2020.

38. Li, B., Qi, P., Liu, B., Di, S., Liu, J., Pei, J., Yi, J., Zhou, B., Trustworthy AI: from principles to practices. *ACM Comput. Surv.*, 96, 4, 474–489, 2022.

39. Zhang, Z., Hamadi, H.A., Damiani, E., Yeun, C.Y., Taher, F., Explainable artificial intelligence applications in cyber security: State-of-the-Art in Research. *IEEE Access*, 10, 93104–93139, 2022.

Application of Artificial Intelligence in Risk Assessment and Mitigation in Banks

Ankita Srivastava*, Bhartrihari Pandiya and Navtika Singh Nautiyal

National Forensic Sciences University, Gandhinagar, Gujarat, India

Abstract

The banking industry encounters several difficulties in efficiently handling the risks linked to lending, investment, and financial activities. Given the swift progress in technology, the utilization of artificial intelligence (AI) has become a valuable asset for banks to improve their risk evaluation and reduction procedures. The objective of this research is to identify and analyze the various aspects of AI application in risk assessment and mitigation in banks and to highlight the emerging research areas for future research and provide suggestions to bank community for mitigating risk. Scopus database was considered for performing the literature search, as it is widely accepted and authentic. The description of the various data like most cited authors, subject-wise division, country-wise analysis, etc., was done and results graphically. Bibliometric analysis was done using VOSviewer software. After conducting a thorough examination and assessment of various research studies, certain elements of artificial intelligence in the banking sector were comprehended. The future research topics, organized into clusters, have the potential for deeper exploration using real-world data sets. By carefully reviewing the selected research papers, several observations were made regarding the field of AI in banking, which in turn opened up new avenues for research. The research paper also discussed important theoretical implications such as formulating the role of artificial intelligence in evaluating risk mitigation of cognitive biases and human limitations and comprehension of data-driven decision-making processes.

Keywords: Artificial intelligence, banking, risk assessment, risk mitigation, bibliometric analysis

---

*Corresponding author: ankita.srivastava@nfsu.ac.in

Ambrish Kumar Mishra, Shweta Anand, Narayan C. Debnath, Purvi Pokhariyal and Archana Patel (eds.) Artificial Intelligence for Risk Mitigation in the Financial Industry, (27–52) © 2024 Scrivener Publishing LLC

2.1   Introduction

The use of artificial intelligence (AI) in the banking sector to manage risk has gained significant attention recently [1–3]. There has been an agreement on AI being the third largest technical revolution in economic history after the industrial revolution of the 19th century and of computer science in the 20th [4]. Banks experienced a transformation in banking practices and philosophy during the 1960s and 1980s, marking a shift from traditional banking [5, 6]. Banking 1.0 relied on traditional and historical banking and gave way to Banking 4.0, which includes cutting-edge technology employed in various sectors of banks, including the usage of AI technologies. Since the turn of the 20th century, banks have undergone an exhaustive revolution, encompassing deregulations, task automation for bankers, digitization of branch offices, and the development of innovative technologies [7–9]. One of the most important and revolutionary developments in finance in this century is fintech [10].

The combination of "finance" and "technology" formed the term "fintech" [11]. The goal of this financial technology deployment is to increase the efficiency and innovation of current services. The World Economic Forum of Geneva considered this fintech transition as the Fourth Industrial Revolution due to its significant influence. Recent research by consultants [12] found that AI can boost the value of the global banking sector by up to USD 1 trillion annually. Ross [13] projected that the global financial services sector would increase at a compound annual growth rate (CAGR) of 6% to reach USD 28.529 trillion by 2025–2030. This is mostly due to the extensive use of AI in the restructuring of banking operations, especially after recovering from COVID-19.

Financial institutions must adopt technological developments in the contemporary banking landscape in order to keep up with the evolving demands of their customers and an increasingly competitive market [14–19]. Artificial intelligence has been a major driver of many emerging technologies in the era of today's banking [20], resulting in creative disruptions of banking channels (such as automated teller machines, online banking, and mobile banking), services (such as check imaging, voice recognition, and chatbots), and solutions (such as AI investment advisers and AI credit selectors).

2.2   Transitions in Banking Due to AI

The transition from relying on human judgment to a robotized inquiry of client information is an outstanding indication of inventive technical advances that have significantly transformed the financial industry [21]. This development allowed the banks to seize nearby markets and opened them up to nationwide competition with other banks and financial institutions. In addition, proposals for retail loans are frequently evaluated using credit score tools built utilizing comprehensive authentic credit card information vaults [22, 23]. With this automated process, moneylenders can make loans without being physically present, which significantly lowers their guarantee and transaction expenses [24]. Because of this reliance on intricate data, endorsing appears simple to outside parties. Thus, it works with ancillary industry sectors to securitize retail advances, allowing non-bank companies that require finance to compete through capital market financing.

Given the increasing importance of cutting-edge technology in the financial sector, many fintech companies combine automated retail client analysis with more user-friendly interfaces to provide customers with more useful support at reduced costs [25, 26]. Peer-to-peer lending platforms, for instance, have emerged as alternative authoritative structures that attract borrowers with an enhanced fundamental loan application process. They examine these applications using credit rating tools and then directly connect financially sound borrowers with financial backers [27, 28]. Some of the areas of application of AI in banking are as follows:

a) **Customer Interface:** Virtual customer support is being tested by a variety of industry players as a way to provide an alternate type of customer service support, answering inquiries to respond to user questions, linking users to useful services, and providing pertinent text and speech suggestions. According to our research, the use of chatbots (text, speech, and video) by banks and concierge apps has been the most common usage of AI. Chatbots from a lot of commercial banks are accessible on mobile Facebook Messenger, Telegram, WhatsApp, and Twitter.

b) **Customer Insights and Personalization:** The researchers report that AI algorithms use cognitive tools to provide more personalized solutions to clients to foresee their needs and expectations and provide recommendations that are specific to them. Such process monitors content, behavior, and data sources and creates models from which practical information about people and content can be provided. It also matches products and services to customers' behavioral patterns and makes it easier to deliver customized advice on the basis of digital profiles and transactional history. For instance, YayPay, a start-up, uses machine learning (ML) to forecast client activity by looking at his or her past payment behavior and habits.

A neural network approach was utilized by Arif *et al.* [29] to research the obstacles that prevent clients from using Internet banking. In their 2019 study, Belanche *et al.* [30] look into what influences the adoption of AI-driven technology in the banking industry. Payne *et al.* [31] investigate the factors that influence the use of mobile banking services with AI integration. Furthermore, bank marketers have discovered a chance to employ AI to more effectively segment, target, and position their banking products and services.

c) **Business and Strategy Insights:** A deep understanding of the vast amounts of data that banks and other financial institutions retain and have at their disposal is made possible by AI technology. Such evaluation can enable more in-depth and timely insights into internal processes and external market trends, guiding prospective departmental strategies. For instance, a deeper understanding of customer data might help portfolio and marketing strategy. Business intelligence tool G-Square's Robo analytics tool, G-square Narrator, offers the user prescriptive analysis and useful business insights. In turn, this makes it easier to spot possibilities, gaps, and growth-oriented initiatives for financial companies. The world of digital payments is one area where the application of AI analytics can provide significant insights because there is a wealth of transaction data (users' transactions, queries, and requirements) at hand. Medhi and Mondal [32] emphasized the usage of AI-driven models to forecast outsourcing success.

d) **Facilitating Backend Processes:** AI is being used to support backend office processes, which can include enormous volumes of rule-based, highly organized, and methodical work. Customer onboarding, compliance monitoring, automated writing of investment/earning reports, and functional information extraction from pertinent financial documents are all examples of "intelligent automation" that can be performed using AI technologies. For instance, Signzy offers AI-assisted onboarding services to banks. Although the details of these "variety of jobs" have not been made public, there have been reports that SBI uses IBM Watson to carry them out [33]. ICICI has chosen an internal solution and is using its Software Robotics program to help with data entry, text mining, and literary formatting.

e) **Innovations:** Fintech has significantly affected the monetary system by potentially eliminating the need for involvement from third parties like banks. Blockchains and cryptocurrencies have the potential to disrupt the current economic system, since they are too young and immature to make strong predictions. Artificial intelligence systems and higher security spending may be able to reduce the risk of money laundering brought on by information and communications technology (ICT) in the financial industry [34]. By reducing data duplication and safeguarding it from fraud, blockchain can enable banks to safely communicate customer data across their organization and work on the authorized interaction [35]. As it enables both consumers and businesses to carry out transactions directly and access the same record of trades updated using cryptography, the use of blockchain innovation can enable banks to speed up the time for settlement [36]. The anticipated benefits of digital currencies and blockchain technology are sufficient to spark significant interest from tech-savvy individuals, large financial institutions, and, shockingly, crucial government administrations.

f) **Algorithm Trading:** The securities market has found use for AI's capacity to handle enormous amounts of unstructured data and intricate mathematical models and calculations, along with automations. The potential for such technologies to further facilitate algorithmic trading is being investigated, in addition to the wealth management applications. Companies like Trade Rays are using AI technologies to offer user-friendly algorithmic trading services.

g) **Wealth Management:** Despite the fact that wealth management companies had been among the least technologically savvy segments of the finance industry, they now run the risk of being rendered redundant in many fields as a result of the growing use of digital technologies that offer algorithm-based portfolio management advice [37]. Machine learning is used in predictive models to evaluate data and identify trends that might guide potential investors in selecting the best product for their portfolio and provide information on price changes in the future. In other applications, AI-based systems examine a user's income, savings, and spending in order to create a financial plan that is effective and meets his or her needs [38].

h) **Credit Lending Process:** Research on AI in the banking sector started developing following the dot com bubble and the advent of Web 2.0. This may have been spurred on by thoughts that artificial intelligence was used to forecast movements in the stock market and choose stocks [39–41]. At this point, credit and loan analysis was the main application of AI in the banking sector according to the literature [42, 43]. Building a quick and dependable AI platform is crucial in the initial phases of AI adoption [44]. A neural network technique was used by Baesens *et al.* [40] to more accurately predict loan defaults and early repayments. Using data mining, Ince and Aktan [41] examined credit scores and discovered that artificial intelligence-driven data mining was better than conventional approaches. In a similar way, Khandani *et al.* [43] discovered that machine learning-driven models were effective in assessing the risk of consumer lending.

Banks do not suffer only from credit risk. There are many other risks pertinent to this industry. A few risk categories are given in Table 2.1.

Table 2.1 Various kinds of risks in banks.

Credit risk	Repayment of loans as per schedule and in full is crucial for a bank to remain profitable. AI-powered credit risk management technologies comprehensively examine the borrower's eligibility and credit history and look for any potential red flags.
Fraud risk	Fraud risk refers to the potential for any unforeseen material, economic, or social losses brought on by either internal or external actors engaging in fraud. To recognize, comprehend, and mitigate fraud risks and prevent threats before they have an impact on the organization or its clients, organizations can carry out a fraud risk assessment. This process makes use of AI technologies and data analytics.

(Continued)

Table 2.1 Various kinds of risks in banks. (*Continued*)

Operational risk	Financial losses brought on by human error or failures in internal corporate procedures are referred to as operational risk. For instance, extending a loan in excess of the sum of money that the borrower was authorized for is a typical error. These procedures can be automated by new digital technology, which helps to decrease errors in current processes.
Market risk	Risk managers closely monitor market aspects that could affect customer behavior using AI technologies. For instance, a borrower's financial destiny could be impacted by geopolitical upheaval, global epidemics, or economic downturns. This information is used by banks and other financial institutions to predict changes and make better choices regarding investments.
Liquidity risk	Banks are required to make it possible for consumers to withdraw money from their accounts. Liquidity risk is the possibility that the bank will not be able to give consumers access to their money. AI can assist banks in making sure there are sufficient reserves accessible to meet the requirements of the clients.
Cybersecurity risk	Cybersecurity hazards are more common than ever in today's rapidly evolving digital environment. AI is used by banks and other financial services providers to precisely pinpoint data point vulnerabilities, preventing criminal activity that could result in data breaches and other cyberattacks.
Reputational risk	The probability of increased deposits in banks depends on the customer perception of safe and secured fund management in banks. Therefore, establishing a bank's reputation is crucial to gaining dependable and devoted clients. With regard to data reporting, privacy, and security rules, digitization aids banks in automating and ensuring compliance.

Source: inscribe.ai

2.3   Risk Assessment and Mitigation through Artificial Intelligence

The volumes of data that surged in recent years and are anticipated to soar even further in the years to come are frequently used in the financial services industry. By 2025, society as a whole is anticipated to produce 463 exabytes of data every day globally, up from the predicted average of 1.7 MB of data created by each human in 2020 [45]. The data that banks may utilize to create more precise risk models enhance decision-making and spot suspicious behavior or transactions in real time can be found in such big complicated data sets. However, humans are unable to accurately analyze this volume of data on their own. In order to efficiently process massive volumes of data and uncover crucial insights that can improve decision-making, lower risk, and improve the customer experience, banks are turning to technology. The possibility, effects, and tolerable levels of potential incidents are determined by a risk assessment. The basic goal of risk assessment is to analyze potential opportunities or avoid risk-related undesirable outcomes [46].

Banks have been able to identify and mitigate risk in a variety of methods that are more efficient and timelier through the use of artificial intelligence and associated technologies.

2.3.1   Fraud Recognition

a) *Fraudulent applications:* The fraudulent applications for loans can be verified by using ML algorithms that assist banks in spotting anomalies and irregularities in loan applications. Today's digital environment allows criminals to steal identities and create false loan or credit requests. Banks generally struggle to strike the right balance in processing applications fast and guaranteeing that the application and its supporting documentation are accurate without the aid of AI- or ML-enabled models.

b) *Real-time transaction fraud detection:* Manual fraud detection techniques, which mainly rely on human analysts, are no longer a viable or effective solution given the explosion of digital transactions occurring in the modern world. Businesses can stop potentially fraudulent transactions or require proof before continuing—thanks to real-time data analysis offered by AI-enabled risk management tools and methodologies. The AI or ML models are believed to get smarter over time for all types of fraud detection like loan fraud, transaction fraud, etc. It means that when models process more data, they are able to analyze it with more accuracy, which helps them improve over time and lowers the frequency of false positives in the system.

2.3.2   Regulatory Compliance Management

Within the financial industry, complying with local, national, and international rules is a crucial and challenging task. Large data sets must be examined, numerous factors must be examined, and precise documentation must be provided to the proper authorities. These processes are automated using machine learning, which guarantees their effectiveness and accuracy. As a result, banks can significantly reduce their costs by maximizing their resources and avoiding fines or penalties. In the compliance system, ML technology can reduce the frequency of false warnings, ensuring that problems are handled manually by a person only when necessary.

2.3.3   Credit Risk Modeling

The credit risk of each person is evaluated by banks using AI, ML, and deep learning. A personalized risk score is generated by these models and neural networks using a wide range of inputs, including the person's existing assets, prior behavior data, personal information, and other characteristics that may affect his or her capacity to repay a loan.

2.3.4   Insider Threat Prevention

In order to spot early indications of fraud, insider trading, data theft, and other financial crimes and malfeasance, traders' and other financial professionals' behavior is also monitored using AI and related techniques and technology. In order to discover and notify the organization of potential hazards and wrongdoing, AI-enabled systems can log, monitor, and analyze phone logs, email traffic, time cards, and vacation itineraries.

2.4   General Banking Regulations Pertaining to Artificial Intelligence

Banking regulations play a crucial role in ensuring the safe and responsible use of artificial intelligence applications in risk assessment and mitigation within the banking industry. Significantly, there are no specific comprehensive laws dedicated solely to governing AI in banking at the global level. However, various existing laws and regulations provide a framework for regulating AI applications in the banking sector. These regulations focus on areas such as data protection, consumer rights, financial stability, and ethical considerations. While the specific regulations may vary between jurisdictions, here are some of the general considerations [47]:

a) **Data Privacy and Security:** Banks must adhere to data protection regulations, such as the General Data Protection Regulation (GDPR) in the European Union or the California Consumer Privacy Act (CCPA) in the United States, to safeguard customer information used in AI risk assessment. They need to ensure proper data collection, storage, processing, and encryption techniques to protect against unauthorized access or breaches. These regulations aim to protect the privacy and security of individuals' data.

b) **Explicability and Transparency:** AI models used in risk assessment should be explainable and transparent, particularly when decisions impact customers. Regulatory bodies often require banks to be able to explain the factors and rationale behind an AI-based risk assessment to ensure fair treatment and avoid biases or discrimination.

c) **Financial Regulations:** Existing financial regulations, such as the Basel III framework, govern banks' risk management practices. These regulations require banks to have appropriate risk assessment and mitigation strategies, which could include considerations related to AI applications. Regulators often provide guidance on how AI should be implemented in risk assessment, taking into account factors such as model validation, explainability, and stress testing.

d) **Anti-Money Laundering (AML) and Know Your Customer (KYC) Regulations:** Banks are subject to AML and KYC regulations, which require them to verify the identity of their customers and monitor transactions for potential money laundering or terrorist financing activities. AI can be used to enhance these processes, but banks must comply with relevant regulations while implementing AI-based solutions.

Markets in Financial Instruments Directive (MiFID) II mandates that fund companies strengthen six components of data gathering in order to ensure the security of fund transactions. For instance, consumers can be requested to submit a certificate of income in order to avoid money laundering. The Money Laundering, Terrorist Financing, and Transfer of Funds Regulations of 2017 also mandate that businesses keep client assets in safe custody. In accordance with these regulations, businesses must create and maintain detailed records for at least 5 years. It includes private data about connections, order processing, reports, assets, and so forth. GDPR, however, gives data subjects the right to an immediate deletion of their personal information.

The information controller must comply with the data subject's right to request that all personal information pertaining to them be erased immediately. This rule conflicts with the MiFID II rule, which states that a firm must keep all records related to its MiFID activity for at least 5 years. The main consideration is the information's intended use. Is it being gathered for the goal of enforcing the law, fulfilling guarantee responsibilities, creating new goods, or doing research in order to create RegTech.

e) **Fair Lending and Discrimination:** Banks must ensure that their AI models for risk assessment do not violate fair lending laws or discriminate against protected groups. Regulatory guidelines often require banks to perform regular audits to assess potential biases and take corrective actions when necessary. Banks must comply with consumer protection laws and regulations that ensure fair treatment of customers. These laws often require transparency and accountability when using AI in decision-making processes that impact consumers, such as loan approvals or credit scoring.

f) **Model Validation and Testing:** Regulators often mandate rigorous validation and testing procedures for AI models used in risk assessment. Banks are required to demonstrate the reliability and accuracy of their models, including ongoing monitoring and validation processes to ensure they continue to perform as expected.

g) **Governance and Risk Management:** Banks should establish robust governance frameworks and risk management practices to oversee the development, implementation, and monitoring of AI models. This includes having clear accountability, risk mitigation strategies, and processes for managing potential AI-related risks.

h) **Flash Crash:** The capital markets experienced a market crash before AI was involved, and the restrictions put in place to prevent a repeat mostly focus on human behavior. Systemic risk becomes the primary worry when machines are engaged, so market safety regulations must be adopted to offer security. Regulators in the EU and UK have put in place measures to lessen the possibility of an AI-related flash disaster. When stock orders are withdrawn, for instance, algorithmic trading can cause a "flash crash," which intensifies price losses quickly. The UK's Financial Conduct Authority [48] and the Prudential Regulation Authority began actively monitoring high-frequency trading after the flash crisis in 2010.

Under the "Markets in Financial Instruments Directive (MiFID) II" and the "Markets in Financial Instruments Regulation (MiFIR)," collectively referred to as "MiFID II and MiFIR," the EU controls HFT activity. Three key strands make up MiFID II. First, it establishes a new operational framework for investment firms' algorithmic trading. Second, it broadens its application to include all companies using algorithmic trading, especially specialized companies that use high-frequency trading. Third, it places operational demands on trading venues, including exchanges and platforms.

i) **Ethical Considerations:** Regulatory guidelines may emphasize ethical considerations when deploying AI in risk assessment. Banks should ensure that their AI models align with ethical standards, promote fairness and transparency, and avoid unethical practices, such as manipulation or exploitation of customer data. Some countries and organizations have published ethical guidelines for AI that can serve as a reference for banks in their AI implementation. For example, the European Commission has released the Ethics Guidelines for Trustworthy AI, which promotes principles like transparency, fairness, and accountability in AI systems. It is important to note that banking regulations can vary significantly across jurisdictions, and these considerations may not cover all specific requirements. Banks should consult with legal and regulatory experts to ensure compliance with applicable laws and guidelines in their respective regions. AI regulations and guidelines are evolving rapidly, and new laws specific to AI may be introduced in the future. It is advisable for banks to stay updated on regulatory developments in their jurisdictions and consult legal experts to ensure compliance with applicable laws and regulations.

The growth of AI is exponential and so its application. In the light of the above discussion, this research aims:

1. To identify and analyze the various aspects of AI application in risk assessment and mitigation in banks and how literature has evolved in this research context
2. To highlight the emerging research areas for future research and provide suggestions to the bank community for mitigating risk.

2.5   Methodology

2.5.1   Bibliometric Analysis

The purpose of this research is to offer an overview of current research in the area of AI in banking. There is a need for reviewing the qualitative and quantitative research in order to organize the previous findings related to usage of AI in banking for risk assessment and mitigation. Bibliometric analysis can be of help in such cases where the present literature can be analyzed [49, 50] because it provides a systematic and transparent understanding of the research [51]. This concept was first introduced as a scientific technique to observe a research area's evolution over time with respect to a multidisciplinary approach [52]. These analyses help in the identification of impact on the basis of author data, research domain data, journal data, and emerging themes [53]. VOSviewer is one of the useful software that helps in conducting bibliometric analysis [54]. Kumar et al. [55] conducted bibliometric assessment technique to evaluate the development of fintech documents from the perspectives of the variety of documents produced in this field, development of yearly publishes with important indexes, leading journals and publishers, top-cited papers, largest number of papers produced from top nations, and frequently used keywords. Thus, bibliometric analysis was done for identifying the research themes in the area.

The recent trends in the area of AI in banking for risk assessment and mitigation will also be explored with the help of bibliometric analysis in this research. It will help to showcase qualitative and quantitative analysis. The various emerging research areas will also be highlighted leading to upcoming research angles.

For the bibliometric analysis, Scopus database was considered for performing a literature search. The final search query that was used was as follows: TITLE-ABS-KEY ("Artificial Intelligence" AND "Credit Risk") AND (LIMIT-TO (SUBJAREA, "BUSI") OR LIMIT-TO (SUBJAREA , "DECI") OR LIMIT-TO (SUBJAREA , "ECON") OR LIMIT-TO (SUBJAREA , "SOCI")) AND (LIMIT-TO (LANGUAGE , "English")).

The number of total data points collected was 107. A full record of the bibliographical information, all citation information, and abstract and related information was downloaded as a CSV file for further analysis. The description of the bibliometric data, most cited authors, subject-wise division, country-wise analysis, etc., was done that showed the results. Figure 2.1 shows the analysis of research published to date. Figure 2.2 denotes the most cited authors. Figure 2.3 shows publications' affiliation country-wise, and it is evident that countries like China, United States, and India are leading centers of research in that area. Figure 2.4 shows documents by academic classification types where most work has been

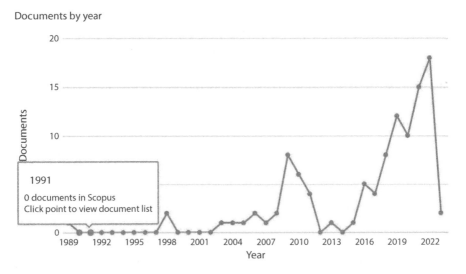

Figure 2.1 Documents year-wise.

Author	Documents	Citations
baesens b.	3	101
martens d.	3	101
vanthienen j.	3	101
mues c.	2	57
ansell j.	2	65
boujelbene y.	2	30
danenas p.	2	27
garsva g.	2	27
hu y.-c.	2	65
khemakhem s.	2	30
lee m.	2	9
li j.	2	59
teng h.-w.	2	9
wang h.	2	52
wu d.	2	52
yu l.	2	190
chi g.	2	10
wang s.	2	162
zhang z.	2	33

Figure 2.2 Most cited authors.

Documents by country or territory
Compare the document counts for up to 15 countries/territories.

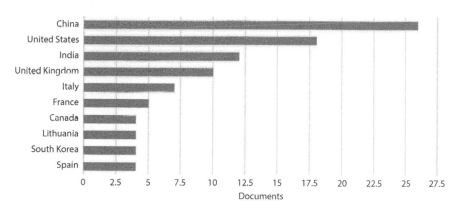

Figure 2.3 Publication country-wise.

Documents by type

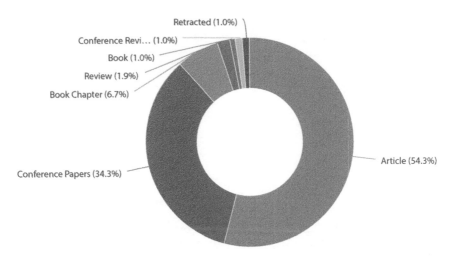

Figure 2.4 Documents by type.

published in the form of articles and conference papers. Figure 2.5 shows the publication growth year-wise, and it is visible how the publication trend in this topic has grown in the recent few years.

Figure 2.6 depicts the keyword co-occurrence network analysis in which the macro clusters have been identified after the bibliometric

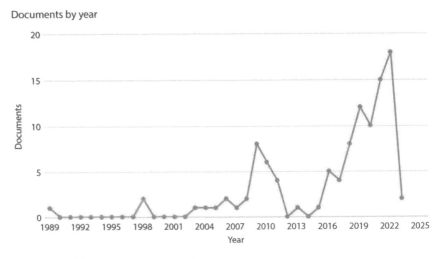

Figure 2.5 Publication growth year-wise.

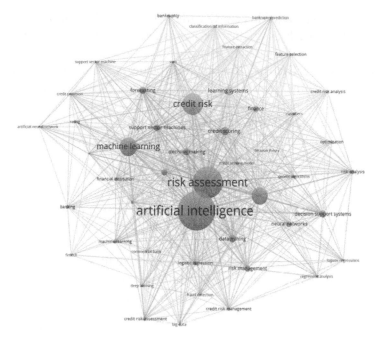

Figure 2.6 Co-occurrence keywords.

analysis. The different colors visible in the co-occurrence diagram show the connectivity with the related keywords in the cluster. There are five colored clusters, viz., Yellow, Red, Green, Blue, and Violet. The co-occurrence keyword artificial intelligence and risk assessment are the biggest in size that indicates that these words are the central theme and the rest of the keywords are related to it. The optimization algorithm detects communities in huge networks by the combination of nodes using heuristics [56]. The keyword co-occurrence analysis offers a distinctive understanding through several areas and its application in a few domains of research.

2.5.2   Co-Occurrence Analysis

In co-occurrence network analysis as depicted in Figure 2.6, the keywords are classified into five clusters in different areas as discussed below:

- Cluster 1 (Blue) - This cluster represents the central themes having biggest sized keywords Artificial Intelligence and Risk Assessment. The research that discusses decision-making in commercial banks has also been identified. The technological aspects of deep learning, big data, and data mining are also covered in this cluster. Important functions and action related such as credit risk assessment and fraud detection have been discussed in this cluster.

- Cluster 2 (Red) – The technical aspects of the topic such as Machine Learning, Support Vector Machine (SVM), Artificial Neural Network, Fintech, etc., have been focused in this cluster. Forecasting mechanisms and credit provisions in banking and financial institutions have also been discussed.
- Cluster 3 (Yellow) – The central mode in this cluster is of the keywords Learning systems from which the other keywords such as Feature extraction and selection emanate. The Classification of information is also an important keyword constituting this cluster.
- Cluster 4 (Green) – The keywords Credit scoring model and Credit risk management are the central constructs in this cluster. The decision support system is a very important node because decisions based on inputs from data are taken and risk is assessed and lowered. The risk analysis and management are done based on such inputs. Tools such as logistic regression are used for the process of classification.
- Cluster 5 (Violet) – The central node is Credit risk that is connected to Neural networks and Optimization algorithms. The Bankruptcy prediction can be done using these tools and models.

2.6 Theoretical Implications

Conceptualizing the role of artificial intelligence in risk assessment can have several theoretical implications. The integration of AI technologies into existing risk frameworks can advance risk theory by considering AI's role in risk assessment. This involves exploring how AI techniques, like machine learning algorithms and predictive analytics, can enhance traditional risk assessment approaches, leading to improved risk prediction, identification, and evaluation. By conceptualizing AI's role in risk assessment, there are theoretical implications for enhancing risk management practices. This includes understanding how AI can enable more accurate and timely risk identification, automate real-time risk monitoring, and facilitate the development of proactive and adaptive risk mitigation strategies. Theoretical contributions can provide insights into how AI can overcome cognitive biases and human limitations in risk decision-making. Furthermore, understanding the implications of data-driven decision-making in risk assessment is crucial. This involves examining the challenges and opportunities associated with using large amounts of data, such as data quality, privacy, and biases. Additionally, considering the ethical and social implications of AI in risk assessment is essential. This includes discussions on fairness, transparency, accountability of AI algorithms, and the potential impacts on privacy and security. Theoretical contributions can help identify ethical challenges and guide the development of responsible AI practices. Overall, conceptualizing AI's role in risk assessment can contribute to advancing risk theory, enhancing risk management practices, addressing cognitive biases and human limitations, understanding data-driven decision-making, and examining ethical and social implications. These theoretical contributions shape the foundations of AI in risk assessment and guide future research and practice in this field.

2.7   Managerial Implications

The managerial implications have been discussed based on the overall summary of the researchers and the themes identified from bibliometric analysis. The utilization of artificial intelligence in risk assessment and mitigation within the banking sector carries several managerial implications. Some essential considerations for bank managers have been identified and discussed. AI has the potential to enhance the precision of risk assessment by examining extensive data sets and uncovering patterns and correlations that human analysts may overlook with improved accuracy. This can lead to more precise risk evaluations, empowering managers to make well-informed decisions. With efficient risk monitoring, AI-powered systems can continuously monitor and analyze diverse data sources, such as transaction records, market data, and news feeds, to swiftly identify potential risks in real time. Managers can leverage this capability to promptly detect and address emerging risks, thereby minimizing the impact on the bank's operations. AI algorithms can aid in the development of early warning systems that identify signals or patterns indicating potential risks or market disruptions. By proactively detecting such indicators, bank managers can take preventive measures and implement risk mitigation strategies well in advance. Operating in a heavily regulated environment, banks must prioritize compliance as a crucial aspect of risk management. AI can automate compliance monitoring by analyzing transactions, customer behavior, and regulatory changes, ensuring adherence to regulations. This reduces the burden on managers and helps mitigate compliance risks. AI can assist in tailoring risk models by analyzing historical data and identifying risk factors specific to a bank's operations, customer base, and market segment. This empowers managers to create risk assessment frameworks that align closely with the bank's unique risk profile. AI-powered risk assessment systems can optimize resource allocation by identifying high-risk areas that require increased attention, allowing managers to allocate resources accordingly. This enables managers to focus on critical risks, optimizing the allocation of time, budget, and personnel and improving overall risk management efficiency.

AI can provide managers with comprehensive and timely risk insights, enabling data-driven decision-making. By leveraging AI-generated risk assessments, managers can evaluate the potential impact of various risk scenarios and assess mitigation strategies more effectively. A different but important consideration was of ethical area where the implementation of AI in risk assessment necessitates addressing ethical concerns such as privacy and algorithmic biases. Managers must ensure that AI systems comply with regulatory and ethical standards, and they should monitor algorithms to prevent biases or discriminatory practices. Implementing AI systems for risk assessment necessitates a competent workforce capable of handling and interpreting insights generated by AI. Managers should prioritize investing in training and upskilling their employees to effectively utilize AI tools and harness the advantages of AI-driven risk management. Additionally, introducing AI-based risk assessment systems may call for organizational changes, such as redefining roles and responsibilities, integrating AI into existing processes, and fostering a culture that embraces AI. Managers need to plan and execute change management strategies to ensure a smooth transition and maximize the effectiveness of AI technologies. Overall, the usage of AI for risk assessment and mitigation in banks presents significant managerial implications, requiring proactive planning, collaboration between humans and machines, and continuous monitoring to ensure the optimal utilization of AI technologies for risk management purposes.

2.8   Future Scope

The combination of artificial intelligence and machine learning in the field of finance intersects with various emerging and established disciplines like dynamic programming, financial econometrics, pattern recognition, probabilistic programming, and statistical computing [57]. AI, with the support of advancements in computational power and data handling capabilities, has become a crucial aspect of computational engineering, making plug-and-play algorithms more accessible through open-source platforms [58]. The widespread adoption of AI and ML in the finance industry highlights the significant demand and numerous research opportunities in this field. In terms of strategy, as AI continues to expand in the banking industry, financial institutions should evaluate how their internal stakeholders perceive the benefits of incorporating AI, the importance of leadership, and other factors that influence AI adoption within the organization. Therefore, future research should focus on exploring various elements, such as the role of leadership, that impact the integration of AI technologies within organizations. Furthermore, as AI becomes more prevalent and accepted, it brings about internal challenges. Consequently, it is recommended to investigate the diverse organizational hurdles, such as organizational culture, that arise from AI adoption. To facilitate the integration of AI-driven decision-making, professionals in the banking industry are encouraged to enhance their utilization of AI in credit scoring, analysis, and loan approval processes. This approach aims to mitigate risks, reduce expenses, and improve the overall customer experience. However, it is advised to incorporate AI not only to enhance internal procedures but also as a tool, like chatbots, to improve customer service for simpler tasks. By doing so, employees can dedicate their efforts to other impactful business activities. Additionally, utilizing AI as a marketing segmentation tool is proposed to effectively target customers and provide them with optimal solutions.

2.9   Conclusion

The themes identified in the clusters can serve as a future scope for upcoming researchers. Various researchers have worked in different dimensions of this field and discussed their findings. Upon comprehensive screening and evaluation of the research works, some aspects of AI in banking were understood. The abovementioned upcoming research themes through clusters can be further explored with empirical data sets. A thorough reading of the finally selected research papers gave a few insights into the area of AI in banking, paving the way for emerging research areas. These findings have been discussed in a summarized form with respect to the role of AI in banking for risk assessment and mitigation. The utilization of machine-readable data has significant implications for both financial systems and financial research. The financial services industry is increasingly relying on computational methods, supported by advanced hardware and software, to enable machines to develop complex models that can effectively evaluate new information. This transformation, driven by the adoption of artificial intelligence, is profoundly reshaping trading and investment decisions. At the same time, financial research is acknowledging the importance of understanding the economic effects of AI. Researchers are also recognizing the value of AI techniques as tools for investigating established topics and research questions in the financial field. AI has become a critical technology in financial scholarship, yet a comprehensive review examining its impact on financial systems is currently lacking. Encouraging further research in finance is crucial to deepen our understanding of how AI influences financial systems.

Additionally, AI algorithms are being used by banks to improve their AML and fraud detection systems. Fraud detection is accelerated and made more affordable by anomaly detection utilizing AI-based technologies. Financial institutions have benefited greatly from the application of AI in AML and fraud detection because they are mandated by law to report cases of fraud or money laundering. On the other hand, using rule-based non-AI algorithms to identify phony accounts and red-flag suspicious transactions is more slower and results in a lot more false positives. Additionally, autonomous AI agents that are proactive and reactive are being used to stay ahead of the money launderers' constantly evolving techniques.

Although the autonomous AI agent strategy is gaining ground, AML detection ultimately still requires human AML expert evaluation and final decision-making. The question of whether it is preferable to eliminate humans from the detection process will present itself to policymakers once the technology matures though.

References

1. Mhlanga, D., Financial inclusion in emerging economies: The application of machine learning and artificial intelligence in credit risk assessment. *Int. J. Financ. Stud.*, 9, 3, 39, 2021.
2. Lee, J.C. and Chen, X., Exploring users' adoption intentions in the evolution of artificial intelligence mobile banking applications: the intelligent and anthropomorphic perspectives. *Int. J. Bank Mark.*, 40, 4, 631–658, 2022.
3. Popkova, E.G. and Parakhina, V.N., Managing the global financial system on the basis of artificial intelligence: Possibilities and limitations, in: *The Future of the Global Financial System: Downfall or Harmony*, vol. 6, pp. 939–946, Springer International Publishing, 2019.
4. Baldwin, R., *The Globotics Upheaval: Globalisation, Robotics and the Future of Work*, Weidenfeld & Nicolson, Hachette, UK, 2019.

5. Grady, J. and Weale, M., The traditional banking system, in: *British Banking*, pp. 1960–8566–93, Springer, UK, 1986, https://doi.org/10.1007/978-1-349-07535-5_5.
6. Mester, L.J., Traditional and nontraditional banking: An information-theoretic approach. *J. Bank. Financ.*, 16, 3, 545–566, 1992. https://doi.org/10.1016/0378-4266(92)90044-Z.
7. Chen, A.H. and Mazumdar, S.C., A dynamic model of firewalls and non-traditional banking. *J. Bank. Financ.*, 21, 3, 393–416, 1997. https://doi.org/10.1016/S0378-4266(96)00049-0.
8. Panova, G., Evolution of traditional banks' business models. *Int. Rev.*, 1–2, 146–152, 2021. https://doi.org/10.5937/intrev2102148p.
9. Thakor, A.V., Information technology and financial services consolidation. *J. Bank. Financ.*, 23, 2, 697–700, 1999. https://doi. org/10.1016/S0378-4266(98)00104-6.
10. Goel, P., Kulsrestha, S., Maurya, S.K., Fintech unfolding: Financial revolution in India. *Thail. World Econ.*, 40, 2, 41–51, 2022.
11. Ashta, A., Fintech–technology in finance: Strategic risks and challenges, in: *Innovation Economics, Engineering and Management Handbook (Vol. 2)*, Wiley, India, 2021, https://doi.org/10.1002/9781119832522.ch15.
12. Consultants, M., *Benefits of Artificial Intelligence in the Banking Sector*, Millinium Consultants, Kuala Lumpur, Malaysia, 2022, Available online: https://www.millenniumci.com/benefits-of-artificial-intelligence-in-the-banking-sector.
13. Ross, S., What percentage of the global economy is comprised of the financial services sector. *Investopedia*, 2015, 5, 2015. Available online: https://www.investopedia.com/ask/answers/030515/what-percentage-global-economy-comprised-financial-services-sector.asp.
14. De Oliveira Santini, F., Ladeira, W.J., Sampaio, C.H., Perin, M.G., Online banking services: A meta-analytic review and assessment of the impact of antecedents and consequents on satisfaction. *J. Financ. Serv. Mark.*, 23, 3, 168–178, 2018.
15. Eren, B.A., Determinants of customer satisfaction in chatbot use: Evidence from a banking application in Turkey. *Int. J. Bank Mark.*, 39, 2, 294–331, 2021.
16. Hua, X., Huang, Y., Zheng, Y., Current practices, new insights, and emerging trends of fnancial technologies. *Ind. Manage. Data Syst.*, 119, 7, 1401–1410, 2019.
17. Rajaobelina, L. and Ricard, L., Classifying potential users of live chat services and chatbots. *J. Financ. Serv. Mark.*, 26, 2, 81–94, 2021.
18. Valsamidis, S., Tsourgiannis, L., Pappas, D., Mosxou, E., Digital banking in the new era: Exploring customers' attitudes, in: *Business Performance and Financial Institutions in Europe*, pp. 91–104, Springer, Cham, 2020.
19. Yang, A.S., Exploring adoption difculties in mobile banking services. *Can. J. Adm. Sci./Revue Can. Des. Sci. L'administration*, 26, 2, 136–149, 2009.

20. Feliciano-Cestero, M.M., Ameen, N., Kotabe, M., Paul, J., Signoret, M., Is digital transformation threatened? A systematic literature review of the factors influencing firms' digital transformation and internationalization. *J. Bus. Res.*, 157, 113546, 2023.
21. Dobrescu, E.M. and Dobrescu, E.M., Artifcial intelligence (Ai)-the technology that shapes the world. *Global Economic Observer*, 6, 2, 71–81, 2018.
22. Rajan, D.P., Baswaraj, D., Velliangiri, S., Karthikeyan, P., Next generations data science application and its platform, in: *2020 International Conference on Smart Electronics and Communication (ICOSEC)*, pp. 891–897, IEEE, September 2020.
23. Garg, N., Gupta, M., Jain, N., Emerging need of artificial intelligence applications and their use cases in the banking industry: case study of ICICI bank, in: *Revolutionizing Business Practices Through Artificial Intelligence and Data-Rich Environments*, pp. 140–161, IGI Global, India, 2022.
24. Gupta, A. and Xia, C., A Paradigm shift in banking: Unfolding Asia's FinTech adventures, in: *Banking and Finance Issues in Emerging Markets*, vol. 25, pp. 215–254, Emerald Publishing Limited, 2018.
25. Knewtson, H.S. and Rosenbaum, Z.A., Toward understanding FinTech and its industry. *Manage. Finance*, 46, 8, 1043–1060, 2020.
26. Popelo, O., Dubyna, M., Kholiavko, N., World experience in the introduction of modern innovation and information technologies in the functioning of financial institutions. *Balt. J. Econ. Stud.*, 7, 2, 188–199, 2021.
27. Ashta, A. and Biot-Paquerot, G., FinTech evolution: Strategic value management issues in a fast changing industry. *Strateg. Change*, 27, 4, 301–311, 2018. https://doi.org/10.1002/jsc.2203.
28. Turiel, J.D. and Aste, T., Peer-to-peer loan acceptance and default prediction with artificial intelligence: P2P default prediction with AI. *R. Soc. Open Sci.*, 7, 6, 1–17, 2020. https://doi.org/10.1098/rsos. 191649rsos191649.
29. Arif, I., Aslam, W., Hwang, Y., Barriers in adoption of internet banking: A structural equation modeling-neural network approach. *Technol. Soc.*, 61, 101231, 2020.
30. Belanche, D., Casaló, L.V., Flavián, C., Artifcial intelligence in FinTech: Understanding robo-advisors adoption among customers. *Ind. Manage. Data Syst.*, 119, 1411–1430, 2019.
31. Payne, E.H., Peltier, J., Barger, V.A., Enhancing the value co-creation process: Artifcial intelligence and mobile banking service platforms. *J. Res. Interact. Mark.*, 15, 68–85, 2021.
32. Medhi, P.K. and Mondal, S., A neural feature extraction model for classifcation of frms and prediction of outsourcing success: Advantage of using relational sources of information for new suppliers. *Int. J. Prod. Res.*, 54, 20, 6071–6081, 2016.
33. Srivastava, K., Paradigm shift in Indian banking industry with special reference to artificial intelligence. *Turk. J. Comput. Math. Educ. (TURCOMAT)*, 12, 5, 1623–1629, 2021.

34. Couchoro, M.K., Sodokin, K., Koriko, M., Information and communication technologies, artificial intelligence, and the fight against money laundering in Africa. *Strateg. Change*, 30, 3, 281–291, 2021. https://doi.org/10.1002/jsc.2410.

35. Osmani, M., El-Haddadeh, R., Hindi, N., Janssen, M., Weerakkody, V., Blockchain for next generation services in banking and finance: Cost, benefit, risk and opportunity analysis. *J. Enterp. Inf. Manage.*, 34, 3, 884–899, 2021. https://doi.org/10.1108/JEIM-02-2020-004.

36. Hassani, H., Huang, X., Silva, E., Banking with blockchain-ed big data. *J. Manage. Anal.*, 5, 4, 256–275, 2018. https://doi.org/ 10.1080/23270012.2018.1528900.

37. Srivastava, M., Artificial intelligence to disrupt wealth management business: PwC. *Business Standard*, June 7, 2017. Retrieved from http://www.business-standard.com/article/companies/.

38. Chugh, and Jaiswal, How AI is disrupting the banking sector in India. *Silicon India*, April 12, 2018. Retrieved from: https://technology.siliconindiamagazine.com/viewpoint/ceo-insights/how-ai-isdisrupting-the-banking-sector-in-india-nwid-9820.html.

39. Tseng, C.C., Comparing artifcial intelligence systems for stock portfolio selection, in: *The 9th International Conference Of Computing in Economics and Finance*, pp. 1–7, July 2003.

40. Baesens, B., Van Gestel, T., Stepanova, M., Van den Poel, D., Vanthienen, J., Neural network survival analysis for personal loan data. *J. Oper. Res. Soc.*, 56, 9, 1089–1098, 2005.

41. Ince, H. and Aktan, B., A comparison of data mining techniques for credit scoring in banking: A managerial perspective. *J. Bus. Econ. Manage.*, 10, 3, 233–240, 2009.

42. Kao, L.J., Chiu, C.C., Chiu, F.Y., A Bayesian latent variable model with classification and regression tree approach for behavior and credit scoring. *Knowl.-Based Syst.*, 36, 245–252, 2012.

43. Khandani, A.E., Kim, A.J., Lo, A.W., Consumer credit-risk models via machine-learning algorithms. *J. Bank. Financ.*, 34, 11, 2767–2787, 2010.

44. Larson, E.J., *The Myth of Artifcial Intelligence,* Harvard University Press, USA, 2021.

45. Maune, A., Intention to use mobile applications in competitive intelligence: An extended conceptual framework. *J. Intell. Stud. Bus.*, 11, 2, 6–29, 2021.

46. Myšková, R. and Doupalova, V., Approach to risk management decision-making in the small business. *Proc. Econ. Financ.*, 34, 329–336, 2015.

47. Krausova, A., Intersections between law and artificial intelligence. *Int. J. Comput. (IJC)*, 27, 1, 55–68, 2017.

48. FCA, Safe custody services and money laundering, 2017c. https://www.fca.org.uk/frms/money-laund ering/safe-custody-services. Accessed 25 Nov 2019.

49. Liu, Z., Yin, Y., Liu, W., Dunford, M., Visualizing the intellectual structure and evolution of innovation systems research: A bibliometric analysis. *Scientometrics*, 103, 1, 135–158, 2015.

50. Sun, Y. and Grimes, S., The emerging dynamic structure of national innovation studies: A bibliometric analysis. *Scientometrics*, 106, 1, 17–40, 2016.

51. Aria, M. and Cuccurullo, C., bibliometrix: An R-tool for comprehensive science mapping analysis. *J. Informetr.*, 11, 4, 959–975, 2017.

52. Pritchard, A., Statistical bibliography or bibliometrics. *J. Doc.*, 25, 348–349, 1969.

53. Sarin, S., Haon, C., Belkhouja, M., Mas-Tur, A., Roig-Tierno, N., Sego, T., Carley, S., Uncovering the knowledge flows and intellectual structures of research in technological forecasting and social change: A journey through history. *Technol. Forecast. Soc. Change*, 160, 120210, 2020.

54. Van Eck, N.J. and Waltman, L., Text mining and visualization using VOSviewer, 2011. arXiv preprint arXiv:1109.2058.

55. Kumar, A., Srivastava, A., Gupta, P.K., Banking 4.0: The era of artificial intelligence-based fintech. *Strateg. Change*, 31, 6, 591–601, 2022. https://doi.org/10.1002/jsc.2526.

56. Kumar, T., Vaidyanathan, S., Ananthapadmanabhan, H., Parthasarathy, S., Ravindran, B., Hypergraph clustering by iteratively reweighted modularity maximization. *Appl. Netw. Sci.*, 5, 1, 1–22, 2020.

57. Dixon, M.F., Halperin, I., Bilokon, P., *Machine Learning in Finance: From Theory to Practice*, Springer International Publishing, USA, 2020.

58. Corbet, S., Goodell, J.W., Gunay, S., Kaskaloglu, K., Are DeFi tokens a separate asset class from conventional cryptocurrencies?, *Ann. Oper. Res.*, 322, 2, 609–630, 2023.

3

Artificial Intelligence and Financial Risk Mitigation

Raja Rehan*, Auwal Adam Sa'ad and Razali Haron

IIUM Institute of Islamic Banking and Finance (IIiBF), International Islamic University Malaysia (IIUM), Kuala Lumpur, Malaysia

Abstract

The former approaches for financial risk mitigation are warranted to be revamped, as they are no longer effective. Nevertheless, the continuous advancement in fintech has developed artificial intelligence (AI), whose powered techniques are considered to be the most effective to identify and mitigate financial risk. Visibly, the financial sector as a whole is drastically altered by artificial intelligence, which gives rise to several procedures to mitigate probable financial risks. In this context, this chapter presents the AI-based financial risk detection process, which involves the main steps used to detect financial risk and then classify its types. Likewise, the established ongoing artificial intelligence-based financial risk mitigation process contains several steps that are used to lessen potential risk. Also, the strategies used by artificial intelligence to mitigate dissimilar sorts of financial risks are discussed in great detail in this chapter. Overall, this chapter discusses how quickly this modern technology provides benefits in terms of mitigating financial risks. As well, by adopting developed artificial intelligence-based financial risk identification and mitigation procedures, financial institutions can accurately evaluate massive information and identify financial risk factors, thus laying a more scientific, accurate, and comprehensive decision-making foundation for financial risk mitigation and management.

Keywords: Artificial intelligence, financial risk, risk mitigation, fraud detection, risk management

Corresponding author: rajarehan@iium.edu.my

Ambrish Kumar Mishra, Shweta Anand, Narayan C. Debnath, Purvi Pokhariyal and Archana Patel (eds.) Artificial Intelligence for Risk Mitigation in the Financial Industry, (53–80) © 2024 Scrivener Publishing LLC

3.1   Introduction

The digital marathon, which began with the emergence of the Internet and has led enterprises through several stages of digitalization, is currently in its artificial intelligence (AI) phase, which is recognized as machine-based intelligence [1]. Technically, AI-based advanced technologies are developed to permit machines especially computers to do what typically human minds can do and then make them able to behave like humans [2]. The field of AI has a dynamic history that commenced in the 1950s with the Dartmouth Workshop, where this technical term, i.e., artificial intelligence, was coined [3]. However, the phase of the 1960s and 1970s in which the advancement of machine learning and expert computer-based systems were offered laid the groundwork for AI [4]. An AI winter rose between the period of 1970s and 1980s in which the arena of AI experienced remarkable advances. After that, AI resurrected in the 21st century, motivated by big data analysis and better computing power, and brought machine learning back into the spotlight. Visibly, AI-based applications became mainstream in the mid of 2010, with simulated assistants and numerous AI-powered structures in businesses. Also, during this phase, the social and moral implications of AI gained attention. The history of AI is characterized by continuing advancements, ethical considerations, and the unceasing quest for generating brainy machinery. Most recently, AI and ML-based models like GPT-3, which is established by OpenAI, robotic process automation (RPA), which is being used to mechanize continuous repetitive tasks, generative adversarial networks (GANs) that can produce accurate and inspired content, counting music, text, and images are some topical trends and progress that have been detected in the ground of AI [5].

Visibly, AI-based applications are diverse and observed in numerous areas, counting simulated personal assistants, recommendation systems, autonomous vehicles, medical diagnosis, etc. Hence, as technology advances, AI continues to have a profound impact on various businesses, transforming the way people live, work, and interact with machines [6]. In the same vein, AI is also rapidly adopted by the financial sector for its several applications and services to stay updated on technological advancement. The execution of AI in the finance sector has experienced substantial growth and alteration over the decades. At first, AI in the finance sector focused only on rule-based professional systems for completing tasks like the detection of fraud and scoring of credit. Though, with the arrival of big data and improvements in machine learning, AI has gradually involved handling more difficult financial tasks [7]. Nowadays, AI in the financial sector is executed to provide dissimilar financial services and applications such as sales forecasting, customer service, asset management, the predication of financial data, credit scoring, algorithmic trading, combating money laundering, financial analysis, fraud detection, and many more counting, assessing, and then mitigating risk factors [8]. However, the advancement of AI also introduces dissimilar interconnected risks that need to be wisely managed [9]. For instance, there is a risk of insufficient privacy and security of data, job displacement, and its economic impacts, limited interpretability, and biased models that can lead to defective policymaking and financial losses. In addition, the dependence on AI-based systems and procedures for critical financial decisions and operations upsurges cybersecurity-related threats, data breaches, and illegal access, possibly resulting in financial fraud and damage to reputation [10]. Thus, mitigating and managing these AI-based risks need ensuring data accessibility and interpretability challenges, executing vigorous cybersecurity procedures, and launching effective governance frameworks to guide the development and deployment of AI in the financial sector.

Evidently, the financial sector has benefited greatly from AI and it has also brought a lot of risk assessment and mitigation procedures for this industry. Technically, risk assessment is measuring and evaluating potential risks that are related to certain financial transactions, investments, or finance-related business decisions [11]. Likewise, risk mitigation is a tactic used by businesses to prepare for and lessen the effects of financial threats confronting businesses [12]. Before AI, financial institutions and firms manually assess risk by using traditional approaches such as evaluating financial data and information. However, now, by using AI-powered tools, businesses can get more accurate outcomes for the existing and forthcoming financial risks [13]. The AI-powered procedures aid firms in making defensible choices regarding financial transactions including loans, investments, savings, insurance, and stock market trading. Hence, firms and individuals can reduce their losses and boost the utmost returns in any area of finance by using AI-powered risk mitigation strategies. As a whole, AI certainly offers huge benefits to the financial sector that outweigh the connected risks. Clearly, the use of AI in the financial sector particularly in the banking industry has been escalating dramatically on a global scale. According to Allied Market Research, the value of AI in the banking industry was estimated to be approximately USD 3.88 billion in the year 2020 and is anticipated to rise up to USD 64.03 billion by 2030 [14]. A far greater figure is also anticipated for total AI market value that postulates that AI's estimated value, i.e., USD 207 billion, is expected to surge rapidly by 788% and hit USD 1.870 trillion by 2030 [15]. Below, Figure 3.1 presents some core benefits delivered by artificial intelligence to the financial sector.

Figure 3.1 AI in the financial sector. (Source: Authors' own elaboration).

This chapter discovers the recent adoption of artificial intelligence and its implications as an advanced tool in the financial sector to mitigate and manage financial risks. In addition, it also delivers a detailed background on AI development, competencies, advantages, disadvantages, and recent challenges that artificial intelligence carries for the financial sector and its policymakers.

3.2   Artificial Intelligence, Financial Sector, and Risk Mitigation

Undeniably, the evolution and development of AI in the financial sector are a long story. The financial sector has rapidly adopted and utilized artificial intelligence in three phases (Table 3.1). Formerly, the financial sector relies on traditional rules and regulations to make any finance-related decisions. Then, after introducing the preliminary finance-related AI-powered systems, the sector gradually accepted and integrated AI-powered models into dissimilar financial services [16]. Afterward, AI is quickly integrated with the sector, and it enhanced the sector's capability to offer high-quality financial services. Thus, financial products and service descriptions are being reformed by AI [17]. In addition to contributing more effective ways, it has also sped up, accelerated, and reinvented conventional processes to make them more effective in handling data and enhancing the customer's experience [18]. Thus, in the recent epoch, AI has become a vital part of our daily routine tasks by introducing and having its advanced applications in dissimilar fields.

Table 3.1 AI development phases in the financial sector.

Phase I: absence of AI model	Phase II: few AI models	Phase III: existence of multiple AI models
The financial sector depends on traditional rules and regulations to make financial decisions.	The financial sector slowly accepts the newly introduced AI models and merges them with dissimilar financial practices such as risk management and control, credit decision, and anti-money laundering.	The financial sector began to integrate AI-powered models into their day-to-day activities such as controlling and mitigating financial risk, stocks and investments prediction, fraud detection, and process automation.

Remarkably, AI-based technologies can examine capital market financial data, financial news for stock predictions, and market historical patterns to adopt rapidly the best trading choices. Thus, it potentially enhances investment performance. AI-based robo-advisors provide automated advice for investment and portfolio management [19]. Moreover, natural language processing (NLP) procedures have permitted AI to examine massive amounts of financial bulletins, financial data, and corporate sector filings to suggest investment decisions. In addition, AI-grounded chatbots and simulated assistants have heightened customer connections and support. Another important aspect of AI technologies is that they are assisting financial institutions to combat money laundering by evaluating their transactions and recognizing doubtful patterns [20]. Moreover, some other AI procedures, like data mining and machine learning, permit financial institutes to extract insights from big databases [21]. Undeniably, AI creates a new world of financial services and brings abundant benefits; nevertheless, it also comes up with numerous hindrances and challenges for the financial sector [22]. Noticeably, AI-based financial systems are prone to security risks such as cybersecurity threats. Also, AI-powered tools in the financial sector involve widespread data collection and investigation. This increases privacy-related concerns, as the financial information of entities and individuals is required to be protected and tightly handled [23]. Importantly, these drawbacks can be lessened via responsible AI practices such as adopting a financial risk detection process. The AI risk detection procedure allows financial institutions to execute advanced data analysis and machine learning techniques to recognize possible risks.

Also, continuous monitoring and inspecting AI methods, robust measures for cybersecurity, and adopting a regulatory framework to handle and address all sorts of unique challenges of AI in the industry of finance [24].

3.2.1   AI and Financial Risk Detection Processes

Notably, AI-powered tools help out the financial sector to detect all sorts of financial risks [25]. AI tools and processes for the financial sector are used to analyze massive amounts of data to detect and identify forms and anomalies indicative of fraudulent activities. Typically, AI procedures used machine learning models that used historic data to notice fraudulent transactions in real time, thus helping financial institutions to prevent and mitigate fraud risks [26].

Figure 3.2 below displays the process that AI uses to evaluate financial risk. Analytically, large volumes of historical and other dissimilar types of data, economic indicators, customer transaction records, etc., are used by AI systems to recognize possible risk factors, notice anomalies, and uncover patterns that humans might overlook. Remarkably, AI algorithms are trained to handle data quality issues, model biases, security vulnerabilities, and ethical concerns [27]. Thus, by applying AI-powered procedures, potential risk and its type can easily be recognized. Additionally, AI lines

Figure 3.2 AI-grounded financial risk detection procedure. (Source: Authors' own elaboration).

up different types of risks such as credit risk, market risk, and liquidity risk by considering their possible influence and possibility of occurrence. Also, by analyzing historical data and patterns, AI-powered algorithms measure the probable impact of each risk-based factor on past events or similar situations [28]. These algorithms allocate weights or scores to dissimilar types of risks. This enables risk prioritization based on their estimated risk levels. Subsequently, after measuring the potential influence and possibility, both, AI can provide valuable insights to prioritize risks effectively and allocate appropriate resources for mitigation efforts [29].

Notably, AI risk detection procedures help financial concerns to measure the creditworthiness and risk analysis of their customers by evaluating credit-based histories, financial statements, and other relevant financial data. AI-powered systems detect and measure risks by executing their competencies in data analysis and pattern recognition [30]. This assists them in streamlining procedures of loan underwriting and making more accurate lending decisions [31]. Additionally, the AI risk detection procedure benefits by providing precise and timely recognition of risks. This enables businesses to proactively address, handle, and mitigate possible threats, minimize financial losses, develop decision-making, and improve overall risk mitigation effectiveness.

3.2.2 AI and Financial Risk Recognition Techniques

Undoubtedly, AI plays an important role in financial risk identification and mitigation by offering advanced tools and techniques such as risk assessment, fraud detection, stress testing, credit risk analysis, portfolio management, market risk analysis, algorithm trading, and regulatory compliance [32]. Importantly, by using process automation, AI automates numerous tasks and plans involved in risk management and mitigation processes. AI-powered algorithms examine the vast volume of data, recognize patterns, and detect irregularities in real time that allow for proactive risk recognition and mitigation. Thus, by automating tasks such as data assessment, verification, and evaluation, AI reorganizes risk management and mitigation procedures [33]. The core techniques and tools executed by AI to mitigate financial risk are enlightened below:

3.2.2.1   Risk Assessment and Prediction

To identify and tackle financial risk, AI algorithms examine large volumes of real-time and historical data and detect potential risks [34]. Remarkably, AI predicts future market trends by executing machine learning approaches after the assessment of credit default possibilities. The machine learning-based approaches enable AI to evaluate and predict financial risks [35]. AI assesses and predicts risk by employing innovative machine learning-based algorithms and techniques after analyzing big data, i.e., real-time and historical data. Technically, during the development phase, AI models are trained to evaluate historical data that enable them to learn patterns and relations. Therefore, these models can examine newly added data, assess financial risk factors, and then after evaluation make predictions [36]. This assessment contains detecting probable anomalies, assessing possibilities of certain consequences, or classifying financial risks based on predefined standards [37]. The AI-powered systems offer valuable insights and recommendations to financial decision makers, also inform them of risk-managing approaches and implement suitable risk mitigation measures.

3.2.2.2   Fraud Detection and Anticipation

Noticeably, AI-powered tools assess fraudulent activities by employing innovative algorithms and machine learning procedures to examine large volumes of data and detect patterns, irregularities, and all dissimilar indicators that indicate fraudulent behavior [38]. Scientifically, by training on historical fraud-related cases and big data, AI-powered models can notice possible fraud by comparing recent transactions and actions against the learned patterns. Moreover, AI-based systems easily recognize suspicious actions, flag fake transactions, and produce alerts for further inquiry [39]. Interestingly, the nonstop learning ability of AI permits it to adapt and improve fraud recognition accuracy over time. This enables businesses to proactively recognize and mitigate probable fraudulent actions, diminish financial losses, and provide shelter against reputational damage [40].

3.2.2.3   Risk Modeling and Stress Testing

AI risk modeling and stress testing involve the use of AI procedures to measure, evaluate, and monitor possible risks and weaknesses within financial systems. Fundamentally, AI-powered tools simulate and evaluate diverse situations such as economic downturns or risky market circumstances to measure the resilience of existing financial systems and investment portfolios. Notably, by stress-testing tactics, institutions can identify weaknesses and numerous risk factors to develop contingency plans [41]. Typically, AI risk models evaluate available historical data, financial market movements, and other related factors to recognize risk features and measure their impact on the complete risk profile [42]. Additionally, these AI models simulate numerous stress situations, such as downturns of financial markets, worst economic shocks, or risky events, to estimate the resilience and weaknesses of the system under hostile circumstances. Consequently, by applying AI-powered algorithms, businesses gain insights into the possible impact of dissimilar risk aspects, enhance risk exposure, and develop vigorous risk mitigation approaches [43]. Notably, AI-powered risk modeling and stress testing permit businesses to mitigate and manage risk more efficiently, improve decision-making, and support their overall risk-managing framework.

3.2.2.4   Portfolio Optimization and Asset Allocation

AI portfolio optimization and asset allocation comprise the use of AI-powered algorithms to regulate the optimal allocation of financial assets within an investment portfolio. Technically, by considering multiple variables and constraints, AI-powered tools suggest optimal asset allocations for investors that balance risk and return that reduce the overall risk exposure in investment portfolios [44]. Thus, by evaluating historical data, financial market trends, risk and return profiles, and all other relevant aspects, AI-powered models can easily recognize the best mix of assets that produce a maximum return and minimize risk. Also, these models consider numerous parameters, such as instability, and probable returns of each financial asset to develop portfolios that attain the required investment aims [45]. Essentially, AI-powered systems continuously learn from newly added data and trends in capital markets. These practices allow them to adapt and enhance investment portfolio allocations and adjustments over time [46]. Thus, AI-powered portfolio asset allocation and optimization offer stakeholders data-driven insights, help them with investment decisions, attain asset diversification, and enhance the risk–return trade-off in their investment portfolios [47].

3.2.2.5   Regulatory Compliance

Notably, AI cares about regulatory compliance by systematizing and streamlining all sorts of compliance procedures, enhancing precision, and improving effectiveness [48]. Likewise, AI-powered algorithms examine complex regulatory frameworks, extract relevant information from regulatory documents, and identify compliance requirements applicable to specific business activities [49]. Also, AI-powered systems monitor and examine massive amounts of financial data in real time to distinguish probable compliance defilements, flag doubtful dealings, and produce alerts for supplementary investigation. Additionally, AI supports conducting Know Your Customer (KYC) procedures on anti-money laundering and all types of data privacy-related compliances by systematizing data authentication, identity confirmation, and risk assessment. Moreover, by executing AI in regulatory compliance, businesses can stay up-to-date with altering rules and regulations, lessen manual struggle, confirm adherence to compliance-related obligations, and minimize dissimilar risks such as financial penalties, legal costs, and reputational damage [50].

3.2.2.6   Cybersecurity and Data Privacy

Visibly, in the last few years, AI has improved cybersecurity by evaluating network systems traffic, recognizing probable threats, and replying in real time to avoid cyberattacks and data breaches. Also, AI plays a key role in preserving data secrecy and cybersecurity by bolstering defenses, detecting and replying to threats, and guaranteeing compliance with privacy regulations [51]. Furthermore, AI-powered systems can also be used to examine network data traffic and observe users' behavior and logs of systems to recognize patterns revealing cybersecurity and threats, such as malware, phishing efforts, or unauthorized contact. Hence, by adopting machine learning-based algorithms, AI uninterruptedly learns from innovative data and acquaints its protection mechanisms to handle threats [52]. Moreover, AI-driven systems are able to improve data secrecy by mechanically recognizing and redacting complex information and certifying compliance with data safety rules and regulations [53]. In addition, AI provides support in anomaly appreciation, user authentication, and threat intellect, providing businesses with real-time visions and practical actions to defend against cyberattacks and protect data privacy [54].

3.2.2.7   Chatbots and Customer Service

AI-powered chatbots and simulated assistants offer customer service, response to investigations, and support with basic banking connections [55]. The natural language processing algorithms permit chatbots to recognize and reply to client inquiries efficiently, improve client satisfaction, and reduce the need for human involvement. Importantly, AI-powered chatbots can potentially handle and reduce various risk areas for enterprises of all sizes, making them a workable and affordable solution for a variety of situations. By using natural language processing and machine learning abilities, AI-powered chatbots are considered best for risk measurement, management and mitigation [56]. Also, because of their 24/7 accessibility and data analysis capability, AI chatbots offer valuable support in classifying, handling, and mitigating risks within the finance and more specifically in the banking industry.

3.2.2.8   Loan Underwriting and Processing

AI-facilitated loan underwriting and processes play an important role in handling and mitigating financial risk. Technically, AI-powered algorithms automate document authentication, measure creditworthiness, evaluate real-time available financial data, notice fraud, and permit exact risk assessment [57]. By streamlining the procedure of loan approval and adopting machine learning, financial organizations can make knowledgeable decisions, confirm steadiness, and reduce human blunders. Moreover, AI-based systems also support portfolio evaluation and management, monitoring customer repayment behavior, noticing possible defaults, and permitting proactive risk management and mitigation [58]. Eventually, AI-powered loan endorsing and processing improve risk managing and mitigation practices, efficiency of lending processes and reduces financial risks.

3.3   Financial Risks and AI Mitigation Practices

AI plays a substantial role in measuring and mitigating financial risks. It can evaluate large amounts of data, recognize patterns, and make financial predictions, thus enhancing risk evaluation and decision-making procedures. Hence, some core types of financial risks where AI can be applied are credit risk, market risk, fraud risk, operational risk, compliance risk, and liquidity risk.

3.3.1   Credit Risk and Artificial Intelligence

Credit risk is one of the key concerns in the financial sector, since it requires careful consideration while determining the possibility when the issued loan will be repaid [59]. Therefore, credit risk scoring is one of the key analytical ways for banks and other financial institutions to measure credit risk [60, 61]. Conventionally, financial institutions have used standard logit, linear, and probit regressions to evaluate credit risk [62, 63]. The former financial crisis indicates that conventional methods for credit risk scoring do not deliver comprehensive and conclusive predictions for forthcoming financial fiascos. Though, by using machine learning and data analytics, financial institutions can automate credit risk assessment processes, detect early warning signs of default, and make more informed lending decisions. Moreover, AI-powered tools' capabilities in credit risk management improve efficiency, enhance risk assessment accuracies, and facilitate proactive measures to mitigate credit-related losses [64].

3.3.2   Market Risk and Artificial Intelligence

Market risk is a significant concern for the financial sector, encompassing the potential for losses arising from adverse movements in financial markets. Typically, it includes risks associated with interest rates, equity prices, foreign exchange rates, commodity prices, liquidity, and systemic factors [65]. Notably, financial institutions mitigate market risk by engaging in approaches such as asset–liability management, portfolio diversification, predictive modeling, currency hedging, liquidity forecasting, stress testing, and network analysis [66]. These tactics are often maintained by AI-driven tools and analytics. Technically, these AI-powered tools optimize risk–return profiles, manage exposure to market variations, and guarantee the stability and resilience of the financial sector and institutions during market uncertainties. Moreover, AI can examine market trends, social media sentiment, news, and all other dissimilar types of data sources to forecast market activities and recognize potential risks. Market risk and AI are closely intertwined in the financial sector. AI technologies play a crucial role in assessing, managing, and mitigating market risk by analyzing vast amounts of data, identifying patterns, and trends and predicting market movements [67].

3.3.3   Liquidity Risk and Artificial Intelligence

Liquidity risk arises when banks are not able to meet their short-term obligations. Principally, liquidity risk is an important concern for banks, as they rely heavily on preserving adequate liquidity to ensure that they meet payment withdrawals, loan disbursements, and other operational and financial needs [68, 69]. Remarkably, liquidity risk and AI intersect to help out the financial sector to manage efficiently and mitigate possible liquidity-related challenges. AI-based technologies examine large volumes of data, counting cash flow patterns, financial market situations, and exterior factors, to estimate liquidity needs and recognize possible liquidity gaps. Therefore, by employing AI algorithms, the financial sector can enhance cash management approaches, improve liquidity prediction accuracies, and systematize liquidity risk monitoring. Moreover, AI-driven tools provide real-time insights, allowing financial institutions to proactively address liquidity risks, adjust cash management strategies, and enhance liquidity positions [70]. Hence, by merging AI's analytical capabilities with inclusive risk management and mitigation frameworks, financial institutions can enhance their ability to maintain sufficient liquidity levels and navigate potential liquidity stress events more effectively.

3.3.4   Operation Risk and Artificial Intelligence

Operational risk is an important concern in the financial sector and mentions the potential for losses that arise from insufficient or failed interior procedures, systems, officials, people, or exterior events [71]. Technically, mitigating operational risk in finance involves various strategies such as a strong risk management framework, process automation, employee training and awareness, business continuity planning, cybersecurity measures, and vendor management [72]. Visibly, operational risk and AI interconnect in the finance sector, offering opportunities to improve operational flexibility and mitigate possible risks. Remarkably, AI-powered tools are used to mechanize and enhance interior procedures, reduce human error, and enhance operational productivity [73]. Furthermore, machine learning-based algorithms are used to examine big data and detect irregularities and classify probable operational risks in real time, permitting practical risk mitigation and management. Also, AI-powered tools can support cyber-security by detecting and replying to existing cyber threats rapidly. AI enables compliance monitoring, thus helping the financial sector to classify and address probable controlling risks [74]. Hence, by involving robust AI-powered tactics, financial institutions are now able to knob operational risk, enhance risk mitigation policies, and preserve a vigorous operational structure.

3.3.5   Compliance Risk and Artificial Intelligence

Compliance risk pertains to probable financial losses, lawful consequences, reputational damage, or other hostile penalties resulting from a failure of complying with the applicable rules, regulations, business ethics, or interior strategies [75]. Precisely, it rises when businesses or the individual interrupts or fails to follow the legal and governing necessities, counting those connected to financial services and operations, data safety, anti-money laundering, customer protection, etc. [76]. Notably, the implementation of AI-powered tools within an organization improves regulatory compliance efforts to mitigate and control compliance risk. Mostly, AI technologies offer competencies that streamline compliance procedures, improve accuracy, and mitigate compliance risks [77]. Thus, AI is utilized to systematize regulatory monitoring and reporting, permitting real-time identification of possible compliance violations. Moreover, AI-based machine learning algorithms also examine vast amounts of data to indicate patterns, anomalies, and suspicious activities, facilitating proactive risk management and fraud detection. Also, AI-driven tools support directing Know Your Customer procedures, checks to control anti-money laundering, and confirming data secrecy compliance [78]. Executing AI for compliance risk mitigation and management, businesses can boost efficiency, decrease human error, and respond to governing necessities promptly, thus mitigating possible legal, reputational, and financial risks.

Importantly, it is observed that despite benefits, AI is also prone to several financial risks. Firstly, for training, AI-powered models depend on historical data, thus, if the underlying data comprise inaccuracies, imperfect information, and biases, it will lead to defective forecasts and conclusions. This will result in huge financial losses and improper risk evaluations [79]. Secondly, AI-powered models are not accustomed to unexpected situations or speedily altering financial market conditions, as they are characteristically trained on only historical data [80]. Technically, this inflexibility leads to unsuitable risk mitigation and management policies that can detect evolving risks. Moreover, the increasing complexity of AI-powered systems makes them vulnerable to combative attacks, which can be exploited for malicious determinations, producing financial damage [81]. Lastly, extra dependence on AI without human involvement and authentication can lead to complications, where serious risks may go unobserved or unaddressed. Hence, to mitigate these sorts of risks, financial organizations need vigorous data governance practices, continuous monitoring and validation of AI-powered systems, human oversight, and suitable risk mitigation and management outlines that account for all sorts of AI-specific risk and challenges.

3.4   AI and Financial Risk Mitigation Procedures

Fundamentally, for risk mitigation, AI implements numerous steps and tactics such as big data collection, data analysis, risk assessment, decision support, and continuous assessment to lessen risk potential adverse impacts. Thus, the overall process for the mitigation of risk in AI includes several steps such as the following:

3.4.1   Identification and Assessment of Risks

AI risk mitigation procedures begin by identifying and assessing potential risks [82]. Fundamentally, the AI risk mitigation process comprises considering both types of risks that are technical and non-technical risks that contain data quality, security weaknesses, ethical concerns, model bias, and controlling compliance [83]. Technically, AI assists in identifying and measuring risks by leveraging its abilities in data analysis and pattern recognition. It evaluates large data to identify possible risk factors, notice irregularities, and expose patterns that humans might overlook [84]. Also, AI algorithms are competent to check data quality matters, constructed model biases, security vulnerabilities, and moral concerns. Moreover, by applying machine learning measures, AI-powered tools can help in identifying and predicting the possibility and potential impact of dissimilar types of risks that are because of historical data and patterns. For instance, AI-powered patterns have significant impacts on credit risk assessments. As a result, banks and other financial institutions can do thorough credit risk analysis, evaluate consumer behavior, and finally confirm the customers' capacity and ability to repay the loans [85]. Similarly, liquidity risk is another devastating threat to financial institutions. Specifically, banks are in severe financial danger from liquidity risk, which, if understated or handled inaccurately, might have irrecoverable implications [86]. Notably, liquidity risk specifies the bank's incapability to provide clients with access to their own deposited cash [87]. To deal with this issue, AI is measured as the best tool that could help banks to improve the assessment of liquidity risk [88]. Thus, AI facilitates risk identification, assessment, and evaluation by automating risk scoring and providing real-time monitoring and alerts, enabling timely intervention and mitigation actions.

3.4.2   Risk Prioritization

Once the risk identification and assessments are done, AI focused on those risks that have the maximum potential for harm or disruption to the financial project [89]. Historically, financial decisions are largely dependent on grouping and assessing descriptive base analytics such as financial reports and dashboards, which only contain past information. Thus, this information cannot handle big quantity of data, which is warranted for accurate forthcoming risk predictions. However, AI procedures that can handle and assess vast quantities of data are now able to predict future risks [90]. Subsequently, AI ranks dissimilar kinds of risks by seeing their potential influence and possibility of occurrence. By examining historical data,

AI-powered algorithms measure the possible impact of each type of identified risk that is based on former similar financial situations. In addition, AI used machine learning procedures to evaluate the possibility of each risk by recognizing related pointers and correlations. These AI-powered algorithms assign weights to dissimilar types of identified risks, permitting the ordering of risks based on their intended risk stages [91]. Moreover, AI-powered robo-advisors are also used to evaluate anticipated financial risk classes for each individual and institution. Technically, AI algorithms are executed to assess big data and measure the returns of operational financial products and services that help to classify accurate levels for each anticipated risk [92]. Consequently, by considering both, the possible influence and likelihood, AI delivers valuable understandings to rank risks efficiently and assign appropriate properties for risk mitigation efforts [93].

3.4.3   Developing Risk Mitigation Policies

After identifying potential risks, AI develops substantial policies to mitigate or lessen its influence. This comprises applying procedural controls, implementing best practices, improving data collection and preprocessing procedures, or creating compliance and governance frameworks [94]. Technically, AI includes massive amounts of information and evaluates historical patterns to develop effective risk mitigation policies. Given identifying risk-related elements such as the risk nature, existing resources, and business objectives, AI develops risk mitigation policies [95]. Technically, these policies are developed to mitigate financial risks through technical controls, such as applying security measures or data anonymization procedures, or best practices for handling specific risks. Furthermore, AI can also assist in measuring the possible effectiveness of dissimilar mitigation methods through simulations or analytical modeling, aiding in the adoption of the most suitable risk mitigation policies [96]. Though, it is imperative to note that the last decision-making and strategy preparation should include human proficiency and judgment to confirm ethical deliberations and controlling compliance are sufficiently addressed. Notably, when AI-based policies are developed for mitigating financial risks, it is also required to pay special attention to AI-associated risks like data protection and cost of execution. Technically, developing and implementing AI systems and policies have both negative and positive impacts. Trustworthy AI risk mitigation policies are safe, secure, explainable, fair, and enhance system privacy [97].

3.4.4   Implementation of Risk Control Policies

Once AI-powered risk mitigation policies are developed and finalized, the next step is to put them into action. This includes applying several technical measures such as security protocols, system privacy and protections, and authentication procedures. Also, it is required to ensure that appropriate policies, guidelines, and procedures are communicated and followed by the project team [98, 99]. Moreover, AI-powered risk control policies are implemented by employing advanced algorithms and machine learning procedures to examine vast amounts of historical data and recognize possible risks [100]. Importantly, applied AI policies are required to continuously monitor and evaluate numerous aspects such as the behavior of users, system weaknesses, and exterior threats [101]. Based on this analysis, AI can autonomously impose predefined policies and strategies such as access controls, irregularity recognition, and response mechanisms to manage and mitigate financial risks successfully. Precisely, AI improves risk control procedures and vigorously alters processes to address evolving threats and financial risk in real time, confirming AI as an active and robust approach to risk management and mitigation [102].

3.4.5   Monitor and Evaluate Risk Mitigation Procedures

After the implementation of risk control policies, it is obligatory to continuously monitor the financial projects for probable risks and assess the efficiency of the applied risk mitigation controls. Technically, monitoring and evaluating AI-powered risk mitigation measures contains a comprehensive framework that includes continuous monitoring, periodic evaluations, and performance analysis [103]. Moreover, this evaluation process also contains monitoring the AI system's performance, outputs, and connections with the financial market environment to detect any potential risks or deviations from desired outcomes. Thus, regular assessments should be conducted to measure the efficiency of the risk mitigation procedures, recognizing any gaps or areas of development. Furthermore, KPIs, i.e., key performance indicators, are recognized to measure the AI system's performance against predefined benchmarks, and feedback loops are required to be executed to gather and integrate user responses [104]. Hence, by combining real-time monitoring, periodic assessments, and response mechanisms, businesses can easily confirm the continuing efficiency of AI risk mitigation procedures and make obligatory alterations to improve the system's general risk management and mitigation capabilities [105].

3.4.6   Testing and Validation

Visibly, AI conducts rigorous testing and authentication of AI models to mitigate risks through numerous tactics. First, businesses employ varied and representative data sets during the testing period to confirm that the AI model learns from a wide range of examples and situations [106]. This helps classify potential biases and declines the risk of the model making biased or discriminatory forecasts. Second, businesses employ rigorous testing procedures, counting stress testing, cross-validation, and holdout testing to assess the model's presentation and robustness [107]. Remarkably, this helps to recognize any probable weaknesses or boundaries of the AI model. In addition, businesses can employ procedures such as sensitivity analysis, real-world simulation, and adversarial testing to evaluate the model's response to dissimilar inputs and situations. Hence, systematic testing of the AI model's performance before launching, coupled with responses from users and domain specialists, contributes to continuing risk mitigation efforts [108]. Particularly, by conducting severe testing and validation, businesses can boost the reliability, accuracy, and fairness of AI models, thus mitigating possible risks related to their deployment.

3.4.7   Continuously Improving the Risk Mitigation Process

Typically, risk mitigation is a continuous procedure [109]. Therefore, it is essential to regularly reassess risks and adapt the mitigation measures through the AI project life cycle. Principally, AI-based risk mitigation procedures repeatedly improve through iterative learning orders that leverage data collection, algorithmic improvements, feedback loops, domain expertise incorporation, adaptive learning, real-time monitoring, and a human-in-the-loop approach. Thus, by examining real-world data and outcomes, AI-based systems enhance their risk assessment capabilities and improve procedures for better correctness. Importantly, the continuous response from users permits AI to adapt and evaluate developing risks [110]. Moreover, adaptive learning ensures that the AI system stays up-to-date with topical information. Also, human fault and iterative development cycles improve the AI-powered model's competence and performance, resulting in uninterruptedly improving risk management and mitigation procedures [111].

Figure 3.3 displays the AI financial risk mitigation procedure. The constructed risk mitigation procedure is an ongoing process that starts with the identification of risk and ends up with the risk mitigation and identification process. Here, after the identification of a new risk, the process again

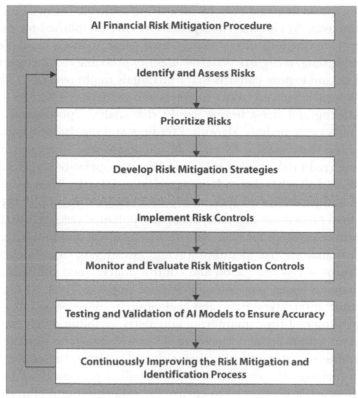

Figure 3.3 AI financial risk mitigation procedure. (Source: Authors' own elaboration).

starts from the beginning to identify and assess the new risk. By treating AI risk mitigation procedure as a continuous procedure, businesses can adjust to changing situations, proactively address possible new forms of risks, and guarantee that AI risk mitigation systems are ongoing and effective, dependable, and aligned with business goals and prospects.

3.5   Conclusion

Financial risk identification and mitigation is one of the core fields in the area of finance with robust expansion during the last few decades, but the desire for more progress is continuously growing. This is one of the main causes why AI has become pivotal in today's world of financial risk management and mitigation. The amazing advantage of AI is that it becomes marvelous after the combination of machine learning and big data. Technically, due to this amalgamation, AI risk detection procedures are now able to speedily capture financial risks by measuring available financial information. Moreover, AI risk detection procedures are established for noticing fraudulent transactions in real time, which helps financial institutions to evaluate big data, recognize patterns, identify probable risk factors, notice anomalies, and expose patterns that individuals might overlook. Also, AI adopts several advanced tactics to assess and manage risk factors such as risk modeling and stress testing, credit risk analysis, portfolio management, market risk analysis, algorithm trading, and regulatory compliance. By adopting these tactics, AI plays an important role in measuring and mitigating credit risk, market risk, liquidity risk, operational risk, compliance risk, and all other dissimilar types of financial risks. Thus, by offering accurate and predictive analysis on big data sets in a fraction of the time, AI-powered procedures can easily recognize potential risks. AI also implements numerous steps for financial risk management and mitigation such as big data analysis, risk identification and assessment, risk prioritization, development of risk mitigation and control policies, and continuous risk assessments to lessen risk potential adverse impacts. Thus, AI facilitates risk identification, assessment, and evaluation by automating risk scoring and providing real-time monitoring and alerts, enabling timely intervention and mitigation actions. Moreover, AI-powered systems support financial institutions in strengthening their risk mitigation strategies, improving decision-making, and enhancing overall resilience in evolving financial risks. However, it is essential to ensure the robustness and ethical use of AI systems while maintaining human oversight and validation to mitigate potential risks associated with AI itself. As a whole, AI is playing a momentous role in mitigating financial risk through its capability to scrutinize vast amounts of financial data, recognize patterns, and make predictions. Without a speck of doubt, AI is the future of the finance sector. It is moving at a rapid pace to make financial processes simpler and risk-free.

References

1. Xu, X., The influence of artificial intelligence on the financial industry. Artificial intelligence based commercial risk management framework for SMEs. *Sustainability*, 11, 16, 4501, 2023.
2. Boden, M.A. (Ed.), *Artificial Intelligence*, Elsevier, Academic Press, San Diego, USA, 1996.
3. Maciel, L., ChatGPT and the ethical aspects of artificial intelligence. *Rev. Gest.*, 30, 2, 110–112, 2023.

4. Liu, Z. K., Thermodynamics and its prediction and CALPHAD modeling: Review, state of the art, and perspectives. Calphad, Elsevier, USA, 82, 102580, 2023. https://doi.org/10.1016/j.calphad.2023.102580

5. Richardson, S., Cognitive automation: A new era of knowledge work? *Bus. Inf. Rev.*, 37, 4, 182–189, 2020.

6. Hussain, M., Mir, M., Musharaf, S., Sajid, S., Examining the role of artificial intelligence in determining sustainable competitive advantage: Evidence from the pharmaceutical sector of Karachi Pakistan. *J. Future Sustain.*, 3, 1, 23–34, 2023.

7. Bauguess, S.W., *The Role Of Big Data, Machine Learning, And AI in Assessing Risks: A Regulatory Perspective*, SEC Keynote Address: OpRisk North America, June 21, 2017, 2017.

8. Pal, T., The exploratory study of machine learning on applications, challenges, and uses in the financial sector, in: *Advanced Machine Learning Algorithms for Complex Financial Applications*, pp. 156–165, IGI Global, Hershey, Pennsylvania, USA, 2023.

9. Turchin, A. and Denkenberger, D., Classification of global catastrophic risks connected with artificial intelligence. *AI Soc.*, 35, 1, 147–163, 2020.

10. Manheim, K. and Kaplan, L., Artificial intelligence: Risks to privacy and democracy. *Yale J.L. Tech.*, 21, 106, 2019.

11. Faustman, E.M. and Omenn, G.S., Risk assessment, in: *Casarett and Doull's Toxicology: The Basic Science of Poisons*, pp. 107–128, 2008.

12. Perri, M., Guta, A., Kaminski, N., Bonn, M., Kolla, G., Bayoumi, A., Strike, C., Spotting as a risk mitigation method: A qualitative study comparing organization-based and informal methods. *Int. J. Drug Policy*, 111, 103905, 2023.

13. Nguyen, D.K., Sermpinis, G., Stasinakis, C., Big data, artificial intelligence and machine learning: A transformative symbiosis in favour of financial technology. *Eur. Financial Manage.*, 29, 2, 517–548, 2023.

14. Baquero, J.A., Burkhardt, R., Govindarajan, A., Wallace, T., Derisking AI by design: How to build risk management into AI development, McKinsey & Company, MCKinsey Analytics, 1-12, 2020.

15. Baltrusaitis, J., *Finbold News*, 2023. Available at: https://finbold.com/ai-sector-to-become-a-trillion-dollar-market-in-the-next-5-years/, (Accessed on: 3-June-2023).

16. Sawwalakhe, R., Arora, S., Singh, T.P., Opportunities and challenges for artificial intelligence and machine learning applications in the finance sector, in: *Advanced Machine Learning Algorithms for Complex Financial Applications*, pp. 1–17, 2023.

17. Ganesh, A.D. and Kalpana, P., Future of artificial intelligence and its influence on supply chain risk management–A systematic review. *Comput. Ind. Eng.*, 108206, 2022.

18. Kabza, M., Artificial intelligence in financial services–benefits and costs, in: *Innovation in Financial Services*, pp. 183–198, Routledge, England, 2020.

19. Yudkowsky, E., Artificial intelligence as a positive and negative factor in global risk, in: *Global Catastrophic Risks*, vol. 1, p. 184, 2008.
20. Kaswan, K.S., Dhatterwal, J.S., Kumar, N., Lal, S., Artificial intelligence for financial services, in: *Contemporary Studies of Risks in Emerging Technology, Part A*, pp. 71–92, Emerald Publishing Limited, United Kingdom, 2023.
21. Williams, T., Artificial intelligence in finance with examples: An ultimate guide, 2023. Available at: https://www.theknowledgeacademy.com/blog/artificial-intelligence-in-finance/, (Accessed on: 28-May-2023).
22. Steimers, A. and Schneider, M., Sources of risk of AI systems. *Int. J. Environ. Res. Public Health*, 19, 6, 3641, 2022.
23. Aleksandrova, A., Ninova, V., Zhelev, Z., A survey on AI implementation in finance, (cyber) insurance and financial controlling. *Risks*, 11, 5, 91, 2023.
24. Park, Y.J. and Jones-Jang, S.M., Surveillance, security, and AI as technological acceptance. *AI Soc.*, 1–12, 2022.
25. Menoni, S. and Margottini, C., *Inside Risk: A Strategy for Sustainable Risk Mitigation*, Springer Science & Business Media, Germany, 2011.
26. Coombs, C. and Chopra, R., Artificial intelligence and data analytics: Emerging opportunities and challenges in financial services, 2019.
27. Choi, D. and Lee, K., An artificial intelligence approach to financial fraud detection under IoT environment: A survey and implementation. *Secur. Commun. Netw.*, 2018, 2–15, 2018.
28. Giudici, P., Fintech risk management: A research challenge for artificial intelligence in finance. *Front. Artif. Intell.*, 1, 1, 2018.
29. Auger, S.D., Jacobs, B.M., Dobson, R., Marshall, C.R., Noyce, A.J., Big data, machine learning and artificial intelligence: A neurologist's guide. *Pract. Neurol.*, 21, 1, 4–11, 2021.
30. Alhaddad, M.M., Artificial intelligence in banking industry: A review on fraud detection, credit management, and document processing. *RRST*, 2, 3, 25–46, 2018.
31. Danenas, P. and Garšva, G., Support vector machines and their application in credit risk evaluation process, 2010. Available online: https://www.researchgate.net/publication/235659762_support_vector_machines_and_their_application_in_credit_risk_evaluation_process (accessed on 31 May 2023).
32. Schuett, J., Risk management in the artificial intelligence act. *Eur. J. Risk Regul.*, 1–19, 2023.
33. Cheatham, B., Javanmardian, K., Samandari, H., Confronting the risks of artificial intelligence. *McKinsey Q.*, 2(38), 1-9, 2019.
34. Dananjayan, S. and Raj, G.M., Artificial intelligence during a pandemic: The COVID-19 example. *Int. J. Health Plan. Manag.*, 35(5), 1260, 2020.
35. Berk, R.A., Artificial intelligence, predictive policing, and risk assessment for law enforcement. *Annu. Rev. Criminol.*, 4, 209–237, 2021.
36. Singh, T.P., Nandimath, P., Kumbhar, V., Das, S., Barne, P., Drought risk assessment and prediction using artificial intelligence over the southern Maharashtra state of India. *Model. Earth Syst. Environ.*, 7, 2005–2013, 2021.

37. Assaad, R. and El-adaway, I.H., Evaluation and prediction of the hazard potential level of dam infrastructures using computational artificial intelligence algorithms. *J. Manage. Eng.*, 36, 5, 04020051, 2020.
38. Balamurugan, E., Flaih, L.R., Yuvaraj, D., Sangeetha, K., Jayanthiladevi, A., Kumar, T.S., Use case of artificial intelligence in machine learning manufacturing 4.0, in: *2019 International Conference On Computational Intelligence And Knowledge Economy (ICCIKE)*, IEEE, pp. 656–659, 2019.
39. Bao, Y., Hilary, G., Ke, B., Artificial intelligence and fraud detection, in: *Innovative Technology at the Interface of Finance and Operations: Volume I*, pp. 223–247, 2022.
40. Bhatore, S., Mohan, L., Reddy, Y.R., Machine learning techniques for credit risk evaluation: A systematic literature review. *J. Bank. Financ. Technol.*, 4, 111–138, 2020.
41. Crockett, D., Kelly, C., Brundage, J., Jones, J., Ockerse, P., A stress test of artificial intelligence: Can deep learning models trained from formal echocardiography accurately interpret point-of-care ultrasound? *J. Ultrasound Med.*, 41, 12, 3003–3012, 2022.
42. O'Halloran, S. and Nowaczyk, N., An artificial intelligence approach to regulating systemic risk. *Front. Artif. Intell.*, 2, 7, 2019.
43. Jacobs Jr., M., The validation of machine-learning models for the stress testing of credit risk. *J. Risk Manage. Financ. Inst.*, 11, 3, 218–243, 2018.
44. Babaei, G., Giudici, P., Raffinetti, E., Explainable artificial intelligence for crypto asset allocation. *Finance Res. Lett.*, 47, 102941, 2022.
45. Adebiyi, S.O., Ogunbiyi, O.O., Amole, B.B., Artificial intelligence model for building investment portfolio optimization mix using historical stock prices data. *RAMJ*, 16, 1, 36–62, 2022.
46. Chan, M.C., Wong, C.C., Tse, W.F., Cheung, B.K.S., Tang, G.Y.N., Artificial intelligence in portfolio management, in: *Intelligent Data Engineering and Automated Learning—IDEAL 2002: Third International Conference, Proceedings*, Manchester, UK, August 12–14, 2002, vol. 3, Springer Berlin Heidelberg, pp. 403–409, 2002.
47. Bartram, S.M., Branke, J., Motahari, M., *Artificial Intelligence in Asset Management*, CFA Institute Research Foundation, United States, 2020.
48. Kingston, J., Using artificial intelligence to support compliance with the general data protection regulation. *Artif. Intell. Law*, 25, 4, 429–443, 2017.
49. Lee, J., Access to finance for artificial intelligence regulation in the financial services industry. *Eur. Bus. Organ. Law Rev.*, 21, 731–757, 2020.
50. Vasista, K., Regulatory compliance and supervision of artificial intelligence, machine learning and also possible effects on financial institutions. *IJIRCCE*, e-ISSN, 9, 2320-9801, June 13, 2021.
51. Bertino, E., Kantarcioglu, M., Akcora, C.G., Samtani, S., Mittal, S., Gupta, M., AI for security and security for AI, in: *Proceedings of the Eleventh ACM Conference on Data and Application Security and Privacy*, pp. 333–334, 2021.

52. Vähäkainu, P. and Lehto, M., Artificial intelligence in the cyber security environment, in: *ICCWS 2019 14th International Conference on Cyber Warfare and Security: ICCWS 2019*, Academic Conferences and Publishing Limited, Oxford, Japan, p. 431, 2019.

53. Wirkuttis, N. and Klein, H., *Artificial Intelligence in Cybersecurity*, Cyber, Intelligence, and Security, Japan, vol. 1, pp. 103–119, 2017.

54. Li, J.H., Cyber security meets artificial intelligence: A survey. *Front. Inf. Technol. Electron. Eng.*, 19, 12, 1462–1474, 2018.

55. Quah, J.T. and Chua, Y.W., Chatbot assisted marketing in financial service industry, in: *Services Computing–SCC 2019: 16th International Conference, Held as Part of the Services Conference Federation, SCF 2019, Proceedings*, San Diego, CA, USA, June 25–30, 2019, Springer International Publishing, pp. 107–114, 2019.

56. Newlands, M., 10 ways AI and chatbots reduce business risks, entrepreneur, 2017. Available at: https://www.entrepreneur.com/science-technology/10-ways-ai-and-chatbots-reduce-business-risks/305073, (Accessed on 6-June-2023).

57. Perel, M. and Plato-Shinar, R., AI-based consumer credit underwriting, in: *Artificial Intelligence in Finance*, pp. 151–176, Edward Elgar Publishing, 2023.

58. Riikkinen, M., Saarijärvi, H., Sarlin, P., Lähteenmäki, I., Using artificial intelligence to create value in insurance. *Int. J. Bank Market.*, 36, 6, 1145–1168, 2018.

59. Berrada, I.R., Barramou, F.Z., Alami, O.B., A review of Artificial Intelligence approach for credit risk assessment, in: *2022 2nd International Conference on Artificial Intelligence and Signal Processing (AISP)*, IEEE, pp. 1–5, 2022.

60. Ghodselahi, A. and Amirmadhi, A., Application of artificial intelligence techniques for credit risk evaluation. *IJMO*, 1, 3, 243, 2011.

61. Lynn, T., Mooney, J.G., Rosati, P., Cummins, M., *Disrupting Finance: FinTech and Strategy in the 21st Century*, p. 175, Springer Nature, Germany, 2019.

62. Altman, E., II, Financial ratios, discriminant analysis and the prediction of corporate bankruptcy. *J. Finance*, 23, 4, 589–609, 1968.

63. Van Thiel, D. and Van Raaij, W.F.F., Artificial intelligence credit risk prediction: An empirical study of analytical artificial intelligence tools for credit risk prediction in a digital era. *J. Risk Manage. Financ. Inst.*, 12, 3, 268–286, 2019.

64. Bussmann, N., Giudici, P., Marinelli, D., Papenbrock, J., Explainable machine learning in credit risk management. *Comput. Econ.*, 57, 203–216, 2021.

65. Carrillo Menéndez, S. and Hassani, B.K., Expected shortfall reliability—added value of traditional statistics and advanced artificial intelligence for market risk measurement purposes. *Mathematics*, 9, 17, 2142, 2021.

66. Groth, S.S. and Muntermann, J., *An intraday market risk management approach based on textual analysis*, vol. 680-691, Decis. Support Syst., 50(4, 2011.

67. Strader, T.J., Rozycki, J.J., Root, T.H., Huang, Y.H.J., Machine learning stock market prediction studies: Review and research directions. *JITIM*, 28, 4, 63–83, 2020.
68. Braun, J., Hausler, J., Schäfers, W., Artificial intelligence, news sentiment, and property market liquidity. *J. Prop. Invest. Finance*, 38, 4, 309–325, 2020.
69. Satheesh, M.K. and Nagaraj, S., Applications of artificial intelligence on customer experience and service quality of the banking sector. *Int. Manage. Rev.*, 17, 1, 9–17, 2021.
70. Tang, S.M. and Tien, H.N., Impact of artificial intelligence on vietnam commercial bank operations. *Int. J. Soc. Sci. Econ. Invent.*, 6, 07, 296–303, 2020.
71. Jarrow, R.A., Operational risk. *J. Bank. Financ.*, 32, 5, 870–879, 20082008.
72. Moosa, I.A., *Operational Risk Management*, Palgrave Macmillan, New York, 2007.
73. Doumpos, M., Zopounidis, C., Gounopoulos, D., Platanakis, E., Zhang, W., Operational research and artificial intelligence methods in banking. *Eur. J. Oper. Res.*, 306, 1, 1–16, 2023.
74. Helo, P. and Hao, Y., Artificial intelligence in operations management and supply chain management: An exploratory case study. *Prod. Plan. Control*, 33, 16, 1573–1590, 2022.
75. Losiewicz-Dniestrzanska, E., Monitoring of compliance risk in the bank. *Proc. Econ. Financ.*, 26, 800–805, 2015.
76. Kim, A.C., Lee, S.M., Lee, D.H., Compliance risk assessment measures of financial information security using system dynamics. *Int. J. Secur. Its Appl.*, 6, 4, 191–200, 2012.
77. Butler, T. and O'Brien, L., Artificial intelligence for regulatory compliance: Are we there yet? *J. Financial Compliance*, 3, 1, 44–59, 2019.
78. Carlos, R.C., Kahn, C.E., Halabi, S., Data science: Big data, machine learning, and artificial intelligence. *J. Am. Coll. Radiol.*, 15, 3, 497–498, 2018.
79. Brynjolfsson, E., Rock, D., Syverson, C., Artificial intelligence and the modern productivity paradox: A clash of expectations and statistics, in: *The Economics of Artificial Intelligence: An Agenda*, pp. 23–57, University of Chicago Press, United States, 2018.
80. Marda, V., Artificial intelligence policy in India: A framework for engaging the limits of data-driven decision-making. *Philos. Transact. R. Soc. A*, 376, 2133, 20180087, 2018.
81. Melnychenko, O., Is artificial intelligence ready to assess an enterprise's financial security? *J. Risk Financ. Manage.*, 13, 9, 191, 2020.
82. Hosam, O., Intelligent risk management using artificial intelligence, in: *2022 Advances in Science and Engineering Technology International Conferences, ASET*, IEEE, pp. 1–9, 2022.
83. Aziz, S. and Dowling, M., Machine learning and AI for risk management, in: *Disrupting Finance: FinTech and Strategy in the 21st Century*, pp. 33–50, 2019.
84. Ozili, P.K., Big data and artificial intelligence for financial inclusion: Benefits and issues, in: *Artificial Intelligence Fintech, and Financial Inclusion*, 2021.

85. Mhlanga, D., Financial inclusion in emerging economies: The application of machine learning and artificial intelligence in credit risk assessment. *Int. J. Financ. Stud.*, 9, 3, 39, 2021.

86. Tavana, M., Abtahi, A.R., Di Caprio, D., Poortarigh, M., An artificial neural network and bayesian network model for liquidity risk assessment in banking. *Neurocomputing*, 275, 2525–2554, 2018.

87. Chen, Y.K., Shen, C.H., Kao, L., Yeh, C.Y., Bank liquidity risk and performance. *Rev. Pacific Basin Financial Mark. Policies*, 21, 01, 1850007, 2018.

88. Boukherouaa, E.B., Shabsigh, M.G., AlAjmi, K., Deodoro, J., Farias, A., Iskender, E.S., Ravikumar, R., *Powering the Digital Economy: Opportunities and Risks of Artificial Intelligence in Finance*, International Monetary Fund, United States, 2021.

89. Singh, S., Risk assessment for AI projects, 2021. Available online: https://www.linkedin.com/pulse/risk-assessment-ai-projects-sonu-singh/, (Accessed on 31-May-2023).

90. Go, E.J., Moon, J., Kim, J., Analysis of the current and future of the artificial intelligence in financial industry with big data techniques. *Glob. Bus. Finance Rev. (GBFR)*, 25, 1, 102–117, 2020.

91. Bevz, R. and Domanska, O., Artificial intelligence (AI) for credit risk management in banking, 2022. Available at: https://www.avenga.com/magazine/ai-for-credit-risk-management/, (Accessed on 31 May 2023).

92. Dowd, K., *Measuring Market Risk*, John Wiley & Sons, New Jersey, United States, 2007.

93. Dumitrascu, O., Dumitrascu, M., Dobrotă, D., Performance evaluation for a sustainable supply chain management system in the automotive industry using artificial intelligence. *Processes*, 8, 11, 1384, 2020.

94. Goltz, N. and Mayo, M., *Enhancing Regulatory Compliance by Using Artificial Intelligence Text Mining to Identify Penalty Clauses in Legislation*, vol. RAIL, 1, p. 175, 2018.

95. Kabašinskas, A., Šutiene, K., Kopa, M., Valakevičius, E., The risk–return profile of Lithuanian private pension funds. *Econ. Res. Ekon. Istraz.*, 30, 1611–1630, 2017.

96. Garvey, C., AI risk mitigation through democratic governance: Introducing the 7-dimensional AI risk horizon, in: *Proceedings of the 2018 AAAI/ACM Conference on AI, Ethics, and Society*, pp. 366–367, 2018.

97. AI, N., *Artificial Intelligence Risk Management Framework (AI RMF 1.0)*, National Institute of Standards & Technology, USA, 2023.

98. Mandala, G.N., Buddhi, D., Arumugam, M., Harbola, S., Othman, B., Almashaqbeh, H.A., A critical review of applications of artificial intelligence (AI) and its powered technologies in the financial industry, in: *2022 2nd International Conference on Advance Computing and Innovative Technologies in Engineering (ICACITE)*, IEEE, pp. 2362–2365, 2022.

99. Milojević, N. and Redzepagic, S., Prospects of artificial intelligence and machine learning application in banking risk management. *J. Cent. Bank. Theory Pract.*, 10, 3, 41–57, 2021.

100. Lui, A. and Lamb, G.W., Artificial intelligence and augmented intelligence collaboration: Regaining trust and confidence in the financial sector. *Inf. Commun. Technol. Law*, 27, 3, 267–283, 2018.

101. Borghi, R. and De Rossi, G., The artificial intelligence approach to picking stocks, in: *Machine Learning For Asset Management: New Developments and Financial Applications*, pp. 115–166, 2020.

102. Dupont, L., Fliche, O., Yang, S., *Governance of Artificial Intelligence in Finance*, Banque De France, Paris, France, 2020, Available at: https://acpr.banque-france.fr/sites/default/files/medias/documents/20200612_ai_governance_finance.pdf, (Accessed on: 28-May-2023).

103. Pan, Y. and Zhang, L., Roles of artificial intelligence in construction engineering and management: A critical review and future trends. *Autom. Constr.*, 122, 103517, 2021.

104. Riikkinen, M., Saarijärvi, H., Sarlin, P., Lähteenmäki, I., Using artificial intelligence to create value in insurance. *Int. J. Bank Mark.*, 36, 6, 1145–1168, 2018.

105. Žigienė, G., Rybakovas, E., Alzbutas, R., Artificial intelligence based commercial risk management framework for SMEs. *Sustainability*, 11, 16, 4501, 2019.

106. Dorofee, A.J., Walker, J.A., Alberts, C.J., Higuera, R.P., Murphy, R.L., *Continuous Risk Management Guidebook*, Carnegie Mellon Univ., Pittsburgh PA, 1996.

107. Som, A. and Kayal, P., AI, Blockchain, and IOT, in: *Digitalization and the Future of Financial Services: Innovation and Impact of Digital Finance*, pp. 141–161, Springer International Publishing, Cham, 2022.

108. Kusumo, K.P., Kuriyan, K., Vaidyaraman, S., García-Muñoz, S., Shah, N., Chachuat, B., Risk mitigation in model-based experiment design: A continuous-effort approach to optimal campaigns. *Comput. Chem. Eng.*, 159, 107680, 2022.

109. Aziz, S. and Dowling, M.M., Machine learning and AI for risk management, in: *Disrupting Finance: FinTech and Strategy in the 21st Century*, T. Lynn, G. Mooney, P. Rosati, M. Cummins (Eds.), PSDBET, pp. 33–50, 20192018.

110. Addo, A., Centhala, S., Shanmugam, M., *Artificial Intelligence for Risk Management*, Business Expert Press, New York, United States, 2020.

111. Wirtz, B.W., Weyerer, J.C., Kehl, I., Governance of artificial intelligence: A risk and guideline-based integrative framework. *Gov. Inf. Q.*, 39, 4, 101685, 2022.

4

Artificial Intelligence Adoption in the Indian Banking and Financial Industry: Current Status and Future Opportunities

Deepthi B. and Vikram Bansal*

Atal Bihari Vajpayee School of Management and Entrepreneurship, Jawaharlal Nehru University, New Delhi, India

Abstract

In the current era of digitization and fast technological development, the manner in which money is managed is experiencing rapid change. As a direct consequence of this, the use of technologies such as artificial intelligence (AI) and machine learning (ML) has developed into an absolute need for the banking and financial sector all over the world. In line with the global trends, the Indian banking and finance sector is increasingly embracing AI and ML-based solutions for its day-to-day operations. The purpose of this research is to give a complete overview of the recent advancements and upcoming trends in the adoption of AI and ML in the Indian banking and financial industry. In addition, the study also looked into the various challenges faced by management to implement these latest developments. The goals of this research are accomplished by the use of secondary data obtained from a variety of sources, including journal papers, books, interviews, blog posts, and newspaper stories, among others. In addition, primary data were gathered from industry professionals by means of in-depth interviews about the difficulties inherent in the implementation of AI technology. According to the findings, banks are increasingly using AI and ML-based apps in the front-end operations in order to give the greatest customer experience possible. However, banks are looking at the possibility of using technologies based on AI in the Know Your Customer and Compliance departments in the near future. According to the results, the most significant obstacles to using AI technologies in the banking

Corresponding author: vikrambansal@jnu.ac.in

Ambrish Kumar Mishra, Shweta Anand, Narayan C. Debnath, Purvi Pokhariyal and Archana Patel (eds.) Artificial Intelligence for Risk Mitigation in the Financial Industry, (81–102) © 2024 Scrivener Publishing LLC

business are a lack of human resource experience, support from senior management, awareness of the uses of AI, and financial resources.

Keywords: Artificial intelligence, banking, systematic literature review, Indian banking and finance industry, bibliometric analysis

4.1   Introduction

In today's world, marked by rapid digitization and the ongoing fourth industrial revolution, the use of cutting-edge technology is an absolute must in every industry. One of the industries that is known for being quick to adopt new technology is the global banking and financial sector [1]. Banks and financial institutions in order to remain relevant and agile in a market that is very competitive, they need to make use of technology; yet, providing superior service to their customers is of utmost importance. Because of this, the business and technology practices of the bank will need to undergo significant revision. For one thing, most transactions used to take place with cash in the past. However, in modern times, they are device-driven. Artificial intelligence (AI) is one of the emerging technologies that is extensively used in all fields at present. In practically every sector of the economy, including banking and finance, artificial intelligence has emerged as a key driver of significant disruption. AI is an umbrella phrase that refers to the use of a computer to simulate intelligent behavior with little human interaction [2]. The general consensus is that AI began with the development of robots. The name robot is derived from the Czech word "robota," which refers to biosynthetic devices used for forced labor. In particular, the functioning of AI systems requires the intake of massive amounts of labeled training data, the inspection of such data in the search for correlations and patterns, and the utilization of such trends in order to formulate predictions about upcoming states. The development of artificial intelligence relies on programming for three cognitive abilities: learning, reasoning, and self-correction [3].

In this 2006 study [4], John McCarthy gives the following definition of artificial intelligence, despite the fact that several other definitions of AI have been proposed over the course of the last few decades. He mentioned AI as "It is the science and engineering of making intelligent machines, especially intelligent computer programs. It is related to the similar task of using computers to understand human intelligence, but AI does not have to confine itself to methods that are biologically observable." In a word, artificial intelligence is a discipline that enables problem-solving by combining computer science with extensive information. This combination is called big data. In addition, it incorporates the subfields of machine learning and deep learning, both of which are commonly referenced in the context of artificial intelligence. These fields are composed of AI algorithms that strive to develop expert systems that can make predictions or classifications depending on the data that are fed into them [5]. The terms "deep learning" (DL) and "machine learning" (ML) are sometimes used interchangeably; nevertheless, there are important distinctions between the two that should be made clear. Deep learning is really considered to be a subfield of machine learning, as was previously stated. Both deep learning and machine learning are considered to be subfields of the larger area of artificial intelligence.

Throughout banking history, institutions have been notoriously sluggish to adopt AI technology in their daily operations. Today, AI is mostly applied for front-end operations, risk management, and fraud detection. Globally, the majority of financial institutions are still in the early stages of rolling out AI throughout their whole organizations, having started with just a few use cases. Some of the reasons go back in time and may be connected to obsolete operating concepts, old legacy systems, data silos, or a disorganized and haphazard AI approach. In line with the trend in other sectors, the banking and finance industry has followed the lead of other sectors by incorporating AI-based applications into day-to-day business operations [1]. The use of artificial intelligence in banking applications and services has, in point of fact, made the industry more customer-focused and technologically relevant. Customers who are used to using new technology in their day-to-day lives have an expectation that banks would provide experiences that are smooth. Banks have extended their industrial landscape to include retail, information technology (IT), and telecommunications in order to match these expectations and allow services such as mobile banking, e-banking, and real-time money transfers. The banking industry has incurred additional expenses as a result of these technological improvements, despite the fact that they have made it possible for clients to access the vast majority of financial services at their convenience whenever and wherever they want [6]. Companies that are active in the banking and financial business in India have begun using AI-based applications across a variety of their departments in order to bring their practices in line with those of the global banking and financial industry. However, compared to industrialized nations, this adoption rate is much lower. As a consequence, the current study is aimed to achieve the following objectives.

1. To understand the recent advancements and upcoming trends in the utilization of AI and ML in the Indian banking and financial industry.
2. To investigate the challenges to the adoption of AI-based technologies in the Indian banking and financial industry.

4.2   Literature Review

In today's contemporary business environment, artificial intelligence has developed into a crucial industrial disrupter that is present in practically every sector. The current state of the art in artificial intelligence is only superficially similar to this symbolic method. Throughout the course of the 20th century, the vast majority of significant commitments and methods were discarded. Human intelligence served as the primary model for early attempts at automating previously manual processes. This is maybe the most notable aspect of these early efforts. The goal was to first determine the processes that are operating in our own intellect and then devise a method for automating those processes in order to create computer programs that are capable of mimicking intelligent human behavior. Nevertheless, in today's world, the majority of academics are more interested in creating automated processes that can undertake well in complex problem domains using whatever methods are feasible rather than through human-like methods. This is because of the nature of the problems that are faced in the world [7]. This section offers an in-depth analysis of the

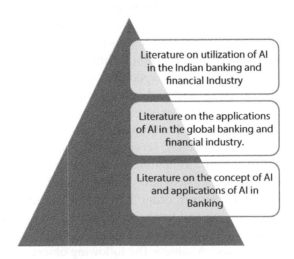

Figure 4.1 Structure of the literature review. Source: Authors.

existing literature on the use of AI-based technologies in the global banking and financial sector. The framework of the literature review is presented in the Figure 4.1.

4.2.1 Introduction to AI

Artificial intelligence is a broad subfield of computer science that focuses on the development of intelligent computers that are able to carry out activities that would normally need the participation of intelligent people. Because of the many advantages it provides to business operations, artificial intelligence is now one of the most widely used technologies available. However, artificial intelligence is not a novel concept and neither is it a novel technology for academics. This technology has been around for a lot longer than most people realize. Even yet, there are tales spoken about mechanical men in the mythology of the ancient Greeks and Egyptians. The following is a list of significant events in the history of artificial intelligence that characterize the path from the first generation of AI to the most recent advancement.

In 1943, McCulloch and Pits [8] carried out the initial experiments in what is now known as artificial intelligence. They put out an idea for a model of synthetic neurons [8]. According to the available evidence, John McCarthy [4] was the first person to use the phrase "artificial intelligence" and organize a conference on the subject [9]. However, the phrase "artificial intelligence," on the other hand, does not have a single definition that is universally recognized. The capacity of robots to execute particular activities, which need the intellect shown by people and animals, is what we mean when we talk about artificial intelligence. It is common practice to attribute this term to Marvin Minsky and John McCarthy [4] from the year 1955, who are also referred to as the pioneers of this field. Artificial intelligence is all around us in today's environment. AI can be found in almost every aspect of modern life, from virtual assistants like Amazon's Alexa to the Internet's ability to anticipate what it is we may want to purchase next. Another use of artificial intelligence is the development of self-driving automobiles. There are two main classifications that may be used in artificial intelligence: narrow AI and general AI. Narrow AI, sometimes known as weak AI, is an application of artificial intelligence technology that enables a high-functioning system that duplicates human intellect for a specific purpose, and maybe even exceeds it [10]. Narrow AI may be seen in action everywhere from identifying offensive information on the Internet to recognizing people in photographs to answering basic questions from customers.

General AI yet remains simply a notion. The goal of general artificial intelligence is to create a system that is as malleable and versatile as human intellect. In a nutshell, artificial general intelligence (AGI) refers to the intelligence possessed by machines that enables them to perceive, learn, and carry out intellectual activities in a manner that is comparable to that of humans. An artificial general intelligence attempts to tackle problems of any complexity by modeling human thought and behavior [11]. As described earlier, the evolution of artificial intelligence is dependent on programming for three cognitive abilities: learning, reasoning, and self-correction.

Learning: In this aspect of AI programming, the major focus is on the collecting of data and the establishment of rules on how to change the data into information that can be utilized. In other words, the transformation of raw data into information that can be used. The rules, which are also known as algorithms, provide the computer equipment that is being used step-by-step instructions on how to carry out a certain action.

Reasoning: When it comes to the programming of AI, this particular aspect places a focus on choosing the suitable algorithm in order to get the intended outcome.

Self-correction: Programming AI often entails the incorporation of components such as this one, which are designed to ensure that the algorithms are continually improved and produce the most accurate results that are feasible [3].

The development of artificial intelligence and machine learning are intertwined and interdependent processes. The creation of intelligent systems may be accomplished with the help of these two technologies. Machine learning is an application or subset of artificial intelligence that enables machines to learn from data without being explicitly programmed. Artificial intelligence is a larger concept that aims to create intelligent machines that can simulate human thinking capability and behavior. On a more specific level, AI is a concept that aims to create machines that can simulate human behavior (Figure 4.2).

Arthur Samuel, who is considered to be one of the pioneers of machine learning, provided the definition of machine learning as a "discipline of research that offers computers the capacity to learn without being explicitly programmed." The figure demonstrates that ML is a subset of AI. This indicates that all ML algorithms may be categorized as being under the umbrella of AI. On the other hand, this does not work in the other direction, and it is essential to keep in mind that not all AI-based algorithms are ML. This is comparable to the fact that a rectangle is always a square, but not every square is always a rectangle [1]. The primary distinction between AI and ML is that the latter enables computer systems to automatically

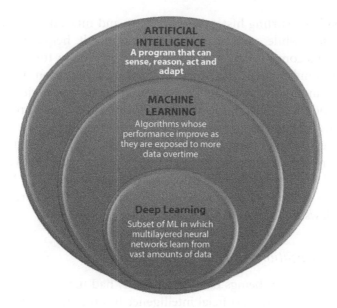

Figure 4.2 Difference between AI and ML. Source: Authors.

learn from their experiences and better themselves by using data rather than being expressly programmed to do so.

The next level of machine learning is called "deep learning." It is a sub-field of machine learning that takes its cues from the way in which human brains function. Deep artificial neural networks are what most people have in mind when they hear the phrase "deep learning"; however, this is not always the case. Learning by example is something that comes easily to humans, and DL trains computers to do the same thing. Figure 4.2 shows the difference between AI and ML.

4.2.2 Applications of Artificial Intelligence

Artificial intelligence is becoming more useful, and it is also gaining a lot of attention. Today, AI systems are being put to use in a wide variety of different ways in the real world. The following are few of the most typical examples:

4.2.2.1 AI Applications in e-Commerce

The technology of artificial intelligence is utilized to construct personalization, which allows to have a more meaningful interaction with clientele.

The individual's surfing history, preferences, and interests are taken into consideration while making these suggestions. It helps improve the organization's connection with its consumers, which in turn encourages increased brand loyalty from those customers. In addition, while doing their shopping online, users may have a better experience with the aid of chatbots and virtual shopping assistants. Natural language processing is used to ensure that the communication comes through in the most natural and personable manner. In addition, these assistants are able to participate in real-time conversation with your consumers. Moreover, the use of artificial intelligence has the potential to help e-commerce businesses address two of the most major challenges they face: credit card theft and bogus reviews.

4.2.2.2   Applications of AI in Education

Even though human beings have traditionally had the greatest impact on the education industry, artificial intelligence has recently started to make inroads into the field in a more subtle way. The use of artificial intelligence may assist educators with non-educational jobs, such as task-related responsibilities, such as planning and enabling parent and guardian contacts and regular problem feedback facilitation, as well as managing enrollment. Artificial intelligence may be used to facilitate the digitization of information such as video lectures, conference guides, and textbook introductions [12]. Additionally, utilizing AI technology, hyper-personalization methods may be used to monitor the data of students in a comprehensive manner. Additionally, it is possible to quickly build habits, teaching materials, alerts, study guides, flash notes, frequency of review, and other similar things.

4.2.2.3   AI Applications in Agriculture

It is anticipated that the global population will reach over 9 billion by the year 2050, which would need an increase in agricultural output of at least 70% in order to satisfy the demand. In this context, the use of the most recent technical advancements in order to make farming more productive remains one of the most important necessities. In recent years, the use of artificial intelligence has become more noticeable in the agriculture industry. The adaptability, high performance, accuracy, and cost-effectiveness of AI in agricultural settings are the primary selling points of this technology [13].

4.2.2.4   Artificial Intelligence in the Banking and Financial Industry

The use of artificial intelligence by contemporary enterprises represents a major advancement in the process of digitalization and transformation. The environment in which we live is increasingly being permeated by artificial intelligence, and financial institutions have already begun incorporating aspects of this technology into the goods and services they provide [14]. If we look back at previous technological breakthroughs in the banking industry, we can see that banks are often early adopters of new information technology prospects. This is not just true for the back office, which has been using current technology for quite some time (for example, to process payments), but it is also true for the front-end of the business. One of the oldest implementations of information technology in banking is the automated teller machine, sometimes known as an ATM. These machines eliminated the need for bank workers to do duties that were routine, such as checking account balances and processing cash withdrawals. They made it simpler for customers to have access to regular banking services, which resulted in increased financial institutions' operational effectiveness [14].

Data are critical to practically every aspect of a bank's operation, from the more conventional areas of deposit taking and lending to more modern areas such as investment banking and asset management. Therefore, autonomous data management that does not include human participation presents banks with significant opportunity to increase their speed, accuracy, and overall efficiency. The following are the major areas into which potential applications of AI in banking may be divided: 1) apps focused on customers in the front office; 2) applications focused on operations in the back office; 3) applications focused on trading and portfolio management; and 4) applications focused on regulatory compliance [15]. The various uses of AI in banking is depicted in Figure 4.3.

According to the Mckinsey report titled "Building the AI bank of the future" [16], banks globally are increasingly adopting AI-based technologies to improve customer experiences and in back-office processes. Banks across the globe are increasingly using AI technologies in the form of chatbots on websites and humanoid robots in bank branches. By incorporating chatbots into banking applications, financial institutions are able to guarantee that they are accessible to their clients at all hours of the day and night. Additionally, since chatbots are able to analyze client behavior, they may provide individualized customer care and make appropriate recommendations for financial services and products in accordance with that behavior [1, 14]. For instance, Erica, a chatbot developed by the Bank

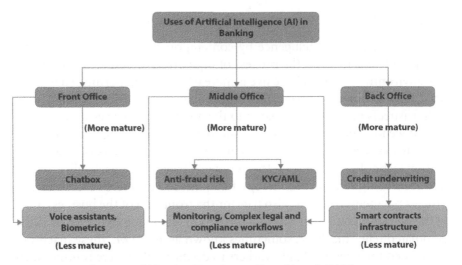

Figure 4.3 Applications of AI in banking. Source: Deepthi *et al.* (2022).

of America, is considered to be one of the most successful instances of AI used in mobile banking applications.

In addition, banks and other financial organizations all around the world are increasingly turning to AI in order to make decisions about the provision of loans and credit. In order to establish a client's creditworthiness, an AI-based loan and credit system may analyze the behavior and patterns of a consumer, even if the customer has a limited credit history. In addition to this, the system issues an alert to banks on certain practices that may raise the likelihood of a default occurring. In a nutshell, technologies of this kind are playing a significant part in the transformation of the future of consumer finance [15]. AI is also being evaluated for use in Know Your Customer (KYC) procedures, which authenticate the identification of customers. The documents submitted by customers are analyzed by AI algorithms, which then determine whether or not the material can be trusted by comparing it to data obtained from the Internet. In the event that AI algorithms discover discrepancies, they will raise a warning signal, which will result in a more thorough KYC check being carried out by bank workers [14]. Existing financial technology tools can, with enough time and development, eventually develop into full AI solutions. Robo-advisors, which allow complete automation in some asset management services, and online financial planning tools, which assist clients make better educated consumption and saving choices, are two good examples. Both of these types of services may be found online.

4.2.2.5   Utilization of AI in the Indian Banking and Financial Industry

In the era of the digital revolution, banks will find themselves in a position of competition with the assistance of fintech businesses by utilizing advanced technologies that augment or even restore human employees with sophisticated algorithms. Customers who are used to using new technology in their day-to-day lives have an expectation that banks would provide experiences that are smooth. In order to fulfill these expectations, financial institutions have expanded their business scope to include retail, information technology, and telecommunications in order to offer services such as mobile banking, online banking, and real-time money transfers. The banking industry has incurred additional expenses as a result of these technological improvements, despite the fact that they have made it possible for clients to access the vast majority of financial services at their convenience whenever and wherever they want [16]. Indian banks and financial institutions are progressively integrating artificial intelligence technology in their banking operations, which is consistent with the trend seen in the worldwide banking and financial sector [15]. In recent years, a variety of banking and financial institutions have formed partnerships with various fintech businesses, and these partnerships have resulted in the testing and implementation of various proof-of-concept strategies in day-to-day business operations. Therefore, the banking and finance sector in India views AI projects as potentially lucrative and successful businesses. However, this adoption is less in comparison with that of developed nations.

According to a study conducted by Malali and Gopalakrishnan [15], the Indian banking and finance industry would benefit greatly from the use of AI in the future because of the rapid pace at which AI-powered technologies are working toward the growth of the financial sector and making things simpler for clients. Therefore, in the approaching days, it will restore the human being and will provide more expedient services along with the most appropriate remedies at a cost that is reasonable.

4.3   Research Methodology

The primary purpose of the present research is to get an understanding of the existing level of AI and ML usage in the Indian banking and finance sector as well as the potential opportunities that lie ahead. In addition, the purpose of the research is to analyze the obstacles that prevent firms in the Indian banking and financial sector from adopting these technologies. We have utilized two types of research techniques to achieve the research objectives mentioned above. The first is the method of desk research that was used in order to get an understanding of the present standing and potential future applications of AI. In order to understand the challenges to the AI adoption, we adopted a qualitative research design.

Desk research is gathering and analyzing information that already exists and is simple to get, such as firm data, published government reports, and material that can be found in various publications like newspapers, journals, and journal articles, among other sources. The desk research was conducted in four phases (Figure 4.4). During the first phase of the desk research process, which consisted of doing a preliminary study on the topic in order to define the core components of this research, including its objective and method, the following steps were taken: During the second phase of the project, we conducted a literature study on the subject of AI applications in the banking and financial sector throughout the world. During Phase 3, we examined all of the papers that were pertinent to the present state of AI adoption and future opportunities in the Indian banking and financial business. This was done so that we could better understand the situation. In Phase 4, we have provided the outcomes of our investigation.

In addition, the study has utilized the qualitative research design to explore the challenges in the AI adoption in the Indian banking and financial industry. The findings of qualitative research represent real-life worlds "from the inside out" or from the perspective of the individuals who take part in the study [16]. As a result, we have applied qualitative research methodology to investigate the various challenges to adopt AI-based applications in the Indian banking and financial industry. We have done in-depth interviews with executives working at both the middle-level and top-level positions. In order to make sense of the information obtained

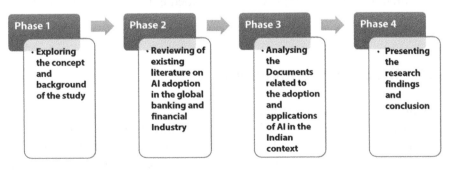

Figure 4.4 Research process. Source: The Author.

from in-depth interviews, we conducted interpretations using narrative analysis. The Labov-defined narrative is one method of recapitulating past experience by matching a verbal sequence of clauses to the sequence of events that (it is inferred) actually occurred. The term "narrative analysis" refers to a group of different analytic approaches that are used to analyze written or visual data that are presented in a story-like format. The belief that individuals create tales to help them organize and make sense of their lives and that the storied narratives they give are useful and meaningful is a prevalent presumption underlying narrative research approaches.

4.4   Findings of the Study

4.4.1   Current Status of AI-Based Application Adoption in the Indian Banking and Financial Industry

The results of the study revealed that when it comes to the use and adoption of artificial intelligence within the banking and financial industry, Indian banks are now in the lead. The same goes for non-bank lenders, insurance players, and payment providers, all of whom are following suit and progressively profiting from the same factors. According to a poll that was conducted by PWC and FICCI, the banking industry in India is in the lead when it comes to the implementation and adoption of all new use cases for artificial intelligence. AI applications are used to increase revenues for institutions that are trying to get ahead of the curve on the adoption of AI. This can be accomplished by increasing the level of personalization of services offered, embedding intelligence in automation, and forming partnerships with digital ecosystems. AI is assisting non-bank financial companies (NBFCs) in expanding their credit offerings and achieving exponential growth in a variety of areas, including collection analytics, credit scoring, customer churn reduction, fraud detection, and risk mitigation. AI is being used by NBFCs, according to the companies' statements, to determine the creditworthiness of applicants, to speed up the collection process, and to determine the residual profitability of customers who are at danger of leaving the company.

According to the research published by PWC and FICCI, AI is assisting firms in the insurance industry in improving their decision-making and providing superior service to their customers. Auto insurance businesses are employing AI-based services for tasks such as new policy creation, renewal, and claim inspection. Another insurance company is supplying insurance companies with AI-powered solutions for claim assessment and fraud detection.

When it comes to Indian banks, banks are extensively using AI to enhance customer service experience through chatbots. For example, the SBI Intelligent Assistant (SIA), which is an AI-powered smart chat assistant, responds immediately to client inquiries and assists them with day-to-day banking chores much as a person would. In a similar manner, HDFC Bank's smart chatbot known as "Eva" collaborates with Google Assistant on millions of Android devices to answer questions from clients and improve the quality of services that are offered to those customers [17].

According to the findings, the recent COVID-19 epidemic sped up the process of artificial intelligence adoption among Indian banks. The use of artificial intelligence has allowed banks to better manage high-speed data, which has resulted in the acquisition of valuable insights. Additionally, banks have been able to improve the quality of their services by implementing features such as digital payments, AI bots, and biometric fraud detection systems. During the COVID-19 pandemic, organizations have automated their day-to-day operations in order to better understand COVID-19-impacted datasets and to exploit these datasets in order to enhance the experience of stakeholders [18]. According to the data that are currently accessible, financial institutions in India are also using AI-based robo-advisors. By doing an analysis of the customer's shared financial history and data, a robo-advisor makes an attempt to get an understanding of the customer's current financial situation. The customer inputs his or her analysis and desired outcomes into the robo-advisor, and it then makes investment suggestions for a specific product or share based on them.

In addition, artificial intelligence is becoming more helpful to enterprises in the banking and financial sector of India in monitoring internal risks or breaches and suggesting remedial steps, which ultimately results in the avoidance of data theft or misuse. Moreover, AI is assisting lenders in the development of novel ways of lending systems that are supported by a strong credit scoring model, even for those persons or companies with a low credit history. This is possible because AI is helping lenders come up with the approaches [18]. The findings suggest that financial institutions are using AI for compliance management. When carried out by hand, these procedures take a great deal more time and need a significant financial commitment; nevertheless, banks often have an internal compliance staff to deal with issues of this kind. Deep learning and natural language processing are two areas of AI that are being used to help financial institutions interpret new compliance requirements and enhance their decision-making process.

4.4.2   Future Opportunities in the Adoption of AI-Based Applications in the Indian Banking and Financial Industry

There are a variety of applications for artificial intelligence within the financial sector. According to a poll conducted by OpenText, approximately 80% of financial institutions are aware of the advantages of artificial intelligence, 75% of these institutions are currently using this technology, and approximately 46% have plans to use AI-based solutions in the near future. It is becoming more important for businesses to include AI-driven solutions into their development plans in order to maintain their position as market leaders. This technology helps to reduce operational expenses while simultaneously enhancing customer assistance and automating business procedures [19].

Despite the fact that Indian banks and other financial institutions are making active use of AI in a variety of areas, there is still space for improvement in this deployment. According to the results of the research, Indian banks are progressively employing apps based on artificial intelligence in the front-end operations in order to improve the quality of customer care. Indian banks will need to embrace artificial intelligence more and weave it into their business strategy if they want to retain a strong competitive advantage. For example, artificial intelligence can be built on machine learning, and it acquires knowledge over a period of time; as a result, it ensures the highest accuracy in calculations and in examining large amounts of data. AI possesses the ability to establish process automation to fields wherever it is necessary, as well as clear thoughts, smart analytics, and clear reasoning. As a consequence, applications of AI are capable of being applied effectively in risk assessment. Additionally, AI may be effectively applied for the identification of fraudulent activity and defaulting chances of loan before disbursement. In the context of the Indian banking industry's struggle with high rates of nonperforming assets (NPAs), banks have the potential to effectively analyze the data of customers in advance in order to minimize NPA rates.

Despite the fact that applications of AI are being increasingly employed in financial advising services, there is still potential for growth in this field. In its 2017 report, PWC discussed the potential role that robo-advisors may play in the not-too-distant future. The research showed that insurance firms may make use of technologies that are equipped with AI to collect evidence and evaluate the data in an intelligent manner in order to guarantee the quality of the findings. Technologies that are empowered with AI are able to understand the behavioral outlines of users or consumers in order to recognize unexpected behaviors and convey the warning indicators of unusual transactions and some types of issues. These sorts of technologies play a significant part in the administration of claims; in particular, ML approaches assist to skip over a number of phases in the process of claim settlement [20].

In addition, technologies based on AI may be applied in the provision of services related to wealth management. Applications powered by AI have the ability to either complement human skills by taking care of low-value activities or proactively take on responsibilities that are more strategic for enterprises. In any case, the application of AI to the management of assets ensures a substantial degree of accuracy in projections by conducting an analysis of billions of alternative scenarios and data points. In order to provide superior management and support, AI algorithms are already being used to do research on specific customers' portfolios. For instance, AI may be used to assist in the decision-making process about stocks, where computer learning may be used to estimate, after taking into account hundreds of indicators, the link between the risks and returns connected with a company's shares. In addition, compliance management is a potential use of technology based on AI. Businesses possibly have the ability to clean and understand different data pieces with the assistance of AI, which may simplify day-to-day processes linked to governance and compliance. According to Gartner's predictions, by the end of the year 2024, one-third of businesses will have moved on from the pilot stage and will be operationalizing AI in wealth management. In the future, applications of AI may include tax planning and the integration of AI into already existing wealth management systems in order to enhance their customers' perceptions of them.

4.4.3   Challenges to the Deployment of AI in the Indian Banking and Financial Services Industry

In order to have a comprehensive understanding of the banking and financial business in India, we spoke in-depth with 25 experienced individuals. Ten of these 25 professionals were managers at the intermediate level of management, and 15 of these professionals were managers at the top level of management. Seven of the participants were employed by Indian public sector banks, 15 of the participants were employed by brokerage organizations, and three of the participants were employed by insurance firms. Only middle-level and top-level executives were included in the sample because we felt that these individuals would be best able to describe the difficulties they face when attempting to implement AI-based technology into their day-to-day operations.

The narratives of the participants suggest that AI-based solutions are very advantageous for the businesses operating in the banking and financial sector of the Indian economy. One of the participants, a bank manager, has shared opinions that AI-based solutions are really useful for reducing wasted time and increasing precision. Participant 7, who is an AVP at a brokerage firm, believes that AI-based solutions have the ability to foresee market swings and also have the potential to successfully aid in compliance management. Despite this, all 25 participants were in agreement that there are many obstacles to overcome before AI-based applications can be successfully implemented in their respective firms.

Participant 3 (institutional dealer) mentioned that "Well, due to the lack of trained employees, our company is not utilizing many AI applications."

The Indian banking and finance business has a very low adoption rate of AI-based applications, and one of the primary reasons for this is the difficulties in managing human resources. The high expense of educating employees and the absence of AI-based competence in staff members are important difficulties relating to human resources.According to Participant 7 who works as a senior manager in one of the leading banks in India, "Very less people know about the AI-based applications in our organization."

Another key obstacle to the use of AI-based technologies in the Indian banking and financial business is the widespread ignorance about the many AI-powered applications now available. The implementation of AI is being hampered, in particular, by the dearth of information that exists among those who make decisions.

Participant 17 (general manager in a leading brokerage company) has expressed that "AI implementation threatens the data privacy of our clients."

The adoption of artificial intelligence has hurdles in terms of data privacy and data safety. These days, the firm views the problem of safeguarding the personal information of customers as one of its highest priorities. Having an effective cybersecurity system may assist businesses in protecting the information that relates to the privacy of their customers.

4.5 Conclusion

One of the technologies that has seen widespread adoption in today's modern-day corporate environment is artificial intelligence. Artificial intelligence is being used in almost every sector. Machines and technology powered by artificial intelligence have the ability to solve problems

and make decisions like the human mind. In ways that complicate tele-
ological accounts, artificial intelligence should be considered part of the
history of human intelligence. According to these accounts, symbolic
AI should emerge naturally and inexorably from efforts made over the
course of several centuries to reduce human reasoning to a logical for-
malism. In this day and age, when the digital revolution is in full swing,
applications of AI are rapidly being seen in the e-commerce, agricultural,
banking and finance, and healthcare sectors.

One of the first industries in the world to fully embrace AI was the
banking and finance sector. The banking and financial services industry
is quickly being taken over by technologies that use machine learning
and artificial intelligence. AI and ML have provided the banking industry with a new approach to satisfy the expectations of its consumers, who
are searching for more efficient, convenient, and secure methods to access,
save, spend, and invest their money. As a result, it is up to the various
financial institutions to respond appropriately to the demand of the new
age. These days, customers are a savvy bunch in general. They have come to
the conclusion that acquiring technological knowledge needs not be costly
or time-consuming, since everything is now included inside a smartphone,
which an average person can simply use. Applications that are powered
by AI are becoming an increasingly common practice in India's front-end
operations. Chatbots are being used by Indian financial institutions to
improve the experience their customers have with artificial intelligence.
The Know Your Customer department, compliance management, and risk
assessment might be potential future uses of artificial intelligence in Indian
banks. In addition, in the not-too-distant future, financial institutions may
use AI to determine credit judgments and identify fraudulent activity.

Findings indicated that compared to banks, wealth management and
trading companies are employing AI at a far lower rate than is the case in
banking. Applications of artificial intelligence that may be used in these
companies in the near future include robo advising, portfolio management, and the automation of trading activities. It was found that AI-based
apps may drastically save costs, save time, and help with effective decision-
making, according to the main data that were acquired from the participants. The use of artificial intelligence in the Indian banking and financial
industry is minimal despite the fact that AI has many benefits for these
institutions. This is due to the many difficulties that are connected with the
deployment of AI. When one takes into account the computing expenses
and the technological data infrastructure that runs behind artificial intelligence, the real execution of AI is a business that is both complicated
and expensive. In addition, problems with maintaining data security are

making it difficult to use AI. Due to the large quantity of data that have been acquired and the fact that they include sensitive and private information, extra security measures need to be put into place. The qualitative interviews that were carried out with the executives brought to light a variety of difficulties linked with the implementation of AI. The participants were of the opinion that the deployment of AI-based applications is experiencing problems in terms of human resources, such as a shortage of qualified people, issues connected to knowledge and awareness, and concerns related to the protection of data. As per the findings, training the existing employees or recruiting the experts who has the AI knowledge is a costly affair. In addition, participants have raised concern that the deployment of AI in several areas may result in the loss of jobs and resistance from current human resources. The participants were of the opinion that if these challenges could be overcome, then AI-based solutions might be applied in the Indian banking and financial industry more effectively.

To summarize, artificial intelligence will not only make banks more powerful by automating their knowledge workers, but it will also make the whole process of automation sophisticated enough to eliminate the threat posed by cyberattacks and the rivalry posed by companies in the fintech industry. AI is essential to the procedures and operations of the bank because it continually adapts to new circumstances and develops new capabilities without requiring significant human participation. AI will make it possible for financial institutions to optimize the use of both human and machine skills, which will allow for greater operational and cost efficiency as well as the delivery of more tailored services. For banks, realizing all of these advantages is no longer an idealistic goal for some distant time in the future. Leaders in the banking industry have already taken the necessary steps to realize these advantages by adopting AI and exercising due care in doing so.

References

1. Deepthi., B., Gupta, P., Rai, P., Arora, H., Assessing the dynamics of AI driven technologies in Indian banking and financial sector. *Vision*, 1–15, 2022.
2. Hamet, P. and Tremblay, J., Artificial intelligence in medicine. *Metabolism*, 69, S36–S40, 2017.
3. Burns, E., What is artificial intelligence (AI)? Definition, benefits and use cases. *SearchEnterpriseAI*, 2022. Retrieved 28 September 2022, from https://www.techtarget.com/searchenterpriseai/definition/AI-Artificial-Intelligence.

4. McCarthy, J., Minsky, M.L., Rochester, N., Shannon, C.E., A proposal for the dartmouth summer research project on artificial intelligence, August 31, 1955. *AI Mag.*, 27, 4, 12–12, 2006.

5. Ibm.com., What is artificial intelligence (AI)?, 2022. https://www.ibm.com/cloud/learn/what-is-artificial-intelligence. Ibm.com. Retrieved 7 October 2022, from Bawack, R.E., Wamba, S.F., Carillo, K.D.A., Akter, S., Artificial intelligence in e-commerce: A bibliometric study and literature review. *Electron. Mark.*, 32, 1, 297–338, 2022.

6. Khurshid, A., Banking on artificial intelligence (AI). *Wipro*, 2021. Wipro. com. Retrieved 28 September 2022, from https://www.wipro.com/business-process/why-banks-need-artificial-intelligence/#:~:text=AI%20also%20enables%20banks%20to,to%20a%20wider%20customer%20base.

7. Floridi, L., *The 4th Revolutional How the Info Sphere is Reshaping Human Reality*, Oxford University Press, Oxford, 2016.

8. McCulloch, W.S. and Pitts, W., A logical calculus of the ideas immanent in nervous activity. *Bull. Math. Biophys.*, 5, 4, 115–133, 1943.

9. Andresen, S.L., John McCarthy: Father of AI. *IEEE Intell. Syst.*, 17, 5, 84–85, 2002.

10. Todorova, M., "Narrow AI" in the context of AI implementation, transformation and the end of some jobs. *Nauchni Trudove*, 4, 15–25, 2020.

11. Kanade, V., What is general artificial intelligence (AI)? Definition, challenges, and trends. *Spiceworks*, 2022. Retrieved 29 September 2022, from https://www.spiceworks.com/tech/artificial-intelligence/articles/what-is-general-ai/.

12. Tahiru, F., AI in education: A systematic literature review. *J. Cases Inf. Technol. (JCIT)*, 23, 1, 1–20, 2021.

13. Eli-Chukwu, N.C., Applications of artificial intelligence in agriculture: A review. *Eng. Technol. Appl. Sci. Res.*, 9, 4, 4377–4383, 2019.

14. Kaya, O., Schildbach, J., AG, D.B., Schneider, S., *Artificial Intelligence in Banking*, Artificial Intelligence, USA, 2019.

15. Malali, A.B. and Gopalakrishnan, S., Application of artificial intelligence and its powered technologies in the Indian banking and financial industry: An overview. *IOSR J. Humanit. Soc. Sci.*, 25, 4, 55–60, 2020.

16. Banking on artificial intelligence (AI). *Wipro*, 2021. Wipro.com. Retrieved 7 October 2022, from https://www.wipro.com/business-process/why-banks-need-artificial-intelligence/.

17. Kumar, V., Banking of tomorrow: Top Indian banks using artificial intelligence, 2021. Analyticsinsight.net. Retrieved 30 September 2022, from https://www.analyticsinsight.net/banking-of-tomorrow-top-indian-banks-using-artificial-intelligence/.

18. Nataraj, P., How are Indian banks adopting digitisation and AI? *Analytics India Magazine*, 2022. Retrieved 30 September 2022, from https://analytics indiamag.com/how-are-indian-banks-adopting-digitisation-and-ai/.

19. Use of artificial intelligence in banking world today. *Finextra Res.*, 2021. Retrieved 7 October 2022, from https://www.finextra.com/blogposting/20688/use-of-artificial-intelligence-in-banking-world-today.
20. Park, J.Y. and Dhanabalan, T., What makes customers repurchase grocery products from online stores in Korea. *Int. J. E-Bus. Res. (IJEBR)*, 15, 4, 24–39, 2019.

5

Impact of AI Adoption in Current Trends of the Financial Industry

S. C. Vetrivel[1*], T. Mohanasundaram[2], T. P. Saravanan[1] and R. Maheswari[1]

*[1]Department of Management Studies, Kongu Engineering College,
Perundurai, India*
*[2]Department of Management Studies, M. S. Ramaiah Institute of Technology,
Bengaluru, India*

Abstract

The banking industry is undergoing a transformation with the adoption of AI technologies. AI technologies help banks in real-time analysis of their vast data and make them more efficient, secure, and profitable. AI technologies enable banks to understand customer behavior, detect fraud, and make informed decisions about investments and loans. In this chapter, we explored the key aspects of real-time analysis of banking data with AI technologies, including their benefits, challenges, and the future implications. By analyzing transaction records in real time, AI algorithms can detect unusual patterns and flag suspicious activity before it results in financial losses. This can help banks reduce their exposure to fraud and enhance their reputation for security and reliability. Cross-selling opportunities, targeted promotions, and tailored recommendations are possible by AI real-time consumer data analysis. As a result, customer engagement and loyalty could increase. However, as the accuracy of AI outcomes depends on the quality of data, banks have to invest in data management systems and processes. The need for human intervention will be reduced if certified AI professionals can be found who have the knowledge to develop and operate AI algorithms that can recognize increasingly complex patterns, analyze outcomes, and integrate them into bank operations.

Keywords: Artificial intelligence (AI), financial industry, automation, machine learning, data analytics, risk management, customer experience, fintech innovation

*Corresponding author: scvetrivel@gmail.com

Ambrish Kumar Mishra, Shweta Anand, Narayan C. Debnath, Purvi Pokhariyal and Archana Patel (eds.) Artificial Intelligence for Risk Mitigation in the Financial Industry, (103–132) © 2024 Scrivener Publishing LLC

5.1   Introduction

The transformation brought by innovative technologies in the past few decades is mind-blowing. Technology has drastically changed our societies and our day-to-day lives. Technology is now on the cusp of moving beyond augmentation that replaces a human capability and into augmentation that creates superhuman capabilities (Gartner, 2019) [1]. This section of the chapter brings out the overview and importance of artificial intelligence (AI), and AI's impact on traditional financial services.

5.1.1   Brief Overview of AI Technology

Artificial intelligence is a broad term for computer systems that are designed to simulate human intelligence and behavior. AI systems can learn, reason, solve problems, and interact with their environment. Examples of AI technology include machine learning, natural language processing, computer vision, robotics, and automated reasoning. AI can be used to automate tasks, improve decision-making, and supplement human intelligence. AI technology is becoming increasingly important in industries ranging from healthcare to finance (Qin *et al.*, 2019; Rajan, 2019) [2, 3]. Figure 5.1 demonstrates the overview of artificial intelligence.

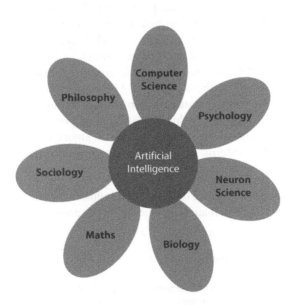

Figure 5.1 Overview of artificial intelligence.

5.1.2   Importance of AI Adoption in the Financial Industry

AI adoption in the financial industry offers numerous benefits, including greater accuracy and efficiency in decision-making, improved customer experience, better risk management, and improved fraud detection. AI can help financial institutions to better understand customer needs, identify trends, and predict customer behavior, enabling them to make more accurate and timely decisions. Additionally, AI-driven automation can reduce operational costs as well as reduce human error and increase operational speed. AI can also help financial institutions detect and prevent fraud, as well as protect customer data. AI adoption in the financial industry is therefore essential for organizations to remain competitive and succeed in the digital age.

5.1.3   Impact of AI on Traditional Financial Services

A clear vision of the future financial landscape will be critical to good strategic and governance decisions (World Economic Forum, 2018) [4]. AI has had a great impact on traditional financial services. AI technologies enable financial services to offer more personalized services to customers, automate and simplify processes, reduce costs, and support regulatory compliance. AI solutions can help detect and prevent fraud and money laundering, analyze financial data to identify trends and opportunities, and provide insights into customer behavior. AI can also enable financial services to identify and offer more tailored products and services to customers, helping them make better decisions and achieve greater financial success.

5.2   AI-Based Trading and Investment Management

AI-based trading and investment management makes use of AI algorithms to make decisions related to trading and investing. This technology can be used to automate the process of analyzing market conditions and making investment decisions. AI-based trading and investment management systems can be used to identify patterns in market data, identify trends, and make decisions based on these patterns and trends. AI-based trading and investment management can also be used to automate the process of portfolio optimization, portfolio rebalancing, and risk management. AI-based trading and investment management can reduce costs and improve accuracy in the decision-making process.

AI-based trading and investment management is a rapidly growing technology that is being used to automate the process of trading and investment decisions. AI technology uses sophisticated algorithms to analyze market data and make predictions about future price movements. AI-powered trading and investment management can help investors make more informed decisions while reducing their risk exposure. AI-based trading and investment management systems can also assist in optimizing portfolio allocations and minimizing trading costs. AI-based trading and investment management tools are becoming increasingly popular as they are able to provide investors with greater insight into the markets, allowing them to make more informed decisions and better manage their portfolios.

5.2.1   Role of AI in Trading and Investment Management

AI has become an increasingly important part of trading and investment management. AI can be used to analyze large amounts of data quickly and accurately, helping traders and investors make informed decisions. AI can also be used to automate trading activities, reducing the amount of time and effort required by traders and investors. AI can also help identify new trading and investment opportunities, as well as identify potential risks. AI can also be used to monitor the performance of investments, helping investors make more informed decisions. In addition, AI can be used to develop customized portfolios for investors, helping them to maximize their return on investment.

5.2.2   AI-Powered Robot-Advisory Services

AI-powered robot-advisory services are computer-driven technology tools that use algorithms and artificial intelligence to provide automated financial advice to investors. They are designed to help individuals make more informed data-driven decisions about their investments. Robo-advisors can provide personalized investment advice tailored to an individual's risk profile and financial goals and can help create a portfolio of low-cost, tax-efficient investments. They can also offer advice on tax planning, retirement planning, and other financial topics.

5.2.3   AI-Based Risk Management and Portfolio Optimization

AI-based risk management and portfolio optimization are two of the most powerful tools available to investors today. By leveraging the power of AI, investors can actively manage their portfolios and make informed decisions based on real-time data and market trends. AI-based risk management and portfolio optimization can help investors identify and manage risk factors, optimize portfolio allocations, and identify potential opportunities for higher returns. AI-based risk management and portfolio optimization can also be used to identify potential sources of revenue and to forecast future market conditions. Ultimately, these tools can help investors maximize their returns and minimize their losses.

5.3   Fraud Detection and Prevention

AI is expected to be able to help accounting practitioners to improve their performance and develop services they provide (Rohmah *et al.*, 2022) [5]. Fraud detection and prevention in the financial industry are critical elements in ensuring the safety of customers and their finances. Financial institutions must be proactive in monitoring and preventing fraudulent activities to protect their customers from potential losses. One of the most common methods that financial institutions use to detect and prevent fraud is by monitoring customer transactions. This can be done by flagging suspicious transactions, such as those with large amounts or those that occur in multiple locations. Financial institutions can also use analytics to detect patterns in customer spending and flag transactions that do not match these patterns. In addition to monitoring customer transactions, financial institutions can also use data security solutions such as encryption, tokenization, and authentication to protect customer data and prevent fraud. These solutions help to ensure that customer data are secure and protected, making it harder for criminals to gain access to customer accounts. Financial institutions can work with law enforcement to investigate and prosecute fraudsters, as well as to develop new methods of fraud detection and prevention. Financial institutions can also work with credit bureaus and other companies to share information about fraudulent activity, allowing them to better identify and prevent fraud in the future.

5.3.1   Role of AI in Fraud Detection and Prevention

AI has a huge role to play in fraud detection and prevention in the financial industry. It can detect suspicious activities and transactions by using algorithms to identify patterns and anomalies. AI can also be used to analyze large amounts of data quickly, helping to identify patterns that may indicate fraudulent activity. AI can also be used to monitor the activity of customers and accounts in real time, helping to detect and prevent fraudulent transactions before they happen. Additionally, AI can be used to send out alerts when suspicious activity is detected, allowing organizations to take immediate action.

5.3.2   Real-Time Fraud Monitoring Using AI

Real-time fraud monitoring using AI in the financial industry can be achieved by using a range of advanced machine learning and artificial intelligence techniques. These techniques are used to detect and analyze any anomalous financial activity, ranging from suspicious transactions to fraudulent accounts. AI can help financial institutions detect suspicious behavior in a fraction of the time it would take a human analyst to manually review the data. AI-driven fraud detection algorithms can be configured to look at various data sources such as transaction data, client behavior, and previous fraudulent activity in order to identify any suspicious activities. AI models such as decision trees, neural networks, and support vector machines (SVMs) can be used to analyze the data and develop predictive models that can identify patterns in the data that might indicate fraudulent activity. AI models can also be used to assess the risk of a given transaction and alert financial institutions of potential fraud. Additionally, AI can also be used to detect unauthorized access to financial accounts, as well as detect changes in account activity that may indicate malicious activity. The use of AI can be combined with other security measures, such as two-factor authentication, to further strengthen the security of financial accounts.

5.3.3   Machine Learning-Based Fraud Prevention Techniques

a) Rule-Based Methods: Rule-based approaches rely on a set of predefined rules to identify possible fraud. The rules are designed to detect suspicious behavior such as large transactions, unexpected changes in user profiles, and unusual changes in account activity.

b) Anomaly Detection: Anomaly detection is a process of identifying outliers in a dataset. This method of fraud detection can be used to detect unusual patterns of financial transactions that may indicate fraudulent activities.

c) Transaction Monitoring: Transaction monitoring is a process of tracking financial transactions for suspicious activities. The system will flag any suspicious transactions and alert the financial institution, so that they can take necessary actions.

d) Behavioral Analytics: Behavioral analytics analyzes user behaviors and patterns to detect fraud. It uses machine learning algorithms to identify recurring patterns or anomalies that may indicate fraud.

e) Natural Language Processing (NLP): Natural language processing is a process of analyzing textual data to identify patterns and detect fraud. It can be used to detect fraudulent activities such as fake reviews and phishing emails.

f) Network Analytics: Network analytics is a process of analyzing large datasets to detect patterns of fraudulent activities. It uses machine learning algorithms to identify relationships between different entities in a network.

5.4   Customer Service and Personalization

AI has the potential to revolutionize customer service in the financial industry. By applying AI-driven technologies like natural language processing and machine learning, customer service representatives can more quickly and accurately identify customer needs and provide personalized customer experiences. For example, AI can be used to automate customer support with chatbots that can provide instant responses to customer questions and quickly resolve issues. AI can also be used to monitor customer interactions and detect customer sentiment, allowing customer service representatives to proactively address customer concerns. Additionally, AI can be used to personalize customer experiences by analyzing customer data and providing tailored product recommendations. AI can be used to automate processes like fraud detection and credit scoring, allowing banks to more quickly and accurately assess customer risk and provide better financial services.

AI is revolutionizing the customer service and personalization in the financial industry. By leveraging AI, financial institutions can provide more personalized services to their customers. AI can analyze customer data and provide tailored services to their specific needs. AI can also enable financial institutions to monitor customer behavior and identify potential fraud. AI can be used to automate customer service tasks such as answering customer queries, responding to customer emails, and performing customer surveys. Live chat services and chatbot functionality are considerably expanding within financial sector organizations, and customer demand is growing (Rajaobelina and Richard, 2021) [6]. AI-based chatbots can be used to provide personalized customer support. AI can also be used

Figure 5.2 AI application in personalized financial advice.

to recommend financial products to customers based on their individual needs and preferences. Finally, AI can be used to provide personalized financial advice to customers, as displayed in Figure 5.2.

5.4.1   AI-Powered Chatbots for Customer Service

Chatbots in the financial industry can be used to help customers with a variety of tasks, such as finding account information, making payments, and providing customer service. A chatbot powered by artificial intelligence technologies can interact with customers in natural language and understand customer intent, which can greatly improve customer experience. AI chatbots can also provide personalized recommendations to customers based on their financial data, such as credit scores, spending habits, and investment goals. Moreover, AI chatbots can be used to automate repetitive tasks, such as data entry and customer service inquiries, to free up employees to focus on high-value activities.

5.4.2   Personalized Recommendations and Offerings Using AI

a)   Automated Investment Advice: AI can be used to provide personalized investment advice to customers based on their individual risk profiles, goals, and preferences.

AI algorithms can analyze historical data to develop an understanding of the customer's financial situation and provide recommendations on the best investments and strategies to pursue.

b) Automated Credit Rating: AI can be used to determine credit ratings for customers based on their financial profiles and past transaction history. AI algorithms can evaluate customer data such as income, payment history, and available assets and liabilities to generate an accurate credit score.

c) Automated Portfolio Rebalancing: AI can be used to automatically rebalance portfolios in order to optimize returns and minimize risk. AI algorithms can analyze the performance of the portfolio over time and make recommendations on which assets to buy, sell, or hold.

d) AI-Powered Financial Planning: AI can be used to create personalized financial plans for customers based on their current financial situation and future goals. AI algorithms can analyze customer data such as income, expenses, investments, and liabilities to create a customized plan that is tailored to their individual needs.

e) AI-Driven Algorithmic Trading: AI can be used to identify profitable investment opportunities in stocks, commodities, currencies, and more. AI-driven algorithmic trading systems can make decisions based on real-time data and react to market changes faster than humans.

f) Intelligent Portfolio Management: AI can be used to analyze complex market conditions and identify optimal portfolio strategies. AI-driven portfolio management solutions can help financial advisers and investors make better, more informed decisions.

g) AI-Driven Investment Recommendations: AI can be used to generate personalized investment recommendations based on individual risk profiles and financial goals. AI-enabled investment advice can help investors make smarter decisions with their money.

h) AI-Driven Fraud Detection: AI can be used to detect suspicious financial transactions and identify potential fraud. AI-driven fraud detection solutions can help financial institutions reduce their risk of fraud and protect their customers' money.

i) AI-Driven Customer Segmentation: AI can be used to segment customers based on their financial behavior, spending
habits, and other factors. AI-driven customer segmentation
solutions can help financial institutions target their offerings more effectively.

5.5 Compliance and Regulatory Reporting

AI has the potential to revolutionize compliance and regulatory reporting
in the financial industry. AI-powered software can automate the collection, analysis, and reporting of data, reducing manual work, improving
accuracy, and enhancing the speed of the process. AI can also be used
to identify anomalies or suspicious activity in data, alerting financial
firms to potential risks or compliance breaches. AI-based systems can
also help financial firms reduce the risks associated with misreporting
by providing more accurate, timely, and comprehensive reports. Finally,
AI can be used to better analyze and understand financial data, helping
financial firms to develop more strategic and proactive compliance strategies. AI can be used to automate and improve the accuracy of regulatory and compliance reporting in financial services. AI-driven solutions
can help financial institutions to detect and prevent fraudulent activities and noncompliance with regulations. AI can also be used to identify
patterns in customer data, monitor transactions, and detect suspicious
activities. AI can be used to automate the process of preparing regulatory
filings and compliance reports, making them more accurate and efficient.
Additionally, AI can be used to monitor customer behavior and detect
anomalies to ensure compliance with financial regulations. AI can also be
used to automate the process of managing customer data and providing
insights into customer behavior. Figure 5.3 exhibits that AI can be used
to detect and prevent money laundering activities and other financial
crimes.

a) Automated Document Processing: AI-based automated
document processing solutions enable businesses to quickly
and accurately process large volumes of regulatory documents. This allows businesses to quickly identify any potential risks associated with the documents and take corrective
action.
b) AI-Powered Risk Management: AI-powered risk management solutions enable financial organizations to detect and

Figure 5.3 AI in regulatory compliance.

address potential risks associated with regulatory compliance. By leveraging machine learning and natural language processing technologies, these solutions can be used to identify potential risks, analyze customer data, and develop strategies to mitigate the risks.

c) Automated Compliance Monitoring: AI-based solutions can be used to automate compliance monitoring processes. By leveraging machine learning algorithms, these solutions can scan and analyze large amounts of data to detect any potential violations or discrepancies in the regulatory framework.

d) Automated Reporting: AI-powered reporting solutions can help financial organizations to quickly and accurately generate regulatory reports. By leveraging machine learning algorithms, these solutions can scan and analyze large amounts of data to generate insightful reports.

e) AI-Based Fraud Detection: AI-based fraud detection solutions can be used to detect and prevent financial frauds. By leveraging machine learning algorithms, these solutions can quickly identify any suspicious activities or transactions and take necessary action.

5.5.1 Streamlining Regulatory Reporting with AI

AI is being used to streamline regulatory reporting in the financial industry by reducing the time and effort associated with manual data entry and analysis.

AI-driven automation can help identify trends and insights and can reduce the time to prepare and submit reports. AI can also automate the identification and analysis of data, as well as the preparation of reports, helping to reduce errors and streamline the regulatory reporting process. AI can also help to identify potential issues and risks, as well as compliance issues, enabling firms to take action before they become major problems. By reducing the amount of manual labor involved in regulatory reporting, AI can help financial institutions increase efficiency and reduce costs.

5.5.2   Risk Assessment and Compliance Monitoring Using AI

AI can be used to improve the risk assessment and compliance monitoring process in the financial industry. AI-driven approaches can help automate the process of identifying, assessing, and monitoring risk by providing insights into complex datasets and uncovering trends that would be difficult to detect with traditional methods. AI can be used to detect patterns in data that may indicate a potential risk or compliance issue, as well as to identify suspicious behavior or transactions that need to be investigated further. AI can also help financial service providers better understand their customers by providing insights into their behaviors and preferences, enabling them to tailor their services accordingly. AI-driven approaches can also help automate the process of monitoring for compliance with regulations and internal policies, thereby reducing the risk of regulatory fines or sanctions.

5.6   Impact of AI on Employment in the Financial Industry

The impact of AI on employment in the financial industry is complex. On one hand, AI technologies have the potential to make financial services more efficient, improve customer experience, and reduce costs of operations. On the other hand, AI could potentially replace some financial jobs and reduce the need for human labor in the industry. To accurately assess the impact of AI on employment in the financial industry, it is important to consider both the positive and negative impacts on jobs. The positive impacts of AI on employment in the financial industry include increased productivity and efficiency. AI-driven solutions can automate tedious and repetitive tasks, which can help improve operational efficiency and reduce the need for manual labor. AI can also help financial services companies analyze customer data, identify trends, and better anticipate customer needs, which can improve customer experience. The potential negative impacts of AI on employment in the financial industry include job displacement and wage stagnation. AI technologies have the potential to replace some of the tasks that are currently done by human labor, such as customer service, loan processing, and fraud detection. This could lead to job displacement and a decrease in employment in the industry. Furthermore, AI-driven solutions can reduce the cost of operations, which could lead to wage stagnation for employees. Fintech powered by AI enables sustainable financial landscape in the future (He & Zhao, 2020) [7].

5.6.1   Potential Job Displacement Due to AI Adoption

AI adoption in the financial industry can lead to potential job displacement. Figure 5.4 depicts AI in job displacement. There was a strong perception that AI and automation may result in workforce reduction. Autor and Salomons (2018) [8] assessed whether rapid automation has served to dampen aggregate labor demand or overall wage growth and found that every firm in an industry undergoing technological progress might substitute capital for labor in a subset of tasks. While automation will eliminate very few occupations entirely in the next decade, it will affect portions of almost all jobs to a greater or lesser degree, depending on the type of work they entail (Chui *et al.*, 2016) [9]. Since AI can process large amounts of data quickly and accurately, it has the potential to automate processes and take on mundane tasks that financial professionals currently do. This could

Figure 5.4 AI in job displacement.

mean that some jobs, such as financial analysts and loan officers, could be replaced by machines. Additionally, AI can help detect and prevent fraud more quickly and effectively than humans, which could lead to a reduction in the need for fraud analysts and investigators. The emergence of AI could also lead to fewer jobs in the customer service sector, as AI-powered chatbots can handle customer inquiries more quickly and efficiently than human employees. Ultimately, AI could lead to a dramatic reshaping of the financial industry, leading to job displacement and a need for new job roles that require more technical or creative skills.

5.6.2   Opportunities for New Roles and Skills in the Industry

- AI Consultant: Companies will need experts to help them develop, implement, and maintain their AI systems.
- Data Scientist: Data scientists will be needed to help companies analyze data and build AI models.
- AI Engineer: Companies will need specialists to help design, develop, and deploy the AI systems.
- Risk and Compliance Specialist: With AI being used to automate many processes, companies need specialists to ensure that their AI systems meet all regulatory requirements.
- AI Product Manager: Companies will need specialists to help them manage their AI products and ensure that they are meeting customer needs.
- AI Auditor: Companies will need experts to audit the accuracy of their AI systems and ensure that they are operating correctly.
- AI Trainer: Companies will need experts to create and deliver training programs to teach employees how to use their AI systems.
- AI Strategist: Companies will need specialists to help them develop strategies and plans to make the most of their AI investments.

5.6.3   The Need for Reskilling and Upskilling the Workforce

Businesses can increase performance by decreasing errors, enhancing quality and speed, and, in certain circumstances, attaining results that are beyond the capacity of humans by automating certain tasks (McKinsey Global Institute, 2017) [10]. The rapid development of artificial intelligence is revolutionizing the financial industry. AI technology is transforming the financial industry by automating mundane tasks, allowing faster and more accurate decisions, and providing access to data-driven insights. This is leading to an increased demand for new skills and capabilities. Financial professionals need to be reskilled and upskilled in order to understand and effectively use AI technologies. Reskilling and upskilling the financial workforce are essential if the industry is to remain competitive. Financial professionals must understand how to use AI technologies to improve their performance and create more value for their clients. They must also be able to interpret the data generated by AI technologies to identify opportunities and risks. Furthermore, financial professionals must be able to use AI technologies to build innovative products and services. The reskilling and upskilling of the financial workforce must also include soft skills, such as communication and problem-solving. Financial professionals must be able to communicate effectively with clients and colleagues and work collaboratively and creatively to solve complex problems. To ensure the successful and effective use of AI technologies in the financial industry, companies must provide their employees with the necessary training and resources. They must also create a culture of continuous learning to ensure that employees are continuously developing their skill. Financial organizations should prioritize reskilling and upskilling the workforce to ensure that employees are able to leverage AI technology to the fullest. This can involve providing employees with the necessary training, workshops, and certifications to understand and use the technology. Additionally, financial organizations should consider investing in tools and technologies that will help users more easily transition to AI technology.

5.7   Ethical and Social Implications of AI Adoption

The ethical and social implications of AI adoption in the financial industry are significant. As AI technology advances, it will shape how financial decisions are made, how financial products and services are developed, and how financial information is used. This could lead to potential issues related to privacy, trust, fairness, and transparency. First, AI technology has the potential to impact how financial decisions are made by automating decisions that were traditionally made by humans. By utilizing algorithms to automate decisions, financial institutions are able to reduce costs, increase efficiency, and make decisions more quickly. However, this could lead to potential ethical issues related to privacy and fairness. Automated

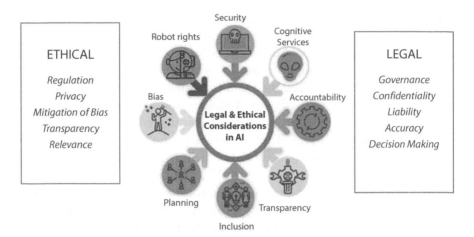

Figure 5.5 AI in ethical and legal considerations.

decisions can lead to biased results, which could negatively impact vulnerable populations. Second, AI technology has the potential to shape the development of financial products and services. For example, AI can be used to identify customers' needs, design products, and develop marketing strategies. While this could increase efficiency and reduce costs, there is also a risk that AI-driven products and services could be designed without consideration for ethical implications. Finally, AI technology has the potential to shape how financial information is used. AI can be used to analyze large amounts of data to identify patterns, which can be used to make predictions about the future. Figure 5.5 shows the role of AI in ethical and legal considerations.

5.7.1   Ensuring Transparency and Accountability in AI Decision-Making

- Establish and enforce clear regulations around the use of AI in the financial industry. These regulations should include requirements for the disclosure of algorithms used to make decisions and that all AI decisions are subject to review and approval by a human decision-maker.
- Implement regular audits of AI decision-making. These audits should be conducted by independent third parties and should assess the accuracy, fairness, and transparency of AI-based decisions.

- Ensure transparency and accountability in AI decision-making by requiring financial institutions to document their decision-making processes and publish the results of their audits.
- Encourage financial institutions to use AI responsibly and adopt best practices, such as responsible data collection, to ensure that customers and stakeholders are treated fairly and ethically.
- Establish an AI ombudsman or commission to investigate complaints or reports of potential misuse of AI and to recommend corrective measures.
- Establish an AI ethics committee to review AI-based decisions and to ensure that they comply with ethical and legal standards.
- Educate stakeholders on the implications of AI decision-making and the importance of transparency and accountability.
- Encourage financial institutions to implement robust policies and procedures that ensure transparency and systematic compliance.

5.7.2   Ethical Concerns Around AI Adoption in Finance

- Unfairness: AI algorithms can amplify existing biases, leading to unfair decisions and outcomes. For example, AI-driven loan decisions can be based on incomplete or inaccurate data that may contain racial or gender biases, leading to discrimination in lending decisions.
- Security: AI systems can be vulnerable to malicious attacks and data breaches, which can have disastrous consequences for financial institutions.
- Privacy: AI systems can store and process sensitive personal data, which create ethical issues around privacy.
- Exploitation: AI may be used to manipulate markets and manipulate prices, which can result in unfair outcomes for consumers.
- Job Loss: AI can replace some jobs, leading to job losses and financial hardship.
- Regulatory Compliance: AI systems may not be compliant with existing financial regulations, leading to costly fines and legal issues.

5.7.3   Addressing Potential Biases and Discrimination in AI-Based Financial Services

a) Developing Fair and Transparent AI Algorithms: AI algorithms used in financial services should be designed to reduce bias and discrimination. This can include incorporating fairness criteria into algorithms, such as avoiding the use of demographic data in automated decisions. Additionally, AI algorithms should be transparent, so that stakeholders can understand how decisions are being made and intervene if needed.

b) Incorporating Human Oversight: AI algorithms should be designed with human oversight, including periodic monitoring for bias and discrimination. This could include requiring that humans review the decisions made by algorithms and intervene if needed.

c) Collecting and Analyzing Data: Financial institutions should collect and analyze data to identify potential biases and discrimination in AI-based financial services. This could include conducting audits and surveys to assess the impacts of their AI algorithms on different demographic groups.

d) Offering Education and Training: Financial institutions should offer education and training to employees to help them better understand and identify potential biases and discrimination in AI-based financial services. This could include providing resources and guidance on how to identify and address potential biases and discrimination.

5.8   Future of AI Adoption in the Financial Industry

The future of AI adoption in the financial industry looks very promising. AI has already been adopted to a great extent, with applications ranging from automated customer service to fraud detection. Research suggests that AI will become increasingly prevalent in the financial industry, as it offers significant benefits such as cost savings, better customer experience, and improved security. AI will be used to automate mundane processes such as account opening and customer service, as well as more complex tasks such as portfolio management and risk management. AI can also be used to detect fraud in real time and to make better decisions about investments

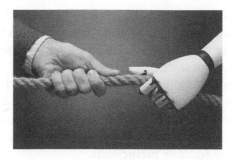

Figure 5.6 AI in decision-making.

and loan applications. AI can also be used to analyze large amounts of data and generate insights, helping to make better decisions. In addition, AI can be used to personalize customer experiences, providing them with tailored services and recommendations. This could make customers more likely to engage with their financial service provider and make them more likely to continue using their services. Overall, AI is set to become a major part of the financial industry in the near future. Financial institutions are already using AI in various areas, and the trend is expected to continue. AI can help financial institutions become more efficient, improve customer service, and make better decisions as shown in Figure 5.6.

5.8.1 Emerging Trends and Technologies in AI Adoption in Finance

a) Automated Trading: Automated trading is the use of computers to automatically execute trades on financial markets. Automation helps to improve financial decision-making and reduce costs associated with manual trading. Automated trading can be used in both long- and short-term investing strategies.

b) Machine Learning: Machine learning is the use of algorithms to uncover patterns and gain insights from large sets of data. Machine learning can be used to make predictive models, identify new trading opportunities, and automate trading decisions.

c) Natural Language Processing: Natural language processing is the use of technology to understand and interpret human language. NLP can be used to interpret news articles, identify sentiment in customer feedback, and automate document processing.

d) Blockchain: Blockchain technology is a distributed ledger that is used to store and record transactions. Blockchain can be used for verifying transactions, tracking assets, and creating smart contracts.

e) Quantum Computing: Quantum computing is the use of quantum mechanical phenomena, such as superposition and entanglement, to perform calculations. Quantum computing can be used to optimize trading strategies and to make more accurate predictions.

5.8.2   Opportunities for Innovation and Growth in the Industry

- Automation and AI: Automation and artificial intelligence are transforming the financial industry. Automation and AI can be used to streamline processes, reduce costs, and improve customer experiences.
- Blockchain Technology: Blockchain technology has the potential to revolutionize the financial industry by improving security, privacy, and accuracy. It can also be used to create new financial products and services.
- Online Banking: Online banking is becoming increasingly popular with customers and is providing new opportunities for banks to expand their reach and serve customers better.
- Mobile Banking: Mobile banking is becoming more popular with customers and is providing new opportunities for banks to increase customer engagement and provide a better user experience.
- Digital Payments: Digital payments are transforming the way customers make payments and are providing new opportunities for banks to create innovative payment solutions.
- Big Data: Big data are transforming the financial industry by providing banks with the opportunity to gain insights into customer behavior and preferences. This can be used to create new products and services tailored to customer needs.
- Cybersecurity: With the increasing threats posed by cybercriminals, banks must invest in cybersecurity to protect their customers' data.
- Social Media: Social media provides banks with a platform to build relationships with their customers and create opportunities for growth.

5.8.3   Challenges and Limitations to Widespread Adoption of AI

- Regulatory Uncertainty: Regulatory uncertainty is a major challenge to widespread adoption of AI in the financial industry. Regulatory bodies are struggling to keep up with the rapid pace of technological development, and this lack of clarity can be a deterrent for firms considering investing in and implementing AI solutions.
- Security Concerns: With the increasing prevalence of cyberattacks and data breaches, financial institutions are understandably cautious about relying on AI for critical decisions. AI systems are vulnerable to malicious attacks, and financial institutions must be able to guarantee the security and reliability of their systems before they can adopt AI.
- Cost: Implementing AI-driven systems requires significant up-front costs. Companies must invest in training and developing AI algorithms, acquiring data, and integrating AI systems into existing infrastructure. These costs can be prohibitive for smaller institutions.
- Lack of Talent: Finding the right talent to develop and manage AI systems is another challenge facing the financial industry. AI experts are in high demand, and financial institutions may struggle to find qualified personnel to build and maintain their systems.
- Trust: Financial institutions must also build trust with their customers and ensure that AI-driven decisions are fair and equitable. Companies must be transparent about how their AI systems work and ensure that their systems are designed to be unbiased and reliable.

5.9   Case Studies on AI Adoption in the Financial Industry

5.9.1   ICICI Bank

ICICI Bank is another Indian financial institution that has adopted AI. The bank is using AI to improve its customer experience by using predictive analytics to anticipate customer needs. For example, the bank uses AI to predict customer preferences based on past transactions and provide personalized services to customers. ICICI Bank has also implemented AI-based chatbots for customer service. The bank also uses AI to detect fraud and automate its operations.

5.9.2   HDFC Bank

HDFC Bank, India's second-largest bank, has been a leader in the adoption of artificial intelligence technologies. The bank has been leveraging AI to improve its customer experience and enhance its operational efficiency. It has implemented several AI solutions, including chatbots, facial recognition technologies, and machine learning algorithms, to automate its processes and services. The bank has developed a chatbot, named Eva, to provide customers with personalized banking services. Eva understands customer queries and provides customers with accurate and timely responses. It can help customers with various banking activities, such as balance inquiry, fund transfer, bill payments, and more. HDFC Bank has also implemented facial recognition technology to improve security and authentication processes. The bank's "Smart Lock" feature uses facial recognition to allow customers to unlock their mobile banking app without entering a password. It also uses AI-based facial recognition technology to detect and alert the bank in case of any suspicious transactions.

5.9.3   Bank of America

Bank of America is one of the largest banks in the world, and it has been using artificial intelligence to improve its operations. The bank has used AI to automate various tasks such as compliance checks and customer support. This has enabled the bank to be more efficient and accurate in its operations. Bank of America has also used AI to improve its risk management process. The bank has deployed AI algorithms that can identify patterns in customer data and alert the bank to potential risks. This has enabled the bank to be more proactive in managing risks, and it has resulted in improved profitability. The bank has also used AI to improve its customer service. AI algorithms have been deployed to analyze customer data and identify patterns that can help the bank better understand customer needs. This has enabled the bank to provide more personalized customer service and enhance customer satisfaction.

5.9.4 Real-World Examples of Successful AI Adoption in Finance

- Automated Trading: Automated trading is the use of algorithms to automate the trading process, allowing for faster decision-making and improved risk management. This is a popular form of AI adoption in finance, as it helps traders make more informed decisions and reduces the potential for human error.
- Fraud Detection: AI is being used to detect fraudulent transactions and money laundering activities faster and more accurately. AI technology can quickly analyze large amounts of data and detect suspicious patterns, making it an invaluable tool in the fight against financial fraud.
- Credit Scoring: AI-powered credit scoring is becoming increasingly popular as it reduces the time it takes to assess creditworthiness. AI algorithms are able to quickly analyze large amounts of data and identify patterns that can be used to determine a person's creditworthiness. This can help lenders make better decisions about approving loans and other financial products.
- Investment Optimization: AI can help investors make better decisions by providing them with sophisticated insights into the markets. AI-powered investment optimization tools can monitor the markets and recommend the best investments based on the investor's goals and risk profile.

5.9.5 Impact of AI on Business Operations and Customer Experience

The impact of AI on business operations and customer experience in the finance industry is profound. AI can be used to automate processes and reduce costs, improve customer service, and increase accuracy and efficiency. The researchers in finance and information systems have started to analyze the impact of digital progress on the financial sector (Gomber et al., 2017) [11]. AI can also help banks and financial institutions better understand customer behavior and provide personalized advice and services. AI can also help detect financial fraud and reduce risks. Additionally, AI can be used to provide predictive analytics and sentiment analysis, helping financial institutions better understand market trends and customer needs.

AI can be used to create more engaging customer experiences, such as chatbots and virtual assistants, which enable customers to have convenient and personalized experiences.

The impact of AI on business operations and customer experience in the finance industry is far-reaching. AI can help streamline operations and automate processes, allowing financial services firms to reduce costs and improve customer service. AI-driven automation can also help financial services firms to better manage customer data and provide personalized experiences. AI can also be used to detect fraud and identify suspicious transactions, helping to protect customers and financial institutions from loss. AI-driven chatbots and virtual assistants can also be used to provide customers with quick and accurate responses to their questions, helping to improve customer satisfaction and loyalty. Finally, AI can be used to provide financial advice and recommendations based on customer data, allowing customers to make more informed decisions about their finances.

The finance industry is one of the industries that are most affected by the introduction of artificial intelligence. AI has already started to revolutionize the way financial services are delivered, from banking and lending to investment and insurance. AI is transforming the financial services industry by providing new opportunities for cost reduction, improved customer experience, risk mitigation, and more accurate decision-making. AI can also provide an edge in areas such as fraud detection, customer segmentation, and customer profiling.

AI can improve business operations in the finance industry in several ways. AI can be used to automate mundane tasks such as data entry and reconciliations, freeing up time for employees to focus on more complex tasks. AI can also be used to improve customer experience by providing more personalized services and reducing response times. AI can also help financial institutions reduce costs by automating processes and reducing operational errors. AI can also help financial institutions better manage risk. AI-driven algorithms can be used to identify suspicious activities and detect potential frauds. AI can also be used to monitor and evaluate market trends, identify potential opportunities, and recommend investments. In addition to improving business operations, AI can also be used to improve customer experience in the finance industry. AI-powered chatbots and virtual assistants can be used to provide quick and personalized responses to customer inquiries. AI can also be used to personalize customer interactions and provide tailored services based on customer needs.

The use of AI in the finance industry is still in its early stages, but it is already having a huge impact on business operations and customer experience.

As AI technology continues to evolve, it will become even more important for financial institutions to leverage AI to remain competitive.

5.9.6   Lessons Learned From AI Implementation in the Financial Industry

- Data Accuracy Is Paramount: AI models rely heavily on the accuracy of data and the quality of the data used to train the model. It is essential to ensure that all data used are up-to-date, accurate, and complete.
- Think Beyond Automation: Financial institutions should use AI to help them make more informed decisions and provide better customer service, not just automate mundane tasks.
- Utilize AI to Personalize Products: AI can be used to personalize financial products to meet the needs of individual customers and offer tailored advice.
- Consider the Long-Term Impact: AI has the potential to disrupt the way financial services are delivered, and it is important to consider the long-term impacts of AI on the industry.
- Leverage AI for Cybersecurity: AI can be used to detect fraud, prevent cyberattacks, and protect customer data.
- Monitor AI Performance: Financial institutions should monitor the performance of their AI models to ensure that they are performing as expected.

5.10   Conclusion and Future Directions

The implementation of AI in the financial industry has revolutionized the way businesses operate. AI has enabled financial institutions to automate processes and make better decisions in a fraction of the time. AI is being used in areas such as fraud detection, customer segmentation, and portfolio management. AI has also enabled the development of more accurate prediction models to improve risk management and compliance.

The future of AI in the financial industry is bright. AI will continue to be used to automate processes and make better decisions. It can also be used to create more personalized customer experiences, reduce operational costs, and improve fraud detection and compliance. AI-powered tools are also being used to improve customer segmentation, portfolio management, and asset allocation. AI is also being used to develop new financial services and products. AI-powered tools can be used to provide more accurate recommendations and insights to customers. In addition, AI can be used to develop new investment strategies and risk management techniques. Finally, AI is being used to improve the security and privacy of financial services. AI-powered algorithms are being used to detect suspicious activity and reduce the risk of fraud. AI can also be used to improve the security of customer data. The future of AI in the financial industry is very promising. AI will continue to be used to automate processes, improve decision-making, and create more personalized customer experiences. AI will also be used to develop new services and products, improve security and privacy, and provide more accurate insights and recommendations.

5.10.1   Summary of the Key Findings and Insights from the Chapter

AI technology can be applied to a variety of financial services and processes, including portfolio management, risk management, customer service, algorithmic trading, and fraud detection. AI can provide more accurate and timely insights and predictions, helping financial services firms better manage risk and improve customer service. AI and machine learning can help financial services firms automate and streamline processes and reduce manual labor costs. AI technologies can be used to identify and target new customer segments, enabling financial services companies to better understand their customer base. AI can help financial services firms develop personalized customer experiences and increase customer loyalty. AI can improve the accuracy and speed of financial services firms' decision-making processes. AI implementation can help financial services firms comply with regulations and enhance security. AI can help financial services firms identify and address potential ethical issues.

AI has the potential to revolutionize the financial industry by enabling faster and more accurate decisions and cost savings. AI can be used to improve efficiency, accuracy, and transparency in areas such as fraud detection, compliance, customer service, and trading. AI can also be used to identify and manage risks, develop personalized customer experiences, and foster innovation. AI-based technology can provide faster and more accurate insights into financial data and help financial institutions make better decisions. AI can be used to automate tasks and processes, such as account opening and handling customer inquiries. AI can also be used to create predictive models for market analysis and trading. The use of AI in the financial industry is still in its early stages, and many challenges still exist, such as data privacy, security, and ethical considerations. AI can be used to create new products and services, such as robo-advisors and auto-mated investment services. AI can help financial institutions gain compet-itive advantage by providing better customer insights and enabling more personalized experiences.

5.10.2   Recommendations for Future Research and Development in AI Adoption in Finance

- Develop algorithms that can accurately assess risk and reward when incorporating AI into financial decision-making.
- Investigate the use of AI-based tools for automating and optimizing financial processes.
- Develop methods to better assess the impact of AI adoption in finance on consumer protection and financial stability.
- Develop ways to use AI to enhance financial literacy and financial decision-making in consumer populations.
- Explore the potential of AI in fraud detection and other areas of financial risk management.
- Investigate the use of AI for financial advice and portfolio management.
- Research the use of AI for better understanding of financial markets and for better prediction of market trends.
- Investigate the use of AI for improving the accuracy and speed of financial transactions and reducing costs.
- Develop ways to use AI for better analysis of alternative data sources.
- Research the use of AI for improved compliance and regu-latory reporting.

5.10.3   The Role of Policymakers, Regulators, and Industry Leaders in Shaping the Future of AI in Finance

The policymakers, regulators, and industry leaders have a vital role to play in shaping the future of AI in finance. For instance, policymakers and reg-ulators can create frameworks that define the ethical, legal, and governance standards for the use of AI in financial services. This could include intro-ducing regulations that ensure that AI-driven decisions are transparent, accountable, and compliant with data privacy laws. Industry leaders can also help shape the future of AI in finance by investing in research and development, innovating new strategies and products, and setting new standards for the use of AI in financial services. Additionally, they can provide guidance and support to financial institutions looking to adopt AI-driven solutions, as well as promote ethical considerations in the development and implementation of these solutions. Industry leaders can help to foster collaboration between financial institutions, regulatory and policymaking bodies, and technology providers to ensure that the right tools and approaches are developed and deployed in a responsible and effective manner. They can set the standards, frameworks, and regulations that will ensure that AI is used responsibly, safely, and ethically. They can also provide guidance to industry on how to use AI responsibly and how to handle data privacy and consumer protection. Additionally, they can promote the development of best practices for AI in finance, such as by establishing guidelines for the use of AI in financial services and systems. Policymakers, regulators, and industry leaders can help to promote the development of AI technologies and services that are tailored to the needs of the industry and that can help to create financial services that are more accessible, affordable, and secure.

Policymakers can promote the responsible use of AI technologies through laws and regulations that ensure that financial institutions are compliant with consumer protection and anti-money laundering requirements. Regulators can use their authority to ensure that financial institutions are transparent about their use of AI and that the technology is used safely and responsibly. Industry leaders can also help to shape the future of AI in finance by investing in the development of new technologies and working to ensure that AI is used ethically and responsibly. Additionally, they can collaborate with policymakers, regulators, and other stakeholders to create and implement industry-wide standards and best practices. Finally, they can help to educate the public about the potential applications of AI in finance and promote its responsible use.

5.11   Conclusion

The adoption of artificial intelligence has had a profound impact on the current trends of the financial industry. AI technologies have revolutionized various aspects of financial services, including risk assessment, fraud detection, customer service, and investment strategies. By leveraging advanced algorithms, machine learning, and data analytics, financial institutions have been able to enhance efficiency, accuracy, and decision-making processes. AI-powered chatbots and virtual assistants have improved customer experiences, while algorithmic trading and robo-advisors have transformed investment practices. However, challenges such as data privacy, ethics, and regulatory concerns continue to accompany the widespread adoption of AI in finance. Overall, the integration of AI into the financial industry has opened up new opportunities, reshaped traditional practices, and paved the way for a more technologically advanced and data-driven future.

References

1. Gartner, Top 10 strategic technology trends for 2020. *Intelligent Automation*, 2019. Retrieved from https://www.gartner.com/en/newsroom/press-releases/2019-10-21-gartner-identifies-the-top-10-strategic-technology-trends-for-2020.
2. Qin, Z., Liu, Q., Cao, J., Shu, K., Intelligent finance: A convergence of AI, blockchain, and cloud computing. *IEEE Intell. Syst.*, 34, 6, 2–9, 2019.
3. Rajan, R.G., Finance and technology: Fintech as an enabler of financial inclusion. *J. Financial Serv. Res.*, 56, 1, 157–162, 2019.
4. World Economic Forum, *The New Physics of Financial Services–How Artificial Intelligence is Transforming the Financial Ecosystem*, 2019, Retrieved from https://www.weforum.org/reports/the-new-physics-of-financial-services-how-artificial-intelligence-is-transforming-the-financial-ecosystem/.
5. Rohmah, K.L., Arisudhana, A., Nurhantoro, T.S., The future of accounting with artificial intelligence: Opportunity and challenge. *ICoSTEC*, 2022, Retrived from https://www.researchgate.net/publication/368772154_The_Future_of_Accounting_With_Artificial_Intelligence_Opportunity_And_Challenge.
6. Rajaobelina, L. and Ricard, L., Classifying potential users of live chat services and chatbots. *J. Financ. Serv. Mark.*, 26, 2, 81–94, 2021. https://doi.org/10.1057/s41264-021-00086-0.
7. He, W. and Zhao, Y., FinTech as a facilitator for sustainable finance: A systematic review. *Technol. Forecast. Soc. Change*, 160, 120241, 2020.
8. Autor, D.H. and Salomons, A., Is automation labor-displacing? Productivity growth, employment, and the labor share. *J. Econ. Perspect.*, 35, 3, 33–66, 2021.
9. Chui, M., Manyika, J., Miremadi, M., Where machines could replace humans—and where they can't (yet). *McKinsey Q.*, 1, 1–10, 2016. Retrieved from https://www.mckinsey.com/capabilities/mckinsey-digital/our-insights/where-machines-could-replace-humans-and-where-they-cant-yet.
10. McKinsey Global Institute, *A Future That Works: Automation, Employment, and Productivity*, McKinsey & Company, Atlanta, GA, United States, 2017.
11. Gomber, P., Koch, J.-A., Siering, M., Digital finance and FinTech: Current research and future research directions. *J. Bus. Econ.*, 87, 5, 537–580, 2017.

6

Artificial Intelligence Applications in the Indian Financial Ecosystem

Vijaya Kittu Manda[1]* and Khaliq Lubza Nihar[2]

[1]*Perspectives in Business Management & Economics, Visakhapatnam,
Andhra Pradesh, India*
[2]*Department of Finance, GITAM School of Business, GITAM Deemed to be
University, Visakhapatnam, India*

Abstract

The Indian banking and financial services (BFS) ecosystem uses artificial intelligence (AI) primarily in five major areas—customer service/engagement (chatbot), robo advice, general purpose/predictive analytics, cybersecurity, and credit scoring/direct lending. While initial AI applications focused on support functions, they evolved to help in decision-making over time. As web servers capture and collect a huge quantum of customer data, companies are taking advantage of artificial intelligence, big data analytics, and machine learning. The technology trio is helping financial companies, particularly startups, build innovative products, monitor, manage risk, and provide superior customer services. Indian startups made their mark by successfully demonstrating AI use cases that suit the Indian atmosphere. On the other hand, financial regulators promote and recommend using AI in a limited way (such as in regulator sandbox areas) that fosters innovative financial engineering and product development and brings in the safety and security of customer data and monies. This research article updates how the Indian financial ecosystem uses artificial intelligence in various dimensions.

Keywords: Chatbots, financial ecosystem, use cases, creditworthiness, RegTech, financial frauds, risk management, AGI

Corresponding author: vijaykittu@hotmail.com; ORCID: https://orcid.org/0000-0002-1680-8210
Khaliq Lubza Nihar: ORCID: https://orcid.org/0000-0001-6272-3579

Ambrish Kumar Mishra, Shweta Anand, Narayan C. Debnath, Purvi Pokhariyal and Archana Patel (eds.) Artificial Intelligence for Risk Mitigation in the Financial Industry, (133–158) © 2024 Scrivener Publishing LLC

6.1   Introduction

Three technology trends related to artificial intelligence (AI) became evident in the early 2020s. Firstly, artificial intelligence came out of its AI winter slumber sleep that was prominently visible during the 1980s and 1990s. During that time, technological development and progress were prolonged. However, today, it gained a fantastic pace in growth and development. Secondly, AI transformed into a technology that almost every institution in every sector and industry wishes to use in its activities. It became a key differentiator among competitors in any industry [1]. AI is not growing in isolation but is in cohesion with the disruption technologies, such as machine learning (ML), deep learning, natural language processing (NLP), computer vision, robotic process automation (RPA), blockchain technology, edge and quantum computing, Internet of Things (IoT), augmented reality (AR), and virtual reality (VR). Figure 6.1 shows how AI integrates with other technologies to build the banking and financial services application stack.

In April 2023, India surpassed China to become the most populous country in the world and has a 74% digital and financial literacy rate. India is a startup nation and home to some of the finest unicorns. Financial innovations and open banking systems, such as UPI, UPI Lite, and RuPay, have spearheaded the Indian fintech revolution. India houses 50,000 startups, of which 2,100 are in the financial technology (fintech) stream. Both open

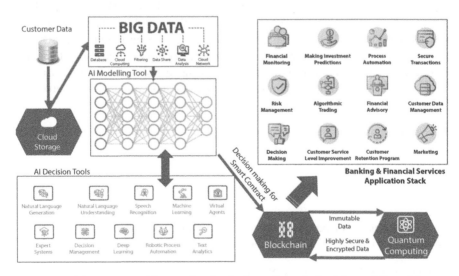

Figure 6.1 AI integrates with several technologies to form the banking and financial services application stack.

banking and generative AI are regarded as the two biggest disruptors in the Indian banking system. Key factors that show the growth of the fintech sector are increasing adoption of digital payments, government initiatives to promote financial inclusion, and rising smartphone penetration. The Indian fintech is a stream that continuously offers first-level AI use cases for corporates. These startups received significant funding and patent filings centered around AI. While the private sector was essentially the implementor of technology in the early days [2], the public sector banks (PSBs) and even governmental, institutional institutions later joined the implementation race facilitated by the policies, rules, and regulation support from the regulators and government. The 2018–2019 Indian Union Budget speech mandated NITI Aayog to establish the National Program on AI, and the Union Budget 2022–2023 accelerated the use of AI in government offices. NITI Aayog released a discussion paper on a national strategy for AI and was instrumental in branding #AIforAll [3].

The COVID-19 pandemic tripled the number of active customers on digital channels in public sector banks—from 3.4 lakh crores in 2019–2020 to 7.6 crores in 2020–2021. This development led to opportunities and challenges for banking and financial services (BFS) regulators to ensure financial safety and stability without sacrificing the enthusiasm to encourage financial innovations. AI became a tool to foster digital financial inclusion [4]. Since the pandemic-led lockdowns, various institutions have expressed immense interest in AI-based implementations. AI-based technologies were also responsible for financial institutions to detect and deter fraud during the pandemic times [5].

While there are many definitions of artificial intelligence, here is a definition mentioned in the *Report of the Working Group on Digital Lending, including Lending through Online Platforms and Mobile Apps* by the Reserve Bank of India (RBI). Artificial intelligence is the "information technology (IT) systems that perform functions requiring human capabilities. AI can ask questions, discover and test hypotheses, and make decisions automatically based on advanced analytics operating on extensive data sets." [6].

Stakeholders in the financial ecosystem include developers, government, investors, users, consulting entities, and academic institutions [7].

6.2 Literature Review

Enormous academic research has already dealt with AI in the banking and financial services industry. Three key research themes identified connecting AI and banking are strategy, process, and customer [8]. Current academic research on AI in BFS revolves around banking, investments, securities, market making, customer relationships, lending, risk management, and compliance with understudied insurance [9]. AI, blockchain, and cloud computing formed an ABC technology triad that changed the face of the banking sector [10]. An examination of 90 articles using the TCCM (Theory, Context, Characteristics, and Methodology) framework finds academic research on AI in customer-facing financial services regarding the role of regulations, ethics, and policy concerned, especially in insurance and pension [11]. A systematic literature review (SLR) finds that the key AI challenges in the banking sector are job loss and user acceptance concerns, privacy breaches, creativity, adaptability loss, restrictive implementation and operational requirements, digital divide, availability of vast quality data, AI-business strategy alignment, and loss of emotional "human touch" [12].

6.3   Evolution: From Operations to Risk Management

Banking and financial services are known as high AI adapters and leading sectors compared to other sectors [6]. Indian AI implementations have evolved from front-end customer support services such as providing product data for prospective customers by sales and marketing teams, onboarding new customers, and chatbots used in credit decision-making shifting to middle-office functions like checking and ensuring compliance for Know Your Customer (KYC)/anti-money laundering (AML). AI now deals with risk management initiatives such as fraud detection and surveillance by regulators [13]. Banks were seen using AI in five areas [14]:

1. Customer service/engagement (chatbot)
2. Robo advice
3. General purpose/predictive analytics
4. Cybersecurity
5. Credit scoring/creditworthiness/direct lending

AI systems are now used not just in traditional banking systems but also in those involving cryptocurrencies [15] and decentralized finance (DeFi) [16].

6.4   Banking Services

The Indian banking sector is competitive, and technology usage can enable banks to build on their competitive edge. Banks—both public sector (led by

SBI, Canara Bank, and Central Bank) and private sector banks (led by ICICI Bank, HDFC Bank, Kotak Mahindra Bank, and Axis Bank)—began embracing AI to build their competencies and improve operational efficiencies to beat the competition and sustain their lead as first movers into AI space. At a meeting of directors of Indian banks, RBI informally asked the banks to adopt AI and blockchain, saying that the technologies are inevitable for sustainable growth, stability, and future readiness of banks [17]. Large-sized banks have been making massive shifts toward AI in recent times. Banks use NLP-based sentiment analysis in customer conversations and AI-driven personalization of services, and efforts are on to improve customer experience in a virtual banking experience. AI becomes essential in future banking service offerings involving Metaverse and Banking 5.0.

AI and NLP power global banking software today. Leading players like CoreCard Software (market share of 23.71%), Misys (8.27%), Morningstar Principia (6.17%), and Infosys Finacle (4.09%) are using AI in core banking, payment, treasury, and wealth management modules. For example, Infosys Finacle Assist (part of EdgeVerve Systems, a wholly owned subsidiary of Infosys) uses AI and NLP to enable banks to automate customer service and other back-end processes. There are three components in an AI software:

1. **Natural language processing** to understand customer questions and transactional requests
2. **Machine learning** to learn from customer interactions, especially over time
3. **Sentiment analysis** to understand the emotional tone of customer conversations

Chatbots are of two types—rule-based and AI-based. AI-based chatbots can understand complicated functionality and contextual awareness that require less training data and can perform the task for the customer without human assistance [18]. Studies show that chatbots reduce costs, provide personalized services, improve customer satisfaction, increase efficiency, and enhance security. The global market for chatbots in the banking and financial services sector is expected to grow from $1.2 billion in 2021 to $4.5 billion by 2026. NASSCOM is India's trade body and tech industry chamber of commerce. NASSCOM projects that the market for chatbots in the banking and financial services sector will grow from $1.2 billion in 2021 to $4.5 billion by 2026.

A report by Juniper Research has determined that the utilization of chatbots in the banking sector is projected to result in global operational cost savings of $7.3 billion by 2023.

According to Ernst and Young's Report, it is predicted that the amalgamation of chatbots and other artificial intelligence-based virtual assistants with human consultation will be so flawlessly executed that clients cannot distinguish between the two services by 2030.

A PWC report says several Indian financial institutions collaborated with fintech to build proof of concepts (POC) and test implementation to see the various facets of AI.

India's largest bank, State Bank of India, conducted the "Code for Bank" hackathon to encourage the development of innovative AI-based applications. One such exciting application is to take camera pictures of customers' faces and instantly tell if the customer is happy or sad. Consent from customers and staff is taken considering ethical considerations. The application allowed the branch to get feedback and improve its service delivery. The bank uses an AI-based chatbot called SIA to address inquiries on banking products and services.HDFC Bank launched Eva (Electronic Virtual Assistant) in 2017. Eva is a chatbot developed by Bengaluru-based Senseforth AI Research that eliminated the need for customers to search, browse, or call for product information. The chatbot was reported to have answered over 2.7 million customer queries between March 2017 and March 2018 with an 85% accuracy rate.

Axis Bank introduced its AI-powered chatbot "Axis Aha!" on June 7, 2018. As of March 2023, Axis Aha has over 10 million registered users and has processed over a billion transactions. The tool is estimated to have helped customers save Rs. 100 crores in fees, and 90% of its users gave positive feedback.

HDFC Bank has developed an in-store application/humanoid robot called the IRA ("Intelligent Robotic Assistant") for usage at bank branches. It was developed in partnership with Asimov Robotics and was first deployed in a branch in Mumbai in January 2017. Since then, it has been deployed in about 100 branches, answered 1 million customer queries, and helped them complete over 100,000 transactions. IRA has received over 90% positive feedback from customers. Apart from routine AI and NLP functions, the tool can intelligently navigate, avoid obstacles, and guide customers to the relevant counter by learning dynamically.

In February 2020, ICICI Bank launched its iPal, where the chatbot was also helping with financial transactions. SBI Card launched its virtual assistant for customer support and services called ELA (Electronic Live Assistant) in 2018.

Union Bank of India has partnered with Intellect Design Arena Ltd. to automate and elevate their enterprise-wide cash flows. The bank has chosen a cash management system built on eMACH.ai to achieve this goal.

This strategic partnership with Intellect will provide UBI with a fully integrated cash and payment management platform, which is expected to enhance the experience and operational efficiency of its corporate customers [19].

AI can help banks understand customer behavior patterns and offer advisory services, making cross-sell products and services more accessible. Long-term deposits are essential for banks because they provide stable funding sources, allow banks to use that money to lend at higher interest rates, and, more importantly, meet regulatory requirements. Applications that use AI and machine learning models are seen helping telemarketers to market long-term deposits with close to 92.48% accuracy [20].

6.5 Payment Systems

The Indian economy made rapid strides by moving from a cash-centric to a cashless digital economy. In the last two decades, technical and infrastructure advancements were vital for RBI to introduce low-cost, accessible, and all-inclusive payment services [21]. Digital payments have become the favorite mode of payment by millennials (34% of the Indian population) and Gen Z generation (27% of the Indian population). AI bots and biometric fraud detection systems need high-speed data connectivity and computational power to provide effective digital financial services. Typical online payment fraud detection systems overcome risk and cost with three models: machine learning-based fraud detection, economic optimization of machine learning results, and a risk model to predict the risk of fraud while considering countermeasures [22]. Generative AI was seen enhancing existing fraud detection capabilities, allowing organizations to see new dimensions to the topic of fraud detection such as gaining deeper understanding of user behaviors and to prevent fraudulent activities proactively. Experts say that generative AI has lots of promises to address fraud detection in UPI, for example. The number of frauds involving UPI transactions was increasing—from 77,000 cases in FY 21 to 84,000 in FY 22 and approximately 95,000 cases in FY 23 [23].

Banks understand the significance of using AI in their operations and have heavily invested in digital infrastructure, sometimes at the direction or request of the RBI. It is estimated that by the year 2025, 71.7% of payment transactions are likely to happen through digital devices. IDC estimates that 40% of payments in India will be optimized using AI-derived routing by 2025. Boston Consulting Group says that the digital payment market will increase to $10 trillion by 2026. Industry-grade AI use cases and implementations were available to Indian fintech immediately.

Bank of Baroda has incorporated artificial intelligence into its operations to optimize currency chests and for the predictive maintenance of automated teller machines (ATMs). The AI system integrates both external sensors and internal data related to failures. The bank has also developed two adaptive learning modules to enhance workforce development strategies. These modules have been designed for individual officers considering their learning rates and specific training requirements.

DBS Bank's Digibank is based on AI-backed intelligent banking services to customers. Since its introduction in 2020, the bank has seen a 47% increase in repeat usage and is bringing 20% of new customers at the branch level. Customers were able to manage their finances better, and the bank is benefiting from higher engagement, retention, and transactions.

Leading wallet service provider Paytm (One97 Communications) feels that artificial general intelligence (AGI) is ready for further innovation. The digital payment company sees more opportunities to bring efficiency in business, especially in loan disbursal business, and wishes to build an AI-first offering. Its October 2021 acquisition of CreditMate helped Paytm gain an additional revenue stream. CreditMate is an AI and ML-driven data collection platform that helps lenders collect overdue payments from borrowers and has banks, NBFCs, and fintech companies as its clients.

The number of payment-related disputes has increased manifold in recent times, so much so that the RBI was compelled to release an Online Dispute Resolution (ODR) circular on August 6, 2020. This need has led to the development of an AI-assisted chargeback/dispute automation system.

The AI-assisted chargeback team helps the institution handle a high volume of chargebacks. The operations team will be able to concentrate its efforts on improving customer experiences and retention. With API triggers, AI leads the communication channels, document collection, and validation, allowing the acquirer to achieve an end-to-end seamless connection. Setting up AI models to resolve dispute cases within TAT will contribute to optimizing efforts and lowering operational costs [24]. HDFC Bank is one of the first Indian banks to implement an AI-based ODR system. They partnered with Singapore-based ODR provider Disc MED to provide an AI-powered resolution of customer complaints and disputes. SBI has partnered with technology company Koinearth to build an AI-enabled ODR platform to handle customer grievances related to digital banking services. The platform uses NLP and machine learning to analyze customer issues and recommend resolutions.

National Payments Corporation of India launched an AI virtual assistant to boost digital payments. Developed by CoRover, PAi provides 24/7 assistance on NPCI products like FASTag, RuPay, UPI, and AePS, aiming to increase the adoption of digital payments among Indian citizens.

6.6   Digital Lending

Digital lenders can use artificial intelligence, big data analytics, and machine learning to understand customer needs better, perform timely underwriting, and improve fraud detection. The ability to handle high amounts of low applications and the ability to process them with lesser processing time and capacity has become the nature of the day. Loan process time was reduced from days to hours. Not just that. The documentation and related requirements became more simplified. For example, South India Bank used actyv. ai's AI-powered enterprise SaaS platform to build a loan-based product that used GST data analytics to determine loan eligibility [25]. Such tools can help banks plan for larger and quicker book building and improve organizational ROI because the overall operational costs are reduced. The first step toward this is to use automation to convert analog data on the loan application form to a digital file. Once digital, different entities in the lending company start using different parts of the data to finally arrive at a collective decision with the help of various AI modules. Customer data for a bank can be of an individual or a business. Data for an AI system is collected from emails, chat messages, voice transcripts, relationship manager notes, the bank's database (CRM, transaction history), alternative data collected from social media, audit reports, and annual reports for businesses. With cloud computing and big data, AI makes data available for the organization hundred times better.

Some areas of its potential uses can be customer analytics, underwriting, and fraud detection. India's upcoming Personal Data Protection Bill mentions various technical aspects of personal data protection. Stakeholders recommend implementing model risk management strategies to alleviate potential repercussions from adopting sophisticated data and artificial intelligence-based financial models, particularly concerning financial stability. This suggestion aligns with impending regulatory frameworks to be introduced in more mature geographies, such as the United States.

Indian financial services providers are more open to embracing AI. For example, Poonawalla Fincorp's new management took up a digital-first tech-led format of offering financial services and intended to use AI and ML extensively in the next growth phase. The company wishes to use AI for automated voice-based collections, digital assistant for customer self-service, transaction recon engine, automated outbound sales calls, and inbound voice assistant [26].

Banks like Yes Bank use AI and machine learning algorithms to digitize and streamline the customer identification process, which helps the bank manage identity. They use optical character recognition (OCR) and face recognition technology for a secure and seamless verification process.

AI allows businesses to make faster decisions [27]. Finance companies must race time to make quick lending decisions to beat the competition. Chinese lenders have a clear edge in making a lending decision in just 30 seconds. Indian companies typically take days but are learning quickly and improving their racing to reach such speeds.

Insufficient data and the inability to check for correctness are significant constraints in credit lending in unbanked populations and places with negligible or low financial inclusion. AI can access public data to deal with information asymmetry and allow credit to households [28].

According to Linson Paul, chief technology officer of Muthoot Microfin Ltd., rural microfinance institutions (MFIs) in India have started using AI and ML to automate certain processes such as credit scoring and loan application processing. The integration of AI and ML into rural microfinance operations has improved the bottom lines of MFIs. They have improved their efficiency, reduced their operational costs, and improved the quality of their loan portfolio [29].

6.7   Credit Scoring/Creditworthiness/Direct Lending

AI deployment, particularly in developing credit risk models, is essential for credit scoring considering modern complexities in evaluating and generating a credit score. Some Indian platforms using this include CreditVidya, ZestMoney, Lendingkart, KredX, and Capital Float. Traditional credit scoring models rely on a limited set of data points such as credit history, income, and employment status to determine an individual's creditworthiness. AI-based credit scoring models, on the other hand, can leverage an extensive and diverse set of data points due to their AI-rooted algorithms to assess credit risk.

Alternative data sources such as social media activity, online behavior, and sensor data from smartphones and wearable devices are used to pull the relevant data points for further analysis. Analyzing these data, AI models can identify patterns and correlations that may predict credit risk. These models can also continuously learn and improve as new data become available.

One advantage of AI-based credit scoring models is that they can provide more accurate credit risk assessments, especially for individuals with little or no credit history. They can also help reduce the risk of bias in credit decisions by removing human judgment. However, it is essential to ensure that these models are transparent, justifiable, and understandable so that individuals understand how their creditworthiness is being assessed and can challenge them in case of discriminatory or unfair decisions. AI tools were able to analyze the customer profile and suggest the right strategy to be used by the lender to recover their lent money resulting in quicker cash collections [30]. Models that help in financial crisis prediction (FCP) are now available to predict or forecast businesses to whom lenders give money [31]. The domain of collections and recovery has been a matter of concern for many businesses, especially the banking sector, with increasing non-performing assets. Several other startups and established companies also use AI and machine learning algorithms for credit underwriting and risk assessment.

Banks are using AI to assess credit risk, particularly in the context of retail loans and credit cards. ICICI Bank uses AI to assess the risk of borrowers defaulting on loans. The bank's AI system analyzes various factors, including the borrower's credit history, income, and employment history, to determine the likelihood of default. This information is used to make more informed lending decisions. The approach has become essential given the rise of new credit models in India, such as microfinance and peer-to-peer lending. RBI regulates P2P lending platforms in India through the Master Directions for NBFC Peer-to-Peer Lending Platform issued in 2017. As of March 8, 2023, there are 25 RBI-registered P2P lending platforms in India.

6.8 Stockbrokers and Wealth Management

Indian stockbrokers are found to be using AI for algorithm trading, predictive analytics and generation of trading signals, market data analysis, risk management, chatbots and virtual assistants, sentiment analysis, and robo-advisory services. Zerodha (such as in small case portfolio design), Upstox, and Angel Broking (AQR tool) are three prominent Indian stockbrokers already using AI. Algorithm trading has extensive use of AI. The volume of algorithmic trades accounts for approximately 50%–60% of the total trading volume in the Indian stock market. Robo-advisory services are still nascent in India. Studies on Indian robo-advisory services focused on investor awareness, attitude, and perception. They found that Indian individual investors believe that human intervention is necessary to gauge the investors' emotions, thus making the service offering only a supplementary service [32]. The robo-advisory market in India is expected to grow at a CAGR of 14.01% from 2023 to 2027, reaching a value of US$56.58 billion by 2027. Kuvera, IndWealth, and Goalwise are some key robo-advisory players in the Indian market.

6.9   Mutual Funds and Asset Management

Artificial intelligence and machine learning are beginning to transform the Indian mutual fund industry. These technologies are being deployed to improve operations, portfolio management, customer service, and new product development.

Most AI applications in the sector focus on automating and optimizing core operations. Machine learning algorithms are used for tasks like monitoring funds for regulatory compliance, tracking market movements, screening new investments, and automating fund accounting. This helps mutual funds operate with higher efficiency, lower costs, and fewer errors.

AI is also aiding mutual fund managers in researching and analyzing investment opportunities. Advanced data analytics and machine learning models can uncover market trends, identify undervalued stocks, and optimize asset allocation strategies. This data-driven approach enhances portfolio performance and risk management.

For customers, AI is powering virtual assistants, chatbots, and robo-advisors that provide 24/7 access to fund information, portfolio recommendations, and investment advice. These AI solutions aim to simplify the investing process, engage younger customers, and reduce customer acquisition costs.

AI is expected to play an even bigger role in new product development. Mutual funds are exploring using machine learning to create completely automated "robo-funds" that make investment decisions without human input.

While still nascent, AI applications show promise in helping Indian mutual funds improve different facets of their business—from the back office to the front office. However, the industry must focus on building in-house AI capabilities, acquiring the right talent, and responsibly governing these technologies to realize their long-term benefits fully.

6.10   Insurance Services

Indian insurance companies are seen using AI in automating claims processing and management, predicting claims and fraud detection, personalizing insurance products, underwriting, risk assessment and pricing of policy premiums, marketing, and sales and in providing customer support. Life Insurance Corporation of India (LIC), HDFC Life, and ICICI Lombard are key players that reported using AI to offer insurance services.

According to an article [33], the Indian insurance industry can leverage AI technology to analyze vast amounts of data and make predictions based on those data. AI algorithms can analyze customer behavior and preferences to develop personalized insurance policies. The technology can also be used to detect fraudulent claims, saving insurers hundreds of crores each year. Another article on India AI states that accurate assessment of risk is the foundation of the insurance industry. AI and ML can offer an advantage to early adopters here—in two disparate areas. Data (and actuarial tables) are used to come up with accurate models of risk, whether it is health insurance, life insurance, or even motor insurance.

A 2020 report by Boston Consulting Group and the Federation of Indian Chambers of Commerce & Industry (FICCI) mentioned that the COVID-19 pandemic has accelerated digital adoption in the Indian insurance sector. This includes increased use of AI, machine learning, and data analytics tools.

According to a 2019 report by PwC, 85% of insurance CEOs globally said that AI was already part of their business model or would be within the next 2 years. While this statistic is not specific to India, it provides an idea of the extent to which AI is being incorporated into the insurance industry.

The Indian insurance industry is expected to grow at a CAGR of 15% from 2022 to 2027, increasing the use of AI in the insurance sector. Market analysts say that the use of AI in the Indian insurance industry is expected to grow at a CAGR of 25% from 2022 to 2027. The Indian insurance industry spent $1 billion on AI in 2022 and is expected to spend $5 billion by 2027.

6.11   Indian Financial Regulators

A solid financial system can be built only under the guidance of an able regulator. Indian regulators increasingly use artificial intelligence to enhance their regulatory capabilities and improve financial sector oversight.

The Reserve Bank of India and the National Payments Corporation of India (NPCI) have a close working relationship in the payment and settlement systems of the country. While the former builds a central information registry about individuals, corporations, and organizations accessing banking services, the latter collates transactional data about UPI. These data mines are rich in big data to identify patterns that help prescribe the optimal use of credit, detect frauds, and prevent financial crimes.

An RBI report suggested that there could be a use of Regulatory Technology (RegTech) and Supervisory Technology (suptech) tools that help replace rules written in a natural legal language with computer codes and use artificial intelligence for regulatory purposes [7]. RBI has been a front-runner and has called for expression of interest from firms interested in building the tools for it. It also uses existing in-house capabilities to develop tools without depending on a vendor.

The Reserve Bank of India has identified seven global consultancy firms to help it in using AI and ML in regulatory supervision [34]. The firms will help the central bank in developing a framework for using AI and ML in regulatory compliance. The framework will be used to identify areas where AI and ML can be used to improve regulatory compliance and supervision. The seven firms shortlisted are Accenture Solutions Private Limited, Boston Consulting Group (India) Pvt. Ltd., Deloitte Touche Tohmatsu India LLP, Ernst and Young LLP, KPMG Assurance and Consulting Services LLP, McKinsey and Company, and Pricewaterhouse Coopers Pvt. Ltd.

To ease business and enable Digital India, DGFT launched an AI chatbot to assist exporters, importers, and the public. Named VAHEI, it answers foreign trade policy and DGFT queries. Users can check application/authorization status and access notifications, notices, and circulars. For simple queries, VAHEI provides text responses; for complex queries, it identifies relevant Foreign Trade Policy/Handbook of Procedure sections. If no direct response is found, VAHEI references related PDF sections.

Instances of existing applications:

1. **Onboarding Customers:** Human complicity is regarded as a key reason for most banking frauds. AI-based onboarding technologies have human-like intelligence to documents/data and cannot be compromised on the quality of work. KYC compliance is no longer document-based but can involve complex data formats such as biometric, voice, and video-based content. The RBI amended the KYC norms on January 9, 2020, allowing banks and other lending institutions regulated by it to adopt a video-based customer identification process (V-CIP) as a consent-based alternate method of identity verification for customer onboarding [35]. Signzy is an onboarding technology company that uses image extraction, classification, object detection, validation, forgery check, video-based identity verification, and liveliness check.

2. **Fraud Detection:** RBI uses AI-powered fraud detection tools for transaction monitoring and fraud case identification. The RBI has also set up a specialized unit, the Central Fraud Monitoring Cell, to analyze and investigate suspicious

transactions using AI-based tools. HDFC Bank reportedly uses AI to analyze billions of transactions daily to identify patterns that may indicate fraud. The system identifies potential fraud and alerts a human banker who can investigate further. Axis Bank leveraged artificial intelligence technologies to address certain issues within the contemporary security landscape and achieve substantial business benefits. The bank deployed AI-driven solutions to challenges arising from the fast-changing threat environment to yield meaningful impact and value for the enterprise. Implementing artificial intelligence capabilities enabled Axis Bank to bolster security protections, enhance fraud detection, and optimize risk management strategies. These technology-based initiatives equipped the organization with advanced tools to navigate the complexities of the present security climate while furthering key business objectives. Artificial intelligence provided the bank with innovative solutions and insights that translated into substantive gains for overall performance and operations. There are three AI modules that a fraud detection system would have: Unstructured Data Pre-Processing, Similarity Analysis, and Named Entity Recognition [36]. Unstructured Data Pre-Processing involves text preprocessing. This will be in three stages: cleaning, annotation, and normalization. Cleaning removes extraneous words and characters through stop-word elimination, capitalization standardization, and other techniques. Annotation applies tagging schemes and structural markup, including part-of-speech labeling. Normalization standardizes terms and linguistic units via stemming, lemmatization, and other methods to reduce inflectional forms. These preprocessing steps prepare the raw text for further natural language procedures. Similarity Analysis uses cosine similarity, the cosine of the angle between document vectors, to quantify the similarity of term vector-represented documents. This popular information retrieval and clustering metric measures the correlation between document term vectors. Cosine similarity is one of the most common measures applied to textual information, especially in document retrieval and grouping applications. Named Entity Recognition identifies relevant nouns—people, places, organizations—in input text-like sentences and paragraphs.

The algorithm scans articles, revealing the significant entities discussed. Tags enable automated article categorization
within hierarchies, facilitating content discovery. Named
Entity Recognition thus automates the organization of
unstructured text around key entities mentioned.

3. **Risk Assessment and Market Surveillance Systems**:
The Securities and Exchange Board of India (SEBI) uses
AI-based risk assessment tools to identify potential market
risks and monitor compliance by market participants. SEBI's
Annual Report 2020-21 has spoken of the regulator's commitment to invest in technology to enhance its monitoring,
investigation, and policymaking capabilities. SEBI has also
set up a specialized unit, the Integrated Market Surveillance
System, to monitor market activity using AI-based tools. Its
PINAKA (Picture-based Information News Accumulator
and Key information Analyser) helps scan the stock suggestions and recommendations aired in business media
and condense them into a database [37]. The Association of
Mutual Funds in India (AMFI) directed all its member fund
houses to submit the use of AI-based systems in the prescribed format within 30 calendar days from the end of the
quarter. The AI usage practices are to be monitored because
they are considered "black boxes," and their behavior cannot
be quantified easily [38].

4. **Consumer Protection:** The Insurance Regulatory and
Development Authority of India (IRDAI) uses AI-based
chatbots to provide customer support and resolve poli-
cyholder queries. The IRDAI has also set up a specialized
unit, the Consumer Affairs Department, to monitor consumer complaints and improve consumer protection using
AI-based tools.

5. **Compliance Monitoring:** The Ministry of Corporate Affairs
(MCA) under the Government of India is using AI-based
tools to monitor compliance by companies with various regulatory requirements, such as filing financial statements and
disclosing corporate information. The MCA has also set up a
specialized unit, the National Financial Reporting Authority,
to oversee compliance by auditors using AI-based tools. AI
chatbots are seen helping return filers meet statutory compliance requirements on the MCA 21 portal, which is pro-
claimed the backbone of corporate companies in India [39].

The e-governance infrastructure necessary for the portal was built by Tata Consultancy Services in the first phase and by Infosys Limited in the second phase.

Overall, the use of AI by Indian regulators is aimed at improving regulatory effectiveness, reducing compliance costs, and enhancing consumer protection in the financial sector. However, ensuring these tools are transparent, explainable, and subject to appropriate oversight is essential to avoid potential biases or errors.

6.12   Challenges in Adoption

Like all technologies, AI also comes with a few challenges requiring serious consideration before real-life implementation. Some key challenges that management will have to consider include:

1. **Data Privacy and Security:** AI models require large volumes of data for training. This data often contain sensitive information, making data privacy a critical concern. Banks must comply with data privacy laws such as the GDPR in Europe or CCPA in California, which restrict how personal data can be used. Data security is another challenge, as the data used and generated by AI systems could be a target for cyberattacks. Countries like India are in various stages of bringing data protection legislation. The provisions of the Digital Personal Data Protection Bill, 2022, should be considered by system designers in building AI systems.

2. **Data Quality:** AI models can function properly only when trained with good data. In other words, good data are the foundation for a strong AI system. Banks must ensure that their data are high quality and accurate to get the most out of AI-powered solutions. Chatbots allowed to self-train based on banking customer queries will initially have a poor success rate but tend to provide better support over time. Similarly, AI-backed data analytics could give incorrect product recommendations, but over time, it will improve. Banks will need patience as the systems get integrated to get the most out of it.

3. **Bias in AI Algorithms:** Bias introduced in training data, intentional or otherwise, will make the AI system learn and

reproduce these biases, leading to potentially unfair decisions. In banking, this could mean unfair loan approvals or credit scoring. This factor is required to be more important when an AI model designed for a different geography or jurisdiction is installed and implemented in another.

4. **Explainability and Transparency:** Many AI models, especially deep learning models, are often called "black boxes" because their inner workings are not easily interpretable. This lack of transparency can be a challenge in banking, where explainability of decisions (like why a loan was rejected) is often legally required.

5. **Regulatory Compliance:** Banks and financial institutions operate within a heavily regulated environment. Ensuring that AI complies with relevant laws and regulations is a significant challenge. This includes regulations related to fairness, transparency, and privacy. Software code written by generative AI needs several levels of checking even before an algorithm trading system built using it goes to the approval of stock exchanges. The recent sandbox regulations issued by various financial regulators in India bring in some degree of freedom and the ability to innovate AI-based products and services.

6. **Skills Gap:** There is a high demand for AI talent but a supply shortage. Banks may struggle to find or retain the talent to develop and maintain their AI systems. Considering the growing usage of AI in financial services, the National Institute of Securities Markets (NISM) has begun offering courses and study modules on AI.

7. **Integration with Existing Systems:** Many banks and financial institutions have legacy systems that may not easily integrate with modern AI solutions. This can make implementing AI technologies difficult and expensive. Many banks have sophisticated complex IT infrastructures that have evolved over decades. Successfully deploying new AI applications often requires effectively interfacing them with existing core banking systems, risk management platforms, data warehouses, and other components. This integration task is further complicated by differences in data formats, APIs, and integration protocols between new AI systems and legacy technologies. Banks must invest in data pipelines, middleware, and application programming interfaces

to allow AI solutions to tap into existing data sources while feeding results back into core applications. Proper AI integration planning and testing are crucial to ensure compatibility, performance, and stability across the entire IT ecosystem.

8. **Ethical Considerations:** Using AI in decision-making processes in banking raises legal and ethical considerations [40]. With so much at stake, ethical considerations should be front and center when using AI to impact people's economic lives and livelihoods. For example, should an AI be allowed to make decisions that could negatively impact a person's financial well-being? Who was involved in the ethical review and governance of the AI solution? Did it include diverse stakeholders beyond just technical and business experts?

9. **Reliance on Vendors:** Many banks may rely on external vendors for their AI solutions. This can lead to issues around data privacy and theft, fear of cyberattacks, difficulties in system integration, and a lack of internal AI capabilities. AI applications for fraud detection, risk analysis, and customer service now underpin many digital business strategies. However, most banks outsource AI model development and software implementation to tech firms. This model concentrates knowledge and skills in the hands of a few vendor companies, creating potential bottlenecks and single points of failure. If a key vendor goes bankrupt, suffers a data breach, or loses key engineers, affected banks could experience severe disruptions. The industry must strive for greater in-house AI capabilities and diversify its vendor base to mitigate these risks. This, of course, comes at a cost and requires considerable time and effort. Studies have shown that while some banks may use just one or two primary vendors to build an initial AI solution, many rely on a broader network of 5–10 or more vendors to provide the full spectrum of required capabilities and resources. The optimal number of vendors depends on each bank's unique circumstances and risk management strategies.

10. **Scalability:** While an AI model might perform well on a small scale or in a controlled environment, scaling up to handle the vast quantities of data processed by large financial institutions can be challenging. The scalability of artificial intelligence systems is crucial for widespread deployment

in large financial institutions. As banks operate at a massive scale, AI models and infrastructure must be capable of handling huge volumes of data, transactions, and decisions. Distributed computing architectures are necessary to scale AI technologies across the organization. Cloud-based platforms facilitate flexibility and access to computing power, but banks must ensure security, privacy, and compliance. To achieve scalability, automated machine learning techniques dynamically adjust models and algorithms. Modular designs also combine separate AI systems, strengthening solutions' overall scalability and coverage. For banking AI to reach its full potential, a centralized computing infrastructure must be in place to construct, implement, and monitor AI on a broad operational level, enabling system-wide scalability and coordinated intelligence. With robust and scalable AI, banks can achieve far-reaching transformation.

11. **Cost:** AI-based systems require a lot of capital expenditure on the part of the bank. Since systems built on AI will need more power and up-to-date infrastructure, cost factors require serious consideration. The implementation of artificial intelligence systems within financial institutions incurs significant capital expenditures. While AI technologies promise increased automation and scalability, the initial investment required to develop AI models and infrastructure is substantial. The costs include hardware, software, and staff with data science and machine learning expertise. Adopting AI solutions demands multi-million-dollar transformation projects and an ongoing commitment to maintenance and enhancement for banks. Despite the costs, many banks see AI as essential to competitive survival and choose to fund large technology budgets. If implemented effectively, AI can transform business processes to reduce operational expenses and boost productivity. The high costs of AI are a barrier, but many banks see the investment as a strategic necessity to achieve long-term efficiency and retain market leadership.

12. **Governance:** Proper AI governance mechanisms are to be built, addressing responsibility as to who monitors, controls, and supervises the design, development, deployment, and evaluation of AI models. Policies and controls must ensure that AI is fair, accountable, transparent, and secure.

AI models should be checked for bias and adverse impact on protected groups for fair lending. Accountability means determining human responsibility for AI decisions and outcomes. Transparency requires explaining why AI made a specific decision. Security necessitates protecting AI systems and data from breaches and cyber threats. Ethical AI should respect customer privacy while improving services. Governance frameworks help balance innovation with risk management. With well-designed governance, AI can boost banking while upholding key principles. Effective governance and oversight build trust in AI.

6.13 Conclusion

An examination is done through this study as to how and in which areas are the Indian banking and financial services using artificial intelligence. The study is vital because AI is a leading disruption technology and, as previous research has suggested, has the potential to help the industry grow. Indian banks (compared to financial services) are the early adopters of the technology, with chatbots and back-office implementations in their early days. Though laggard, the financial services sector caught up with AI as the technology evolved from its early AI winter days and back-office adoptions to credit and lending decision-making. Not just BFS service providers but the Indian financial regulators too are seen extensively using AI. The study takes a practical approach to observe from the ground-level industry-level perspective. Certain challenges feared by the service providers were identified and discussed, highlighting potential future research on the topic.

References

1. Mahalakshmi, V., Kulkarni, N., Pradeep Kumar, K.V., Suresh Kumar, K., Nidhi Sree, D., Durga, S., The Role of implementing Artificial Intelligence and Machine Learning Technologies in the financial services Industry for creating Competitive Intelligence. *Mater. Today Proc.*, 56, 2252–2255, 2022. https://doi.org/10.1016/j.matpr.2021.11.577.
2. Ranjan, S., Gupta, R., Gupta, A., Artificial intelligence in financial acumen: Challenges and opportunities. *Cosmos J. Eng. Technol.*, 10, 1, 23–27, 2020.

3. NITI Aayog, *National Strategy for Artificial Intelligence [Discussion Paper]*, NITI Aayog, 2018. https://www.niti.gov.in/sites/default/files/2023-03/National-Strategy-for-Artificial-Intelligence.pdf.

4. Mhlanga, D., Industry 4.0 in finance: The impact of artificial intelligence (AI) on digital financial inclusion. *Int. J. Financial Stud.*, 8, 3, 45, 2020. https://doi.org/10.3390/ijfs8030045.

5. Sinha, M., Chacko, E., Makhija, P., AI based technologies for digital and banking fraud during covid-19, in: *Integrating Meta-Heuristics and Machine Learning for Real-World Optimization Problems*, E.H. Houssein, M. Abd Elaziz, D. Oliva, L. Abualigah (Eds.), vol. 1038, pp. 443–459, Springer International Publishing, 2022, https://doi.org/10.1007/978-3-030-99079-4_17.

6. Achary, R., Artificial intelligence transforming indian banking sector. *International Journal of Economics and Management Systems (IJEMS)*, 6, 19–31, 2021.

7. RBI, *Report of the Working Group on Digital Lending including Lending through Online Platforms and Mobile Apps*, Reserve Bank of India (RBI), 2021, https://www.rbi.org.in.

8. Fares, O.H., Butt, I., Lee, S.H.M., Utilization of artificial intelligence in the banking sector: A systematic literature review. *J. Financ. Serv. Mark.*, 28, 835–852, 2022. https://doi.org/10.1057/s41264-022-00176-7.

9. Herrmann, H. and Masawi, B., Three and a half decades of artificial intelligence in banking, financial services, and insurance: A systematic evolutionary review. *Strateg. Change*, 31, 6, 549–569, 2022. https://doi.org/10.1002/jsc.2525.

10. Vijai, C. and Nivetha, P., ABC technology—artificial intelligence, blockchain technology, cloud technology for banking sector. *Adv. Manage.*, 13, 4, 19–24, 2020. https://papers.ssrn.com/sol3/papers.cfm?abstract_id=3758718.

11. Hentzen, J.K., Hoffmann, A., Dolan, R., Pala, E., Artificial intelligence in customer-facing financial services: A systematic literature review and agenda for future research. *Int. J. Bank Mark.*, 40, 6, 1299–1336, 2022. https://doi.org/10.1108/IJBM-09-2021-0417.

12. Ghandour, A., Opportunities and challenges of artificial intelligence in banking: Systematic literature review. *TEM J.*, 4, 1581–1587, 2021.

13. Malali, A.B. and Gopalakrishnan, S., Application of artificial intelligence and its powered technologies in the indian banking and financial industry: An overview. *IOSR J. Humanit. Soc. Sci.*, 25, 4, 55–60, 2020.

14. Endless Origins, *How are Indian Banks Adopting Digitisation and AI?*, April 11, 2022, https://analyticsindiamag.com/how-are-indian-banks-adopting-digitisation-and-ai.

15. Choithani, T., Chowdhury, A., Patel, S., Patel, P., Patel, D., Shah, M., A comprehensive study of artificial intelligence and cybersecurity on bitcoin, crypto currency and banking system. *Ann. Data Sci.*, 11, 103–135, 2022. https://doi.org/10.1007/s40745-022-00433-5.

16. Sadman, N., Ahsan, M.M., Rahman, A., Siddique, Z., Gupta, K.D., Promise of AI in DeFi, a systematic review. *Digital*, 2, 1, 88–103, 2022. https://doi.org/10.3390/digital2010006.

17. FE Digital Currency, Indian banks support mass adoption of AI and blockchain. *Financ. Express*, May 31, 2023. https://www.financialexpress.com/business/blockchain-indian-banks-support-mass-adoption-of-ai-and-blockchain-3109371/.

18. Sadekov, K., Types of chatbots: Rule-based chatbots vs AI chatbots, April 11, 2023. https://mindtitan.com/resources/guides/chatbot/types-of-chatbots/.

19. Express Computer, Union Bank of India partners with Intellect to bolster transaction banking with an advanced Cash Management System built on eMACH.ai, May 17, 2023. https://www.expresscomputer.in/news/union-bank-of-india-partners-with-intellect-to-bolster-transaction-banking-with-an-advanced-cash-management-system-built-on-emach-ai/98104/.

20. Borugadda, P., Nandru, P., Madhavaiah, C., Predicting the success of bank telemarketing for selling long-term deposits: An application of machine learning algorithms. *St. Theresa J. Humanities Soc. Sci.*, 7, 1, 91–108, 2021. https://journal.stic.ac.th/index.php/sjhs/article/view/296.

21. Uma, V.R., Poola, K., Kallarakal, T.K., Nair, B.B., B. J., S, G., Understanding the Technological Evolution in Electronic Payments System in India and the Acceptance. *Int. J. Process Manage. Benchmarking*, 1, 1, 1, 2023. https://doi.org/10.1504/IJPMB.2023.10054809.

22. Vanini, P., Rossi, S., Zvizdic, E. *et al.*, Online payment fraud: From anomaly detection to risk management. *Financ. Innov.*, 9, 66, 2023. https://doi.org/10.1186/s40854-023-00470-w.

23. Live Mint, Gen AI boosts financial fraud detection, June 15, 2023.

24. Krishna Dev, P., Streamlining dispute resolution: How ai-driven odr solutions can drive customer retention & operational efficiency. *Inc42*, June 10, 2023. https://inc42.com/resources/streamlining-dispute-resolution-how-ai-driven-odr-solutions-can-drive-customer-retention-operational-efficiency/.

25. ANI, South Indian bank partners with actyv.ai to offer gst-based loans and wins digital CX awards, June 9, 2023. https://www.aninews.in/news/business/business/south-indian-bank-partners-with-actyvai-to-offer-gst-based-loans-and-wins-digital-cx-awards20230609154202/.

26. Srikanth, R., We are experimenting with several AI use cases: Kandarp Kant, CTO, Poonawalla Fincorp Limited. *Express Comput.*, July 11, 2022. https://www.expresscomputer.in/exclusives/we-are-experimenting-with-several-ai-use-cases-kandarp-kant-cto-poonawalla-fincorp-limited/88186/.

27. Madhavi, *Artificial Intelligence in Business Decision Making*, Ph.D. Thesis, Maharishi University of Information Technology, 2021, http://hdl.handle.net/10603/384942.

28. Mhlanga, D., Financial inclusion in emerging economies: The application of machine learning and artificial intelligence in credit risk assessment. *Int. J. Financial Stud.*, 9, 3, 39, 2021. https://doi.org/10.3390/ijfs9030039.

29. BFSI Network, AI/ML helps rural MFIs to improve financial inclusion: Linson Paul, CTO Muthoot Microfin Ltd, May 27, 2023. https://bfsi.elets-online.com/ai-ml-helps-rural-mfis-to-improve-financial-inclusion-linson-paul-cto-muthoot-microfin-ltd/.

30. Kshetri, N., The role of artificial intelligence in promoting financial inclusion in developing countries. *J. Glob. Inf. Technol. Manage.*, 24, 1, 1–6, 2021. https://doi.org/10.1080/1097198X.2021.1871273.

31. Pradeep Mohan Kumar, K., Dhanasekaran, S., Hephzi Punithavathi, I.S., Duraipandy, P., Kumar Dutta, A., Pustokhina, I.V., Pustokhin, D.A., Bird swarm algorithm with fuzzy min-max neural network for financial crisis prediction. *Comput. Mater. Contin.*, 73, 1, 1541–1555, 2022. https://doi.org/10.32604/cmc.2022.028338.

32. Bhatia, A., Chandani, A., Atiq, R., Mehta, M., Divekar, R., Artificial intelligence in financial services: A qualitative research to discover robo-advisory services. *Qual. Res. Financial Markets*, 13, 5, 632–654, 2021. https://doi.org/10.1108/QRFM-10-2020-0199.

33. The Week Focus, The A.I age in the Indian insurance sector begins. *Week*, April 8, 2023. https://www.theweek.in/focus/leisure/2023/04/08/the-ai-age-in-the-indian-insurance-sector-begins.html.

34. PTI, RBI shortlists 7 global consultancy firms to use AI, ML to improve regulatory supervision, December 12, 2022. https://economictimes.indiatimes.com/industry/banking/finance/banking/rbi-shortlists-7-global-consultancy-firms-to-use-ai-ml-to-improve-regulatory-supervision/articleshow/96159388.cms.

35. RBI, *Master Direction—Know Your Customer (KYC) Direction, 2016 (Updated as on May 04, 2023)*, Master Directions, Reserve Bank of India, 2023, https://www.rbi.org.in/Scripts/BS_ViewMasDirections.aspx?id=11566.

36. Balaji, S., Innovate2Transform: Axis bank addressing financial crime management with AI & ML, May 29, 2023. https://indiaai.gov.in/article/innovate2transform-axis-bank-addressing-financial-crime-management-with-ai-ml.

37. Saha, S., SEBI to use AI scanner PINAKA to examine stock tips on TV channels, December 2, 2022. https://analyticsindiamag.com/sebi-ai-scanner-pinaka-to-examine-stock-tips-on-tv-channels/.

38. PTI, Mutual funds to submit details about artificial intelligence-based systems. *ET CIO*, May 10, 2019. https://cio.economictimes.indiatimes.com/news/government-policy/mutual-funds-to-submit-details-about-artificial-intelligence-based-systems-on-quarterly-basis-sebi/69264158.

39. Taxscan, Artificial intelligence to be used for compliance under companies act: MCA introduces chatbox to assist with statutory filings, May 14, 2022. https://www.taxscan.in/artificial-intelligence-to-be-

used-for-compliance-under-companies-act-mca-introduces-chatbox-to-assist-with-statutory-filings/174952/.

40. Nizioł, K., The challenges of consumer protection law connected with the development of artificial intelligence on the example of financial services (chosen legal aspects). *Proc. Comput. Sci.*, 192, 4103–4111, 2021. https://doi.org/10.1016/j.procs.2021.09.185.

7

The Extraction of Features That Characterize Financial Fraud Behavior by Machine Learning Algorithms

George X. Yuan[1,2,3], Yuanlei Luo[4‡], Lan Di[5†], Yunpeng Zhou[3],
Wen Chen[3], Yiming Liu[3] and Yudi Gu[6*]

¹College of Science, Chongqing University of Technology, Chongqing, China
²Business School, Chengdu University, Chengdu, China
³Shanghai Hammer Digital Tech. Co. Ltd. (Hammer), Shanghai, China
⁴Research Center, China Institute of Ocean Engineering, Beijing, China
⁵School of AI and Computer Science, Jiangnan Univ., Wuxi, China
⁶Center of Information Construct and Management, Jiangnan University, Wuxi, China

Abstract

The purpose of this paper is to discuss how to use machine learning algorithms to screen the features and related applications of the characteristic indicators in describing a company's financial fraud behavior under the framework of big data analysis. In particular, we first screen the "characteristic indicator" (features) related to the financial anomalies due to a company's fraudulent financial reports then extract (fraud) features based on the corresponding fraudulent actions. In addition, the validation test is carried out to test the ability of fraud features' (indicators') performance in identifying and providing warning signals on fraud events. Specifically, by extracting the characteristics (features) of fraudulent financial behaviors related to financial frauds, based on traditional (structure) financial data and unstructured corporate governance structures, the associated features (characteristic indicators) in interpreting the risk warning system of corporate governance structures are studied and established in this paper, and then these indicators (features) are applied to the case studies. The results show that the

Corresponding author: udy1215@jiangnan.edu.cn
†*Corresponding author*: dilan@jiangnan.edu.cn
‡*Corresponding author*: luoyuanlei@hotmail.com

Ambrish Kumar Mishra, Shweta Anand, Narayan C. Debnath, Purvi Pokhariyal and Archana Patel (eds.) *Artificial Intelligence for Risk Mitigation in the Financial Industry*, (159–186) © 2024 Scrivener Publishing LLC

features in describing financial frauds and financial anomalies constructed from financial reports to corporate governance could achieve at least minimum purpose in predicting financial fraud with early warning.

Keywords: Machine learning algorithm (MLA), financial fraud behavior, CAFÉ risk assessment, Gibbs algorithm (sampling), early warning system, odds ratio (OR), feature

7.1   Introduction

Financial fraudulence refers to the artificial manipulation or alteration of the financial working report papers and accounting documents used to prepare financial statements by the management authorities of an enterprise, the false disclosure or omission of important financial information, and improper accounting treatment. Financial fraud refers to the intentional disclosure of erroneous or misleading information by corporate management through financial reporting (Abbott *et al.* [1, 2]; Huang *et al.* [3]; Li *et al.* [4]).

By following the SAS No. 99 (AICPA [5]), it states that financial fraud is a legal term (concept) and that auditors should not make judgments about whether a company has fraud, but auditors should focus on material misstatements (or misleading statements) in financial statements because material misstatements in statements are highly correlated with financial fraud. SAS No. 99 also points out that there are two kinds of misrepresentations that can be regarded as financial fraud (Abbott *et al.* [1]; AICPA [5]; Beasley *et al.* [6]; and Beneish [7]):

- First category (I): Artificial manipulation or alteration of working papers and accounting documents to prepare financial statements, false disclosure or omission of important financial information, improper accounting treatment;
- Second category (II): Through the embezzlement or appropriation of company assets.

The first type (I) of financial fraud above is a kind of fraudulent behavior (action) on financial report, while the second type (II) of financial fraud is caused by the company's internal control, audit and other deficiencies, internal corruption, and other factors. In other words, financial fraudulence and financial fraud are two different concepts that are inseparable and not exactly the same, and financial fraudulence is often coexistent with financial fraud for companies.

With focus on the capital market of China, Huang *et al.* [3] conducted a comprehensive study based on 175 fraud events (by 113 companies) that happened between 2010 and 2019 (Table 7.1). A core finding is that the listed companies have manipulated their operating performance through a variety of fraudulent methods, not only including conventional revenue fraud, cost fraud (including cost fraud, expense fraud), but also the frauds of monetary funds, investment income, asset impairment, the accounting reporting for such as non-operating income and expenditure have gradually become the object of management's performance manipulation. By summarizing, they find that financial fraud events in the capital market of China basically could be divided into the following eight categories (Table 7.1).

Firstly, in Table 7.1, we observed the following: First, the purpose of revenue fraud and cost fraud is to improve the company's profit performance and improve the market value expectations of the outside world. Second, in the process of manipulating revenue, in order to meet the hook relationship, the cost and expense are usually adjusted. Third, inflated revenues, expenses, and costs need to be masked by false cash flows. Indeed, based on these basic conditions, multiple forms of financial fraud often occur at the same time period.

Secondly, based on SAS Financial Standard No. 99 (Dunn [8]; Hopwood *et al.* [9]; Summers *et al.* [10]; Wells [11]), an important job and perspective in characterizing and warning financial fraud is to expose companies to "pressure, opportunity, excuses." The 3-part content is also considered as an object, through the algorithmic processing of the fusion of structured

Table 7.1 Financial fraud types caused by 113 companies for the time period from 2017 to 2018.

Fraud types	Quantity	Ratio	Fraud types	Quantity	Ratio
1) Income fraud	77	44%	5) Impairment fraud	13	7.4%
2) Fee fraud	25	14.3%	6) Non-operating income and expenditure fraud	10	5.7%
3) Fraud in monetary funds	24	13.7%	7) Investment income fraud	7	4.0%
4) Cost fraud	17	9.7%	8) Other fraud	2	1.1%

and unstructured data, the characteristics of financial fraud behavior are characterized, and finally the screening of risk characteristic factors of financial fraud is formed.

The purpose of this paper is to discuss the characterization and application of machine learning algorithms for the early warning of corporate financial fraud and financial anomalies under the framework of big data, especially to support the characteristic construction of corporate financial fraud behavior (or in another team, fraudulent actions). Specifically, based on risk factors, a warning system in interpreting companies' governance structures (especially, for financial fraud) is established by the characteristic indicators of financial fraud extracted based on unstructured companies' governance structures and is successfully applied to real case analysis. The case study shows that the characteristic indicator portrayal of financial fraud behavior and financial anomalies constructed from the financial to corporate governance framework can achieve the purpose of predicting financial fraud and early warning. The innovation of this paper is that based on the triangular principle of corporate fraud behavior as the starting point, we originally try to use the big data feature extraction method to build a financial fraud risk assessment system for the company's financial quality and corporate governance structure. The system provides timely early warning of financial fraud, thereby promoting the healthy development of the industry and avoiding potential losses from fraudulent practices.

7.2   The Framework of Gibbs Sampling Algorithm

By incorporating a big data analysis approach to extract the characteristic factors that have the ability to identify the financial fraud behavior of the company, it is first necessary to solve the problem in dealing with insufficient bad samples. In today's development of big data and artificial intelligence technology, the needed "bad samples" can be constructed through artificial intelligence-based machine learning methods and then promoting the work in this regard to the Gibbs sampling algorithm is one of them (Geman and Geman [12]; Li *et al.* [13]; Shi *et al.* [14]; Yang *et al.* [15]; Yuan *et al.* [16–22]).

7.2.1   The Summary of Gibbs Sampling Algorithm

Gibbs sampling (Geman and Geman [12]; Qian *et al.* [23]) is an algorithm used in statistics for Markov chain Monte Carlo (MCMC) specifically for approximating sample sequences from a multivariate probability when it is difficult to sample directly, with the advantage that the sequence of samples produced by the method can be used to approximate the edges of joint distributions and partial variables distribution or computation of integrals (such as the expected value of a variable, but sampling is not required if some variables are already known). Gibbs simulation is used in statistical inference (in particular, the Bayesian inference), which is a randomization algorithm (it is fundamentally different from deterministic algorithms in statistical inferences such as the maximum expectation algorithm). Also, like other MCMC algorithms, Gibbs is sampled from a Markov chain, which is actually the Metropolis and Hastings (MH) method, a special case of Geman and Geman's algorithm [12].

7.2.2   The Framework of Associative Feature Extraction Method

Many classification problems in big data are difficult to get accurate answers. Using the Gibbs stochastic (random) search algorithm under the Monte Carlo simulation framework, it can spend reasonable computing resources to complete the solution of the feature problem in the face of massive data and a certain degree of error tolerance, so as to obtain an approximate solution. The following will introduce how to establish a screening framework and a common analysis process based on Gibbs stochastic search algorithm with five steps below for the convenience of reading in self-containing (see Yuan *et al.* [18, 19]; Yuan [20]; Zeng [23]; and Yuan *et al.* [24] for details):

Step 1: Assuming the characteristic indicators depicting financial fraud follow the Bernoulli distribution, and random sampling is performed to classify the characteristics according to if the coefficient being 0 recorded as 0, otherwise recorded as 1, respectively. Then, the initialized feature space is denoted by:

$$A_0 = (0, 1, 1, \ldots, 0) \in \{0, 1\}^m \tag{7.1}$$

where m represents the number of features in the initialized feature space A_0.

Step 2: Via BIC (see Geman and Geman [9]; or Qian *et al.* [14]) conducts standard random samples to construct a distribution for features, subject to the following formula (based on BIC criteria):

$$P_{BIC}(i_n = 1 \mid I_{-n}) = \frac{exp(-BIC(i_n = 1 \mid I_{-n}))}{exp(-BIC(i_n = 0 \mid I_{-n})) + exp(-BIC(i_n = 1 \mid I_{-n}))}$$

(7.2)

where $P_{BIC}(i)$ is the indicator transfer probability function, i_n represents the nth feature, I_{-n} is in addition to i_n the other feature sets, the number of features in A_0, I_0 represents a subset in A_0, using the formula (Equation 7.2) to ensure that the feature subset shifts to a higher degree of fit. As a result, the salience of the characteristic indicators that ultimately characterize financial fraud behavior can be revealed.

Step 3: In order to ensure the significance of extracted features, we often use sample size error recommended to be less than or equal to 5%, in 2 times' standard derivation; thus, its formula is given as follows:

$$Std(p) = \sqrt{\frac{p(1-p)}{M}} < \sqrt{\frac{1}{4M}}$$

(7.3)

By the formula (Equation 7.3), the sampling size that can be obtained is 400 times' optimization.

Step 4: To extract (highly related) features based on the characteristic factors based on the criteria of the significance for the correlation defined by the value of "odds ratio" (OR) (Yang and Guo [25]), which indicates the ratio of a probability that is presumed to be true to a probability that is presumed to be false. In addition, for general nonlinear models, such as tree models or ensemble models, the intensity of associative features can also be characterized (classified) based on the contribution of factors in the SHAPley algorithm (Li et al. [13]; Yang et al. [15]).

Step 5: Test the effectiveness of the characteristic factors to identify "good or bad." After performing a Gibbs sampling calculation of not less than 400 times, the combination of feature indicators is obtained, $(I^{(1)}, I^{(2)}, \ldots I^{(M)})$, and the frequency of feature occurrence can be obtained by using the ratio of the number of feature occurrences to the total number of samples, and then the influence of features on the model results is analyzed according to the level of frequency. In addition, by using ROC (i.e., receiver operating characteristic) and AUC (i.e., area under the ROC curve) test as an evaluation criterion for the model to measure the significance of the final obtained feature indicators (see Yuan *et al.* [16, 17]).

The above steps complete the implementation process framework for screening characteristic indicators that characterize corporate financial frauds.

7.3   The Framework in Screening Features for Corporate Financial Fraud Behaviors

7.3.1   The Framework of Holographic Risk Assessment Based on the CAFÉ System

The core structure for the "CAFÉ" system representing the so-called CAFÉ evaluation framework is explained as follows: 1) "C" stands for the basic holographic portrait risk assessment of the company; 2) "A" stands for the analysis of the company's financial holographic portrait; 3) "F" stands for holographic profiling analysis of financial behavior; 4) "E" stands for holographic portrait analysis of business ecology (Yuan [19, 20]).

Based on the framework of CAFÉ, the corresponding evaluation process is given by four steps, we have: 1) the initial feature pool, which includes indicator calculation, data preprocessing, that is, data standardization and feature coding; 2) conduct feature extraction based on Gibbs simulation approach; 3) model building based on machine learning algorithms; and 4) the model integration and deployment, including assigned values for key feature indicators plus corresponding score for risk factors with assigned critical values.

7.3.2   The Structure of the Company's Financial Fraud Early Warning Risk System

The early warning solutions for the identification and prevention of the company's financial fraud behavior, combined with the financial fraud triangle theory, this paper analyzes and deals with the following three dimensions: first, the company's own financial indicators (the company's business operations); second, the company's directors, supervisors, and high governance framework; third, support aspects such as internal and external audit management and execution functions of day-to-day management (Figure 7.1).

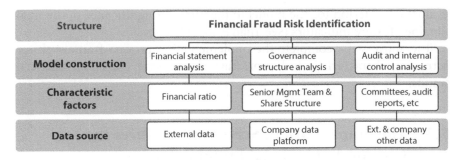

Figure 7.1 The framework of CAFÉ evaluates the company's financial fraud risks.

7.3.3   The Method for Extracting Financial Fraud Characteristics of Listed Companies

Based on the financial statement data of listed companies, this section adopts Gibbs sampling algorithm, screens the characteristic factors that describe the financial fraud risk of companies under the framework of big data, and combines unstructured bad sample information to form an empirical analysis of listed companies as a sample. The data samples of violations disclosed by the CSRC from the beginning of 2017 to the end of 2018 are used as the basic samples for supervised learning, in the case of "bad samples" accounting for approximately 20% of the total sample size. Through algorithmic learning from Gibbs sampling against corporate financial fraud, we filter out the characteristic factors that characterize financial fraud. In this process, by solving the dimensionality disaster problem arising from the collusion relationship of financial statements, a small number of associated characteristic factors (in this paper) are extracted from the financial statement data to characterize the financial fraud risk of listed companies. At the same time, combined with the "odds ratio" (in short, OR) (Wang and Guo [25]) that characterizes financial fraud characteristics as a verification criterion, it is found that these indicators show the characteristics of high correlation with the accounting policy choices and corporate governance of the company where the financial fraud is located.

Inspired by the traditional financial analysis method, this paper will construct the initial feature pool according to the discussion in Subsection 1.2, divide the feature construction method into three categories, static analysis, dynamic (trend) analysis, and interbank comparison, and on this basis, realize the portrayal of the relationship between financial statements and audits, so as to support the screening of characteristic indicators that depict the risk of financial fraud.

7.3.3.1   Static Analysis

Static analysis is the analysis of the financial statement structure, considering the asset–liability structure, income and expense structure, cash flow and income expenses, asset–liability hook relationship, and other factors. When modeling static analysis, you choose to preprocess financial data using the percentage reporting method. It can not only reflect the asset–liability structure of the appraised company but also realize the normalization of the financial data of the appraised company. A small number of companies' financial data, normalized based on a percentage reporting approach, may still have outliers (such as investment returns significantly higher than operating income) and therefore need to be treated for outliers.

7.3.3.2   Dynamic (Trend) Analysis

Dynamic analysis is used to capture unusual changes in a company's financial data. Based on the articulation relationship of the accounting report, the fraud activity whitewashes some financial accounts and usually causes abnormal changes in other financial accounts. On the other hand, considering that financial fraud activities such as inflated assets, fictitious profits, and fictitious cash flows are a very large system engineering, which usually requires the cooperation of multiple departments or even multicompany entities, when the fraud means are difficult to obtain support from various activities such as commerce and taxation, a large amount of asset subtraction usually may occur, resulting in abnormal changes in the financial statement data. In order to capture the above two abnormal changes, based on the change in the most recent year of each financial statement account, and then using the growth rate index formed by the change of the same account in the past 4 years, the degree of abnormality of the change in the financial indicators of the company being evaluated in the current year is measured.

7.3.3.3   Comparison of Peers

Extract the characteristics of financial fraud based on the average performance of the same industry. The samples of the same industry are used as a collection, and then the data in the peer industry are standardized in a Z-score standardized manner, so that the processed data have a fixed mean and standard deviation. In this process, it is not assumed that any financial indicator should follow a normal distribution within the same industry, but defines the difference between a single sample and the average of the same industry by the difference between it and the other samples in the same industry, and then normalizes it through the normal distribution cumulative probability function.

7.3.3.4   *The Insight for the Relationship Between Financial Statements and Audits*

Considering the hook relationship between the financial statements, this paper needs to consider not only the possible abnormalities of the financial data themselves but also the ratio relationship between the various financial statement accounts.

This article is based on the 2018 annual report financial data of 3,459 non-financial entities listed on A-share according to static analysis and dynamic (trend) analysis. Interbank comparison of data processing methods for three modules constructs an initial feature pool (initial factors for nearly 200 financial statement accounts) and then extracts features using Gibbs sampling (Qian *et al.* [23]) by the Gibbs sampling method under MCMC framework at a given sample error tolerance (the sample error is set to 5% in this article). For details, see formula (Equation 7.3) and its description, which allow us to reduce the complexity of NP problems in feature extraction to polynomial complexity screening, which support us to extract features in characterizing corporate financial fraud behaviors.

7.3.4   Feature Extraction Based on AUC and ROC Testing for Financial Frauds

Based on the commonly used financial ratios, percentage reports, and financial statement account growth rates, an initial feature pool of 183 features was constructed (see Table 7.2 for their information) to obtain eight characteristic factors depicting the risk of financial frauds as shown by Table 7.3 below.

The sample data used in this article are based on a ratio of 8:2 for training and test sets, respectively. The correlation between each characteristic factor and financial fraud risk is classified, and the eight characteristics used to characterize the financial fraud risk of the enterprise in Table 7.2 are obtained, and these eight characteristic indicators have a strong correlation with other subjects of the company's finance.

This explains the financial statement accounts that involve factors such as the company's business income, taxation, and company accounting policies (such as asset impairment standards) and accounts that are not easily

Table 7.2 Examples of initial characteristic factors.

#s	Description of features	Significance of related ships
1	Paid-in capital (or equity)/total assets	31.95%
2	Days of non-current asset turnover	25.70%
3	Capital leverage	20.15%
...	...	...
181	Accounts receivable turnover days	0.05%
...	...	...
183	Absorption of cash received from investments/Subtotal of cash inflows from financing activities	0.05%

Table 7.3 The eight features of highly associated features for financial frauds.

Number	Features	Coefficients	p-value	Significant	Odds ratio
0	Constant term	-2.49	0.00%		0.08
1	Deduction of non-net profit growth rate	-0.41	0.00%	82.30%	0.67
2	Growth rate of works under construction	-0.16	0.89%	87.40%	0.85
3	Advance payment growth rate	-0.15	1.05%	59.70%	0.86
4	Where: interest expense (finance expense)/ total operating income	0.30	0.00%	97.90%	1.36

(Continued)

Table 7.3 The eight features of highly associated features for financial frauds. (*Continued*)

Number	Features	Coefficients	p-value	Significant	Odds ratio
5	Net income from investments/ total operating income	-0.15	0.24%	52.90%	0.86
6	Other income/ total operating income	-0.20	0.06%	98.45%	0.82
7	Other receivables (including interest and dividends)/ total assets	0.20	0.00%	99.80%	1.22
8	Long-term borrowings/ total assets	-0.17	0.14%	65.05%	0.84

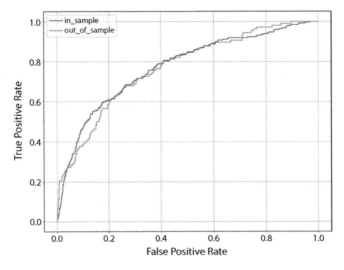

Figure 7.2 The AUC and ROC test for features in depicting financial frauds.

verifiable in the audit (such as advance payments, accounts payable). The risk of financial fraud has a high correlation. In addition, the initial characteristics of the static analysis and interbank comparison method construction also have a high correlation with the financial fraud risk, indicating that under the framework of machine learning, static analysis and interbank comparison can more effectively highlight the financial fraud risk of listed companies. AUC values based on the training set and test set are 0.77 and 0.77, respectively (Figure 7.2).

7.3.5   The Corporate Governance Framework of Financial Fraud Indicators

Considering the classification analysis of the company's major shareholders, management, board of directors and supervisory board according to the shareholding ratio, the identity of the position, and the proportion of internal and external, the CART classification method and the corresponding XGBoost algorithm [combined with the evidence weight, that is, weight of evidence (WOE), are used, and information value (i.e., IV), the amount of information in information value] to explain the impact on the risk of possible fraud on the assessment object, and obtain an unstructured feature assessment index that characterizes the quality of the corporate governance structure (Chen *et al.* [26]; Li *et al.* [4]; Li *et al.* [13]; Yang *et al.* [15]; Yuan [19, 20]). The following are the four characteristics from the perspective of companies' governance in providing early warning information:

(1)   First, the shareholding ratio of major shareholders and representatives of enterprise law is between 5% and 50%;

(2)   Second, the cumulative shareholding ratio of the major shareholder shall not exceed 60%, that is, the sum of the shares of all major shareholders shall not exceed 60%;

(3)   Third, the shareholder sharcholding of management is less than 1%;

(4)   Fourth, the proportion of major shareholders in the board of directors shall not exceed 12% (that is, the proportion of directors participating in the board of directors who are also the major shareholders of the company shall not exceed 12%).

Based on the above two types of indicator systems, combined with the performance analysis based on internal and external audit-related data, we have established a more comprehensive characteristic system that portrays the company's financial fraud behavior (see the illustration in Figure 7.1 for details).

In addition, in the process of constructing and characterizing indicators of corporate (financial) fraud and fraud, we should actually think about a basic question: Why is there always fraud in a company?

In view of this problem, we combined the business situation, violations, cooperation of the audit institution, as well as the auditor's education experience, work experience, etc., to conduct a comprehensive sorting and analysis and used the evidence weight (WOE) of the audit performance index for box analysis (Chen *et al.* [26]; Li *et al.* [4]; Li *et al.* [13]; Yang *et al.* [15]; Yuan *et al.* [19, 20]).

7.4   The Case Study for Financial Frauds from Listed Companies

7.4.1   The Case Study Background

For LQ Industrial Co., Ltd. (herein simplified name "LQ"), in 2021, on January 8, LQ received the Notice of Investigation from the China Securities Regulatory Commission (CSRC). Due to the company's suspected violation of laws and regulations on information disclosure, in accordance with the relevant provisions of the Securities Law of the People's Republic of China, it was decided to file a case investigation against the company. For details, please refer to the Announcement on Receipt of the Notice of Case Filing and Investigation by the CSRC (Announcement No. 2021-010) disclosed by the Company on January 9, 2021.

In this section, our goal is to target the real listed company "Guangzhou LQ" (in short, LQ) by the CSRC in the "Notice of Investigation" by conducting corresponding case studies of its "financial fraud" that occurred during 2020.

7.4.2   The Case Study by Qualitative Analysis

Based on Figure 7.3 and Table 7.4 below, the company's profit indicators show that the company has the possibility of financial fraud under profit pressure.

In addition, LQ has faced a long-term decline in stock prices. Among the top 10 shareholders of LQ, Jiang XX debuted at LQ in the third quarter

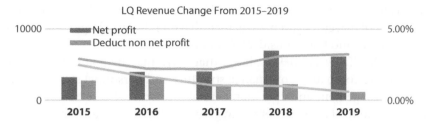

Figure 7.3 The summary of LQ revenue for the time period from 2015 to 2019.

Table 7.4 The summary of LQ 2015–2019's revenue.

Year	Net-profit	Deduct-non net profit	Net profit equity ratio	Equity ratio of non-net profit deduction
2015	3184.07	2707.57	2.89%	2.46%
2016	3927.16	2905.21	2.20%	1.63%
2017	3997.3	1893.11	2.17%	1.03%
2018	6936.67	2219.79	3.10%	0.99%
2019	6135.59	1115.72	3.22%	0.59%

of 2017, buying 3.11 million shares at a cost price of 7.8 per share to 8.1 per share range. As early as the third quarter of 2013, Wu XXX "entered" LQ with a shareholding size of 1.34 million shares. The top 10 shareholders increased their holdings to 6.63 million shares in the following quarter until the beginning of 2015, when the number of shares held remained mostly at 4.8884 million shares to 662.90 between 10,000 shares. The three major shareholders held shares for years and suffered long-term losses, which may put additional pressure on management, further exacerbating the possibility of corporate fraud.

From what is currently known, an important time point for financial fraud is 2018, a year in which the company added 1.01 billion in inventory. According to the company's 2018 annual report, the company has a total of seven directors (in which three are independent), three supervisors (in which one is independent), and the board of directors and the board of supervisors are among the same listed companies in the small- and medium-sized category. At the same time, Vice Chairman Chen XXX has been serving as the general manager for a long time, and the company's board of directors and the management level have a relatively high correlation, so the board of directors and management have a relatively large influence on the company and have considerable control.

Secondly, Table 7.5 below shows that there may be some major loopholes in the company's governance structure and personnel structure, and senior management and core members of the board of directors may have too much control over the company, giving opportunities for the possibility of financial frauds, from the perspective of the triangular theory for LQ to have financial frauds, which made the financial risk of LQ greatly increased.

In addition, in Table 7.5 and Table 7.6, plus the company changed the auditor in 2018 and generated a huge inventory in the same year, from the perspective of the triangular theory of corporate fraud, the company's management attitude and under the pretext of the business environment, LQ has a relatively large possibility of financial fraud.

7.4.3   The Quantitative Analysis Based on the CAFÉ Risk Evaluation System

The evaluation results of the CAFÉ model show that compared with companies in the same industry, LQ's financial quality score in 2017–2019 was 27.48 in turn 22.09, 53.53, its possible financial fraud is a dynamic and cumulative process. LQ's financial fraud should have occurred earlier than 2017, and financial fraud in 2018 is a continuation of the previous behavior. Although the financial quality of the company itself has improved in 2019 compared with before, it is still at a relatively low level in the company's history and in the same industry.

Table 7.5 The summary for the meeting of directors and board of LQ.

Point in time	Board meetings	Meeting by board	Point in time	Board meetings	Meeting of the board
2001/12/31	4	3	......	......	......
2002/12/31	13	7	2015/12/31	9	No information
2003/12/31	9	5	2016/12/31	5	No information
2004/12/31	8	3	2017/12/31	6	No information
2005/12/31	12	4	2018/12/31	9	No information
2006/12/31	9	2	2019/12/31	9	No information

Table 7.6 The summary of rotation for audit committee members from LQ.

Name of the committee	Start the event	End event	Member name
Board of Auditors	2014/6/20	2015/8/18	Lv XX
Same as above	Same as above	Same as above	King XX
Same as above	Same as above	Same as above	Lee XX
Same as above	2015/8/18	2017/6/30	Character XX
Same as above	Same as above	Same as above	King XX
Same as above	Same as above	Same as above	Lee XX
Same as above	2017/6/30	2020/7/30	Character XX

Further from the core indicators of our evaluation system (Table 7.7), we observed the following: "Indicators 1–3" and other core indicators "5 and 6" are highly similar to the "black sample of financial quality" (Table 7.3), which implies that LQ may have inflated its income in order to increase LQ's net profit. Moreover, Table 7.7 indicates that there is possibly

Table 7.7 The summary of LQ index's deviation analysis.

Features	Black samples	White sample	LQ indicator (features) industry deviation			
			2017	2018	2019	Mean
Feature 1	-103.9%	8.1%	-84.5%	-85.1%	-91.1%	-86.9%
Feature 2	9.5%	51.6%	-80.3%	-41.9%	42.3%	-26.7%
Feature 3	-4.7%	34.1%	-1.4%	1967.6%	-42.2%	-21.8%
Feature 4	127.6%	38.2%	-47.1%	-28.8%	16.0%	-20.0%
Feature 5	36.0%	51.1%	-93.5%	-101.2%	-45.3%	-80.0%
Feature 6	30.7%	52.8%	-44.6%	-50.7%	-66.8%	-54.0%
Feature 7	115.5%	41.4%	17.8%	55.3%	19.7%	30.9%
Feature 8	84.6%	85.2%	——	——	2.1%	——

Note: See Table 7.2 for the corresponding serial numbers of indicators (features) used.

an abnormal phenomenon between the deduction of non-net profit and net profit of LQ, which also supports and helps us explain the abnormal performance of related indicators.

Based on the analysis data in Table 7.3, we have a special note that due to the increase of 937 million yuan in advance payments of LQ in 2018 compared with 460 million yuan in the previous year, it is being deducted. This increase is clearly anomalous when non-net profit does not change much, so this value is ignored when calculating the average industry deviation. At the same time, since there is no long-term borrowing in LQ, this may indicate not included in the comparison range by against the average.

By LQ's financial report before 2018, the company's assets totaled 4.813 billion yuan in 2017, an increase of 643 million yuan over 2016. Mainly from the increase in accounts receivable and bills receivable, it seems that one of the common fraud accounts, especially in 2016–2017 (see also Table 7.8 below).

Table 7.8 The deviation test of LQ's corporate governance's features.

Features #	Features for the characteristics of corporate governance structure	LQ indicator	LQ test results
1	The ratio of major shareholders and corporate law representatives is between 5% and 50%.	45.0%	Within the criteria range
2	The cumulative ratio of the major shareholder shall not exceed 60%.	49.0%	Within the criteria range
3	Shareholder of management is less than 1%.	0.0%	Within the criteria range
4	The proportion of major shareholders in the board of directors shall not exceed 12%.	0.0%	Within the criteria range

Table 7.8 shows that LQ's structure falls within the four unstructured feature indicator pre-values established above. Therefore, in view of the performance of LQ's fraudulent behavior, the characteristic portrayal of LQ's financial fraud behavior from the financial to the corporate governance framework discussed in this article has an early warning function.

7.4.4   Case Study Results and Remark

The analysis on the case study shows that the outbreak of a company's financial fraud incident is not a sudden event. In particular, by establishing a comprehensive evaluation system based on features as constructed in this paper, it may help us capable to timely expose and warn the financial fraud behavior, financial abnormal state outbreak of listed companies in the capital market of China.

7.5   Conclusion

In this paper, the machine learning algorithm based on artificial intelligence under the framework of big data depicts the risk characteristic extraction method of financial fraud indicators and unstructured corporate governance structure and constructs a corporate governance structure. The risk warning system of financial fraud requires correlation characteristic indicators and conducts corresponding case studies. The results of this case study show that the behavior of financial fraud at the level of financial and corporate governance framework can actually play a predictive role through the characterization of the ability to identify. Especially under the framework of the fraud triangle principle, the correlation indicators constructed in this paper to support the financial fraud risk assessment system are the release of possible timely warning information on the company's financial fraud behavior.

We also hope that the methods and frameworks discussed in this article can bring different dimensions of thinking to the traditional financial fraud analysis and also look forward to more practitioners and industry experts to use unstructured data under the big data framework to make full use of big data algorithms for this part of the data that was difficult to quantify in the past and provide more data analysis methods and technical means for complex scenarios of finance frauds, or fraudulent behaviors, so as to continuously standardize and promote the benign development of the industry.

Appendix A: The Description for Eight Types of Financial Frauds

The following are the description of typical eight kinds of financial frauds and the accounting subjects involved in the sample companies from 2010 to 2019 from the capital market based on listed companies in China summarized by Huang *et al.* [3].

The following analyzes the main types of financial frauds and the accounting subjects involved in the sample companies from 2010 to 2019 from the , analyzes the usual methods of financial fraud, and points out the severe challenges brought by internal accounting fraud and external cooperation fraud to the audit of certified public accountants.

As can be seen from Table 7.A below, financial frauds mainly focus on the whitewashing and manipulation of the income statement. Revenue fraud has become the "hardest hit area" of financial fraud, accounting for around 68%, which is similar to the findings of COSO's "Financial Fraud Report from 1998 to 2007". During this period, the U.S. listed companies involved in revenue fraud accounted for more than 60% of the total sample companies. Expense and cost fraud became the second and fourth major types of financial fraud, accounting for around 22% and around 15% respectively. What is particularly noteworthy is that the monetary and capital fraud on the balance sheet has become the third type of financial fraud, accounting for around 21%,

We also note that listed companies often manipulate their operating performance through a variety of fraud types, and 113 sample companies

Table 7.A Summary of eight types of financial frauds in the capital market of China.

Income fraud (around 68%);
Expense fraud (around 22%);
Monetary fraud (around 21%);
Cost fraud (around 15%);
Impairment fraud (around 12%);
Non-operating income-expenditure fraud (around 9%);
Investment income fraud (around 6%);
Other fraud (around 2%).

cover 175 types of fraud. In addition to the conventional income, cost and expense fraud, monetary funds, asset impairment, investment income, non-operating income and expenditure and other items have increasingly become the objects of management performance manipulation.

The above top four types of financial frauds appear to be independent of each other on the surface, but are actually related to each other. First, both revenue fraud and cost fraud aim to exaggerate operating performance for the purpose of issuing new shares, refinancing or maintaining listing status. Secondly, in order to satisfy the falsification relationship and avoid revealing loopholes, listed companies usually adjust expenses and cost items while manipulating income. Finally, the inflated income, expenses and costs need to be disguised by false capital flows, and fictitious bank statements, bank statements and bank confirmations become "compulsory courses" to deal with the inspection of CPAs and regulatory authorities. Driven by the huge economic benefits, it seems that the rigorous reconciliation between the statement items contained in double entry bookkeeping can only increase the difficulty and cost of fraud, that is, it absolutely cannot stop the determination and action of counterfeiters.

1. The characteristics of income fraud:

The income fraud in this paper consists of two types: accounting manipulation and transaction fraud. Accounting manipulation fraud is mainly manifested in the management of listed companies through the choice of accounting judgment more favorable to themselves, to achieve the purpose of performance manipulation, the most common is to recognize revenue in advance. Transaction fraud is mainly manifested in the management of listed companies to fabricate transactions to achieve the purpose of falsely increasing income, the most common is through related party customers or hidden related parties, collude to fabricate business and income. Indeed, the most common type of income fraud in the sample companies is transaction fraud, accounting for around 70%.

Income fraud has become a chronic disease of financial fraud in listed companies, and the high proportion of income fraud in transaction fraud indicates that financial fraud in listed companies has evolved from simple and crude accounting fraud to true accounting fraud at any cost. This not only increases the audit risk of certified public accountants, but also means the deterioration of social integrity environment, because there must be a large number of customers, suppliers, related parties and financial institutions behind the transaction fraud income fraud, common fraud. In such a bad credit environment, how can certified public accountants prevent audit failure?

The most effective way to detect revenue fraud is to extend the scope of audit to customers, suppliers, related parties and financial institutions, which is what regulators have tried and tested time and again. Unfortunately, laws and regulations do not endow certified public accountants known as "market economy guard" with the right to audit external transfer, certified public accountants can only passively inquire or inquire by letter, and the effect depends entirely on the other party's honesty and integrity. However, many audit failure cases prove that such honesty and integrity are often unreliable.

2. The characteristics of expense fraud:
The main methods of the expense fraud are externalization of expenses, intertemporal adjustment and current billing. Among the expense fraud methods, the most secret is the expense externalization, but whether it can escape the audit of CPA depends on whether it can get external cooperation from suppliers, related parties and financial institutions. As long as these external parties actively cooperate with the fraud, in the absence of the right to transfer, even if the analytical review work is in place, it is difficult for certified public accountants to find this kind of expense fraud, especially to obtain sufficient audit evidence.

3. The characteristics of monetary fund fraud:
The monetary fund fraud mainly involves the appropriation of funds by related parties (for example, the listed company may create false externalization of funds through the co-management account of the group). The second way in this category is fabricated monetary funds to cover up income fraud (such as falsifying bank receipts, and some other similar ways).

Monetary fund fraud usually requires the cooperation of banks. In the most common fraud cases, the related financial institutions can be found to cooperate with listed companies to provide false bank statements, statements, confirmation letters and other bad phenomena to auditors. The problem of financial institutions cooperating with listed companies to cheat should be paid attention to and rectified, otherwise the quality of accounting information cannot be guaranteed, audit failure is inevitable.

4. The characteristics of cost fraud:
It can be seen that the cost fraud methods are relatively single, but have certain industry dependence. For example, for listed companies in agriculture, forestry, animal husbandry and fishery, it is difficult to verify the input-output ratio of inventory, and the probability of artificially reducing

current operating costs is high. For example, listed companies using the percentage of completion method, such as equipment manufacturing industry and information technology service industry, have a high probability of cost fraud due to their high dependence on the estimate of the completion schedule.

Cost fraud methods are not complicated, and they are accounting manipulation fraud, which is easy to be found. Once certified public accountants find such fraud, they should expand the scope of audit and implement additional procedures to evaluate whether there is a broader and more hidden financial fraud in the listed company.

5. The characteristics of impairment fraud:

It can be seen that the impairment fraud of listed companies is mainly to reduce the provision for the impairment of assets. The common methods are deliberately ignoring the signs of impairment or fictitious payment collection to write down current accounts. It is worth noting that in the case of insufficient basis for impairment, more provision for impairment is the same as less provision for impairment, which is a fraud. Especially in the year after the occurrence of fraud, listed companies "take a big bath" through the provision of huge impairment provisions, often in order to "digest" the fictitious income and profit of the previous year and form false assets. Certified public accountants should hold a high degree of professional skepticism towards such impairment, and check whether there is any fraud in the income and profit items related to the previous year through the asset items involved in the impairment provision.

6 & 7. The characteristics of Non-operating income-expenditure fraud, & Investment income fraud:

These two categories financial frauds are mainly reflected by the following ways, that is, the significant change in the proportion of non-operating income and expenditure (or investment income) in the total profit of the company or the significant change in the absolute amount is achieved without debt restructuring, non-monetary Prostitution and changes in major investment behavior of the company, which is often a fraud that may adjust the value of assets, or use subsidiaries to achieve income adjustment.

8. The characteristics of other fraud:

Those fraud events not covered by seven types of fraudulent practices mentioned above.

Appendix B: The Summary of 12 Classes of Data Types in Describing Financial Fraud Behaviors

Based on the time period from January 2017 to December 2018, the following is the summary for the data which shows that there were around 2,700 bad events happened by around 383 listed companies as given by Table 7.B below for twelve categories of data types in describing "bad events" (actually for eight kinds of financial frauds) by applying the general principle of CSRC's compliance in the practice for the capital market in China summarized by Yuan *et al.* [21, 22], Zeng [23], and Yuan *et al.* [24].

The Summary of 12 Classes of Data Types in Table B1 is as follows:

1. The occupation of corporate assets;
2. False disclosure (others);
3. Non-compliant guarantees (illegal guarantees);
4. Fraudulent listing;
5. Changing the role of funds without authorization;
6. Improper treatment of general accounting;
7. False records (or misleading statements);
8. Delayed disclosure;
9. Fictitious profits;
10. Material omissions
11. Falsely listing assets
12. Others.

Now we give a brief description for each of twelve data types from Table 7.B.

Table 7.B The Summary of 12 classes events from Listed Companies from 2017 to 2018.

The occupation of corporate assets	Changing the role of funds without authorization	Non-compliant guarantees	Fraudulent listing	False disclosure (others)	Falsely listing assets
87	17	60	0	32	4
Improper treatment of general accounting	False records (or misleading statements)	Delayed disclosure	Fictitious profits	Material omissions	Others
30	233	306	15	143	117

(1) The occupation of corporate assets
Occupation of company assets refers to the direct or indirect appropriation of funds and assets of a listed company by controlling shareholders, actual controllers and other enterprises under their control through related party transactions, asset reorganization, advance payment, foreign investment, guarantee, profit distribution and other means, so as to damage the legitimate rights and interests of the company and other shareholders.

(2) False disclosure (others)
False disclosure refers to the disclosure of untrue information by a listed company, that is, untrue records, misleading statements and major omissions by a listed company. False information includes both the false information contained in the financial report disclosed by the listed company and the false information in the voluntary information disclosed by the listed company.

(3) Non-compliant guarantees (illegal guarantees)
Illegal guarantee refers to the external guarantee implemented by the listed company and its holding subsidiaries without the review procedures stipulated in the articles of association.

(4) Fraudulent listing
Fraudulent listing refers to that a company is subject to administrative punishment by the CSRC or transferred to the public security organ for the crime of fraudulent issuance due to false records, misleading statements or major omissions in the application for initial public offering and disclosure documents, which cause the issuer that does not meet the issuance conditions to obtain the issuance approval fraudulently, or has a material impact on the pricing of new shares.

(5) Changing the role of funds without authorization
Unauthorized change of the use of funds refers to the use of funds by listed companies in violation of China Securities Regulatory Commission (CSRC)'s Regulatory Guidelines for Listed Companies No. 2 - Regulatory Requirements for the Management and Use of Funds Raised by Listed Companies.

(6) Improper treatment of general accounting
Improper general accounting treatment refers to the accounting treatment of listed companies that does not meet the requirements of the Accounting Standards for Business Enterprises.

(7) False records (or misleading statements)

False records refer to the records that are inconsistent with the truth in the information disclosure documents, that is, the events that do not objectively occur are fabricated or not eliminated in the information disclosure documents; Misleading statement refers to that although the record of a certain event in the information disclosure document is true, it is easy to be misunderstood due to the defects in the expression, so that investors could not obtain a clear and correct understanding.

(8) Delayed disclosure

Delayed disclosure refers to the behavior of delaying the disclosure of information of a listed company without the prescribed time.

(9) Fictitious profits

Fictitious profit refers to the act of inflating the after-tax profit of an enterprise by means of accounting fraud. Usually, the purpose of accounting fraud is to increase the net profit of the enterprise, so as to inflate the operating performance of the company.

(10) Material omissions

Major omissions refer to the failure of information disclosure documents to record matters that should be recorded according to law, so as to affect investors to make correct decisions.

(11) Falsely listing assets

False listing of assets refers to the act of falsely increasing or reducing the assets of enterprises through accounting fraud. The illegal way of false listing of assets usually also brings false profit at the same time, so the two can occur at the same time.

(12) Others

Any other cases not included as mentioned by 11 categories above.

References

1. Abbott, L.J., Park, Y., Parker, S., The effects of audit committee activity and independence on corporate fraud. *Manage. Finance*, 26, 11, 55–68, 2000.
2. Abbott, L.J. *et al.*, Audit committees and auditor selection. *J. Account.*, 191, 6, 95–95, 2001.

3. Huang, S.Z., Ye, Q.H., Xu, S. *et al.*, Analysis of financial fraud of Chinese listed companies from 2010 to 2019. *Financ. Account. Mon.*, 14, 153–160, 2020.

4. Li, Q. and Ren, C.Y., Research on the construction and early warning of accounting fraud risk index of listed companies. *J. Xi'an Jiaotong University: Soc. Sci. Edition*, 36, 36–44, 2016.

5. AICPA, *Statement of Auditing Standards No.99: Consideration of Fraud in a Financial Statement Audit*, AICPA, New York, 2002.

6. Beasley, M.S., Carcello, J.V., Hermanson, D.R. *et al.*, Fraudulent financial reporting: Consideration of industry traits and corporate governance mechanisms. *Account. Horiz.*, 14, 4, 441–454, 2000.

7. Beneish, M.D., Detecting GAAP violation: Implications for assessing earnings management among firms with extreme financial performance. *J. Account. Public Policy*, 16, 3, 271–309, 1997.

8. Dunn, P., The impact of insider power on fraudulent financial reporting. *J. Manage.*, 30, 3, 397–412, 2004.

9. Hopwood, W.S., Leiner, J.J. *et al.*, *Forensic Accounting and Fraud Examination (2nd Edition)*, McGraw-Hill Education, New York, 2011.

10. Summers, S.L. and Sweeney, J.T., Fraudulently misstated financial statements and insider trading: An empirical analysis. *Account. Rev.*, 73, 1, 131–146, 1998.

11. Wells, J.T., *Corporate Fraud Handbook: Prevention and Detection*, John Wiley & Sons, Inc., Hoboken, New Jersey, 2005.

12. Geman, S. and Geman, D., Stochastic relaxation, Gibbs distributions, and the Bayesian restoration of images. *IEEE Trans. Pattern Anal. Mach. Intell.*, 6, 6, 721–741, 1984.

13. Li, H., Cao, Y., Li, S. *et al.*, XGBoost model and its application to personal credit evaluation. *IEEE Intell. Syst.*, 35, 52–61, 2020.

14. Shi, H.B., Chen, Y.W., Chen, X., A Review on SMOTE Oversampling and its improved algorithm. *CAAI Trans. Intelligent Syst.*, 14, 6, 1073–1083, 2019.

15. Yang, H., Li, L., Fang, Y.F., Cai, F. *et al.*, The extraction of early warning features for the predicting financial distress based on XGboost model and shap framework. *Int. J. Financ. Eng.*, 8, 3, 2141004, 2021.

16. Yuan, G.X., Yan, C.X., Zhou, Y.P., Liu, H.Y., Qian, G.Q., Shi, Y.K., Credit risk analysis of Chinese companies by applying the CAFÉ approach, in: *Data Science, ICPCSEE 2022, Communications in Computer and Information Science*, vol. 1629, Y. Wang, G. Zhu, Q. Han, L. Zhang, X. Song, Z. Lu (Eds.), pp. 475–502, Springer, Singapore, 2022, https://doi.org/10.1007/978-981-19-5209-8_33.

17. Yuan, G.X., Zhou, Y.P., Yan, C.X. *et al.*, The framework for the risk feature extraction method on corporate fraud. *Chin. J. Manage. Sci.*, 30, 3, 47–58, 2022.

18. Yuan, G.X., Zhou, Y.P., Yan, C.X. *et al.*, A new method for corporate financial fraud early warning and risk characteristic screening: based on artificial

intelligence algorithm, in: *Proceedings of the 15th (2020) China Management Annual Conference*, China Management Modernization Research Society, pp. 709–724, 2020.

19. Yuan, G.X., Interpretation of corporate governance structure: A big data method for characterizing the good and bad characteristics of companies. *TGES - Modern Financial Risk Management Platform (TGES 2021) Advanced Offline Seminar: Retail Micro, Inclusive Finance and Risk Management*, Renmin University of China, 2021, https://www.cfrisk.org/course/13131.

20. Yuan, G.X., Using big data to improve credit rating quality and differentiation: An exploration of the holographic risk assessment system of Cafe (CAFE). *Tsinghua Financial Rev.*, 98, 70–74, 2022.

21. Yuan, G.X., Zhou, Y.P., Yan, C.X. *et al.*, The framework for the risk feature extraction method on corporate fraud. *Chin. J. Manage. Sci.*, 30, 3, 47–58, 2022.

22. Yuan, G.X., Zhou, Y.P., Liu, H.Y. *et al.*, The framework of cafe credit risk assessment for financial markets in China. *Procedia Comput. Sci.*, 202, 33–46, 2022.

23. Zeng, T., *Feature Extraction by Gibbs Sampling algorithm and Machine Learning for Corporate Financial Frauds*, Master Thesis (2009853U-MI20-0025), Macau University of Science and Technology, Macau, March 20, 2022.

24. Yuan, X.G., He, H., Liu, H.Y., *et al.*, The framework of Hammer (CAFÉ) credit rating for capital markets in China with international credit rating standards. *Manage Decis. Econ.*, 2023, 1–21, First published: 02 August 2023. https://doi.org/10.1002/mde.3964

25. Wang, J.C. and Guo, Z.G., *Logistic Regression Model*, Higher Education Press, Beijing, 2001.

26. Chen, T. and Guestrin, C., XGBoost: A scalable tree boosting system, in: *KDD '16: Proceedings of the 22nd ACM SIGKDD International Conference on Knowledge Discovery and Data Mining*, August 2016, pp. 785–794, 2016, https://doi.org/10.1145/ 2939672.2939785.

8

A New Surge of Interest in the Cybersecurity of VIP Clients is the First Step Toward the Return of the Previously Used Positioning Practice in Domestic Private Banking

Gusev Alexey

Department of Cybernetics, National Research Nuclear University MEPhI (Moscow Engineering Physics Institute), Moscow, Russia

Abstract

Thanks to the efforts of medium-sized and niche banks, Russian private banking is gradually beginning to return to its usual positioning scheme, "universal VIP bank" against the "VIP club," tested before the introduction of anti-Russian sanctions and before the COVID-19 pandemic. However, further steps will directly depend on how exactly these banks manage to solve the main problem of this positioning, namely, to build an effective risk minimization model for the current organizational and management structure of the VIP client's capital with the promotion of long-term restructuring services. However, now, VIP clients prefer to rigidly insist on the need to preserve the previous structure, which poses a very difficult task for domestic private banking, finding arguments that could convince target customers to change their minds. It is here that the achievements of domestic private banking in the field of profiling VIP clients, rather than proprietary palliative solutions of vendors in the field of cybersecurity, can be quite successful both for organizing effective protection against cyber threats of VIP clients, and for increasing the overall competitiveness in Russian private banking for medium-sized and niche banks.

Keywords: Private banking, VIP clients, intercultural communications, information security, whaling, phishing, cyber hygiene

Email: AIGusev@mephi.ru

Ambrish Kumar Mishra, Shweta Anand, Narayan C. Debnath, Purvi Pokhariyal and Archana Patel (eds.) *Artificial Intelligence for Risk Mitigation in the Financial Industry,* (187–208) © 2024 Scrivener Publishing LLC

8.1   Introduction

Largely due to the activity of medium-sized and niche banks, domestic Russian private banking is gradually beginning to return to its usual positioning scheme: "universal VIP bank" versus "VIP club." Thus, the purpose of the article is to present the modern practice of solving the main task of such repositioning with the promotion of long-term capital restructuring services which will directly depend on how exactly the patronymic players will solve the problems of their VIP clients in the field of cyber hygiene. This topic began to be actively introduced by bankers even before the COVID-19 pandemic, but right now, medium-sized and niche banks have made it the main one in their own positioning.

8.1.1   Cyber Hygiene

- **By 2019, domestic private banking begins to attract target customers using the arguments of cyber hygiene**

Over the past few years, the growth of targeted cyberattacks on Russian business has quite naturally led to an adequate offer of counteraction tools from vendors actively promoting new solutions in the field of information security. However, along with vendors, Russian banks have also approached the practice of continuous provision of cyber hygiene, not only their own but also in relation to their customers. At the very beginning, only individual structural units of the private banking direction were active, trying to help level the risks of cyber threats only to their target VIP clients. Yet, now, it makes sense to talk about a more representative promotion of this banking model to other client units, as well as a wider range of clients themselves, primarily in the corporate sector. And such a statement raises the question of whether bankers should take care of cyber hygiene not only of their VIP clients, but also of the bank's clients as a whole. Moreover, such a statement is based on a direct pragmatic approach initiated and very effectively developed by private banking units even before the COVID-19 pandemic. It was then that cyber hygiene began to be considered in private banking as a further promotion of long-term capital restructuring services for its target VIP client.

It was at the beginning of 2020 that new methods of providing protection against cyber threats for Russian industrial enterprises appeared, primarily for owners and their families, and were even the subject of serious discussion at specialized conferences related to the specifics of the development of domestic private banking in particular. Rigorous debates have developed around rethinking the most serious cyber threats and searching for an adequate industrial enterprise comprehensive protection. Recently, it has been customary to analyze such cyberattacks by using certain software exploits of the external and internal perimeter of protection of a particular business unit where the presence of such exploits is a consequence of more general problems of the corporate structure profile of a typical Russian industrial enterprise [1]. First of all, it is necessary to identify the profile of a typical Russian owner of an industrial enterprise. It is he who, as the owner of a large- and medium-sized business with actual confirmed assets, has been a successful target client of domestic private banking since about the beginning of the century. Just such a private banking client went from a simple potential client relatively quickly to one of the target categories of VIP clients. At the same time, the bank could easily establish long-term relationships with such owners by providing a corresponding product range of private banking.

It is worth taking into account the fact that the upper part of the Russian wealth feast, which is represented by the target categories of domestic VIP clients, was not fully available for targeted search of potential customers. So, the owners of large businesses, representatives of the top management of state-owned companies, and senior officials have long been successfully served in individual banks and financial companies. Therefore, the costs of leveling their loyalty to them in order to fully transfer them to service in their own bank were very high. It is not surprising that private banking has chosen a different position for less wealthy private business owners, with whom it was possible to effectively implement understandable and replicated technologies for attracting service. And first of all, they were wealthy owners of the industrial sector of the economy, representing medium and even small businesses. When working with such clients, domestic private banking began to use specific technologies of effective service, building its new positioning on them. It was called the "corporate loyalty program" because Russian private banking began to attract and serve VIP clients, introducing and managing their business, not limited to just servicing personal wealth as before. The fact is that by this time, the assessment of the total capital of a typical Russian VIP client began to take into account his business, which turned out to be closely related to his personal condition, differing in this from the traditional model adopted in Western private banking, which was used in Russia before.

This allowed domestic private banking to immediately begin building an effective competitive positioning in relation to Western private banking, and leveling the fact that domestic private banking was seriously inferior to Western in the assortment and quality of the product line. To do this, domestic private banking has chosen a narrower appropriate specialization, more suitable for the main target category of VIP clients. As part of this specialization, Russian private banking was able to significantly refine and expand its product range for such VIP clients, not only effectively adapting existing Western private banking products but also developing new ones of its own. This also allowed Russian bankers to successfully compete for attracting and servicing such target customers by the time private banking began to stand out as a separate service of the Russian banking sector.

We are observing the correctness of the choice of such positioning now. Growing uncertainty and far from optimistic assessments of the development of the Russian market after the COVID-19 pandemic reduce the possibilities of choice for a Russian owner who has just managed to adapt to doing business under sanctions. Especially the owner of a business representing just the industrial sector, when it comes not only to long-term medium- and long-term planning but also about simple survival. However, it is in the latter case that domestic private banking can provide such owners with not only medium-term, but also long-term, service through the "corporate loyalty program" maintaining the continuity of its business processes and ensuring the establishment and strengthening of long-term relationships with the bank. And this is exactly what such an owner, previously chosen by domestic private banking as the main target client, should strive for in conditions of economic uncertainty.

In this case, the owner, the owner of such a business, still prefers to retain overall management, tightly controlling decision-making by hired professionally trained top managers [2]. The owner tries to retain full, almost total, control over strategic issues related to the development of his business, and even in the case of delegation of authority to the same top managers, he tries to retain operational control over the business. At the same time, the owner himself is well aware that it is necessary to delegate part of the responsibility to trusted persons. And the number of such proxies already needs to be expanded, assessing trust on the principle of not only maintaining personal loyalty and loyalty to the owner but also taking into account the level of competence over time. In fact, as practice shows, to a greater extent such an owner can relatively trust only his family and close friends, appointing them to top management positions in his own business. But this circle is limited, and with the development of business, even they need to start demonstrating a high level of professional training comparable to hired top managers, so that they simply will not be replaced. But all the same, the circle of people personally loyal to the owner is limited, and over time, he begins to hire more and those with whom he has already encountered in the same business in the past and has become convinced not only of their high professionalism but also that it is also difficult to trust them relatively. But even an accepted hired employee, with excellent recommendations, not to mention top managers, such an owner does not fully trust for some time, often independently engaged in auditing their current activities.

It is certainly not worth talking about the effectiveness of such a management style, especially given the high costs of such intercultural communication. And the control technologies themselves of such almost total control by the owner are not fully technological. So, it is not surprising that they are not always effectively implemented in practice, and this is always an additional cost. Moreover, when the owner's business begins to grow and develop rapidly, the owner is often distracted by a small audit of employees, by the need to maintain operational control over routine operations, simply not being able to pay attention to strategic planning issues that are more significant for his business and missing appropriate opportunities for faster development. They rely on those whom he fully trusts, on family members and friends, it is still possible here. But the greater the instability of the economy, when it is simply necessary not only to understand how to survive, but also to quickly assess the new opportunities provided for development, the more he must rely on top management in these matters, trusting him and delegating part of the authority. And loyalty alone is no longer enough here, we must constantly think about additional education, about constant and continuous retraining. Of course, a certain margin of safety for the most loyal top managers still remains, but they also gradually have to think about retraining because practically since 2009, the Russian economy has been developing in such conditions of almost continuous uncertainty. During this time, even the most loyal representa tives of top management, for example, the same family members, had to radically reconsider their views on compliance with the professional level and seriously think about additional education, not to mention continuous retraining, which can no longer be ignored.

As a result, the owner builds the organizational structure of the business far from optimal on his personal experience, while he has to spend considerable funds and his own efforts to support it. Of course, over time, he gradually becomes convinced that the costs of supporting it are too high, and it is necessary to do at least partial optimization of it, gradually revising his own methods of total control that are becoming obsolete. Nevertheless, it is worth recognizing that such a suboptimal structure turns out to be very viable, having proved in practice that despite the high operating costs, it can still ensure the successful development of large- and medium-sized Russian businesses. At the same time, it is necessary to revise the previously established opinion that such a structure corresponds only to the period of initial accumulation of property and capital formation, mainly for not-so-large Russian businesses.

This is largely due to the fact that it is precisely by ensuring almost total control on the part of the owner that such a structure is initially focused on promptly making not only strategic and tactical but even operational decisions both by the owner himself and with his direct participation. This allows you to quickly and effectively respond to the external competitive environment when appropriate management decision-making is required. Moreover, the decisions agreed by the owner of the business, especially at the operational, not to mention strategic, level, which, as practice shows, ensure sustainable and continuous business development in the conditions of Russian reality. First, this is important for a highly competitive environment, where management decisions agreed with the owner must be made and, most importantly, implemented in a short time. Second, in conditions of high uncertainty, which may also apply to the period of instability and the manifestation of local crisis phenomena (let us recall once again that this is typical for the Russian economy after 2009), the cost of an error in incorrect management decision-making at any level is very high. It is the high degree of control on the part of the owner, and the decision-making by him or with his direct participation, that makes it possible to successfully neutralize the erroneous actions of linear managers. Third, it is important when a business has to resist non-market competition, especially when large state-owned companies or companies with state participation, as well as large private businesses, are trying to carry out an unfriendly merger and absorb the business of our owner. In this case, the owner purposefully offers the least attractive parts of his business for absorption, removing the most attractive ones from under attack, and transferring his assets to them. After all, the fragmentation of the organizational and managerial structure of his business, difficult for the uninitiated, but not for the owner himself, especially when it comes not only to hierarchical, holding, but also network, with many small- and medium-sized businesses, does not allow us to correctly assess what is acquired or provided for absorption as a result. In part, this is also important in the fourth place, when the owner takes out loans or uses external financing, which he will distribute to businesses, which he organizes a deliberate bankruptcy, without fear of reputational losses.

The popularity of such structures in Russian business began to be talked about immediately after the 2008 crisis, when the owners of large- and medium-sized Russian businesses began to actively use them in the conditions of Russian reality. And then the first anti-Russian sanctions, the COVID-19 pandemic, and another anti-sanctions policy and the understanding that the development of the Russian economy in the coming years will not cause much optimism were added to the postcrisis recession. Of course, against this background, it will be necessary to reduce costs, especially quite understandable and excessive ones, due to management optimization, sooner or later, since these costs themselves are obvious for business. But the Russian owner is in no hurry to follow this already global general trend because his business continues to exist and develop very stably and efficiently all these years, therefore, it is not worth radically revising the existing structure, especially to abandon it, which has proven its usefulness for survival by its practice. Enough local, not so painful for the owner, cosmetic optimization, not affecting its basis, no more.

And here, in a long-term competition for the right to carry out the necessary first partial optimization, and then, having demonstrated their skills to the owner, and the second, then the third and all subsequent ones, getting with each step more and more access to understanding the organizational structure of the client's business, and therefore understanding what else he can be offered more, among all specialized legal and it was Russian private banking that won financial consultants. Which is not surprising, since already initially, at the preliminary stage, Russian private banking had a fairly detailed idea of the organizational and managerial structure of the owner's business.

Such an owner, even if he is not currently being serviced in a particular private banking division, falls within the scope of his interests. And as a typical target VIP client of private banking, he is well known for his financial preferences, including as the owner of such a complex structured business with his needs for its optimization. Of course, it could turn out that the private banking division did not have the opportunity to apply optimization schemes already tested earlier on other VIP clients for a new client. Either these schemes had to be further refined, or they did not even exist at all. This was not a big problem because it was easy to attract external counterparties, since the technologies of such attraction that are most suitable for both the bank and the client have already been worked out as part of the testing of open architecture technologies. And among these procedures, the most demanded by customers turned out to be the following: selection of the best counterparty, personalization of the offer, constant monitoring of the quality of service, liability insurance for decisions taken, and nonproliferation of confidential information. Here, immediately differing for the better from its consulting competitors, Russian private banking built its positioning, offering them as a certain standard of quality, to which the owner was already accustomed in private banking and which no one else simply had.

Yes, and Russian private banking began to face a similar partial restructuring of the business for its VIP clients within the framework of local optimization of its organizational and managerial structure of clients more and more often, and for more and more new tasks. So, he could almost constantly demonstrate his successful skills and experience to VIP clients, quite successfully strengthening his competitive position in relation to consultants. It all started with tax optimization programs and regulatory requirements for business deoffshorization, when private banking was able to use and supplement its previous local optimization methods. Later, two amnesties of capital followed and the mechanism of anti-Russian sanctions was launched. Which consistently provided domestic private banking with comfortable enough conditions for further improvement of local optimization methods. Moreover, these developments helped him to replicate his experience further, offering his solutions not only for a narrow group of owners of industrial enterprises but also for VIP clients from other sectors of the economy.

Since about the middle of the last decade, just before the COVID-19 pandemic, Russian private banking has been able to strengthen such positioning by targeting a broader group of target customers, including wealthier ones, forcing them to reconsider their loyalty to even their current financial institutions, including Western private banking. Such clients turned out to be Russian business owners who meet a purely age criterion (age 55–60 years, the business was opened back in the 90s of the last century), who began to think more and more about their departure from active affairs, planning its transfer to heirs, or direct sale (they turned to the latter task more often, especially if the transfer by inheritance was fraught with difficulties). As practice shows, even experience in solving similar tasks for other clients does not allow them to be replicated specifically if these clients are not included in the category of VIP clients. Although analogies are appropriate, an individual approach is much more important here than the ability to adapt existing developments. The ideal adaptation option is possible only if these are clients of a similar category in terms of solvency or VIP clients of private banking. This reduces the capabilities of consultants immediately because it was necessary to demonstrate your portfolio of solutions and proven practice for similar wealthy clients. But private banking, as it turned out, it was enough to go the other way and show that it was enough for him to get partial access to the client's business structure to solve the problem, and he would be able to build the necessary analogies based on the relevant experience of different stages of optimization, whereas other consultants needed to immediately get full access to the inherited or sold. And for this, the client needed to initially trust such a consultant, and it was difficult to immediately earn such trust, which private banking managed just within the framework of less sensitive work schemes for the client [3].

And exactly at the same time, just before the COVID-19 pandemic, Russian private banking got a new argument, absolutely not previously involved, to interest VIP client to proceed with immediate optimization of organizational and management structure of his business—the cyber hygiene of equity. Even now, this argument fits perfectly into the already familiar schemes of "selling fear" to VIP clients (more politically correct, of course, "selling risk management services"). And it is not even that the total number and quality of attacks on Russian business has increased significantly. Simply, taking advantage of the surge of interest in this problem, private banking has very skillfully focused on a certain type of vulnerabilities that is extremely sensitive for a VIP client. It is not even a targeted attack, which is usually backed by highly skilled attackers and from which it is very difficult to defend against. Even with the simplest type of attacks—phishing, it can be easy to gain access to a not too actively protected smartphone of an accountant and a trusted signatory for very sensitive operations for him, in the person of the former wife of a co-owner. And an attack from a low-skilled novice-neophyte hacker who is just learning his craft. Even he can no longer limit himself to a simple standard attack on a simple employee of a small business, but understand that it is necessary to attack part of the organizational and managerial structure of the holding company in which this business is included. There are more opportunities for him here, and the profit from the attacks is significantly higher. Well, if the neophyte stops in time, he will easily realize that the data obtained can be transferred to more trained professionals for a very good commission, who will more quickly, professionally, and effectively open the protection of the illuminated holding that is unattainable for him now. The main thing is not to be greedy, which has been taught for a long time in the darknet, using the example of carders who, massively withdrawing $10 from illuminated cards, should at some point simply understand that they have a platinum card in their hands, from which a more qualified attacker can withdraw at least several thousands, if neophyte directly sells it to him.

On the one hand, cyber hygiene turned out to be a very advantageous marketing move. The identification of typical vulnerabilities further strengthened the loyalty of VIP clients to the private banking division, which allowed him to go quite the beaten path and offer more complex services to such a client in the direction of further optimization of the organizational and managerial structure of his business; fortunately, there was another argument in favor of such a procedure. On the other hand, we are dealing here not with simple phishing but with its kind focused on attacks of VIP clients—whaling, where personalization of the profile of the target of the attack is important. And here, such experience of Russian private banking, especially in the ability to identify various problems of intercultural communication of the target of the attack, could be in demand not only when building adequate protection against the same phishing and its more complex variety but also for further strengthening the positioning of private banking itself. And although the necessary conditions for this were created even before the COVID-19 pandemic, they have only been fully realized now.

- Only medium-sized and niche banks in the Russian private banking market are still interested in observing cyber hygiene by their clients

It is the medium-sized and small niche Russian banks that are now in a situation where they can effectively compete for VIP clients who are starting to withdraw their assets from state-owned and other large banks and are looking for an alternative to their service [4]. This trend was formed also before the COVID-19 pandemic [5]. Since 2015, Russian VIP clients have been forced to repatriate assets previously withdrawn from the country under the pressure of anti-Russian sanctions. This process was slow and continuous. VIP clients withdrew their funds and invested them in Russia exclusively conservatively, preferring to wait out the time and develop the right strategy for the future in deposits, choosing the most reliable and large banks, mainly state-owned banks, for the placement of private banking units. Over time, some of them began to consider riskier and less conservative placement schemes, again through private banking of state-owned banks and only then medium-sized and niche banks [6]. Large banks, represented by state-owned banks, constantly pumped up with assets of new VIP clients from abroad, and realizing that the bulk of their clients have not yet matured to less conservative investments, did not pay attention to the outflow of funds to medium-sized and niche banks for individual products [7]. The target client was quite loyal to state-owned banks, so there was no need to worry about the outflow of some assets against this background. Moreover, for medium-sized and niche banks, the funds withdrawn even by a separate VIP client, unlike state-owned banks, turned out to be so significant that it was worth fighting for them by introducing new technologies for alternative investments.

Over time, state-owned banks would have to respond to such an outflow, and before the COVID-19 pandemic, they even began to think about how to quickly and efficiently build an appropriate product line, since they had resources for this, even in a crisis, not comparable to medium-sized and niche banks in their capabilities. But then, the COVID-19 pandemic broke out, and then, with the introduction, new sanctions also broke out.

VIP clients either completely withdrew their assets to the West or, for the most part, repatriated assets previously remaining in foreign banks back to the country. While the situation has not become more or less predictable, state banks have resumed the usual accumulation of VIP clients' funds in conservative assets, further increasing the customer base, completely ignoring the outflow of the most risky clients, which, although noted last year, has sharply decreased in volume. Only after a while, when the situation around sanctions became more or less clear by this spring, and the development of the economy became more predictable, VIP clients of state banks began to think about how they would have to place their assets and equity inside the country. And this is not only and not so much work with state-owned banks and exclusively conservative investments. Alternatives are required to place personal wealth not only in state-owned banks but by diversifying them across several Russian banks [8] with their private banking, as well as understanding where and how their own business will be serviced.

The total volume of assets of target VIP clients in state-owned banks, and clients who are still, as before the COVID-19 pandemic, are ready to be placed exclusively conservatively, preferring to serve both personal wealth and business in this way, is such that it simply does not make sense to pay attention to another round of asset outflow of an insignificant part of VIP-clients who are more risky from the point of view of investments, and who are thinking about withdrawing part of their business from state-owned banks in order to get higher returns. It would seem that the situation of 2 years ago is completely repeated, except that state banks have more VIP client assets, as well as medium-sized and niche banks are again trying to "sell fear," and the same. But not really. Medium-sized and niche banks already see that the VIP client is think ing not only about diversifying his personal fortune but also about business. And the experience is not just correct, but also effective, if we talk about the subsequent transition of a VIP client to service, over the previous 2 years, the same medium-sized and niche banks have acquired a lot.

Let us start with the fact that the crisis is a crisis, stagnation is stagnation, Western sanctions are sanctions, but business, for those VIP clients who decided to stay in Russia, with all these restrictions, will have to be built here and through domestic banks, there is simply nowhere else! Therefore, on the part of medium-sized and niche banks, another purposeful reversal is now taking place to the very proven model of domestic private banking, where large banks are positioned in the "universal VIP bank" model, and medium-sized and niche banks—in the niche "VIP club," copying technologies from the Swiss private bank, and which have long proved their effectiveness in Russia especially in the crisis situation in the economy, in which we have been almost continuously since about 2008 [9]. Here, the outflow of customers in the near future will be caused precisely by the search for a bank where VIP clients withdrawing part of their assets from state banks will choose banks in which they will receive a significant share in management and control precisely due to the fact that they will immediately become significant customers, and not one of the many VIPs. Well, over time, they will be able to transfer part of their business here, independently controlling the operational risks of the bank. And for clients, such repositioning of medium-sized and niche banks against large ones, when the latter, unlike the former, failed, except in isolated cases, to build a long-term model of investment in industrial assets and finally create an effective system of "corporate loyalty program" (with simultaneous servicing, aggregately, of both personal wealth and their own VIP business of the client), it is quite understandable and especially attractive in terms of their likely transition to service.

And it will not work out right away, the "VIP club" based on trust between its members will be created gradually, so that the outflow from state banks will not be so significant, but constant and increasing! The main thing is that such an outflow is not yet fundamental for state banks, but it is important for medium-sized and niche ones because for the latter, it is a potentially attractive client for whom you can and should fight, since such an opportunity is given.

Nevertheless, VIP clients' business will not be built in the right direction right away, there will be mistakes, someone, as it has already happened in a similar situation in Russian practice, will decide to even completely retire because of this. And this is a task for the same optimization, for the restructuring of capital, which will then be inherited or simply sold (which the domestic private banking has been talking about for a long time, and for which it came up with the whole current restructuring, waiting for a more "massive" generational change of Russian business). And to whom will such a VIP client come for this now? To the one who knows how to solve it at a more advanced stage—to those who managed to deal with the same cyber hygiene, and not only scared, and then, leveling the risks, building effective cyber defense, and reassured other VIP clients, proving that it is possible to work with him! Then VIP clients will think about how to work with the redundant structure and optimize it, reducing the costs of its maintenance so that the continuity of processes is maintained.

And they will think again about medium-sized and niche banks, which do not have a long-standing experience in such optimization, initially focused on the individual owner personally. And not to a wider group of targeted VIP clients from several types of co-owners at once, where their individual preferences may be lost, as with large banks for which such personalization is not yet a priority against the background of more important tasks. In addition, medium-sized and niche banks demonstrate their ability to effectively solve such a task, through arguments familiar to VIP clients, related to the introduction of the right cyber hygiene. The fact is that large banks, in the conditions of sanctions against them directly, have been busy with more important tasks for themselves over the past year, turning to using more familiar and time-tested arguments for optimizing the organizational and managerial structure than those that have not yet been sufficiently tested, related to cyber hygiene.

8.2   VIP Clients

- **Russian vendors within information security are inferior to medium-sized and niche banks in the ability to independently solve the tasks of their VIP clients**

As a result, medium-sized and niche banks now had to cooperate directly with vendors in the field of information security. And it seemed that the best opportunities to close all of the issues of information security of such niche customers (target VIP clients) of domestic private banking in this situation remain with more specialized players, domestic vendors, who have significant resources for this. After all, to level out the vulnerabilities of the VIP client's organizational and managerial structure that have already been identified, it would be enough for them to develop several generalized, wider solutions for the whole group of such niche customers less personalized for each specific VIP client. Especially if we talk about the change of priorities regarding the protection of the same VIP clients, who quickly turned from significant to just niche buyers and customers. At the same time, it does not take into account the fact that quite simple cyber attacks can be quite dangerous for such clients with their identified vulnerabilities. First of all, these are phishing-based attacks, which are very easy to defend against, but even such protection is not yet considered by customers. However, attackers prefer to start with such simple attacks. Only when meeting with a properly built defense, attackers are forced to think about the costs of more complex and targeted attacks, and in the end think about shifting attention to a less protected client. Let us look at this in more detail.

In the spring of 2022, with the beginning of the special operation in Ukraine, the number and quality of attacks on Russian business from outside is expected to increase. To a greater extent, this growth was associated with the simplest and most rapidly scalable external cyberattacks on Russian business in general, with minimal selectivity and not requiring solid qualifications and serious training from the attacker. These include, first of all, phishing and DDoS attacks, for which, by the end of March, Kaspersky Lab recorded an increase of 54% compared to February, and almost 8-fold compared to the same period of the previous year[1]. At the same time, according to StormWall, up to 30% of attacks were carried out from the US territory and 47% from EU countries[2]. It is quite expected that in the spring, these attacks only intensified and became more complicated. Hackers' interest in a rather rare and highly specialized type of phishing like whaling, initially focused on complex personalized attacks of the wealthiest, VIP clients, has grown especially.

Such an unusual interest in such rare attacks was mentioned at both professional financial and banking conferences in the first half of 2022, when issues of the specifics of servicing the target VIP client category of domestic private banking, similar in consistency, and at cybersecurity conferences, including with the participation of the author (CISO FORUM XV[3] and XII MobiFinance-2022[4]). It was noted that the targets of the attacks are quite clear, and they use already established stereotypes in the behavior of VIP clients, which make it easy to identify target vulnerabilities. Moreover, the economy of attacks is determined by the interests of the main stakeholders, including not only hackers and VIP clients themselves but also vendors and banking employees engaged in cybersecurity, as well as the divisions of Russian private banking themselves.

To begin with, the most trained hackers, especially those close to government structures, are initially aimed at substantial profits, and not necessarily monetized into fiat currencies, but even with a significant political component. Having considerable resources, they are ready to go to significant costs in preparation, purposefully and carefully preparing the final attack, at least compensating for the costs incurred. It is quite difficult to defend against such attacks, but by the summer of last year, they simply were not yet prepared to attack Russian business, and the hackers themselves had just begun to reorient themselves to Russia. In addition, the object of their targeted attacks in Russia is the most solvent large business, as well as state-owned companies and government structures, which rarely share the results of attacks on themselves, especially if they are successful. So, such information simply could not have appeared last summer yet. Let us not forget here about the good training of domestic cybersecurity specialists in large businesses, as well as state-owned companies and government structures. Among other things, the vast majority of them belong

---

[1]https://www.kaspersky.ru/about/press-releases/2022_ddos-osada-atak-vsyo-bolshe-ataki-vsyo-dlinnee

[2]https://stormwall.pro/blog-news-hacktivists-started-attacks-on-russian-companies

[3]https://infor-media.ru/events/118/3171/

[4]https://mobifinance.ru/

to the category of enterprises of critical infrastructure, which are initially strictly regulated by the measures taken in relation to the necessary organizational and methodological procedures of cyber defense, which also initially ensures that the overall level of their security is much higher than the average for the same Russian business.

Therefore, the simplest and most scalable general-purpose cyberattacks were immediately used to attack Russian business, which were immediately used not only by beginners but also by experienced hackers. But the gradual strengthening and complication of attacks were directly related to the actions of just experienced hackers who preferred to improve the same phishing and DDoS attacks, using more serious personalization of the client profile and more selective targeting of the client, just presented in the technologies previously rarely used, but here it immediately became very popular—whaling. The corresponding identification of vulnerabilities allowed them to attack Russian business immediately or fix the vulnerabilities found for the future, for more carefully prepared subsequent targeted attacks. And the economics of such an approach is quite obvious, since attacks of greater complexity and on other vectors cannot yet be compared with lower costs with a comparable result from the same phishing and whaling. The fact is that the hourly cost of the work of a trained hacker remains high, making up a significant part of the initial costs. But we still have to add to this the significant costs of the organizational period, the unhurried selection and preliminary testing for the penetration of identified vulnerabilities, as well as the subsequent monetization of profits.

At the same time, the current approach to "urgent import substitution" of means of protection from Western vendors, presented by regulators as a priority task by domestic cybersecurity specialists, still seems to leave the possibility for targeted attacks until the necessary means of protection are developed and implemented. Despite the fact that some vulnerabilities have not yet been identified, and they have yet to be discovered by the same hackers, all this will take time, during which, with strict and stimulating supervision by regulators over the execution of their own orders, sufficient protection can be quickly implemented. However, such hackers can immediately spend part of their resources in another way, on more expensive means of penetration and on a wider range of attack tools themselves, not limited to relatively cheap and easy-to-use phishing and DDoS attacks. Sooner or later, despite the slow but continuous improvement of Russian security tools, these hackers still have a very real chance to detect a vulnerability that has not yet been closed by protection. Since the autumn of last year, as part of the analysis of supply and demand, we have been observing interest in appropriate technologies that allow us to quickly attack such vulnerabilities while their protection is only being built. The offer from qualified hackers is growing, but it is noteworthy that they prefer to provide such vulnerabilities to others, fixing the costs of detecting them, and continuing to use phishing and DDoS. After all, the whole question is how quickly this vulnerability will be eliminated, and whether it is already being eliminated now, which is very important for an attacker. However, for hackers, not everything is so clear.

We should immediately note that within the framework of the "urgent import substitution" strategy, the process of switching to Russian solutions itself is not carried out immediately and may take several years. In addition, such a replacement is being implemented in stages, although continuously, with the gradual introduction of Russian developments that have ceased to be updated and accompanied by Western ones. The preservation of the latter in operation, while they cannot be completely replaced, already in itself represents the original source of vulnerabilities known to everyone, which is why it is necessary to eliminate them as soon as possible, introducing at least some temporary protection solutions, which over time will have to be gradually refined to more or less adequate. Everything is more or less simple when it comes to replacing a separate product, rather than an integral ecosystem of products from Western vendors (especially the previously popular leaders of this market in Russia—Cisco, Check Point and Fortinet), which is much more difficult to replace with a temporary palliative. After all, replacing Western solutions with domestic ones, it is necessary to evaluate not just their compatibility with Western ones, but also to take into account the possibility of a single operation, replaced by domestic solutions within a separate system that somehow replaces the past ecosystem. And this is another cost in the form of significant costs for finding Russian solutions that can work together, when there are not so many resources at all, which significantly reduces the possibilities for protection. It remains to use the same temporary palliatives, hoping that they will not be quickly opened by qualified hackers. And if they are opened, it may turn out that the refinement of a particular vulnerability has already been completed randomly in parallel, and by the time of the attack, the hacker will have to resist a full-fledged or more serious protection, which he had not previously counted on. And the economics of evaluating the profitability of an attack forces hackers to return to the simplest attacks, in the form of the same phishing and DDoS, without using too complex ones.

At the same time, the Russian business in the field of information security has fully adapted to work in such negative conditions and is only improving the technology of using temporary palliatives. After all, since 2014, the entire Russian business has continued to survive in extremely unfavorable and deteriorating conditions of sanctions to the tightening of which it has managed to somehow adapt during all this time. Therefore, when we talk about information security, we should not forget that even before the start of the COVID-19 pandemic, we have already begun, albeit slowly, but quite consciously, to switch to exclusively domestic solutions in advance. Well, then even the Russian business, which had not thought about digitalization before, began to introduce remote work [10, 11], and the need for data cyber hygiene based on just domestic solutions. And even if now individual companies know almost everything about phishing, but still the economy of hacker attacks remains tied to it. The simplest phishing attacks and more complex whaling have already been tested in the first approximation on Russian specifics, so with the development of a special operation in Ukraine, attackers have minimal adaptation for replication in a more massive segment of Russian business [12].

8.3   Cyber Defense Against Simple Threats

- **It is medium-sized and niche banks that are further strengthening their positions not only in the field of domestic private banking but also in building effective cyber defense against simple threats**

Here, just medium-sized and niche banks had to work more closely with vendors in the field of information security. Such generalized, less personalized vendor solutions turned out to be very effective just against fairly simple phishing and DDoS attacks and were easily adapted to the changed conditions later, when the total number increased and their quality (traditional phishing smoothly evolved to whaling) increased. However, these solutions are still too general, and in order to successfully sell them to niche customers, VIP clients by vendors, and a personal approach to each potential customer is still required, radically different from the approach they developed for wider promotion. This is where domestic private banking can be very competitive, by enhancing personalization just by making the promotion of such simple products for VIP client more visible [13]. It was also mentioned by Russian analysts, and not only at specialized seminars on private banking, devoted specifically to the peculiarities of working with Russian VIP clients under sanctions, but also on information security conferences in Moscow (Positive Hack Days 12 Forum[5]), with the active participation of the author as a whaling topic speaker.

Moreover, in this case, it is medium-sized and niche banks that become the only players who will be able to take advantage of the temporary decline in interest in this problem from other traditional competitors and even to further strengthen their positioning in the field of both domestic private banking and implementing effective cyber defense against more or less simple threats. And if we talk in more detail, we should start within the framework of the already mentioned example, it is worth trying to draw the VIP client's attention to the fact that, right now, the number of attacks immediately turns into quality, especially attacks from novice hackers, neophytes, who become the most dangerous. The number of such hackers has grown noticeably over the entire time, since a common politically biased goal has appeared for them. And although their qualifications are not so high, and they use standard, simplest penetration technologies, for example, in the form of the same simple phishing, this is especially dangerous for Russian private banking and domestic VIP clients, since it is these attacks that quickly refocus on typical vulnerabilities.

Moreover, these simplest attacks become very productive precisely because of the increase in the total number of objects of the attacks themselves, from the growing number of novice-neophyte hackers who are simply forced to look for new objects in order not to compete too much with each other! And just with such an increase in the number of small- and medium-sized businesses under attack, simply by virtue of the law of large numbers, not a separate small- and medium-sized business company may suddenly be under attack, but directly part of the VIP client's holding structure. And here we can already talk about a higher probability of subsequent cyberattacks against VIP clients, specifically focusing the attention of customers on them. And it has become much easier to promote such cyber hygiene services to the personal manager of a VIP client of a medium-sized and niche bank than it was 3 or 4 years ago. He gets a good assistant — this is the internal information security unit, which deals with similar tasks to protect the bank itself. And a specialist from such a unit, who can easily be turned into an assistant consultant in a not-so-much bureaucratic by comparison with a large bank, not only deals with similar tasks for a VIP client but also can quite simply and clearly state the most difficult problem to a nonprofessional user in the person of the same VIP client. Moreover, using similar methods of persuasion, as it happened to him more than once in

---

[5]https://phdays.com/program/

his native bank, when he convinced top managers of the bank of the need to introduce certain means of cyber defense.

It should be especially noted that the same top managers have become very competent in matters of information security. But they traditionally act in small- and medium-sized and niche banks as curators of the most important VIP clients for the bank, and along with personal managers can successfully promote the product range of their bank, in this case, just the services of cybersecurity services. In addition, everything together can be scaled due to similar solutions from bank counterparties already here and now. Let us not forget that the Russian bank is initially under strict control of regulators, so the "average temperature in the hospital," if we talk about the bank's security, comparing it with the security of the capital and even the VIP client's business and which it can offer here, is much higher! Therefore, the VIP client is inclined to listen to the advice of the private banking unit especially from medium-sized and niche banks, whose attention from regulators is traditionally high. In addition, he will be able to recommend the most suitable and proven vendor solutions to the client. Let us not forget about the visibility of the presentation for the VIP client of such seemingly simple to develop, but very effective in attacking their typical vulnerabilities, phishing attacks. The same technologies of generative neural networks are sometimes used by the VIP client himself as entertainment, and this does not cause him any rejection! To search for vulnerabilities, it is enough to use the latest modifications of the same ChatGPT when analyzing the profile of the attack object. For example, having before his eyes a list of regulations updated in the last 6 months that the same accountant needs to know, a personal manager, without resorting to the services of a bank security officer sitting right here, next to him, can quickly make a list of topics in direct letters to which this particular accountant, in full compliance with his public data, unequivocally will react by opening an infected email or clicking on an external link. And all this has been presented in real time to VIP clients in recent months, proving the need to pay close attention to cyber hygiene.

However, the current situation is not limited to organizational and managerial structure's optimization but by choosing the further path of development of both the private banking unit itself and the entire bank as a whole. Phishing protection is protection against the simplest attacks. Why stop there only? You can try to scale the bank's already proven solutions to more complicated attacks of VIP clients. This is already a higher level of their loyalty not only for the private banking unit but also for the entire bank as a whole. After all, private banking can even focus on global cyber protection of medium and small business legal entities for the bank's corporate business unit, which allows us to talk about the same cyber protection. However, this is still the specialization of the bank's corporate business, and it is to him that all existing developments of the private banking division should be transferred to improve the efficiency of the bank as a whole. But as practice shows, such a position does not match for large banks, where the private banking unit will be interested right now, when there is serious competition for resources within the bank, to redistribute part of the resources from the corporate department in its favor, even closing part of its functions. And it turns out that right now the heads of medium-sized and niche banks have a good opportunity to move to this more intelligently, without much expense, strengthening the loyalty of their own customers, especially if this task is formulated much more broadly, and not "Why should a bank take care of the cyber hygiene of its VIP clients?" but "Why should a bank care about the cyber hygiene of its corporate clients?" The potential for such a change in the tactics of banking business is already present, but they have yet to realize it.

8.4   Conclusion

Even before the COVID-19 pandemic, it was demonstrated that implementation of protection technologies against the most advanced cyber attacks (whaling as complex targeted phishing) in the Russian industry should be carried out within the profile of the owner. This is where the experience of analyzing intercultural communication by domestic private banking can be quite successful not only with effective protection against whaling-style cyber threats but also to increase its local competitiveness. Finally, now, remaining the only players in Russian private banking, medium-sized and niche banks keep interest in dealing with cyber hygiene issues, they try to strengthen their positioning in the field of both domestic private banking and implementing effective cyber defense against more or less simple threats.

References

1. Gusev, A., New cyberattacks vectors of Russian critical infrastructure enterprises: Domestic private banking sector view within AI protection methods. *Procedia Comput. Sci.*, 169, 205–206, 2020.
2. Tkachenko, I., Pervukhina, I., Zlygostev, A., Modeling the contribution and benefits of company stakeholders. *Manager*, 11, 2–15, 2020. https://doi.org/10.29141/2218-5003-2020-11-2-1.

3. Frolova, E.E., Prospects for the development of private banking in russian commercial banks. *Entrepreneur's Guide*, 13, 76–85, 2020. https://doi.org/10.24182/2073-9885-2020-13-1-76-85

4. Kasyanov, R., Digitalization: Service "robot advisors" in private banking. *Magazine: Banking Serv.*, 4, 25–30, 2020.

5. Gusev, A., New vectors of cyberattacks and new is methods for critical infrastructure enterprises: Russian private banking view. *Mech. Mach. Sci.*, 80, 237–245, 2020.

6. Gusev, A., Domestic private banking solutions can be quite successful as an effective protection against whaling-style cyber attacks which are used as a basis for more complex targeted phishing. *Procedia Comput. Sci.*, 213, 391–9, Jan. 1, 2022.

7. Timokhina, G.S., The study of consumer incentive system on the private banking market. *Bull. South Ural State Univ.*, 12, 237–245, 2018. https://doi.org/10.14529/em180219.

8. Loginov, M. and Usova, N.Y., Private banking pattern in Russia. *Manage. Issues*, 59, 64–77, 2019.

9. Loktionova, Y., Yanina, O., Shinkareva, O., Osobennosti, Features and methods of personal bank service in a segment of private banking. *Economy*, 21, 43–53, 2019. https://doi.org/10.25688/2312-6647.2019.20.2.05.

10. Khominich, I., Savvina, O., Semenov, E., Wealth management industry: factors and trends of modern development in the context of digitalization. *Magazine: Banking Serv.*, 7–8, 22–29, 2020. https://doi.org/10.36992/2075-1915_2020_7-8_22.

11. Starodubtseva, E. and Kasyanov, R., Digitalization in the wealth service segment in private banking. *Magazine: Finances, Money, Investments*, 73, 23–30, 2020. https://doi.org/10.36992/2222-0917_2020_1_23.

12. Gusev, A., Assessment of investment risks by Russian private banking in the post-crisis era. *J. Financial Risk Manage.*, 66, 237–245, 2021. https://doi.org/10.36627/2221-7541-2021-2-2-122-127.

13. Lehto, M., Cyber-attacks against critical infrastructure, in: *Cyber Security: Critical Infrastructure Protection*, pp. 3–42, Springer International Publishing, Cham, Apr. 3, 2022.

9

Determinants of Financial Distress in Select Indian Asset Reconstruction Companies Using Artificial Neural Networks

Shashank Sharma* and Ajay Kumar Kansal

School of Management, Gautam Buddha University, Greater Noida, India

Abstract

An analysis has been performed to examine the financial health of select asset reconstruction companies (ARCs) registered with the Reserve Bank of India (RBI). For the analysis, 10 key firmlevel financial variables have been assessed for the period 2011–2012 to 2019–2020 and analysed through multilayer perceptron artificial neural networks (MLP-ANNs) and popular Altman's Zscore models. In addition, an impact analysis of Insolvency and Bankruptcy Code (IBC) on the capital structure of ARCs has been presented as an additional section. Rationale behind the analysis has been the concern that any contingent financial distress situation in ARCs may trigger a triplebalancesheet problem, which may affect nonfinancial corporates, the banking sector, and ARCs altogether. Findings indicate a gradual rise of financial distress in select ARCs over the last decade and among the selected variables—return on equity, debt to total assets, and return on capital employed surfaced as the most important indicators. Similarly, the MLP-ANN model has returned an average root mean square error of 0.15 with an overall average classification accuracy of 95.4% during the training and testing phases of the model. Furthermore, introduction of IBC may have a significant positive impact on the capital structure of ARCs, and deterrents to financial health of ARCs may include a lack of competitive environment among ARCs, the presence of vintage stressed assets on their portfolio, and a capacity deficit considering the workload.

Corresponding author: inbox2903@gmail.com
Shashank Sharma: ORCID: https://orcid.org/0000-0002-5718-0589
Ajay Kumar Kansal: ORCID: https://orcid.org/0000-0001-8030-0596

Ambrish Kumar Mishra, Shweta Anand, Narayan C. Debnath, Purvi Pokhariyal and Archana Patel (eds.) *Artificial Intelligence for Risk Mitigation in the Financial Industry*, (209–228) © 2024 Scrivener Publishing LLC

Keywords: Financial distress, default, resolution, recovery, revival, stressed assets, corporate finance, artificial intelligence

JEL Classification: G01, G20, G33, G34, G38

Abbreviations

ARCs	asset restructuring companies
AUM	assets under management
EMIS	Financial Database of Companies
EBITDA	Earnings Before Interests, Taxes, Depreciation and Amortization
EBIT	Earnings Before Interests and Taxes
F/Y	Financial Year
GOI	Government of India
MLP-ANN	Multilayer perceptron artificial neural network
NARCL	National Asset Reconstruction Company Limited
NPAs	Nonperforming assets
RBI	Reserve Bank of India
SARFAESI Act, 2002	Securitisation and Reconstruction of Financial Assets and Enforcement of Security Interest Act, 2002
SR	Security receipts

9.1   Introduction

Financial distress has been an intermittent barrier in the well-being of any business entity. After independence, since the inception of the industrialization phase in India, the events of financial distress has been evident in the literature. Nowadays, even in the era of modernday asset quality monitoring and asset classification norms, this inevitable concern still remains. In recent times, the issue of rising nonperforming assets (NPAs) with substantial share of nonfinancial corporates may be a cause of concern caused by financial distress of the corporate sector affecting the banking sector [1].

In addition, in any financial system, an effective resolution framework may have a significant positive impact on the nation's economic growth. Consequently, governments have been proactively involved in the resolution of stressed assets. However, considering the quantum of distress, combined with low revival/recovery rates, channels of resolutions have been overwhelmed [2].

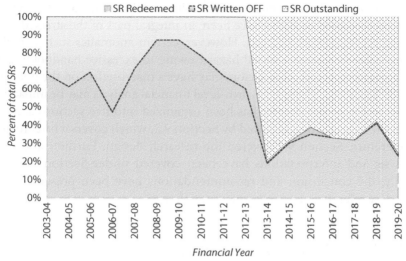

Source: Compiled by the author, data sourced from [4].

Figure 9.1 Security receipts (SRs) held by ARCs.

Additionally, with the enactment of SARAESI Act, 2002, asset reconstruction companies (ARCs) have evolved as a channel of resolution for stressed assets under the regulatory control of RBI. At present, there are 29 ARCs[1] operating in India, including recently set up government-owned company NARCL. Moreover, ARC business operations involve purchasing nonperforming stressed assets from banks in consideration of expertise in resolution, haircuts, management fees, and other incentives.

However, there has been a lack of competitive environment among ARCs, considering the fact that approximately 67.0% and 76.0% of capital base and assets under management (AUM), respectively, have been held by the top 5 ARCs. Furthermore, debt has been a major source of funds in ARCs, particularly from the banking sector, and its profitability has been volatile [3]. Thus, any contingent event of financial distress in the ARCs may trigger a triple balance sheet problem caused by stressed assets of the corporate sector sold to ARCs by banks, with capital borrowings from the banking sector. As evident in Figure 9.1, there has been a marginal number of security receipts (SRs)[2] written off every year.

---

[1] https://rbidocs.rbi.org.in/rdocs/content/DOCs/LSCRCRBI07092016.xlsx
[2] Security receipts (SRs) may be termed as the non-tradable financial instruments transferred by ARCs to the financial institutions in purchase consideration of stressed or nonperforming assets.

Therefore, analysis of the financial health of ARCs may contribute to the existing literature, as ARCs have been an integral part of the stressed asset resolution framework of India. However, certain anomalies such as policy and regulatory changes, moral hazard owing to excessive handholding by the government, and other factors may have a macro-effect on the financial health. Therefore, a long-term firm-level financial analysis may be impactful.

Accordingly, the chapter has been organized into five sections starting from the Introduction followed by Section 9.2, which covers a brief review of literature. Section 9.3 covered the research design. Furthermore, data analysis and interpretations have been covered under Section 9.4, and finally, the conclusion and recommendations have been presented, followed by references and relevant appendices.

9.2   Brief Review of Literature

Extant literature has documented the determinants effecting the financial distress and reconstruction of distressed assets. Accordingly, the literature has been segregated into two sections, where the first part shall discuss the dimensions of financial distress, followed by operations of asset reconstruction.

Empirically, Altman *et al.* (2017) discussed the classification performance of the original Z-score model invented by Prof. Altman for predicting the financial distress in companies, constructed using financial ratios extracted from annual financial reports of the companies and analyzed statistically through multivariate discriminant analysis. The Z-score model has been relevant for over four decades and has been used extensively in the credit rating market as an indicator of financial distress. Key strengths of this model have been its simplicity and accuracy [5].

Bawa *et al.* (2019) analyzed the panel data composed of stressed assets in majority of the Indian banking sector using a set of 31 financial ratios for the period 2007–2014. Findings indicate a significant relationship of firm-level financial information with nonperforming assets, with an overall accuracy of 85.0% [6].

Jan (2021) discussed the use of artificial neural networks (ANNs)[3] in predicting the prospective financial distress in the listed companies of Taiwan, and findings indicate an overall prediction accuracy rate of 94.2%. In addition, to measure the overall potency and determinant ability of the model, sensitivity analysis has been conducted [7].

---

[3] Artificial neural network is a tool, developed using application of artificial intelligence, for classifying and predicting complex problems with greater accuracy.

Additionally, the main objective of distress prediction has been the timely effective resolution of distress, which may prevent the time and cost associated with insolvency proceedings and resultant deterioration of a company's value. Thus, asset reconstruction ensures the revival of the distressed company, while operating as a going-concern entity. In fact, certain alternatives have been followed by Indian ARCs in the reconstruction operations, namely, liquidation, aforementioned going-concern approach, or mixed approaches, according to the requirements of the situation [8]. Moreover, resolution of distressed assets and reconstruction may be conducted by raising new capital or, as an alternative, renegotiating with financial/operational creditors [9]. Accordingly, the approaches followed for the resolution may determine the outcomes of debt restructuring. Moreover, the time and costs involved in insolvency proceedings may impact the probability of effective reconstruction.

Apparently, ARCs may adopt various alternatives to distress resolution, such as settlement of dues of borrower, rescheduling of payments, possession of distressed assets, or enforcement of security interest, as an alternative [10]. Moreover, reconstruction operations may include renegotiations with creditors, *viz.*, out-of-court settlements under section 12A or Pre-packaged insolvency resolution process (PPIRP) to avoid bankruptcy under the legal provisions of IBC, 2016. Empirically, more than 90.0% of distressed companies firstly renegotiate amicably and may file for insolvency as a last resort.

In a similar context, Meher and Puntambekar (2018) analyzed the ARCs, their resolution mechanism, and problems faced by them in India. Findings suggest that the total net worth of all ARCs may not be sufficient to purchase and resolve all of the stressed assets of the Indian banking sector. In addition, there has been a significant correlation between the profitability of ARCs and stressed assets of the banking sector [11].

RBI (2021) discussed the concerns in the asset resolution framework in India, specifically, ARCs. The main concerns have been the absence of competitive environment among ARCs, with 62.0% of the total AUM being managed by the top 3 ARCs. Furthermore, majority of the resolution work has been performed by ARCs just through rescheduling of payments. Therefore, the main purpose of asset reconstruction and resolution may not be realized [12].

9.3   Research Design

During the analysis, a few concerns have surfaced, such as "the underlying risk that the ARCs may face a situation of financial distress themselves" and "expertise of the ARCs in financial distress revival business may mitigate the aforementioned risk of facing financial distress situation."

Accordingly, select objectives have been formulated for the analysis, as follows:

I.   Analyzing the financial health of the asset restructuring companies in India
II. Exploring the financial determinants indicating distress
III. Analyzing the impact of Insolvency and Bankruptcy Code, 2016, on the capital structure of ARCs.

Initially, for the analysis of the first objective, firm-level secondary data composed of annual financials of all 29 ARCs registered with the RBI have been explored from various sources. However, considering the fact that the top 5 ARCs hold majority of the AUM and taking into account the age-related bias, well-established companies incorporated before 2007–2008 have been considered.

Accordingly, a data sample of 12 ARCs has been considered, with data availability for the period of 2011–2012 to 2019–2020[4]. Thus, findings corresponding to these 12 companies may be generalized for the whole population. In addition, financial data have been sourced from the EMIS[5] data repository.

Further to the analysis, 10 key financial ratios have been identified from the review of literature and sourced from the EMIS database. Thus, 108 firm-year observations with total of 1,080 data points[6] have been included in the analysis. In addition to the ratio analysis, Altman's Z-scores, being an important indicator for the probable future financial distress situation, have been also sourced and analyzed.

Furthermore, the second objective has been serviced using an artificial intelligence tool, through constructing a formative "multilayer perceptron artificial neural network (MLP-ANN)" model, to analyze the key financial ratios, with potent determinant ability in explaining the variations in prospective financial distress situations. The rationale behind using MLP-ANN

---

[4] The financial years 2020–2021 and 2021–2022, being an abnormal year owing to the pandemic, have been excluded from the analysis.

[5] EMIS is a subscription-based financial database repository based in London, UK, with data related to companies registered and operating in 197 emerging markets all over the world.

[6] Ten financial ratios of 12 asset reconstruction companies for 9 financial years (2011–2012 to 2019–2020).

has been its efficacy on small sample sizes, absence of underlying assumptions of linearity, normality, and homoscedasticity and outlier management [12]. For the analysis, "financial distress condition" has been taken as a dependent variable that has been transformed into a binary form through observing the Altman's Zscores, where a Z-score less than 0.5 has been coded as "1" indicative of distress and "0" otherwise. Similarly, 10 financial ratios have been selected as covariates. Moreover, financial ratios reflecting the overall profitability, efficiency, liquidity, and leverage of the corporate business have been selected for the analysis. Consequently, ideal values of particular ratios and its ideal expected trend have been presented (Table 9.1).

Additionally, a correlation matrix of the variables considered for the analysis has been presented (Table 9.2).

Table 9.1 Select financial ratios considered for the analysis.

Type	Abbreviation	Ratios	Ideal value	Formula
Profitability	ROA	Return on assets	0.05	Net profit/Average total assets
	ROCE	Return on capital employed	0.20	EBIT/Equity + Long-term liabilities
	NPM	Net profit margin	0.10	Net profit/Total sales
Efficiency	TAT	Total asset turnover	1x	Main business revenue/Average total assets
Liquidity	CR	Current ratio	2x	Current assets/Current liabilities
Leverage	D_TA	Debt-to-total assets ratio	0.50	Total debt/Total assets
	D_E	Debt-to-equity ratio	2x	Total debt/Total equity
	ICR	Interest coverage ratio	1.5x	EBIT/Interest charges
Financial distress indicator		Altman's Z-scores [5]	>0.5= Safe Zone	3.25 + 6.56*Working capital/Total assets + 3.26*Retained Earnings/Total assets + 6.72*EBIT/Total assets + 1.05*Market or book value of equity/Total assets

Source: Compiled by author.

Table 9.2 Correlation matrix of the variables considered for the analysis.

Variables	ROA	ROE	NPM	TAT	CR	QR	D_TA	D_E	ICR
ROA	1.00								
ROE	0.76	1.00							
NPM	0.77	0.45	1.00						
TAT	0.55	0.69	0.15	1.00					
CR	0.08	-0.09	0.01	-0.06	1.00				
QR	0.08	-0.09	0.01	-0.06	1.00	1.00			
D_TA	-0.12	0.23	-0.17	0.11	-0.34	-0.34	1.00		
D_E	-0.19	0.17	-0.21	0.03	-0.30	-0.30	0.89	1.00	
ICR	0.24	0.04	0.32	-0.02	0.08	0.08	-0.25	-0.23	1.00

Source: Computed by author.

In addition, panel regression analysis has been performed through introducing a dummy variable to study the impact of Insolvency and Bankruptcy Code, 2016, on the capital structure of ARCs and presented in Section 9.4.4. Furthermore, the sample adequacy requirements for the MLP-ANN model have been calculated using the 50x rule, where the number of observations must be 50.0 times the number of independent variables [13]. Therefore, 1,080 observations have been twice the prescribed limits for sample adequacy. SPSS software has been used for performing the MLP-ANN analysis, and a conceptual model diagram has been presented in Figure 9.2.

9.4   Data Analysis and Interpretation

9.4.1   Financial Ratio Analysis

Selected annual frequency financial ratios, corresponding to the sample companies have been sourced and analyzed considering ideal values[7] as mentioned in Table 9.1, from 2011–2012 to 2019–2020. Accordingly, all

---

[7] Standard/ideal values may differ from industry to industry. For instance, the Indian NBFC industry average ROA has been approximately 3.0% (RBI, 2021). Thus, for the reliability of analysis, universally acceptable standard values have been considered.

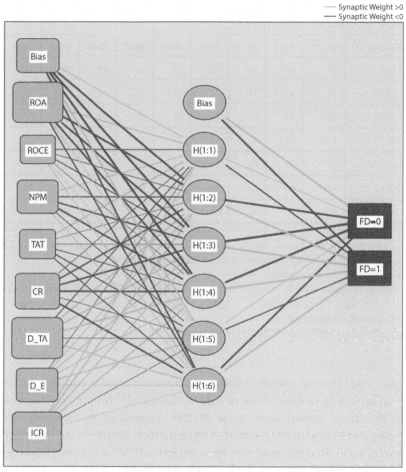

Hidden layer activation function: Hyperbolic tangent
Output layer activation function: Sigmoid

Figure 9.2 Multilayer perceptron artificial neural network model constructed for the analysis. *ROA, return on assets; ROCE, return on capital employed; NPM, net profit margin; TAT, total asset turnover; CR, current ratio; D_TA, debt-to-total assets ratio; D_E, debt-to-equity ratio; ICR, interest coverage ratio. H (1–6) are hidden layers of neural network model, and FD is a binary variable, where "1" indicates financial distress and vice versa. Source: Compiled by the author.

1,080 data points have been analyzed, and the number of companies having values less than ideal values has been presented year-wise (Table 9.3).

Thus, a gradual year-on-year rise of companies having unfavorable ratios, such as return on assets, net profit margin, current and quick ratio, debt to total assets, and interest coverage ratio has been evident in ARC

Table 9.3 Summary table of financial ratio analysis for the period 2011–2012 to 2019–2020 (Number of companies**).

Financial ratios^	2012*	2013	2014	2015	2016	2017	2018	2019	2020
ROA < 0.05	09	07	10	09	10	11	09	08	10
ROCE < 0.20	12	12	11	12	11	12	11	12	11
NPM < 0.10	01	01	00	00	01	00	01	01	03
TAT < 1x	12	12	12	12	12	12	12	12	12
CR < 2x	01	01	05	04	04	05	07	04	05
D_TA > 0.50	05	05	06	09	09	09	09	10	09
D_E > 2x	00	00	01	01	00	02	02	04	02
ICR < 1.5x	00	03	01	01	02	01	01	01	05

*Years mentioned in the table represents corresponding financial years.
** Sample size = Total 12 companies.
^ ROA, return on assets; ROCE, return on capital employed; NPM, net profit margin; TAT, total asset turnover; CR, current ratio; D_TA, debt-to-total assets ratio; D_E, debt-to-equity ratio; ICR, interest coverage ratio.
Source: Compiled by author using data sourced from EMIS.

businesses over the last decade. However, return on capital employed and return on equity have been unfavorable in almost all companies over the studied duration; nonetheless, most of the companies maintained net profit margins. Consequently, establishing a distress situation on the basis of financial ratio analysis may not be sufficient. Thus, Altman's Z-scores being an indicator of distress have been sourced from the database.

9.4.2   Altman's Z-Score Analysis

Altman's Z-scores have been sourced from the EMIS database and presented as an addition to financial ratio analysis. The Z-score model has been constructed with the combination of distinct financial ratios, not considered in former Section 9.4.1. Although Altman has not suggested Zscores primarily for financial companies, however, considering the fact that Z-scores may have been the most popular and accurate indicator in gauging the likelihood of prospective financial distress situations, it may be resourceful as a representation. Additionally, the 3-year moving average trend has been considered and presented for the long-term representation (Table 9.4).

Table 9.4 Altman's Z-scores of selected ARCs for the period 2013–2014 to 2019–2020 (3-year moving average Z-scores*).

Company#	2013–2014	2014–2015	2015–2016	2016–2017	2017–2018	2018–2019	2019–2020
C_1	03.73	02.94	03.29	03.21	03.54	03.50	03.57
C_2	07.20	05.92	06.82	09.23	18.77	35.98	56.84
C_3	01.92	02.09	03.26	06.81	13.64	14.41	12.88
C_4	03.01	03.58	16.97	28.65	41.86	41.97	36.70
C_5	18.74	14.66	21.22	18.31	18.35	07.30	05.70
C_6	20.09	27.59	21.54	13.32	01.25	00.85	00.71
C_7	05.93	11.07	10.11	09.31	02.43	01.27	00.70
C_8	21.24	17.08	04.76	01.56	01.12	01.03	01.14
C_9	11.14	01.10	00.69	00.38	00.23	00.22	00.49
C_{10}	01.61	01.03	00.21	00.20	00.23	00.36	00.50
C_{11}	01.76	00.96	00.24	-00.09	00.06	00.18	00.13
C_{12}	01.14	01.11	01.07	00.92	00.58	00.36	00.05

*Z-score <1.2 = Distress Zone; Z-score = 1.2–2.9 = Gray Zone; and Z-score >2.9 = Safe Zone. The 3-year moving averages have been considered for data smoothening.
#Companies' names are coded (presented in Appendix I).
^Shaded region in the Table represents the financial distress zone.
Source: Compiled by author using data sourced from EMIS.

Findings of Z-score analysis have been visibly in agreement with the financial ratio analysis, as discussed earlier. Therefore, Z-score of less than 1.2 may be considered for classification of distressed companies and to determine the key ratios affecting the distress situation other than ratios considered in the Z-score analysis.

9.4.3   Determinants of Financial Distress in Indian ARCs—Analysis Using MLP-ANN

Considering the presence of financial distress in ARCs, as discussed in former sections, the analysis has been further extended to determine the important indicators that may have been significantly contributing to the distress situation. The group-wise statistics of the variables used in the analysis have been placed in Table 9.5. Consequently, multivariate panel analysis has been performed using MLP-ANN on 10 financial indicators corresponding to 120 firmyear observations for the period 2011–2012 to 20192020. Furthermore, the dependent variable has been transformed into binary form using the Z-score analysis, where a score less than 0.5 has been coded as "1" and "0" otherwise.

Table 9.5 Groupwise descriptive statistics of the variables used in the analysis.

Group A (FD = 0, Z-score >0.5)					
Variable	Sample	Mean	Std. Deviation	Min	Max
FD	94	00.00	00.00	00.00	00.00
ROA	94	03.84	02.56	-00.28	08.82
ROCE	94	08.08	05.25	-00.17	18.26
NPM	94	30.90	20.22	-01.10	73.20
TAT	94	00.12	00.06	00.00	00.23
CR	94	06.49	06.04	00.19	21.98
D_TA	94	00.18	00.20	00.00	00.71
D_E	94	00.39	00.57	00.00	02.86
ICR	94	31.73	70.68	00.98	295.70
Group B (FD = 1, Z-score <0.5)					
Variable	Sample	Mean	Std. Deviation	Min	Max
FD	14	01.00	00.00	01.00	01.00
ROA	14	01.66	01.53	-00.28	05.40
ROCE	14	07.71	05.24	-00.17	18.26
NPM	14	16.00	12.50	-01.10	42.50
TAT	14	00.10	00.04	00.04	00.16
CR	14	00.93	00.99	00.19	03.33
D_TA	14	00.56	00.23	00.03	00.72
D_E	14	02.23	01.17	00.01	03.20
ICR	14	04.96	11.37	00.98	45.50

Source: Computed by author.

Similarly, sensitivity analysis has also been conducted using the 10-fold cross-tabulation technique [14], and the mean normalized importance of the indicators has been obtained. Subsequently, select key determinants have surfaced in the analysis, as presented in Table 9.6. The model details have been placed in Appendix II.

As evident in Table 9.6, return on equity has been the most important determinant, followed by debt-to-total assets ratio with normalized importance of 99.0%, return on capital employed (95.0%), and debt-to-equity ratio (80.0%). Surprisingly, interest coverage ratio has indicated the importance percentage of 58.0%.

Table 9.6 Sensitivity analysis—observed importance of financial factors using MLP-ANN (percent).

Network*	D_TA	D_E	ROA	ICR	CR	NPM	TAT	ROCE
N – 01	1.00	0.44	0.94	0.90	0.61	0.40	0.12	0.06
N – 02	1.00	0.22	0.34	0.44	0.40	0.22	0.32	0.21
N 03	0.38	1.00	0.31	0.13	0.38	0.14	0.32	0.18
N – 04	0.08	1.00	0.11	0.12	0.18	0.10	0.06	0.21
N – 05	0.10	1.00	0.16	0.06	0.19	0.10	0.11	0.13
N – 06	1.00	0.50	0.34	0.78	0.44	0.27	0.10	0.35
N – 07	0.84	0.37	1.00	0.22	0.65	0.59	0.23	0.10
N – 08	0.08	1.00	0.22	0.13	0.31	0.14	0.11	0.17
N – 09	1.00	0.18	0.49	0.58	0.39	0.24	0.19	0.20
N – 10	1.00	0.44	0.94	0.90	0.61	0.40	0.12	0.06
Mean importance	0.65	0.61	0.49	0.43	0.42	0.26	0.17	0.17
Normalized importance (%)	100%	95%	75%	66%	64%	40%	26%	26%

* N - nn represents the number of iterations – for consistent results [14].
ROA, return on assets; ROCE, return on capital employed; NPM, net profit margin; TAT, total asset turnover; CR, current ratio; D_TA, debt-to-total assets ratio; D_E, debt-to-equity ratio; ICR, interest coverage ratio.
Source: Computed by author using data sourced from EMIS. https://www.emis.com/.

Further to the analysis, root mean square error (RMSE) values have been computed at each iteration run of the model for the training and testing phases. Findings indicate the mean RMSE values of 0.14 and 0.16 at the training and testing phases, respectively. Thus, the low values of RMSE indicate a model fit (Table 9.7).

Further to the analysis, the 1,080 observations have been split into a 70:30 ratio for the training and testing samples, respectively [15]. Likewise, the overall classification accuracy of the model has been 97.19% for the training sample and 93.64% for the testing sample, respectively (Table 9.8).

Table 9.7 Summary of root mean square errors during the training and testing phases of the MLPANN model.

Network*	Sum of square error (Training)	Sum of square error (Testing)	RMSE** (Training)	RMSE (Testing)	RMSE (Training) - RMSE (Testing)
N – 01	0.124	0.331	0.041	0.097	0.057
N – 02	0.176	0.381	0.047	0.115	0.068
N – 03	1.551	0.966	0.138	0.183	0.044
N – 04	1.224	1.317	0.130	0.186	0.056
N – 05	1.960	0.992	0.151	0.203	0.052
N – 06	0.520	0.665	0.080	0.151	0.071
N – 07	1.800	0.990	0.162	0.155	0.006
N – 08	2.464	0.408	0.186	0.102	0.084
N – 09	1.137	0.013	0.118	0.022	0.096
N – 10	1.124	0.310	0.122	0.094	0.028
Mean	1.208	0.637	0.118	0.131	
Std Dev	0.770	0.412	0.048	0.055	

* N - nn represents the number of iterations – for consistent results [14].
** RMSE = Root means square errors calculated using formula = square root (sum of square errors/sample size), where the sum of square errors has been computed by the SPPS.
Source: Computed by author using data sourced from EMIS. https://www.emis.com/.

Table 9.8 Classification accuracy of the of MLP-ANN model during the training and testing phases.

Sample	Actual class	Classified class		
		Healthy	*Distressed*	*Total*
Training	Healthy	67 (100.00%)	00 (00.00%)	68 (100.00%)
	Distressed	01 (011.11%)	09 (88.88%)	10 (100.00%)
Average correct classification: 97.43%				
Testing	Healthy	27 (100.00%)	01 (00.00%)	27 (100.00%)
	Distressed	01 (016.16%)	04 (83.33%)	05 (100.00%)
Average correct classification: 96.87%				
Overall	Healthy	94 (98.94%)	01 (01.06%)	95 (100.00%)
	Distressed	02 (13.33%)	13 (86.67%)	15 (100.00%)
Average correct classification: 97.27%				

Source: Computed by author.

9.4.4   Impact of IBC, 2016, on the Capital Structure of Indian ARCs

For the analysis of the impact of the introduction of IBC, 2016, on the capital structure of ARCs, a dummy variable has been introduced across the time series where "1" indicates the presence of IBC and "0" otherwise. Debt-to-total assets ratio has been taken as a proxy for the capital structure, and profit after tax margin has been taken as a proxy for the profitability. Accordingly, the following hypothesis has been assumed for the analysis:

H_1: *There has been a significant impact of X_1 and D_1 on "Leverage" with B_1 and $D_1 \neq 0$.*

where X_1 = *Profitability of ARCs and D_1 = Dummy variable for analyzing the effect of the introduction of IBC, 2016.*

As evident in Table 9.9, independent variables have low correlations. Likewise, panel regression analysis has been performed with time variable 2012–2020, and results indicated that profitability has a significant negative impact on leverage with $T = -1.71$, $p < 0.1$, and there has been a significant positive impact of the introduction of the Insolvency and Bankruptcy Code on the capital structure of ARCs with $T = 5.12$, $p < 0.001$ (Table 9.10).

Table 9.9 Correlation matrix of the variables considered to study the impact of IBC.

Variables	Leverage	Profitability	IBC
Leverage	1		
Profitability	-0.168	1	
IBC	0.334*	-0.147	1
* p < 0.1.			

Profitability, PAT margin; Leverage, debt to total assets.
Source: Computed by author.

Table 9.10 Summary of panel regression analysis.

Leverage	Coef.	Std. Err.	t-value	p-value	[95% Conf Interval]		Sig
Profitability	-0.001	0.001	-1.71	0.087	-0.003	0	*
IBC	0.152	0.030	5.12	0.000	0.094	0.210	***
Constant	0.207	0.062	3.35	0.001	0.086	0.328	***
Mean dependent var		00.233	SD dependent var			0.24	
Overall r-squared		00.126	Number of obs.			108	
Chi-square		32.987	Prob > chi2			0.000	
R-squared within		00.258	R-squared between			0.007	
*** p < 0.01, ** p < 0.05, * p < 0.1.							

Profitability, PAT margin; Leverage, debt to total assets.
Source: Computed by author.

Moreover, $R^{2\ (within)}$ has been 0.258, and tests for assumptions of normality have been placed in Appendix III.

9.5 Conclusion

In the last two decades, a consistent rise in stressed assets may have created roadblocks for the financial system, even before the pandemic occurred. Moreover, institutional resolution of stressed assets has been a time-consuming process, and the efficacy of ARCs in providing an impact through their core business has been moderate over the years. In addition, ARCs hold an average settlement success rate of approximately 27.0% and, surprisingly, approaching the alternate resolution channels for revival of their purchased portfolio of stressed assets. Therefore, proactive corrective measures may be implemented.

Furthermore, the business of ARCs has been concentrated to a few companies, and considering the market size of stressed assets, the presence of untapped business opportunities may exist. In addition, findings indicate that ARCs have been experiencing a rising financial distress situation over the last decade and overdependency on the banking sector may create a triple balance sheet problem, where nonperforming debt corresponding to corporate sector and financial distress in ARCs may have a combined effect on the banking sector.

Furthermore, select financial indicators such as return on equity, followed by debt-to-total assets ratio, and return on capital employed may have been the important determinants of financial distress situation among ARCs in the last decade. In addition, with the introduction of IBC in 2016, there may have been a significant positive impact on the capital structure of ARCs. Accordingly, select key recommendations may be relevant for the longterm financial health of ARCs, as follows:

- Enhanced competitive environment among ARCs
- Proactive efforts in resolution and tracking the life cycle of stressed assets
- Classification and quick resolution of vintage[8] stressed assets
- Close asset quality monitoring over the financial health of ARCs – on continuous basis

References

1. Dhananjaya, K., Corporate distress and non-performing assets in India. *Glob. Bus. Rev.*, 22, 3, 780–796, 2021.
2. Sharma, S. and Kansal, A.K., Insolvency and bankruptcy code, 2016 and resolution process: Retrospect and prospect. *Vinimaya*, XI, III, National Institute of Bank Management, 23, 2022.

---

[8] Vintage stressed assets refer to the substandard stressed assets lying in the financial statements of lenders over larger time frames.

3. Reserve Bank of India Bulletin, vol. LXXV, no. 4, pp. 157–168, April, 2021.

4. *Report of the Committee to Review the Working of Asset Reconstruction Companies*, Reserve Bank of India, Mumbai, Maharashtra, India, 2021.

5. Altman, E., II, Iwanicz-Drozdowska, M., Laitinen, E.K., Suvas, A., Financial distress prediction in an international context: A review and empirical analysis of Altman's Z-score model. *J. Int. Financ. Manage. Account.*, 28, 2, 131–171, 2017.

6. Bawa, J.K., Goyal, V., Mitra, S.K., Basu, S., An analysis of NPAs of Indian banks: Using a comprehensive framework of 31 financial ratios. *IIMB Manage. Rev.*, 31, 1, 51–62, 2019.

7. Jan, C.L., Financial information asymmetry: Using deep learning algorithms to predict financial distress. *Symmetry*, 13, 3, 443, 2021.

8. Datta, S. and Iskandar-Datta, M.E., Reorganization and financial distress: An empirical investigation. *J. Financial Res.*, 18, 1, 15–32, 1995.

9. Outecheva, N., *Corporate Financial Distress: An Empirical Analysis of Distress Risk*, Verlag nicht ermittelbar, Munich, Germany, 2007.

10. Gilson, S.C., *Bankruptcy, boards, banks, and blockholders: Evidence on changes in corporate ownership and control when firms default*, vol. 355-387, *J. Financ. Econ.*, 27, 2, 1990.

11. Meher, B.K. and Puntambekar, G.L., Asset reconstruction companies: An analysis of growth (a case study of ARCIL). *Abhigyan*, 36, 1, 11, 2018.

12. Leong, L.Y., Hew, T.S., Ooi, K.B., Wei, J., Predicting mobile wallet resistance: A two-staged structural equation modeling-artificial neural network approach. *Int. J. Inf. Manage.*, 51, 102047, 2020.

13. Alwosheel, A., van Cranenburgh, S., Chorus, C.G., Is your dataset big enough? Sample size requirements when using artificial neural networks for discrete choice analysis. *J. Choice Model.*, 28, 167–182, 2018.

14. Ooi, K.B. and Tan, G.W.H., Mobile technology acceptance model: An investigation using mobile users to explore smartphone credit card. *Expert Syst. Appl.*, 59, 33–46, October 2016.

15. Gameel, M.S. and El-Geziry, K., Predicting financial distress: multi scenarios modelling using neural network. *IJEF*, 8, 11, 159, 2016.

Appendices

Appendix I Companies considered for the analysis.

Code name	Company name
C_1	ASREC India Ltd. (India)
C_2	Sicom Arc Ltd. (India)
C_3	Pegasus Assets Reconstruction Pvt. Ltd. (India)

C_4	International Asset Reconstruction Company Pvt. Ltd. (India)
C_5	Asset Reconstruction Company India Ltd. (India)
C_6	Phoenix ARC Pvt. Ltd. (India)
C_7	Alchemist Asset Reconstruction Company Ltd. (India)
C_8	Reliance Asset Reconstruction Company Ltd. (India)
C_9	JM Financial Asset Reconstruction Company Pvt. Ltd. (India)
C_{10}	Edelweiss Asset Reconstruction Co. Ltd. (India)
C_{11}	Invent Assets Securitisation & Reconstruction Pvt. Ltd. (India)
C_{12}	Assets Care & Reconstruction Enterprise Ltd. (India)

Source: https://rbidocs.rbi.org.in/rdocs/content/DOCs/LSCRCRBI07092016.xlsx

Appendix II ANN model summary.

Network information			
Input Layer	Covariates	1	ROA
		2	ROCE
		3	NPM
		4	TAT
		5	CR
		6	D_TA
		7	D_E
		8	ICR
	Number of Units	8	
	Rescaling Method for Covariates	Standardized	

Hidden Layer(s)	Number of Hidden Layers		1
	Number of Units in Hidden Layers		6
	Activation Function		Hyperbolic tangent
Output Layer	Dependent Variables		FD
	Number of Units		2
	Activation Function		Sigmoid
	Error Function		Sum of Squares

Source: Compiled by the author

Appendix III Test for assumptions of normality.

Skewness/Kurtosis tests for normality					
Variable	Obs	Pr(Skewness)	Pr(Kurtosis)	adj_chi2(2)	Prob>chi2
resid	108	0.041	0.195	5.66	0.059

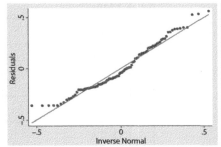 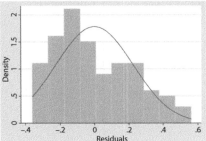

The Framework of Feature Extraction for Financial Fraud Behavior and Applications

George X. Yuan[1,2,3], Shanshan Yang[1*], Lan Di[4†], Yunpeng Zhou[3],
Wen Chen[3] and Yuanlei Luo[5‡]

[1]Business School, Chengdu University, Chengdu, China
[2]College of Science, Chongqing University of Technology, Chongqing, China
[3]Shanghai Hammer Digital Tech. Co. Ltd. (Hammer), Shanghai, China
*[4]School of Artificial Intelligence and Computer Science, Jiangnan University,
Wuxi, China*
[5]Research Center, China Institute of Ocean Engineering, Beijing, China

Abstract

By employing the Gibbs algorithm, we establish a general framework to extract features for the detection of corporate's financial frauds by using a fintech method related to the big data analysis. In the empirical analysis, based on those proxy "bad" samples of events in describing illegal behaviors by these Chinese A-share listed companies released by China Securities Regulatory Commission (CSRC) due to their (black) behaviors mainly violating the Rules of Disclosures and related fraudulent actions during the time period from the beginning of 2017 to the end of 2018, we conducted risk assessment for those highly related risk factors (features) that could provide related risk information on the exposure of financial fraud events by detecting the difference between their financial fraud actions with normal performances in the practices in the capital market of China.

In this paper, by employing the Gibbs sampling method, we are able to extract eight key factors that are highly associated with behaviors of corporate financial frauds, which are as follows: 1) the ROE; 2) the growth construction in process; 3) the growth of advance payment; 4) the interest expense/revenue; 5) the investment income/revenue; 6) the other income/revenue; 7) the other receivables/total assets; and 8) the long-term loan/total assets.

[*]Corresponding author: shanshanyang123@hotmail.com
[†]Corresponding author: dilan@jiangnan.edu.cn
[‡]Corresponding author: luoyuanlei@hotmail.com

Ambrish Kumar Mishra, Shweta Anand, Narayan C. Debnath, Purvi Pokhariyal and Archana Patel (eds.) Artificial Intelligence for Risk Mitigation in the Financial Industry, (229–260) © 2024 Scrivener Publishing LLC

The key contribution of this paper is that a general framework for the extraction of key risk factors that are not only used to provide detecting signals for behaviors of financial fraud but also able to predict fraudulent or related illegal actions is established under ROC and AUC testing based on financial information provided by A-share listed companies in the current capital market of China.

Keywords: Feature extraction, Gibbs sampling algorithm, SAS99, financial fraud, fraud triangle theory, framework of feature extraction, ROC and AUC testing

10.1   Introduction

With the development of financial technology, the rapid development of big data thinking framework and machine learning methods has proposed a new approach and solution for the identification of financial frauds. Today, when quantitative investment is gradually becoming mainstream, Beneish [1] proposed M-score, and the method proposes a preliminary method for modeling the risk of financial fraud based on quantitative analysis. However, in the more general fields on the identification of financial fraud and related risk management, quantitative analysis is a key tool in providing technological guidance for due diligence service in different purposes, so is true for predicting financial fraud risk and other illegal behaviors in the practice. In order to serve the needs of various application scenarios, in the context of big data, a method that can extract features according to the specific needs of different purposes is needed, so as to provide more effective support for application scenarios such as the identification of financial fraud, risk management that serves different goals.

It is well known that the most representative method for the analysis of enterprises' performance is Palepu *et al.* [2], who proposed a comprehensive analysis for the companies in at least four aspects: 1) the strategy; 2) the accounting; 3) the finance; and 4) the prospects. This, namely, is called, the well-known Harvard analysis framework. The core idea of the Harvard analytical framework is based on a multidimensional fusion analysis approach, that is, the analysis of the company should not be carried out alone from the financial or other single aspects but should be based on various aspects of the information to draw comprehensive analysis conclusions, and it also emphasizes the importance of the quality of accounting statements for the evaluation of the company.

The American Institute of Certified Public Accountants (AICPA) [3] defines financial fraud as "deliberately misstatement, omission or disclosure in financial statements to deceive users of financial statements" in its standard SAS99 (and SAS82) "Considerations of Fraud in Financial Statement Auditing." Looking at the global capital market, financial fraud by listed companies is a type of event that cannot be ignored in the practice. In addition, because financial fraud events can bring huge losses to investors, on the other hand, listed companies are usually influential (group or entity) companies, and the chain reaction caused by financial fraud of these companies may evolve into systemic risks (such as ENRON events). The empirical research by Niu et al. [4] on the Chinese market has found that corporate fraud can have a significant impact on the way investors behave, making investors more conservative and thus causing harm to capital markets. Healy and Palepu [5] conducted research on corporate information disclosure from the perspective of information asymmetry, proposed a methodological framework for the analysis and research of company disclosure information, and sorted out and summarized the research on various information disclosure regulations and disclosure channels. In addition, their research has also found many basic problems that have not yet been implemented in industry practice and need to be solved. Defond and Zhang [6] conducted research from the perspective of measuring audit quality, proposing a methodological framework for measuring audit quality, Donovan et al. [7]. On their basis, further research was carried out on the method of audit quality assessment. Yang and Lee [8] conducted a study on corporate fraud risk management from the perspective of forensic accounting and proposed an assessment method based on a balanced scorecard, which provided decision-making tools for corporate governance, anti-fraud, etc. Vanhoeyveld et al. [9] conducted a study of fraud at the tax level, proposing solutions to the problem of VAT fraud through unsupervised anomaly detection. Nurhayati [10] and Goode and Lacey [11] also discussed the link between the company's internal control management system and the risk of financial fraud. Beasley [12] studied the risk of financial fraud in terms of the number of members of the board and supervisory board. Many scholars have conducted financial fraud-related analysis from different perspectives, but the analysis of the company's financial fraud risk involves all aspects of the company's operation, management, finance, legal affairs, corporate governance, information disclosure, and supervision; so, in practice, the company's fraud risk screening requires complicated professional analysis and supporting due diligence according to different target characteristics.

Under the framework of big data, the goal of this paper is mainly to describe the characteristics of the companies' financial fraud risk, which allow us to provide detecting signals for behaviors of financial fraud and allow us to predict fraudulent or related illegal actions by integrating corporate financial information, accounting information, and ecological information.

In particular, the Gibbs stochastic search method (in short, Gibbs sampling) under the framework of Markov chain Monte Carlo (MCMC) is used to sample a subset of features, and under the condition of given sample error tolerance (assuming a sample error of 5%) (see [13]), the financial fraud feature extraction method based on financial statement data of listed companies and the corresponding feature extraction inference principle are proposed, which are used to solve the dimensionality disaster problem caused by considering the collusion relationship of financial statements (see [13–15]). From the financial statement data and the hook relationship of financial data, the eight risk characteristic factors that are highly associated (correlated) with financial fraud are extracted in this paper, which can effectively portray the financial fraud risk of listed companies. At the same time, combined with the concept of so-called odds ratio (see [16]) for these eight characteristic indicators and their accounting implications, it is found that these eight characteristics that are highly associated (correlated) with the financial fraud risk of listed companies are usually highly associated (correlated) with the company's accounting policy choices, corporate governance, and other factors, which is consistent with the traditional financial statement analysis framework.

Finally, the empirical data results show that the method used in this paper can effectively extract the characteristics of financial fraud, so as to provide technical support for due diligence and risk analysis in scenarios such as auditing, compliance, and investment analysis under the framework of a big data analysis.

10.2   The Feature Extraction for Financial Fraud Behaviors

Financial analysis is an extremely important part of the identification of financial frauds (see [17–25]), but in real-world scenarios, financial fraud activities are highly dynamic and uncertain, requiring a comprehensive analysis of financial and nonfinancial factors to reach a final conclusion. In view of this dynamic and uncertainty, this paper believes that under the framework of big data, the financial fraud risk of a company should be simulated by characterizing the characteristics of financial fraud, rather than qualitatively judging whether a company has financial fraud in its real business activities and information disclosure. However, in order to achieve the characterization of financial fraud risk characteristics under the framework of big data, we first need to construct relatively general initial features in the traditional analysis method or find ways to construct the initial feature set based on artificial intelligence big data analysis. At the same time, considering that the initial feature set may contain more correlation factors, there will be interaction effects between the individual features, so that the feature screening work faces a typical NP problem as discussed by Paz and Moran [26]. In order to overcome NP, this paper uses the method by combing the associated (correlation) rule learning method to establish the Gibbs stochastic (random) search algorithm based on samples in describing financial fraud risk from listed companies under the framework of big data to complete the characteristic screening for fraud events of companies.

10.2.1 Risk Characteristics of Financial Frauds from Listed Companies

The reasons for listed companies to carry out financial fraud activities may be diverse, and their manifestations and implementation means continue to evolve with the development process of society and economy, so financial fraud activities have a high degree of uncertainty and dynamics. Chen and Robinson [18] conducted a study of public financial fraud cases listed in Asia and pointed out that various financial fraud cases show that the inadequacy of corporate governance is an important feature of financial fraud, but due to changes in various factors such as industry characteristics and regulatory requirements, corporate governance issues in each company will also be manifested in a completely different form. Based on the domestic financial fraud sample, a similar conclusion was reached by Ye [24] and pointed out that complex equity structures, lack of traces of capital flows, difficult verification of business links, and high-risk accounting policies are important risk factors for financial fraud, and at the same time, his research also pointed out that because the organizational form of economic activities is also evolving with the pace of social development, moreover, financial fraud in different industries will also have different manifestations and characteristics, and the operating characteristics of many industries are difficult to form general experience and conclusions in a short period of time. Liu [21] systematically elaborated that financial fraud identification needs to be based on financial analysis, fundamental analysis (including macroeconomics, industry characteristics, corporate governance, management capabilities, business characteristics, and other factors), on-site investigation, and comprehensive analysis before reaching a conclusion and pointed out that on-site investigation should be the core link in judging financial fraud. Combined with real cases, for companies with relatively clear business lines including business corporations such as "Yin Gangxia Company," "Lantian Shares Limited," "Kangdexin," "Young Eagle Agriculture," "Animal Husbandry," and related other business partners, analysts can conduct comprehensive analysis of the company's financial data, business data, asset vouchers, and other information to locate the cause of financial fraud and find relevant evidence. However, for diversified groups (including "Delong company"), the intricate network relationship of the group is likely to obscure the relationship between the transmission of benefits, etc., and it is equally difficult to determine whether there is financial fraud in it. In this way, Wang and Yang [23] conducted a classified study of the financial data indicator system in the study of the financial difficulties of listed companies and found that 21 financial ratios such as asset scale, capital structure, and solvency can establish a financial forecast index system. Hong et al. [19] also selected 44 financial fraud companies and 44 companies in the 2004–2013 time period. A listed company with normal operations conducted a comparative verification of financial fraud indicators. Zhou et al. [25] used the company's financial data (interest protection multiple, total asset turnover, etc.) as a micro covariate to study the contagion effect of credit risk of enterprise groups and combined with macro covariate variables to determine the company's default distance. Although the focus of the above articles is different, whether the company has defaults, fraud, and financial difficulties, it is inseparable from the analysis of the company's underlying financial data.

Based on the above research and the relationship between business, financial, and accounting statements, it can be known that all financial fraud activities will leave clues and traces in financial statements and related party information, which makes it possible to use the holographic profiling method of financial big data (also known as Hologram, see Yuan and Wang [15]). It is possible to characterize the financial fraud of public companies in multiple dimensions. In the face of the high uncertainty and dynamics of financial fraud, the characteristic characterization under the framework of big data should not start from the perspective of qualitative judgment but should simulate the risk of financial fraud of listed companies from the perspective of risk measurement. This idea of risk characteristic portrayal can save a lot of time for investment research while avoiding risks more efficiently and can better meet the actual needs of quantitative investment, credit rating, and other practical application scenarios in today's rapid development of financial technology and the gradual domination of quantitative analysis.

10.2.2   The Method for the Identification of Financial Fraud Behavior Based on Financial Analysis

Financial analysis is an indispensable step in the identification of financial fraud, and under the framework of big data, traditional financial analysis methods can also provide the basic idea of building an initial feature pool for the feature extraction of financial fraud. Therefore, the first step in this work needs to sort out the most commonly used financial analysis methods in academia and practice to form indicators for constructing the initial feature pool. Chen and Robinson [18] conducted financial analysis in five dimensions according to inflated profits, exaggerated performance, inflated assets, inflated liabilities, and forged cash flows and detailed how to apply financial ratios in each module for analysis. Ye [24] mainly proposed the analysis method for the two angles of gross profit margin and cash flow, elaborated on the analysis method of accounting methods, accounts receivable, inventory, and other issues in the main business activities of listed companies, and focused on the analysis methods of companies' incomes and expense structures. Combined with the collusion relationship of the financial statements, it is pointed out which changes in assets and liabilities will occur in the presence of profit manipulation. The analysis method proposed by Liu [21] is carried out according to the three modules of static analysis, trend analysis, and inter-industry comparison, of which static analysis is the analysis of financial data and financial indicators at a fixed period or a time point; trend analysis is the analysis of financial data and financial indicators in different periods; and interbank comparison is the comparison of a company's financial data and financial indicators with those of companies in the same industry.

By taking into account those methods and analysis methods mentioned above, the goal of this paper is to establish the framework to extract features for companies' financial fraud events, then the true case study shows that the features established by this paper are able to help us to provide exposure related to fraudulent behaviors from listed companies in the capital markets of China.

10.2.3   The Method for the Feature Extraction

When faced with massive data, the correlation relationship between features automatically discovered by the algorithm is feature extraction.

In statistics, correlation tests can reflect whether there is a linear correlation between features (e.g., using Pearson's correlation coefficient), but the correlation between a large number of features in the framework of big data is nonlinear and difficult to describe by correlation. On the other hand, when facing a high-dimensional feature space, it is difficult to find the most suitable subset of features for modeling through the two-sided correlation between variables, while traversing the feature space will face a typical NP problem [26], the algorithm will lose the computational feasibility in the face of the high-dimensional feature space due to the exponential complexity of the algorithm, and the regularization method will most likely not converge when the dimensionality of the feature space is close to or even exceeds the number of observed samples. In summary, in the context of big data, it is difficult to avoid two difficulties in feature extraction for high-dimensional feature space, one is that the correlation relationship between features (including features and response variables) is not only a linear correlation relationship; the second is the contradiction that the characteristic spatial dimension is too high and the number of observed samples is limited. In order to solve the above two problems, this paper uses the logistic regression method to characterize the financial fraud risk of listed companies, draws on the correlation rules learning algorithm to solve the idea of high characteristic dimension, and reduces the computational complexity under the Gibbs stochastic search (Gibbs sampling) algorithm based on the framework of MCMC simulations under the condition of limited observation sample size.

The association rule learning (see [17] and [27]) is a technology that shows the associated relationship between features in data and is currently widely used in retail, finance, web user behavior analysis, and other fields. For example, analyzing a user's web browsing data may reveal that users who often search for a shaver on a shopping site may also need to search for something else, accurately pushing links to relevant product pages to users. Since these application scenarios often face a feature number greater than the number of observed samples (that is, the abovementioned contradiction that the feature dimension is too high and the number of observed samples is limited), the correlation rule learning usually proposes a solution to this problem.

At present, the most representative association rule mining algorithms including Apriori [28] and Gibbs sampling-based feature mining algorithms. The Apriori algorithm was proposed by Agrawal and Srikant [17], and the basic idea is to use a certain property of the support of the item set to avoid exhausting all candidate sets, thus solving the NP problem of traversing the feature spaces (see [26]). In addition to the Apriori method, using idea for feature mining algorithm based on Gibbs sampling, Qian and Field [29] developed a method to achieve a stochastic sampling of the feature space while ensuring that the sampled stochastic samples can maintain the original information of the features, so as to transform the NP problem into a polynomial-level complexity problem, which solves the problem of correlation rule learning in high-dimensional feature spaces (see [27] and [29]).

In empirical studies, based on the confidence of the association rules, by constructed metastasis probability, Qian *et al.* [27] conducted the study on gene fragment data (including 366 gene-coding regions) of 229 cases (including 39 cases of breast cancer), and better than Apriori algorithm, the 35 important association rules were obtained through 6,000 simulations under the condition of setting the minimum support degree of 0.2 and the minimum confidence degree of 1. However, the Apriori algorithm does not extract valid correlation rules under the condition of setting the same minimum support and confidence.

Gibbs stochastic sampling is a simple and effective MCMC method that has been widely used in both academia and practice. Glasserman [31] has conducted extensive applied research in the field of finance using the MCMC method. Narisetty *et al.* [22] discuss a scalable Gibbs sampling algorithm that supports model selection. Yuan *et al.* [13] applied Gibbs sampling to study the associated characteristics of depicting commodity price trends, and also based on the nature of the Monte Carlo simulation, the number size of simulations to control the error significance between the sample size and the associated characteristic factors of the screening was also established (see [13]).

10.2.4   Gibbs Sampling Method Under the MCMC

As mentioned in Section 10.2.3, many problems under the framework of the big data environment are difficult to get accurate or reliable answers, the use of Gibbs stochastic search algorithm under the MCMC simulation framework can make the face of massive data and under a certain degree of error tolerance spend reasonable computing resources to complete the solution of the problem, get an approximate solution, so this paper establishes the general framework to achieve the extraction of features in describing companies' financial fraud risk factors' screening process by using the Gibbs stochastic search algorithm summarized below by four steps (see [13–15], [25], and [32]).

First Step: Assuming that the financial fraud risk characteristic factor obeys the Bernoulli distribution, the feature (characteristic) space formed by the characteristic factor is initialized, and stochastic sampling is performed, and the characteristics are classified according to whether the coefficient is 0, and the non-0 is recorded as 1, and the 0 is recorded as 0, which can be obtained as follows:

$$A_0 = (0, 1, 1, ..., 0) \in \{0, 1\}^m \tag{10.1}$$

where m represents the number of features in the initialized feature space and represents a subset in the initialized feature space A_0.

Second Step: By BIC [28] (Bayesian Information) criteria to build a standard that supports stochastic sampling, and to construct a distribution function of features, get:

$$P_{BIC}(i_n = 1 \mid I_{-n}) = \frac{exp(-BIC(i_n = 1 \mid I_{-n}))}{exp(-BIC(i_n = 0 \mid I_{-n})) + exp(-BIC(i_n = 1 \mid I_{-n}))} \tag{10.2}$$

where P_{BIC} (i) presents the transfer probability function of indicators (features), P_{BIC} $(i_n = 1 \mid I_{-n})$ denotes all other feature sets except in i_n, I_0 the number of features in A_0, using the formula (10.2) to ensure the indicator (feature) subset shifts to a higher degree of fit, for the purpose in achieving the significance of indicators for financial frauds can be revealed.

Third Step: In turn, the number of samples sampled is determined. The number of samples is determined to reduce computational complexity and allow the results of the final metric significance to be achieved within a tolerable margin of error. In order to ensure the significance of the financial fraud indicator, the sample size error is usually recommended to be no more than 5%, and the corresponding formula is as follows:

$$Std(p) = \sqrt{\frac{p(1-p)}{M}} < \sqrt{\frac{1}{4M}} \tag{10.3}$$

when the *2-sigma* (i.e., 2 *Std* (p)) criterion is used to control the simulation error within 5%, the number of samples M greater than or equal to 400 times can be obtained by the formula (10.3). This number of samples can have the effect of reducing the computational complexity and ensuring the distinctiveness of the features.

Fourth Step: Finally, no less than 400 times' Gibbs sampling is performed, the combination of feature indicators is obtained, and the ratio of the number of feature occurrences to the total number of samples is used to obtain the frequency of feature occurrences, and the influence of features on the model results is analyzed according to the level of frequency. Based on obtained features ($I^{(1)}, I^{(2)}, \ldots I^{(M)}$), we conducted the performance of testing on the ROC (i.e., receiver operating characteristic curve for features) and the AUC testing (area under the ROC curve) as an evaluation criterion for the model to measure the significance (sensitivity) of the resulting feature indicator.

10.3   The Framework of Feature Extraction for Financial Fraud Behavior

Based on the discussion in the previous section, the focus of this section is based on the financial report statement data of listed company using the Gibbs stochastic search (Gibbs sampling) algorithm as a tool to establish a general processing method for the implementation on screening the characteristic factors that describe the risk of financial fraud behaviors for listed companies. In particular, based on the initial set of feature factors that described financial fraud in the financial statements of A-share listed companies with the data samples from January 2017 to December 2018 on the disclosure violations of the financial statements, the characteristics of "financial fraud risk" can be obtained, that is, by solving the dimensionality disaster problem caused by the collusion relationship of financial statements, a small number of associated characteristic factors (actually, eight features) were extracted from the financial statement data to characterize the financial fraud risk of listed companies. At the same time, combined with the odds ratio (see [16], [13–15]) (in short, OR) that was used in classifying highly related features in characterizing fraudulent behaviors as a verification criterion, it is found that these indicators show the characteristics of high correlation with the accounting policy choices and corporate governance of the company where the financial fraud is located.

10.3.1   The Initial Set of Characteristics that Characterizes Financial Fraud Behavior

Inspired by the traditional financial analysis method, we first construct the initial feature pool according to the discussion of 2.2 and divide the feature construction method into three categories: static analysis, dynamic (trend) analysis, and interbank comparison. Then, realize the portrayal of the hook relationship of financial statements, so as to support the screening of characteristic indicators that can portray the risk of financial fraud's behaviors.

(1) Static Analysis

Static analysis is the analysis of the structure of financial statements, considering factors such as asset–liability structure, income and expense structure, cash flow and income expense, and the hook relationship between assets and liabilities. When modeling static analysis, we chose to use the percentage reporting method to preprocess financial data. The use of percentage statements can not only reflect the asset–liability structure of the assessed company but also achieve the normalization of the financial data of the assessed company. A small percentage of a company's financial data may still have outliers (such as investment returns significantly higher than operating income) after normalization based on percentage reporting, so outliers need to be processed before you can participate in modeling.

(2) Dynamic (Trend) Analysis

Dynamic (trend) analysis is used to capture unusual changes in a company's financial data. Based on the hook relationship of the accounting report, the fraud activity whitewashes some financial accounts and usually causes abnormal changes in other financial accounts. On the other hand, considering that financial fraud activities such as inflated assets, fictitious profits, and fictitious cash flows are a very large system engineering, which usually requires the cooperation of multiple departments or even multi-company entities, when the fraud means are difficult to obtain support from various activities such as commerce and taxation, a large amount of asset subtraction may usually occur, resulting in abnormal changes in the financial statement data. In order to capture the above two abnormal changes, we use the change in the most recent year of each financial statement account and then use the growth rate indicator formed by the change in the same account in the past 4 years to obtain a measure of the degree of abnormality in the financial indicators of the company being evaluated in the current year.

(3) Comparison of Peers

That is, it is based on the average performance of the same industry to extract the characteristics of financial fraud, and the specific method is to take the sample of the same industry as a collection and then standardize the data in the peer industry in a Z-score standardized manner, so that the processed data have a fixed mean and standard deviation. It is worth noting that we do not assume that any financial indicator should follow a normal distribution within the same industry but define the difference between a single sample and the average of the same industry by the difference between it and the other samples in the same industry and then normalize it through the normal distribution cumulative probability function.

(4) Portrayal of the Hook Relationship between Financial Statements and Audits

Considering the hook relationship between the financial statements, this article needs to take into account not only the possible abnormalities of the financial data itself but also the ratio relationship between the various financial statement accounts. This article is based on the financial data of the 2018 annual report of entity companies listed on the A-share market (nonfinancial industry) and selects the three major financial statements of 3,459 sample companies from listed companies. As the basic data, the initial feature pool (the initial factor of nearly 200 financial statement accounts) is constructed according to the data processing methods of the three modules of static analysis, dynamic (trend) analysis, and interbank comparison, and then the Gibbs stochastic search method for feature extraction is used (see Yuan *et al.* [14]), and the MCMC simulation is implemented. The Gibbs sampling method under the framework reduces the complexity of NP problems in feature extraction to polynomial complexity screening under the condition of tolerant sample error tolerance (set to less than 5% as shown by Equation 10.3 in Section 2.4). Thus, the extraction of the characteristics of portraying corporate financial fraud is completed.

10.3.2   Extracting Features Related to Companies' Financial Fraud Behaviors

In the development of China's capital market, there are also many cases of financial fraud events from the listed companies (such as "Yin Guangxia Company" and "Lantian Shares Limited"), but these cases are still only a dime a dozen relative to the listed company group, and it is difficult to extract the characteristic factors that effectively portray the risk of financial

CSRC's Announcement on Kangde's Penalty

中国证监会 www.csrc.gov.cn   时间：2019-07-05   来源：证监会

　　2019年1月，康得新复合材料集团股份有限公司（以下简称康得新）因无力按期兑付15亿短期融资券本息，业绩真实性存疑，引起市场的广泛关注和高度质疑，证监会迅速反应，果断出击，决定对康得新涉嫌信息披露违法行为立案调查。

　　经查，康得新涉嫌在2015年至2018年期间，通过虚构销售业务等方式虚增营业收入，并通过虚构采购、生产、研发费用、产品运输费用等方式虚增营业成本、研发费用和销售费用。通过上述方式，康得新共虚增利润总额达119亿元。此外，康得新还涉嫌未在相关年度报告中披露控股股东非经营性占用资金的关联交易和为控股股东提供担保，以及未如实披露募集资金使用情况等违法行为。上述行为导致康得新披露的相关年度报告存在虚假记载和重大遗漏。

　　康得新所涉及的信息披露违法行为持续时间长、涉案金额巨大、手段极其恶劣、违法情节特别严重。证监会已经向涉案当事人送达行政处罚及市场禁入事先告知书，拟对康得新及主要责任人员在《证券法》规定的范围内顶格处罚并采取终身证券市场禁入措施。下一步，我们将充分听取当事人的陈述申辩意见，以事实为依据、以法律为准绳，依法进行处罚；对涉嫌犯罪的，严格按照有关规定移送司法机关追究刑事责任。

　　证监会重申，上市公司及大股东必须讲真话、做真账、及时讲话，牢牢守住"四条底线"，不披露虚假信息，不从事内幕交易，不操纵股票价格，不损害上市公司利益。下一步，证监会将一如既往对上市公司信息披露违法行为依法严查，净化市场生态，努力提升上市公司质量，服务实体经济发展，为打造一个规范、透明、开放、有活力、有韧性的资本市场保驾护航。

Figure 10.1 Notice of CSRC's inquiry on Kangde's penalty (we keep its original form in Chinese here as a reference).

fraud based on these sample data through machine learning methods with a high correlation to financial fraud that are used as a basis for identifying financial fraud samples. However, much of the information related to fraud events is unstructured text processing, which is under the category of big data framework. For example, Figure 10.1 is a general notice of the penalty and prohibition notice issued by the CSRC on the listed company "Kangdexin" on 6 July 2019.

In the 2 years from January 2017 to December 2018, there were 393 listed companies that had "black sample" events, which basically involved the following 12 types of risk events used to describe financial fraud risk scenarios, that are classified as follows under the general principle of SCC's compliance in the practice for capital markets in China, Yuan [13–15]:

(1) Occupation of Company Assets
Appropriation of the company's assets refers to the direct or indirect misappropriation of the funds and assets of the listed company by the controlling shareholder, the actual controller, and other enterprises under their control by using related party transactions, asset restructuring, advance payment, foreign investment, guarantee, profit distribution, and other means, harming the legitimate rights and interests of the company and other shareholders.

(2) False Disclosure (Related to Other)
False disclosure refers to the disclosure of untrue information by a listed company, that is, the listed company makes untrue records, misleading statements, and material omissions. False information includes both false information contained in its disclosed financial reports and false information in voluntary information disclosed by it.

(3) Illegal Guarantee

Illegal guarantee refers to the external guarantee implemented by the listed company and its holding subsidiary without the deliberation procedures stipulated in the articles of association, etc.

(4) Fraudulent Listing

Fraudulent listing refers to the fact that an issuer that does not meet the conditions for issuance has fraudulently obtained the approval of the issuance due to false records, misleading statements, or material omissions in the initial public offering application or disclosure documents, or has a substantial impact on the pricing of the new share offering, and has been administratively punished by the CSRC, or has been transferred to the public security organs according to law for suspected fraudulent issuance.

(5) Unauthorized Change of the Use of Funds

Unauthorized change of use of funds refers to the use of funds by listed companies in violation of the provisions of the Regulatory Guidelines for Listed Companies No. 2—Regulatory Requirements for the Management and Use of Funds Raised by Listed Companies.

(6) Improper General Accounting Treatment

Improper general accounting treatment means that the accounting treatment of listed companies does not meet the requirements of the Accounting Standards for Business Enterprises.

(7) False Statements (or Misleading Statements)

False records refer to making records that are inconsistent with the truth of the facts on the information disclosure documents, that is, the matters that did not occur objectively were fabricated or not excluded from the information disclosure documents. A misleading statement is when a statement of an event in an information disclosure document is true, but it is easily misunderstood due to a defect in the representation, making it impossible for investors to obtain a clear and correct understanding.

(8) Postponement of Disclosure

Deferred disclosure refers to the act of delaying the disclosure of information by a listed company without following the prescribed time.

(9) Fictitious Profits

Fictitious profits refer to the act of inflating the after-tax profits of enterprises through accounting fraud, and usually the purpose of accounting

Table 10.1 The summary of the 12 classes of events from listed companies between January 2017 to December 2018.

Occupation of company assets	Unauthorized change of the use of funds	Illegal guarantee	Fraudulent listing	False disclosure (related to other)	Imaginary assets
87	17	60	0	32	4
Improper general accounting treatment	False statements (or misleading statements)	Postponement of disclosure	Fictitious profits	Material omissions	Other assets
30	233	306	15	143	117

fraud is often to increase the net profit of enterprises, thereby inflating the company's operating performance.

(10) Material Omissions
Material omissions refer to the fact that the information disclosure documents do not record the matters that should be recorded according to law, so as to affect investors to make correct decisions.

(11) Imaginary Assets
Fictitious assets refer to the act of inflating or reducing the assets of an enterprise through accounting fraud, and the violation of fictitious assets usually brings inflated profits at the same time, so the two can occur at the same time.

(12) Other Assets
Any other cases not included as mentioned by the 11 categories above.

During 2 years' time from 2017 to 2018, there were approximately 2,700 events that happened in 383 listed companies as shown in Table 10.1 above for the 12 categories of (incidents) events released by CSRC's compliance in the practice from the capital markets of China.

10.3.3   Features Extracted for Financial Fraud Behavior by AI Algorithms and Empirical Analysis

As shown by Huang *et al.* [20], based on the historical samples of 175 financial fraud behaviors caused by 113 listed companies for the time from 2010 to 2019, they find that almost all of financial fraud behaviors by listed companies in the capital market of China can be classified by eight types as shown by Table 10.2 below (see **Appendix A** for details of their description).

Based on information provided in Table 10.1 and Table 10.2, we are able to construct approximately 1,000 proxy samples in describing issuers' financial anomalies, if we think the eight types of financial frauds would be regarded as the "proxy samples" for (default) bad behaviors of listed companies, which are represented by approximately 2,700 behaviors summarized by Table 10.1 above, this allows us to reach the minimum enough size of observed samples with the ratio level of approximately 20% (i.e., 1,000/5,000 = 20%, the ratio of 1,000 proxy samples against approximately 5,000 companies listed in the A-shares capital markets of China in the year 2020), which, in turn, would provide strong support for us to model companies financial fraud behavior by extracting the corresponding eight features below (Table 10.3).

In order to achieve extraction for highly related risk features that characterize fraud embedded from the unstructured data, by following the Gibbs sampling algorithm introduced by Section 10.2.4 above, under the integration of the AIC (see [28]), and BIC (see [30]) test standards for the amount of information were used and developed, the Gibbs algorithm is currently a very effective method to support feature extraction from high-dimensional complex systems.

Actually, under the framework for the construction of proxy bad samples above, we are able to obtain the following eight characteristic factors in depicting the risk of financial fraud behaviors as shown by Table 10.3 below

Table 10.2 The list of financial fraud types in the capital markets of China.

Fraud type	# of events	Ratio	Fraud type	# of events	Ratio
1) Revenue fraud	77	44%	5) Impairment fraud	13	7%
2) Expense fraud	25	14%	6) Nonoperating revenue and expenditure fraud	10	6%
3) Cash fraud	24	14%	7) Investment income fraud	7	4%
4) Cost fraud	17	10%	8) Other fraud	2	1%

Table 10.3 The eight features characterize the highly correlated factors of financial frauds.

Serial number	Description of features	Model coefficients	P-value	Relevance significance	Odds ratio
0	Constant term	-2.49	0.00%		0.08
1	Deduct non-return on equity	-0.41	0.00%	82.30%	0.67
2	Growth rate of works under construction	-0.16	0.89%	87.40%	0.85
3	Advance payment growth rate	-0.15	1.05%	59.70%	0.86
4	Where: interest expense (finance expense)/ total operating income	0.30	0.00%	97.90%	1.36
5	Net income from investments/ total operating income	-0.15	0.24%	52.90%	0.86
6	Other income/ total operating income	-0.20	0.06%	98.45%	0.82
7	Other receivables (including interest and dividends)/ total assets	0.20	0.00%	99.80%	1.22
8	Long-term borrowings/ total assets	-0.17	0.14%	65.05%	0.84

(which are based on the pool of 183 initial features given by Table 10.4 below).

Table 10.4 below is a brief summary for the pool of some initial characteristic factors in supporting to describe behaviors of financial frauds and related financial anomalies.

In the process of big data algorithm, the sample data used in this report are 3,459 companies listed in 2018, and according to 80% of them as the training set and 20% as the test set (keeping the proportion of black and white samples in the training set and the test set the same), the correlation between each feature factor and the financial fraud risk is classified by logistic regression model and combined with odds ratio. The eight characteristics of Table 10.3 are derived to characterize the risk of financial fraud of the enterprise.

As can be seen in Table 10.3, we obtained the following eight highly related features, they are: 1) Deduct non-return on equity; 2) Growth rate of works under construction; 3) Advance growth rate; 4) Interest expense

Table 10.4 The list for the pool of initial characteristic factors.

# Serial number	Description of features	Relevance significance
1	Paid-in capital (or equity)/ total assets	31.95%
2	Days of non-current asset turnover	25.70%
3	Capital leverage	20.15%
4	Net worth EBIT rate	18.45%
5	Short-term borrowings/total assets	15.55%
...	...	...
181	Accounts receivable turnover days	0.05%
182	Growth rate of other payables	0.05%
183	Absorption of cash received from investments/Subtotal of cash inflows from financing activities	0.05%

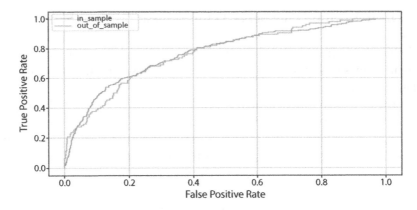

Figure 10.2 The ROC test for the financial fraud risk events.

(finance expense)/gross operating income; 5) Net income from investments/total operating income; 6) Other Income/Total Operating Income; 7) Other receivables (including interest and dividends)/total assets; and 8) the long-term borrowings/total assets, which have a strong correlation with other accounts of the company's finances.

This shows that the risk of financial fraud is highly correlated with financial statement accounts that involve factors such as the company's business income, taxation, and company accounting policies (such as asset impairment standards) and accounts that are not easy to verify in the audit (such as advance payments, accounts payable). In addition, the initial characteristics of the static analysis and interbank comparison method construction also have a high correlation with the financial fraud risk, indicating that under the framework of machine learning, static analysis and interbank comparison can more effectively highlight the financial fraud risk of listed companies. Based on the eight risk characteristic factors used to characterize financial fraud, the ROC test in Figure 10.2 shows that the AUC values based on the training set and the test set are 0.771 and 0.766, respectively, which show that the characteristics we screened out can be more effective in characterizing the financial fraud risk of listed companies.

10.4 The Framework of Characterizations for Companies' Financial Fraud Behavior

This section, based on the "Fraud Triangle Theory" of financial fraud and fraud in the Fraud Auditing Standard (SAS99), combined with the governance framework of the company's board of directors and supervisors, combs and summarizes whether management has the opportunity to participate in the fraudulent performance of financial statements. Combined with the financial fraud risk indicators discussed earlier, effective financial fraud risk warning and management are established. The first statement supports the computational performance of the extraction of the characteristics of the fraud risk.

10.4.1   The Performance of the Extraction for Companies' Financial Fraud Behavior Characteristics

In this section, we discuss the performance of the extraction for companies' financial fraud behavior based on information of listed companies from the capital markets in China.

(1) Data and Initial Feature Description
1) The black and white sample data: The data of inquiry letters issued by the CSRC and the exchange because the listed companies in 2017 and 2018 were questioned because of irregular disclosure or authenticity of the financial reports was screened from the CSMAR's violation penalty data[2], and the listed companies inquired were used as black samples. The remaining companies listed before 1 January 2019 are considered white samples if they are not inquired in the above 2 years.

2) The core indicators of feature data: The feature construction method adopted in this paper is based on the hook relationship of financial statements, and the company may cause data anomalies in other accounts of financial statements to identify financial report abnormalities when whitewashing some financial accounts, so the basic data of the main features are "the main financial ratio of listed companies, the year-on-year growth rate of each financial statement account, and the three parts of the percentage report."

(2) Depict the Numerical Performance of Financial Fraud Risk Characteristic Extraction
Iterative effect of feature extraction: After 2,000 iterations of Gibbs stochastic search (Gibbs), at the beginning of the iteration, the model adopts the "'BIC" rapid descent algorithm as the standard, and the corresponding stochastic analog output value has been stable in the given range (the average

---

[2] "CSMAR" is a database provided by the data company "Shenzhen CSMAR Data Technology Co., Ltd." (http://www.csmar.com/channels/46.html).

value is 2,039.50, standard deviation 6.55), which indicates that the Gibbs stochastic search (Gibbs) algorithm based on the BIC judgment standard is stable.

1) The results of the screening ability of the screening features are selected: the features with correlation significance index higher than 0.5 are selected as the modeling features, and Figure 10.3 is obtained. All eight of the features shown are significantly correlated with the financial fraud risks of listed companies. Combined with the ROC performance of the model (Figure 10.2), it can be seen that the model can effectively identify a sample company with a high risk of financial fraud, and the AUC values inside and outside the sample are 0.771 and 0.766, respectively. At the same time, these eight indicators also portray the risk of whether the company's finances are real from both positive and negative aspects: for example, "the proportion of interest expenses to total operating income and the proportion of other receivables to operating income and the proportion of other receivables to total assets" have a significant positive correlation with the financial fraud risk of listed companies. Other features such as "return on net assets after deduction of fees, growth rate of construction in progress, growth rate of advance payments, proportion of investment income and other income to total operating income, and proportion of long-term borrowings to total assets" have a significant negative correlation with the financial fraud risk of listed companies.

2) The eight characteristics of fraud risk are significant in China's A-share market: Based on this paper, the eight characteristics used to characterize financial fraud are screened out, combined with the 2018 annual report information of 3,459 listed company samples, and through the discrete analysis of the indicators, the high correlation characteristic index values shown in Figure 10.3 are obtained (including 353 black sample companies

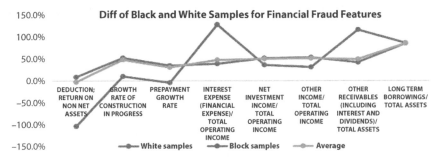

Figure 10.3 The comparison of the average values of the black and white samples of financial fraud illustrated.

and 3,196 white sample companies). The data in Figure 10.3 also show that except for the small significance value of the black and white sample difference corresponding to "long-term borrowing/total assets" (one of the essential reasons for the inclusion of this indicator is that the company's long-term debt ratio is a core basic benchmark for the stable operation of the company), the remaining seven screening features can reflect the significant difference between the black and white samples from the absolute value of the value. This shows that the eight characteristic indicators we screened can identify the phenomenon of financial fraud of the company, and the ROC test for depicting the financial fraud risk model also shows that these indicators have more effective predictive power (the corresponding AUC values in the sample and outside the sample are approximately 0.76), that is, the eight features screened out in this paper can effectively support the detection and prediction of the company's financial fraud behavior (detecting and predicting) function.

10.4.2 The Characterization of Financial Fraud Behavior from Companies' Governance Structure

Taking 3,459 listed entities as a sample, in the case of a relatively reasonable number of supervisory boards (i.e., between five and nine people), the test results show that the number of supervisory boards of the company is not intrinsically related to the company's financial fraud.

Statistical data analysis and test results also show that in the case of a company with a relatively reasonable number of supervisory boards (that is, between five and nine people), the number of the company's supervisory board is not intrinsically related to the company's qualifications, for the general entity enterprise, whether it is in the category A (credit rating from A, AA to AAA) or B (from B, BB to BBB credit rating) or C (from C, CC to CCC credit rating), see Appendix B for their definition of credit rating criteria in detail.

By following Figure 10.4, it is observed that, in general, 25% of left and right companies have seven board members, and approximately 46% of companies have nine board members, and the sum of the two shows that approximately 70% of companies have seven or nine board members. At the same time, for the supervisory board, approximately 80% of the companies have three members of the supervisory board, and the other 14% of the company has five members of the supervisory board.

Credit Rating	Average #	5	6	7	8	9	10	11	12	13	14	15	17	18	Total #
AAA-AA	8.4	7	9	35	13	61	2	9	5	1	0	1	0	0	143
A	8.4	19	20	116	36	225	10	18	9	1	5	3	0	0	462
BBB	8.4	43	31	217	70	402	22	46	19	1	0	7	1	0	859
BB	8.5	26	27	135	68	295	13	48	11	3	3	8	0	0	637
B	8.4	32	30	172	77	359	16	43	16	2	5	4	0	0	756
CCC-C	8.2	41	36	186	55	326	11	32	10	1	1	5	0	1	705
Sum		168	153	861	319	1668	74	196	70	9	14	28	1	1	3562

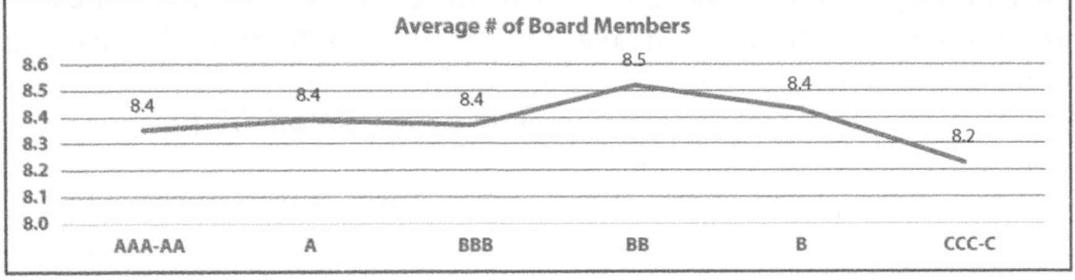

Average # of Board Members

Figure 10.4 The number of directors and supervisors of the companies with credit ratings.

10.5   Conclusion with Remarks

The risk of financial fraud of listed companies will not only cause huge damage to the interests of shareholders but also trigger systemic risks due to the chain reaction of their own business and scale factors. In the practice of the industry, the company's financial fraud risk identification generally needs to be systematic analysis and due diligence from accounting, finance, legal affairs, taxation, internal control management, and other aspects, in today's rapid development of financial technology, under the framework of big data, the company's operation, finance, ecology, and other dimensions of the "holographic portrait" integration processing, in addition to providing more comprehensive due diligence and risk assessment information, but also improve the financial fraud identification and risk management processing capabilities.

In this paper, using the Gibbs stochastic search (Gibbs sampling) method as a tool under the framework of big data, this paper proposes a financial fraud feature extraction method based on the analysis of financial statement data of listed companies, solves the dimensionality disaster problem caused by the hook relationship of financial statements, and extracts eight feature factors from the financial statement data and the two-two interaction items of each financial data to effectively portray the financial fraud risk of listed companies, and the empirical results also show that this method can be more effective in extracting the characteristics of depicting financial fraud. Provide effective technical support for due diligence and risk analysis in audit, compliance, investment analysis and other scenarios.

In the actual scenario, based on big data and artificial intelligence algorithms, with the financial standard No. 99 (SAS.99) standard as the basic framework, the "fraud triangle theory" is combined with structured and unstructured information, and the information of various dimensions of the main company is fully utilized, which can realize the identification and prediction of the company's financial fraud risk, and establish dynamic assessment risk indicators to support dynamic early warning and business management.

Furthermore, it is necessary to start from the governance framework of the company's directors and supervisors, combined with historical information on the bad sample of financial fraud, and the description based on the unstructured 12 classifications, and in particular, how to make full use of deep learning to find out the relationship between the essential characteristics of the following three types of information that characterize the company and financial fraud:

(1) The company's audit committee [effective management, such as the frequency of meetings (problem-solving)];
(2) The members of the Internal Audit Committee and their effectiveness; and
(3) Information on the number of independent outside directors and the effectiveness of their work, etc., which is the focus of our next scientific research work.

Appendix A: The Description of Eight Types of Financial Frauds
The following are the description of typical eight kinds of financial frauds and the accounting subjects involved in the sample companies from 2010 to 2019 from the capital market based on listed companies in China summarized by Huang et al. [20].

Table 10.A The list of description for eight types of financial frauds from the capital market of China.

1. Income fraud (around 68%);
2. Expense fraud (around 22%);
3. Monetary fraud (around 21%);
4. Cost fraud (around 15%);
5. Impairment fraud (around 12%);
6. Non-operating income-expenditure fraud (around 9%);
7. Investment income fraud (around 6%);
8. Other fraud (around 2%).

The following analyzes the main types of financial frauds and the accounting subjects involved in the sample companies from 2010 to 2019 and analyzes the usual methods of financial fraud, and points out the severe challenges brought by internal accounting fraud and external cooperation fraud to the audit of certified public accountants.

As can be seen from Table 10.A above, financial frauds mainly focus on the whitewashing and manipulation of the income statement. Revenue fraud has become the "hardest hit area" of financial fraud, accounting for around 68%, which is similar to the findings of COSO's "Financial Fraud Report from 1998 to 2007". During this period, the U.S. listed companies involved in revenue fraud accounted for more than 60% of the total sample companies. Expense and cost fraud became the second and fourth major types of financial fraud, accounting for around 22% and around 15% respectively. What is particularly noteworthy is that the monetary and capital fraud on the balance sheet has become the third type of financial fraud, which accounts for around 21%.

We also note that listed companies often manipulate their operating performance through a variety of fraud types, and 113 sample companies cover 175 types of fraud. In addition to the conventional income, cost and expense fraud, monetary funds, asset impairment, investment income, non-operating income and expenditure and other items have increasingly become the objects of management performance manipulation.

The above top four types of financial frauds appear to be independent of each other on the surface, but are actually related to each other. First, both revenue fraud and cost fraud aim to exaggerate operating performance for the purpose of issuing new shares, refinancing or maintaining listing status. Secondly, in order to satisfy the falsification relationship and avoid revealing loopholes, listed companies usually adjust expenses and cost items while manipulating income. Finally, the inflated income, expenses and costs need to be disguised by false capital flows, and fictitious bank statements, bank statements and bank confirmations become "compulsory courses" to deal with the inspection of CPAs and regulatory authorities. Driven by the huge economic benefits, it seems that the rigorous reconciliation between the statement items contained in double entry bookkeeping can only increase the difficulty and cost of fraud, that is, it absolutely cannot stop the determination and action of counterfeiters.

1. The characteristics of income fraud:
The income fraud in this paper consists of two types: accounting manipulation and transaction fraud. Accounting manipulation fraud is mainly manifested in the management of listed companies through the choice of accounting judgment more favorable to themselves, to achieve the purpose of performance manipulation, the most common is to recognize revenue in advance. Transaction fraud is mainly manifested in the management of listed companies to fabricate transactions to achieve the purpose of falsely increasing income, the most common is through related party customers or hidden related parties, collude to fabricate business and income. Indeed, the most common type of income fraud in the sample companies is transaction fraud, accounting for around 70%.

Income fraud has become a chronic disease of financial fraud in listed companies, and the high proportion of income fraud in transaction fraud indicates that financial fraud in listed companies has evolved from simple and crude accounting fraud to true accounting fraud at any cost. This not only increases the audit risk of certified public accountants, but also means the deterioration of social integrity environment, because there must be a large number of customers, suppliers, related parties and financial institutions behind the transaction fraud income fraud, common fraud. In such a bad credit environment, how can certified public accountants prevent audit failure?

The most effective way to detect revenue fraud is to extend the scope of audit to customers, suppliers, related parties and financial institutions, which is what regulators have tried and tested time and again. Unfortunately, laws and regulations do not endow certified public accountants known as "market economy guard" with the right to audit external transfer, certified public accountants can only passively inquire or inquire by letter, and the effect depends entirely on the other party's honesty and integrity. However, many audit failure cases prove that such honesty and integrity are often unreliable.

2. The characteristics of expense fraud:
The main methods of the expense fraud are externalization of expenses, intertemporal adjustment and current billing. Among the expense fraud methods, the most secret is the expense externalization, but whether it can escape the audit of CPA depends on whether it can get external cooperation from suppliers, related parties and financial institutions. As long as these external parties actively cooperate with the fraud, in the absence of the right to transfer, even if the analytical review work is in place, it is difficult for certified public accountants to find this kind of expense fraud, especially to obtain sufficient audit evidence.

3. The characteristics of monetary fund fraud:
The monetary fund fraud mainly involves the appropriation of funds by related parties (for example, the listed company may create false externalization of funds through the co-management account of the group). The second way in this category is fabricated monetary funds to cover up income fraud (such as falsifying bank receipts, and some other similar ways).

Monetary fund fraud usually requires the cooperation of banks. In the most common fraud cases, the related financial institutions can be found to cooperate with listed companies to provide false bank statements, statements, confirmation letters and other bad phenomena to auditors. The problem of financial institutions cooperating with listed companies to cheat should be paid attention to and rectified, otherwise the quality of accounting information cannot be guaranteed, audit failure is inevitable.

4. The characteristics of cost fraud:
It can be seen that the cost fraud methods are relatively single, but have certain industry dependence. For example, for listed companies in agriculture, forestry, animal husbandry and fishery, it is difficult to verify the input-output ratio of inventory, and the probability of artificially reducing current operating costs is high. For example, listed companies using the percentage of completion method, such as equipment manufacturing industry and information technology service industry, have a high probability of cost fraud due to their high dependence on the estimate of the completion schedule.

Cost fraud methods are not complicated, and they are accounting manipulation fraud, which is easy to be found. Once certified public accountants find such fraud, they should expand the scope of audit and implement additional procedures to evaluate whether there is a broader and more hidden financial fraud in the listed company.

5. The characteristics of impairment fraud:
It can be seen that the impairment fraud of listed companies is mainly to reduce the provision for the impairment of assets. The common methods are deliberately ignoring the signs of impairment or fictitious payment collection to write down current accounts. It is worth noting that in the case of insufficient basis for impairment, more provision for impairment is the same as less provision for impairment, which is a fraud. Especially in the year after the occurrence of fraud, listed companies "take a big bath" through the provision of huge impairment provisions, often in order to "digest" the fictitious income and profit of the previous year and form false assets. Certified public accountants should hold a high degree of professional skepticism towards such impairment, and check whether there is any fraud in the income and profit items related to the previous year through the asset items involved in the impairment provision.

6 & 7. The characteristics of Non-operating income-expenditure, & Investment income fraud:
These two categories financial frauds are mainly reflected by the following ways, that is, the significant change in the proportion of non-operating income and expenditure, & investment income in the total profit of the company or the significant change in the absolute amount is achieved without debt restructuring, non-monetary abuse and changes in major investment behavior of the company, which is often a fraud that may adjust the value of assets, or use subsidiaries to achieve income adjustment.

Table 10.B The definition of credit rating used for CAFÉ credit risk assessment system.

The classification	Ratings	The definition for credit rating
Investment Grade	AAA	The issuer (company) has the best operating conditions, the highest quality of financial reports, and the highest security.

(*Continued*)

Table 10.B The definition of credit rating used for CAFÉ credit risk assessment system. (*Continued*)

The classification	Ratings	The definition for credit rating
	AA	The issuer's business conditions are very good, the quality of financial reports is high, and the security is high.
	A	The issuer's operating conditions are relatively good, the quality of financial reports is high, and the security is high.
	BBB	The issuer's operating conditions and financial report quality are acceptable, and safety can be basically guaranteed.
Speculative Grade	BB	The issuer's operating conditions are relatively poor, the quality of financial reports is not high, and the security is not high.
	B	The issuer's operating conditions are poor, there may be some problems in the financial report, and safety cannot be guaranteed.
	CCC	The issuer's operating conditions are poor, or the quality of financial reports is low, and the security is poor.
	CC	The issuer's operating conditions are extremely poor, or the quality of financial reports is extremely low, and the security is extremely poor.
	C	The issuer's operations are basically difficult to maintain, and there is basically no security at all. level

8. The characteristics of other fraud:

Those fraud events not covered by seven types of fraudulent practices mentioned above.

Appendix B: The Definition of Credit Rating Grades for CAFÉ Risk Assessment System

The following is the summary in supporting our CAFÉ Assessment System for the credit rating grades.

References

1. Beneish, M.D., The detection of earnings manipulation. *Financial Anal. J.*, 55, 5, 24–36, 1999.
2. Palepu, K.G., Healy, P.M., Bernard, V.L., *Business Analysis & Valuation: Using Financial Statements*, South-Western College Publishing, Cengage Learning Australia, South Melbourne, Vic, 2000.
3. AICPA, *Consideration of Fraud in a Financial Statement Audit: Statements on Auditing Standards No.99*, PCAOB Washington, DC, 2002.
4. Niu, G., Yu, L., Fan, G.Z., Zhang, D., Corporate fraud, risk avoidance, and housing investment in China. *Emerg. Mark. Rev.*, 39, 18–33, 2019.
5. Healy, P.M. and Palepu, K.G., Information asymmetry, corporate disclosure, and the capital markets: A review of the empirical disclosure literature. *J. Account. Econ.*, 31, 405–440, 2001.
6. Defond, M.L. and Zhang, J.A., Review of archival auditing research. *J. Account. Econ.*, 58, 275–326, 2014.
7. Donovan, J., Frankel, R., Lee, J., Issues raised by studying DeFond and Zhang: What should through forensic audit researchers do? *J. Account. Econ.*, 58, 327–338, 2014.
8. Yang, C.H. and Lee, K.C., Developing a strategy map for forensic accounting with fraud risk management: An integrated balanced scorecard-based decision model. *Eval. Prog. Plann.*, 6, 80, 101780, 2020.
9. Vanhoeyveld, J., Martens, D., Peeters, B., Value-added tax fraud detection with scalable anomaly detection techniques. *Appl. Soft Comput.*, 86, 105895, 2020.
10. Nurhayati, Revealing and building the COSO concept and Khalifatullah Fill Ard philosophy to prevent and detect the occurrence of fraud through forensic accounting. *Procedia Soc. Behav. Sci.*, 219, 541–547, 2016.
11. Goode, S. and Lacey, D., Detecting complex account fraud in the enterprise: The role of technical and non-technical controls. *Decis. Support Syst.*, 50, 4, 702–714, 2011.
12. Beasley, M., An empirical analysis of the relation between the board of director composition and financial statement fraud. *Account. Rev.*, 71, 4, 443–465, 1996.
13. Yuan, G.X., Zhou, Y.P., Yan, C.X. *et al.*, The framework for the risk feature extraction method on corporate fraud. *Chin. J. Manage. Sci.*, 30, 3, 47–58, 2022.
14. Yuan, G.X., Liu, H.Y., Zhou, Y.P. *et al.*, Bigdata stochastic search algorithm and application of fund correlation feature mining. *J. Manage. Sci.*, 3, 6, 1–16, 2020.
15. Yuan, G.X. and Wang, H.Q., The general dynamic risk assessment for the enterprise by the hologram approach in financial technology. *Int. J. Financ. Eng.*, 6, 01, 1950001, 2019.

16. Wang, J.C. and Guo, Z.G., *Logistic Regression Model*, Higher Education Press, Beijing, 2001.

17. Agrawal, R. and Srikant, R., Fast algorithms for mining association rules, in: *Readings in Database Systems*, 3rd Edition, Morgan Kaufmann Publishers Inc., Burlington, Massachusetts, 1996.

18. Chen, J.H. and Robinson, T.R., *Asia's Financial Black Hole: The Fatal Weakness Lies In Corporate Governance*, China Machine Press, Beijing, 2015.

19. Hong, W.Z., Wang, X.X., Feng, H.Q., Research on fraud identification of financial reports of listed companies based on logistic regression model. *China Manage. Sci.*, 22, S1, 351–356, 2014.

20. Huang, S.Z., Ye, Q.H., Xu, S., Analysis of financial fraud of Chinese listed companies from 2010 to 2019. *Finance Accounting Monthly*, 14, 153–160, 2020.

21. Liu, S.W., *Identification Technology of False Accounting Statements of Listed Companies*, China Machine Press, Beijing, 2013.

22. Narisetty, N.N., Shen, J., He, X.M., Skinny Gibbs: A consistent and scalable Gibbs sampler for model selection. *J. Am. Stat. Assoc.*, 114, 527, 1205–1217, 2019.

23. Wang, Y. and Yang, S.S., Corporate financial distress prediction based on multi-dimensional efficiency indicators. *Chin. J. Manage. Sci.*, 29, 02, 32–41, 2021. https://doi.org/10.16381/j.cnki.issn1003-207x.2019.1366.

24. Ye, J.F., *Fraud From The Report: Financial Statement Analysis And Risk Identification*, China Machine Press, Beijing, 2018.

25. Zhou, L.G., He, Z.J., Meng, T.C., Research on the contagion effect of credit risk of enterprise groups based on dynamic copula. *Chin. J. Manage. Sci.*, 27, 02, 71–82, 2019.

26. Paz, A. and Moran, S., Non-deterministic polynomial optimization problems and their approximations. *Theor. Comput. Sci.*, 15, 3, 251–277, 1981.

27. Qian, G., Rao, C.R., Sun, X., Boosting association rule mining in large datasets via Gibbs sampling. *Proc. Natl. Acad. Sci.*, 113, 18, 4958–4963, 2016.

28. Akaike, H., A new look at the statistical model identification. *IEEE Trans. Autom. Control*, 19, 6, 716–723, 1974.

29. Qian, G. and Field, C., Using MCMC for logistic regression model selection involving large number of candidate models, in: *Monte Carlo and Quasi-Monte Carlo Methods 2000*, K.L. Fang, H. Niederreiter, F.J. Hickernell (Eds.), pp. 460–474, Springer, Berlin, Heidelberg, 2002.

30. Schwarz, G., Estimating the dimension of a model. *Ann. Stat.*, 6, 2, 461–464, 1978.

31. Glasserman, P., *Monte Carlo Methods in Financial Engineering*, Springer Science & Business Media, New York, 2013.

32. Geman, S. and Geman, D., Stochastic relaxation, Gibbs distributions, and the Bayesian restoration of images. *IEEE Trans. Pattern Anal. Mach. Intell.*, 6, 6, 721–741, 1984.

11

Real-Time Analysis of Banking Data with AI Technologies

S. C. Vetrivel[1]*, T. Mohanasundaram[2], T. P. Saravanan[1] and R. Maheswari[1]

[1]Department of Management Studies, Kongu Engineering College, Perundurai, India
[2]Department of Management Studies, M. S. Ramaiah Institute of Technology, Bengaluru, India

Abstract

The real-time analysis of banking data with artificial intelligence (AI) technologies has the potential to revolutionize the banking industry. This chapter discovers the key aspects of real-time analysis of banking data with AI technologies. One of the key benefits of real-time analysis of banking data with AI technologies is its ability to detect fraudulent transactions quickly and thereby benefiting banks. However, there are also challenges associated with real-time analysis of banking data with AI technologies. One of the biggest challenges is the need for high-quality data. AI algorithms are only as good as the data they are trained on, and poor-quality data can lead to inaccurate insights and recommendations. This invites bankers to spend heavily on data management. Another challenge is the need for skilled AI professionals. Banks must hire or train professionals who have the expertise to develop and implement AI algorithms, interpret results, and integrate them into the bank's operations. This can be challenging in a competitive job market, and banks must be prepared to offer attractive compensation packages and ongoing training to retain their AI talent. As AI algorithms become more advanced, they will be able to analyze larger datasets, detect more complex patterns, and provide even more accurate insights and recommendations.

Keywords: Transformation, real-time, challenge, technologies

*Corresponding author: scvetrivel@gmail.com

Ambrish Kumar Mishra, Shweta Anand, Narayan C. Debnath, Purvi Pokhariyal and Archana Patel (eds.) *Artificial Intelligence for Risk Mitigation in the Financial Industry*, (261–288) © 2024 Scrivener Publishing LLC

11.1   Introduction

The banking industry is constantly looking for ways to improve customer experience, reduce operational costs, and increase revenue. Artificial intelligence (AI) technologies are becoming increasingly important tools for banks to achieve these goals. Real-time analysis of banking data with AI technologies can help banks to identify new opportunities, detect fraud, and make better decisions. AI-driven analytics can be used to gain insights into customer behavior, develop more efficient processes, and increase customer service. By leveraging machine learning, natural language processing, and other AI technologies, banks can quickly analyze banking data and gain valuable insights. This can help banks to better understand customer needs, detect risks, and improve marketing strategies. Researchers around the world are exploring the use of AI in the banking sector (*Fares et al., 2022*) [1] and tracing the consequences of AI for macro control (*Danielsson et al., 2022*) [2]. Real-time analysis of banking data with AI technologies can also help banks optimize customer service, reduce operational costs, and increase revenues. The concept of real-time analysis of banking data with AI technologies is about using artificial intelligence to analyze and interpret banking data in real time. This could include analyzing customer spending patterns, detecting fraud, or predicting future customer behavior. AI-based solutions can help banks make more accurate decisions about how to best serve their customers and make more efficient use of their resources. Additionally, AI technologies can be used to automate mundane tasks such as categorizing transactions, providing customer support, and

Figure 11.1 Data analytics for the prevention of financial fraud. Source: https://www.altair.com/resource/guide-to-using-data-analytics-to-prevent-financial-fraud

offering personalized product recommendations. Figure 11.1 shows the picture of a user applying data analytics to prevent financial fraud.

The purpose of using AI technologies for real-time analysis of banking data is to enable banks to make faster and more informed decisions about their customers, products, and services. This can be used to identify potential fraud, detect changes in customer behavior, detect new opportunities for improved customer service, and provide better insights into customer trends. *Noreen et al. (2023)* [3] found that factors—awareness, attitude, subjective norms, perceived usefulness, and knowledge of artificial intelligence technology—had a significant and positive relationship with the intention to adopt AI in the banking sector. AI can also help banks make more informed decisions about their financial strategies, investments, and risk management. By leveraging the power of AI, banks can become more efficient, agile, and profitable.

11.1.1   The Benefits of Real-Time Analysis of Banking Data with AI Technologies

➤ Increased efficiency: AI technologies can help banks improve the efficiency of their data analysis. By automating the process, AI can quickly scan large datasets for anomalies and insights, allowing for faster decision-making.

➤ Improved accuracy: AI technologies can help banks improve the accuracy of their data analysis. By using predictive models, AI can identify patterns in data that may have been missed by humans, resulting in more reliable and accurate insights.

➤ Reduced costs: AI technologies can help banks reduce costs associated with data analysis. By utilizing AI, banks can reduce labor costs associated with manually analyzing data, as well as the costs associated with storing and maintaining large datasets.

➤ Improved customer experience: AI technologies can help banks create a more personalized customer experience. By analyzing customer data in real time, banks can tailor their products and services to better meet the needs of their customers.

➤ Enhanced security: AI technologies can help banks improve the security of their data. By using predictive models, AI can detect patterns in data that may indicate fraud or other suspicious activities, allowing banks to respond quickly and mitigate any potential losses.

11.1.2   Challenges in Applying AI Technologies to Banking Data

a) Compliance: Banks are subject to strict regulations, making it difficult to use AI technologies such as automated decision-making, which often require large datasets.
b) Data Privacy: Banks must protect sensitive customer information, which may not be suitable for AI technologies.
c) Data Quality: AI algorithms require clean well-structured data, which are not always available from banking systems.
d) Security: Banks must ensure the security of their systems and customer data, which may be vulnerable to malicious attacks when using AI technologies.
e) Legacy Systems: Banks may have legacy systems that are not well-suited to integrating with AI technologies.
f) Adoption: Banks may face challenges in getting employees to adopt AI technologies, as they may require new skills and processes.

The world of banking is shifting faster than ever, with artificial intelligence leading the way in bringing in sea change in the banking industry (Kaur *et al.*, 2020) [4]. The different types of AI technologies that can be used for real-time analysis of banking data are as follows:

o Natural Language Processing (NLP): NLP is a type of AI technology that is used to process and interpret text data. It can be used for real-time analysis of banking data by automatically extracting key information from customer conversations, emails, and other written communications.
o Machine Learning (ML): ML is a type of AI technology that is used to identify patterns and insights from large datasets. It can be used for real-time analysis of banking data by automatically detecting trends and anomalies in customer transactions, detecting fraudulent activities, and predicting customer behavior.
o Robotic Process Automation (RPA): RPA is a type of AI technology that is used to automate repetitive tasks. It can be used for real-time analysis of banking data by automating

the processing of customer requests, transactions, and other back-office operations.

o Computer Vision: Computer vision is a type of AI technology that is used to recognize and classify objects in images and videos. It can be used for real-time analysis of banking data by automatically analyzing customer photos and videos to detect suspicious activities.

o Blockchain: Blockchain is a type of distributed ledger technology that is used to securely store and process data. It can be used for real-time analysis of banking data by providing a secure and transparent platform for transactions and customer data.

11.2   Data Collection and Preprocessing

Data collection is a key step in the development and implementation of AI technologies for banking. Data must be collected, structured, and organized to ensure that AI algorithms can process them properly. This includes gathering data from internal and external sources, such as customer transaction records, market research, and public data. Once the data are gathered, it must be preprocessed in order to ensure accuracy and consistency. This may include cleaning the data, removing outliers, normalizing values, and transforming the data into a format suitable for the AI algorithms. Additionally, data must be labeled in order to properly classify and analyze it. Finally, the data must be split into training and testing sets in order to provide a reliable evaluation of the AI algorithms. The training set is used to train the algorithms, while the testing set is used to evaluate the performance of the algorithms and ensure that they are able to accurately predict the results. By taking the time to properly collect and preprocess the data before applying AI technologies to banking data, organizations can ensure that they are setting themselves up for success. With the right approach, AI can be used to unlock insights and provide actionable business decisions. Figure 11.2 displays the methods involved in AI/ML for data preprocessing.

Data collection is essential for any AI technology applied to banking data. This is because the data collected and preprocessed provide the basis for the model-building process. The model-building process involves identifying and selecting the most relevant features from the preprocessed data, applying the appropriate algorithms, and fine-tuning the model parameters to produce the most accurate and reliable results. This process can

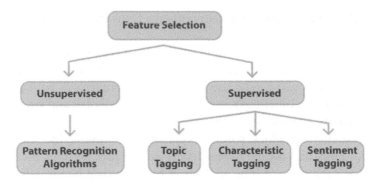

Figure 11.2 AI/ML methods for data preprocessing. Source: https://monkeylearn.com/blog/data-preprocessing/

involve feature selection via univariate or multivariate methods, feature engineering to create derived features, and hyperparameter tuning to optimize the model's performance. Finally, the model is tested against unseen data to evaluate its performance. Data collection and preprocessing also help ensure that the data are accurate and of high quality. This is especially important for AI technologies that use supervised learning algorithms, as the data used for training must be of high quality and accuracy to produce an accurate model. Data preprocessing is also important for AI banking technologies as it helps in cleaning the data, removing noise and outliers, and normalizing the data. This helps the AI technology to better understand the data and provide more accurate results. Data preprocessing also helps reduce the time and resources needed to build the model. Without preprocessing, the model-building process may take longer and require more resources than necessary.

Data collection and preprocessing are the foundation of any successful AI application in banking. With the right data and preprocessing, banks can better understand the customer, identify areas of opportunity, and develop better products and services. Data collection and preprocessing help banks to uncover insights that can inform decisions and strategies. Banks can use the data to identify and understand customer behavior, create personalized experiences, and optimize operations. Additionally, preprocessing allows banks to reduce data errors, clean up data, and make it easier to analyze.

Data collection and preprocessing are also important for ensuring the accuracy of AI models. Without accurate data, AI models can produce inaccurate results, leading to incorrect decisions and strategies. Preprocessing helps to ensure that the data are high-quality, which leads to more reliable results. This helps banks to protect customer data and comply with regulatory requirements. By preprocessing the data, banks can ensure that customer data are anonymized and secure and to protect customers from potential data breaches and helps banks to meet regulatory compliance.

The following are types of banking data that must be collected before applying AI technologies to banking data:

a) Transaction Data: These include information about all customer transactions, such as account balances, funds transfers, deposits, withdrawals, and payments.
b) Client Data: These include demographic information such as age, gender, location, and income.
c) Credit Data: These include credit score, credit limit, and credit history.
d) Risk Data: These include data about customer risk profiles and creditworthiness.
e) Compliance Data: These include data about regulatory and compliance requirements.
f) Marketing Data: These include customer preferences, interests, and behaviors.
g) Security Data: These include authentication and authorization data, fraud detection data, and cybersecurity data.

The steps necessary to prepare the data for analysis before applying AI technologies to banking data are the following:

a) Data Acquisition: Obtain data from multiple sources such as customer databases, transaction records, and credit reports.
b) Data Cleaning: Remove any missing, incomplete, or irrelevant data.
c) Data Exploration: Explore the data to understand its structure and distribution.
d) Feature Engineering: Transform the data into a format that is suitable for machine learning algorithms.
e) Data Split: Split the data into training, validation, and test sets.
f) Model Training: Train a machine learning model on the training dataset.
g) Model Evaluation: Evaluate the model on the validation dataset.

h) Model Selection: Select the best model based on performance metrics.
i) Model Deployment: Deploy the model in production.

Data quality is essential for any successful AI-driven banking application. Poor-quality data can lead to inaccurate analysis, incorrect predictions, and unreliable results. Banks rely heavily on data to make decisions and process transactions. If the data are of poor quality, it could lead to inaccurate decisions and customer service issues.

Data quality is also important for AI-driven banking applications because it helps the AI algorithms learn faster and make better predictions. High-quality data ensure that the AI-driven banking applications are able to learn from the right data and make better predictions. In addition, data quality helps ensure that the AI algorithms are able to identify patterns in the data and make more accurate predictions.

Data quality is also important for AI-driven banking applications because it helps banks ensure compliance with regulations. Banks must adhere to various regulations, such as the General Data Protection Regulation (GDPR) and the Payment Services Directive (PSD2). Banks must ensure that the data they use to build AI-driven applications are accurate and up-to-date. High-quality data help banks meet the requirements of the regulations, reducing the risk of fines and other penalties.

Furthermore, data quality is essential for any successful AI-driven banking application because it helps the AI algorithms learn faster, make better predictions, and ensure compliance with regulations. Banks must invest in data quality initiatives to ensure that their AI-driven applications are able to provide accurate and reliable results.

Underlying methods used to ensure that the data are of a high quality before they are used for analysis while applying AI technologies to banking are as follows:

- o Data Collection: Collecting data from reliable sources is the first step in ensuring high-quality data. This includes gathering data from financial institutions, customer surveys, and transaction records.
- o Data Cleaning: Once the data are collected, it is important to clean them before using them for analysis. This step includes removing any duplicates, correcting errors, and filling in any missing values.
- o Data Transformation: After cleaning the data, it is important to transform them into a format that can be used for analysis.

This includes normalizing data, converting data types, and encoding categorical variables.

o Data Validation: Once the data are transformed, it is important to ensure that the data are accurate and valid. This can be done by performing tests such as cross-validation and unit tests.

o Data Visualization: Data visualization is an important step for exploring the data and discovering patterns. This can be done by creating charts, graphs, and other visualizations of the data.

o Data Analysis: After exploring the data, it is important to analyze them and draw conclusions. This can be done by applying machine learning algorithms and other AI technologies to the data.

11.3   Machine Learning Techniques for Real-Time Analysis

Machine learning is a branch of artificial intelligence that provides systems the ability to automatically learn and improve from experience without being explicitly programmed. It focuses on the development of computer programs that can access data and use them to learn for themselves. Machine learning techniques are commonly used in data analytics, predictive modeling, and optimization.

To enable real-time analysis, machine learning can be used in two major ways: supervised learning and unsupervised learning. Supervised learning involves building a model from labeled data, which is then used to classify new data points. Unsupervised learning is the process of finding patterns in data without any prior labels or predefined rules.

Supervised Learning: Supervised learning algorithms use labeled data to learn from and make predictions. Common supervised learning algorithms include decision trees, support vector machines (SVMs), and artificial neural networks (ANNs). These algorithms are used to classify and predict future outcomes from new data points. Figure 11.3 exhibits the use cases of machine learning in fintech and banking sector.

Unsupervised Learning: Unsupervised learning algorithms do not need labels or predefined rules. These algorithms use statistical methods to explore data and detect patterns and clusters. Common unsupervised

Figure 11.3 Use cases of machine learning in fintech and banking sector. Source : https://intellias.com/5-use-cases-of-machine-learning-in-fintech-and-banking/

learning algorithms include clustering, anomaly detection, and association rules.

Reinforcement Learning: Reinforcement learning is a type of machine learning algorithm that uses rewards and punishments to train the model to learn how to behave in different situations. This type of algorithm is commonly used to control autonomous agents in a virtual environment.

Deep Learning: Deep learning is a subset of machine learning that uses deep neural networks to learn from large datasets. It is used to solve complex problems such as image recognition, natural language processing, and autonomous driving.

These techniques can be used together to create a real-time analysis system that is able to quickly process and analyze data to make predictions and decisions. By combining supervised and unsupervised learning techniques, a system can learn from both labeled and unlabeled data, making them more accurate and efficient. Reinforcement learning and deep learning techniques can be used to further improve the accuracy and speed of the system.

11.3.1   Machine Learning Techniques Used for Real-Time Analysis of Banking Data

> Stream Processing: Stream processing is a type of big data analysis used to analyze large amounts of data in real time. Stream processing systems can be used to identify trends,

detect anomalies, and make predictions as data are being collected. Examples of stream processing technologies include Apache Flink, Apache Spark, Apache Storm, and Apache Kafka.

➤ Supervised Machine Learning: Supervised machine learning is a type of machine learning technique used to predict outcomes and classify data based on labeled data. Supervised machine learning models are trained using labeled data and can then be used to make predictions on new data. Examples of supervised machine learning algorithms include decision trees, support vector machines, and random forests.

➤ Unsupervised Machine Learning: Unsupervised machine learning is a type of machine learning technique used to find patterns and structure in unlabeled data. Unsupervised machine learning models are trained using unlabeled data and can then be used to discover hidden patterns and structure in the data. Examples of unsupervised machine learning algorithms include k-means clustering, hierarchical clustering, and self-organizing maps.

➤ Deep Learning: Deep learning is a type of machine learning technique used to learn complex patterns from large amounts of data. Deep learning models are trained using deep neural networks and can then be used to make predictions on new data. Examples of deep learning algorithms include convolutional neural networks, recurrent neural networks, and deep belief networks.

➤ Anomaly Detection: Anomaly detection is a type of machine learning technique used to detect unusual patterns or behaviors in data. Anomaly detection models are trained using labeled data and can then be used to detect anomalies in new data. Examples of anomaly detection algorithms include k-nearest neighbors, local outlier factor, and one-class support vector machines.

11.3.2   Techniques Used to Evaluate the Accuracy of the Algorithms in Machine Learning for Real-Time Analysis

a) Splitting the Dataset: Splitting the dataset into training and testing sets is one of the most common methods used to evaluate the accuracy of a machine learning algorithm.

The training dataset is used to train the model, and the testing dataset is used to evaluate the performance of the model.

b) Cross-Validation: Cross-validation is another common technique used to evaluate the accuracy of a machine learning algorithm. It is a technique that involves splitting the dataset into multiple parts, training the model on one part and testing it on another part.

c) Confusion Matrix: A confusion matrix is a table that shows the performance of a classifier on a set of test data for which the true values are known. It can be used to evaluate the accuracy of a machine learning algorithm.

d) Classification Report: A classification report is a report that contains the precision, recall, F1 score, and support for each class in the dataset. It can be used to evaluate the accuracy of a machine learning algorithm.

e) ROC Curve: A receiver operating characteristic (ROC) curve is a plot that shows the true positive rate against the false positive rate for a given set of test data. It can be used to evaluate the accuracy of a machine learning algorithm.

11.3.3   Challenges Associated with Applying Machine Learning Techniques to Banking Data

a. Data Imbalance: Banking data are typically highly imbalanced when it comes to class label distribution. This can lead to the machine learning model being biased toward the majority class.

b. Data Quality: Low data quality can be a challenge when applying machine learning techniques to banking data. This is due to the fact that inaccurate or incomplete data can lead to inaccurate predictions and results.

c. High Dimensionality: Banking data can often be high-dimensional, which can be a challenge for some machine learning algorithms.

d. Security: As financial data are sensitive, security is a major concern when applying machine learning techniques to banking data. This means that extra measures must be taken to ensure that the data are secure and protected.

e. Regulatory Compliance: Banks must adhere to a variety of regulations and laws that must be taken into account when using machine learning techniques. This can lead to additional complexity in the development process.

11.4   Natural Language Processing Techniques for Real-Time Analysis

Natural language processing is an area of artificial intelligence that deals with the processing of natural language. It is used to help machines understand and interpret language that people use in everyday life. NLP techniques have been used in various applications such as automated customer service, text analysis, and sentiment analysis.

In the banking industry, NLP techniques can be used to help banks analyze and respond to customer inquiries in real time. Banks can use NLP to identify customer needs, answer questions, and provide timely customer service. NLP can also be used to detect fraud by analyzing customer conversations to determine if suspicious behavior is occurring. Figure 11.4 illustrates the benefits of NLP technique in banking.

NLP techniques can also be used to analyze customer sentiment. Banks can use NLP to monitor customer conversations to identify customer sentiment and track customer satisfaction levels. This can help banks improve customer experience and address customer concerns quickly. NLP can also be used to analyze customer data to identify customer trends and patterns. Banks can use NLP to identify customer needs and preferences and

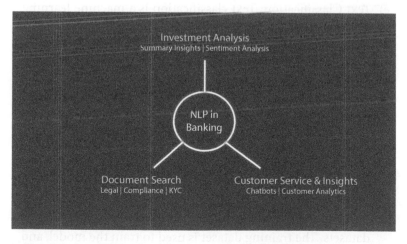

Figure 11.4 Benefits of NLP in banking. Source: https://towardsdatascience.com/natural-language-processing-in-banking-current-uses-7fbbaee837de

develop personalization strategies to better serve their customers. Overall, NLP techniques provide banks with a powerful tool to analyze customer data and respond quickly to customer needs. NLP can help banks improve customer experience, detect fraud, and identify customer trends.

11.4.1   Natural Language Processing Techniques Used for Real-Time Analysis of Banking Data

a) Text Mining: Text mining involves extracting meaningful insights from large volumes of text data. It can be used to identify customer sentiment, trends in customer feedback, and other relevant information.

b) Sentiment Analysis: Sentiment analysis enables the automatic analysis of customer sentiment expressed through text. It can be used to identify customer complaints, feedback, and overall sentiment toward a product or service.

c) Topic Modeling: Topic modeling is a technique that uses machine learning algorithms to identify topics or clusters of related words in a given text. This can be used to identify customer topics of interest and provide more personalized customer experiences.

d) Named Entity Recognition: Named entity recognition is a technique used to identify and classify entities in a text. It is often used to identify customers, products, services, and other relevant entities in customer feedback and other types of data.

e) Text Classification: Text classification is a machine learning technique used to identify the sentiment or category of a given text. It can be used to classify customer feedback or to identify customer groups based on their interests.

f) Text Summarization: Text summarization is a technique used to automatically generate summaries of long text documents. It can be used to quickly identify key topics and customer sentiment in large volumes of customer feedback.

11.4.2   Techniques Used to Evaluate the Accuracy of the Algorithms for Real-Time Analysis of Banking Data

o Data Splitting: The data can be divided into training and test datasets. The training dataset is used to train the model, and the test dataset is used to evaluate the accuracy of the model.

o Cross-Validation: This method is used to evaluate the model's performance on unseen data by splitting the data into multiple subsets and using them for training and testing.

o Confusion Matrix: This is a visual tool used to evaluate the accuracy of the model. It displays the true positive, false positive, true negative, and false negative values of the model's predictions.

o Precision and Recall: These are used to measure how accurate the model's predictions are. Precision is the ratio of true positives over the total number of predicted positives, while recall is the ratio of true positives over the total number of actual positives.

o Area Under the Curve (AUC): AUC is used to measure the accuracy of the model by plotting the true positive rate against the false positive rate. The higher the AUC value, the better the performance of the model.

11.4.3   Challenges Associated with Applying Natural Language Processing Techniques to Banking Data

a) Dealing with Inaccurate Data: Bank data are often noisy and unreliable, which can be difficult to clean and prepare for machine learning algorithms.

b) Understanding Domain-Specific Jargon: Banks often have their own jargon and technical terms that can be difficult to interpret for NLP algorithms.

c) Managing Data Privacy: Banks are heavily regulated and must protect customer data, which can be a challenge when applying NLP techniques that require data sharing.

d) Identifying Meaningful Insights: Natural language processing can be used to generate insights from customer feedback and conversations, but this requires careful analysis to identify meaningful patterns.

e) Dealing with Unstructured Data: Natural language processing techniques are often used on unstructured data, which can be more difficult to work with and analyze than structured data.

f) Developing Accurate Models: Banking data can be highly complex, making it difficult to develop accurate models that can accurately predict outcomes.

11.5   Deep Learning Techniques for Real-Time Analysis

Many researchers explored the real-time application of AI in banking (*Bao et al., 2019; Chen et al., 2020*) [5, 6]. Deep learning is a form of artificial intelligence that is revolutionizing the way that banking data are analyzed in real time. By leveraging multilayered neural networks, deep learning algorithms can process data quickly and accurately, identify patterns and correlations between different elements of the data, and generate actionable insights for banks to use in decision-making.

One way in which deep learning is being used in the banking sector is in fraud detection and risk management. By analyzing transactional data from a variety of sources, deep learning algorithms can identify suspicious behavior that may indicate fraud. This can help banks reduce the amount of fraud losses due to fraudulent activities. *Singh et al. (2020)* [7] explored the real-time analysis of banking data using AI for fraud detection. *Mytnyk et al. (2023)* [8] studied the feasibility for application of AI for identifying fraudulent banking operations and detailed various methods for improving fraud detection accuracy. The fraudulent transactions are scattered with genuine transactions, and simple pattern matching techniques are not often sufficient to detect these frauds accurately *(Lawal, 2021)* [9].

In addition, deep learning is being used to automate the process of customer segmentation. By analyzing customer data, banks can better understand their customers' needs and preferences, allowing them to tailor their services accordingly. This can help banks increase customer loyalty and improve customer experience.

Deep learning techniques provide powerful tools for real-time analysis of banking data. These techniques can be used to identify patterns in the data, detect anomalies, and generate forecasts. For example, they can be used to detect fraud, identify customer segmentations, and understand customer behavior. Additionally, deep learning models can be used to generate predictive analytics models for customer segmentation, customer churn, and customer lifetime value. The use of deep learning for real-time analysis of banking data can also provide insights into customer preferences and trends, enabling banks to tailor their services and products to the needs of their customers. Furthermore, deep learning techniques can be used to identify customer segments and target them with personalized offers. Finally, deep learning can be used to improve customer service by predicting customer needs and providing tailored solutions.

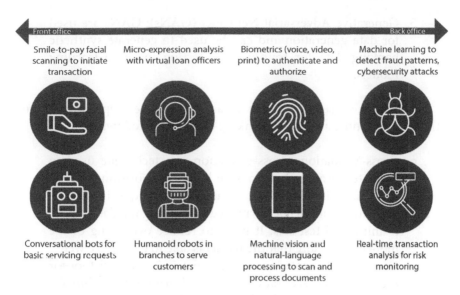

Front office → Back office

| Smile-to-pay facial scanning to initiate transaction | Micro-expression analysis with virtual loan officers | Biometrics (voice, video, print) to authenticate and authorize | Machine learning to detect fraud patterns, cybersecurity attacks |

| Conversational bots for basic servicing requests | Humanoid robots in branches to serve customers | Machine vision and natural-language processing to scan and process documents | Real-time transaction analysis for risk monitoring |

Figure 11.5 Application of AI in banking. Source: https://blog.arrowhitech.com/how-ai-is-used-in-banking/

Figure 11.5 exhibits the application of AI in banking. By using natural language processing and machine learning algorithms, banks are able to better understand customer queries and provide more accurate and personalized responses. This can help banks increase customer satisfaction and create a better customer experience. The types of deep learning algorithms for real-time analysis of banking data are the following:

1. Convolutional Neural Networks (CNNs): CNNs are used for image recognition and classification and can be used to identify patterns in banking data to detect fraud or anomalies.
2. Recurrent Neural Networks (RNNs): RNNs are used for natural language processing and understanding and can be used to analyze text-based banking data for customer sentiment, customer service feedback, etc.
3. Long Short-Term Memory Networks (LSTMs): LSTMs are used for time-series analysis and can be used to detect trends in banking data, such as customer spending patterns, or to predict customer behavior.
4. Autoencoders: Autoencoders are used for anomaly detection and can be used to detect anomalies in banking data, such as fraudulent transactions or customer behavior.

5. Generative Adversarial Networks (GANs): GANs are used for data generation and can be used to generate synthetic banking data for training and testing machine learning models.

The techniques used to evaluate the accuracy of the deep learning algorithms for real-time analysis of banking data are the following:

o Cross-Validation: Cross-validation is a technique used to evaluate the accuracy of a deep learning algorithm for real-time analysis of banking data. This technique is used to evaluate the model performance by splitting the dataset into training and test sets. It helps to reduce overfitting of the model and ensure that the model is able to generalize well.

o Confusion Matrix: A confusion matrix is a useful tool for evaluating the accuracy of a deep learning algorithm for real-time analysis of banking data. This technique provides a visual representation of the model's performance by comparing the predicted labels to the actual labels.

o Receiver Operating Characteristic (ROC) Curve: The ROC curve is a graphical representation of the true positive rate and the false positive rate of a deep learning algorithm for real-time analysis of banking data. This technique can be used to evaluate the model's performance at various probability thresholds.

o AUC-ROC: The AUC-ROC curve is a popular metric for evaluating the accuracy of a deep learning algorithm for real-time analysis of banking data. This technique measures the area under the ROC curve and can be used to determine the model's performance at various thresholds.

o Precision-Recall Curve: The precision-recall curve is a graphical representation of the precision and recall of a deep learning algorithm for real-time analysis of banking data. This technique can be used to evaluate the model's performance at various probability thresholds.

The use of deep learning techniques for banking data can be a tricky situation, as there are many potential risks and benefits associated with it. On the one hand, deep learning techniques can provide banks with more accurate and comprehensive data-driven insights that can help them better manage and optimize their operations. On the other hand, there are fears that the data collected for deep learning models could be used to discriminate against certain groups of people or to build algorithms that could be used to manipulate markets or manipulate customer decisions.

The use of deep learning models also raises questions of data privacy and security, as the data collected to train the models could be potentially used by malicious actors to gain access to sensitive customer information. Additionally, deep learning models may not be able to accurately identify and distinguish between fraudulent activities and genuine ones, thus exposing banks to financial losses due to fraudulent activities.

Overall, there is a need for banks to carefully weigh the risks and benefits of using deep learning techniques for their data before deciding to move forward with their implementation. Banks should also be sure to have the necessary data security and privacy protocols in place to protect customer data, as well as to ensure that the data used for deep learning models are of the highest quality and accuracy.

The main challenge associated with applying deep learning techniques to banking data is data privacy and security. Banking data are highly sensitive and require stringent regulations for access and usage. Deep learning algorithms typically require large amounts of data to be trained, and these data need to be processed and stored securely. In addition, there is a need to ensure that no confidential data are leaked or used for any malicious purposes. Another challenge is the quality of the data. Banking data are often unstructured, which require additional preprocessing and cleaning before being used for deep learning. Finally, deep learning algorithms require a large amount of computing power and time to train, which can be expensive and difficult to manage. According to *Rabbani et al. (2020)* [10], decision-makers in the banking sector should think about modernizing their financial process by utilizing innovation and raising awareness of its use among both current employees and banking clients.

11.6 Real-Time Visualization of Banking Data

Visualizing banking data in real time can be a useful tool for both customers and bankers. It can help customers better understand their financial situation, identify potential opportunities and potential risks, and make more informed decisions about their money. It can also help bankers to gain insight into the customer's financial behavior, monitor customer accounts for any suspicious activity, and detect potential fraud.

The ability to visualize banking data in real time can be achieved by implementing a variety of tools and technologies. These could include financial data visualization tools, such as dashboards, charts, and graphs, which can be used to give customers an overview of their financial situation. Additionally, real-time analytics can be used to detect and monitor customer activity, detect anomalies, and alert bankers when necessary.

Overall, real-time visualizations of banking data can provide customers and bankers with valuable insights that can help improve customer experience, identify potential opportunities and risks, and prevent fraud. Visualizing banking data in real time helps to gain insights into customer behavior, financial trends, and other patterns that can help inform decision-making. It can be used to track spending habits, customer loyalty, and even fraud detection. By visualizing data in real time, banks can quickly identify and address problems, such as customer dissatisfaction or an unusual transaction. It also allows banks to proactively respond to customer needs, so they can provide a better customer experience.

Real-time data visualizations can be used to gain valuable insights into customer behavior and help inform marketing campaigns, product offerings, and customer segmentation. Additionally, it can be used to improve operational efficiency by identifying areas of cost savings, improving customer service, and optimizing processes.

11.6.1   Visualization Techniques Used to Visualize Banking Data in Real Time

- o   Heat Maps: Heat maps are one of the most popular visualization techniques used to visualize banking data in real time. Heat maps allow users to quickly identify trends in the data by using different colors to represent various values. Heat maps can be used to represent the number of transactions, number of customers, amount of deposits, etc.
- o   Pie Charts: Pie charts are another popular visualization technique used to visualize banking data. Pie charts provide an easy way to compare the relative sizes of different categories of data. This helps users to quickly identify which areas are performing better or worse than others.
- o   Bar Graphs: Bar graphs are used to visualize the distribution of data over a period of time. This is especially useful for analyzing trends in banking data over a period of time. Bar graphs can also be used to compare different banks' performance over a period of time.

o Line Graphs: Line graphs are used to visualize the trends in banking data over a period of time. This is especially useful for analyzing the performance of different banks over a period of time.
o Scatter Plots: Scatter plots are used to visualize the relationship between two different variables. This is particularly useful for analyzing the relationship between different banks' performance over a period of time.

The effectiveness of visualizations of banking data in real time depends on the type of data being visualized. For example, if the data consist of customer transactions, a line chart may be used to compare the average transaction amount over time. Alternatively, if the data consist of customer retention rates, a bar chart may be used to compare the retention rate of customers at different levels of service. In addition, if the data consist of customer complaints, a pie chart may be used to show the percentage of customers who experienced a particular problem. Another factor that affects the effectiveness of visualizations of banking data in real time is the accuracy of the data. If the data are inaccurate, the visualization will be misleading. Additionally, the visualization should be user-friendly and easy to interpret. If the visualization is too complex or difficult to understand, it will not be effective in providing insights into the data. The data should be presented in an organized and visually appealing way. An effective visualization should include colors, labels, and other design elements that make the data easier to interpret. Additionally, the visualization should be tailored to the audience and provide insights that are relevant to them.

11.6.2   Techniques Used to Evaluate the Accuracy of the Visualizations of Banking Data in Real Time

a) Cross-Validation: Using cross-validation, predictive models can be tested and evaluated to ensure accuracy. This technique divides a dataset into separate training and test sets, and tests the model against the test set to evaluate the accuracy of the model.
b) Data Clustering: Clustering can be used to group data points into meaningful clusters. This can be used to identify patterns and anomalies in the data that could indicate potential inaccuracies in the visualizations.

c) Statistical Analysis: Statistical analysis can be used to evaluate the accuracy of visualizations by testing for differences between groups or correlations between variables.
d) Visual Inspection: Visual inspection of the data can help identify any potential inaccuracies in the visualization. This involves looking for any patterns or anomalies in the data that could indicate potential problems with the visualizations.
e) Data Mining: Data mining can be used to identify patterns and relationships in the data that could indicate potential inaccuracies in the visualizations. This can be done by looking for correlations between variables or relationships between different sets of data.

11.7   Real-Time Alerting Systems for Banking Data

Real-time alerting systems for banking data play an important role in helping financial institutions keep up with the latest trends and trends in the financial industry. These alerting systems provide banks with a comprehensive view of their data in order to detect fraud, monitor customer behavior, and track financial performance. By providing real-time insight into the data, banks are able to quickly identify and address potential issues that may impact their customers or the overall financial health of the institution.

Real-time alerting systems can also be used to monitor customer transactions, detect suspicious or fraudulent activity, or to alert customers when their accounts are nearing their overdraft limit. Banks can even use these systems to monitor customer account balances and provide customers with tailored advice on how to manage their finances. This helps customers make informed decisions about their finances and can reduce the potential for fraud. Figure 11.6 displays the integrated systems and gateways in banking.

In addition to monitoring customer data, real-time alerting systems can also be used to detect potential security threats. By proactively monitoring the data, banks can detect and address potential cyber threats before they become a problem. This can help banks protect their customers from malicious actors and help them maintain their data security.

Real-time alerting systems are an important tool for banks to have in order to remain competitive in today's ever-changing financial landscape. By monitoring customer data, detecting fraud, and providing tailored advice to customers, banks can ensure that their customers are protected and their financial health is maintained.

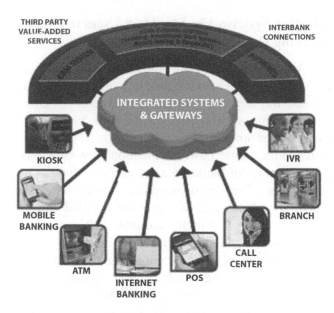

Figure 11.6 Integrated systems and gateways in banking. Source: https://www.inetco.com/wp content/uploads/2013/03/INETCO_MultiChannel-01-300x276.jpg

Real-time alerting systems for banking data are an important tool to help banks stay secure and protect their customers. With the increasing sophistication of cyberattacks, banks must be able to detect unusual activity and suspicious behavior quickly in order to prevent fraud and other security threats. Real-time alerting systems can provide banks with an automated way to monitor their systems and alert them if any suspicious activity is detected.

Real-time alerting systems can use a variety of measures to detect suspicious activity. They can monitor account transactions and flag any transactions that appear to be out of the ordinary. They can also monitor customer activity such as login attempts, account changes, and credit card purchases. Alerts can be configured to be sent to the bank's security team or to the customer directly. *Rahman and Vasimalla (2020)* [11] used machine learning techniques to predict customer churn in banking.

Real-time alerting systems can also be used to detect potential fraud. By monitoring customer accounts for unusual activity, banks can recognize potential fraudulent activities quickly. This can help prevent fraud before it is too late. Overall, real-time alerting systems for banking data are an essential tool for banks to protect their customers and their own operations. By quickly detecting suspicious activity and potential fraud, banks can reduce the financial losses associated with these security threats.

11.7.1 Alerting Systems Used to Alert Users to Changes in Banking Data in Real Time

o SMS Alerts: Many banks are now offering SMS alerts to alert users to changes in banking data in real time. This is a quick and easy way for customers to be notified of any changes in their accounts, such as new transactions, balance updates, overdrafts, or other important events.

o Push Notifications: Push notifications are also becoming a popular way for banks to alert users to changes in their banking data. These notifications can be sent to users' smartphones or tablets and can provide detailed information about any changes in their accounts, such as new transactions, overdrafts, or balance updates.

o Email Alerts: Email alerts are another popular way for banks to alert users to changes in their banking data. These alerts can be sent to customers' email address and can provide detailed information about any changes in their accounts, such as new transactions, overdrafts, or balance updates.

o Voice Alerts: Voice alerts are a more modern way for banks to alert users to changes in banking data in real time. These alerts are sent to customers' phones, in the form of a voice message, and can provide detailed information about any changes in their accounts, such as new transactions, overdrafts, or balance updates.

o Automated Alerts: Automated alerts are a newer way for banks to alert users to changes in banking data in real time. These alerts are generated automatically, based on certain criteria or user-defined parameters, and can provide detailed information about any changes in their accounts, such as new transactions, overdrafts, or balance updates.

11.7.2 Techniques Used to Evaluate the Accuracy of Alerting Systems in Banking Data

❖ False Positive Rate: This measures the rate of false positives, which occur when an alert is triggered for a transaction that is not fraudulent. False positives can cause unnecessary disruption and cost to the customer and the banking institution.

❖ False Negative Rate: This measures the rate of false negatives, which occur when a transaction is flagged as fraudulent but actually is not. False negatives can lead to losses for the bank as well as customers.

❖ Accuracy Rate: This measures the overall accuracy of the alerting system by taking into account both false positives and false negatives.

❖ Precision: This measures the ratio of true positives to all positive predictions.

❖ Recall: This measures the ratio of true positives to all actual positives.

❖ Receiver Operating Characteristic Curve: This plots the true positive rate against the false positive rate to evaluate the performance of a classification system.

11.7.3 Difficulties Associated with Implementing Real-Time Alerting Systems for Banking Data

➢ Data Availability: One of the challenges with implementing real-time alerting systems is the availability of data. Many banking institutions may lack access to timely data that are needed for accurate alerts.

➢ Data Accuracy: Another challenge is the accuracy of data. Without accurate data, the alerting system may not be able to identify fraudulent transactions.

➢ System Complexity: Implementing a real-time alerting system can be complex. The system must be able to process large amounts of data quickly and accurately.

➢ Cost: Implementing a real-time alerting system can be costly. Banks may need to invest in high-end hardware, software, and personnel to make sure the system is up and running.

➢ Privacy: Privacy concerns are a major concern when implementing a real-time alerting system. Banks must ensure that customer data are secure and that data are not being shared with third parties.

11.8 Conclusion

Real-time analysis of banking data with AI technologies is a topic that involves the use of artificial intelligence technologies to analyze banking data in real time. AI technologies such as machine learning and natural language processing can be used to detect patterns in the data and generate meaningful insights. This can be used to identify fraudulent activities and other anomalies. The accuracy of the alerting systems in banking data can be evaluated using various methods such as precision and recall, receiver operating characteristics curve, and confusion matrix. Precision and recall are measures of accuracy and refer to the ability of the system to correctly identify true positives and true negatives. An ROC curve can be used to measure the performance of a classification model by plotting the true positive rate against the false positive rate. The confusion matrix provides a visual representation of the performance of a classifier by showing the number of true positives, false positives, true negatives, and false negatives.

The implementation of real-time alerting systems for banking data can be a challenge due to the need to process large amounts of data in a short period of time. This requires robust computing infrastructure and scalable algorithms that can handle the data load. Additionally, the alerting system needs to be tuned to minimize false positives while ensuring that all suspicious transactions are detected. Finally, the system should be tested regularly to ensure accuracy and reliability. Techniques used to evaluate the accuracy of the alerting systems in banking data typically involve testing the accuracy of the system's predictions. This may include testing the accuracy of the system's identification of fraudulent activity, customer behavior, or other banking-related events. Additionally, accuracy can be evaluated through customer feedback and surveys, as well as by analyzing customer complaints.

The main difficulty associated with implementing real-time alerting systems for banking data is the ability to quickly and accurately detect fraudulent activity or abnormal customer behavior. This requires the system to have access to the latest data in order to detect potential fraudulent activity or customer behavior in a timely manner. Additionally, the system must be able to accurately interpret the data and produce meaningful results. The potential of real-time analysis of banking data with AI technologies is vast. AI technologies can be used to detect and interpret patterns in banking data that could be used to identify fraudulent activity or customer behavior. Additionally, AI technologies can be used to automatically generate alerts in response to changes in banking data. This can enable banks to quickly detect and respond to potential fraudulent activity or abnormal customer behavior.

Techniques used to evaluate the accuracy of alerting systems in banking data include the use of metrics such as precision, recall, and F1 score. These metrics measure the number of true positives, false positives, true negatives, and false negatives generated by the alerting system and are used to determine how accurate the system is in identifying instances of fraudulent activity. Additionally, other metrics such as the receiver operating characteristic curve and area under the curve can be used to evaluate the system's ability to discriminate between legitimate and fraudulent transactions. One of the main difficulties associated with implementing a real-time alerting system for banking data is the need for a continuous and reliable data feed. This is because the system must be able to detect fraudulent activity in real time and respond to changes in patterns of data quickly. As such, the data feed must be able to provide large amounts of data in a timely manner, which can be a challenging task. Additionally, the system must be able to process large amounts of data quickly and accurately in order to generate timely and accurate alerts. This requires the use of high-performance computing and large databases, which can be expensive and difficult to maintain.

Another difficulty associated with implementing a real-time alerting system is the need to have a comprehensive understanding of the data and the rules used to identify fraudulent activity. This is because the system must be able to recognize patterns in the data that indicate fraudulent activity and must be able to accurately distinguish between legitimate and fraudulent transactions. This requires the use of sophisticated artificial intelligence technologies to detect subtle patterns in the data, which can be difficult and time-consuming to develop. Overall, the potential of real-time analysis of banking data with AI technologies is significant, as it can provide banks with the ability to quickly and accurately detect and respond to instances of fraud. However, significant challenges must be overcome in order to implement a successful and reliable alerting system, such as the need for a reliable data feed and a comprehensive understanding of the data and the rules used to identify fraudulent activity.

References

1. Fares, O.H., Butt, I., Lee, S.H.M., Utilization of artificial intelligence in the banking sector: A systematic literature review. *J. Financial Serv. Mark.*, 28, 835–852, 2022. https://doi.org/10.1057/s41264-022-00176-7.
2. Danielsson, J., Macrae, R., Uthemann, A., Artificial intelligence and systematic risk. *J. Bank. Financ.*, 140, 1–9, 2022. https://doi.org/10.1016/j.jbankfin.2021.106290.
3. Noreen, U., Shafique, A., Ahmed, Z., Ashfaq, M., Banking 4.0: Artificial intelligence (AI) in banking industry & consumer's perspective. *Sustainability*, 15, 4, 3682, 2023. https://doi.org/10.3390/su15043682.
4. Kaur, N., Sahdev, S.L., Sharma, M., Siddiqui, L., Banking 4.0: The influence of artificial intelligence on the banking industry & how AI is changing the

face of modern day banks. *Int. J. Manage.*, 11, 6, 577–585, 2020. https://doi. org/577-585. 10.34218/IJM.11.6.2020.049.

5. Bao, Y., Ramesh, A., You, J., Real-time fraud detection in online banking using machine learning techniques. *J. Financial Serv. Mark.*, 24, 1, 41–53, 2019.

6. Chen, J., Wu, L., Liao, H., Xu, J., Real-time data analysis in banking industry based on machine learning, in: *Proceedings of the 2nd International Conference on Computer Science and Application Engineering*, IEEE, pp. 347–352, 2020.

7. Singh, D., Prasad, P., Kumar, A., Real-time analysis of banking data using AI for fraud detection, in: *International Conference on Big Data Analytics and Computational Intelligence*, Springer, Top of Form, pp. 579–587, 2020.

8. Mytnyk, B., Tkachyk, O., Shakhovska, N., Fedushko, S., Syerov, Y., Application of artificial intelligence for fraudulent bankingoperations recognition. *Big Data Cogn. Comput.*, 7, 93, 1–19, 2023. https://doi.org/10.3390/bdcc7020093.

9. Lawal, S., Fraud detection and prevention: A synopsis of artificial intelligence intervention in financial services smart card systems, 2021. https://ssrn.com/abstract=4117507.

10. Rabbani, M.R., Lutfi, A., Ashraf, M.A., Nawaz, N., Watto, W.H., Role of artificial intelligence in moderating the innovative financial process of banking sector: A research based on structural equation modelling. *Front. Environ. Sci.*, 10, 1–16, 2023, https://doi.org/10.3389/fenvs.2022.978691.

11. Rahman, M. and Vasimalla, K., Machine learning based customer churn prediction in banking. *4th International Conference on Electronics, Communication and Aerospace Technology (ICECA)*, 2020, https://doi.org/10.1109/ICECA49313.2020.9297529.

12

Risks in Amalgamation of Artificial Intelligence with Other Recent Technologies

K. Sathya[1]* and A. Hency Juliet[2]

[1]Department of Computer Applications, Faculty of Science and Humanities, SRM Institute of Science and Technology, Kattankulathur, Chengalpattu, Tamil Nadu, India
[2]Department of Computer Applications, SIMATS, Saveetha University, Chennai, Tamil Nadu, India

Abstract

There are various risks while amalgamating two or more technologies. While doing sentiment analysis using artificial intelligence (AI) technique to monitor human activities online, the privacy of humans is affected. Applying AI technique in hospitals for taking care of elderly patients with the help of a robot caretaker affects the quality of life, and there is no contact with the human being. Practicing plenty of algorithms for self-driving cars instead of human decisions may cause mass accidents. In amalgamation of AI and the medical industry, AI sometime recommends wrong medicine to the patient, fails to predict the tumor on a radiological scan, and assign a single bed to two different patients. Another risk of a smart home is that all gadgets are associated, normally connected with the owner's account. Hence, hacking a single device can provide access to the personal data of the smart home owner. AI has no creative thinking; this is the big disadvantage of AI. It never thinks out of the box, it behaves as per the human instructions even though it produces results with increased speed and accuracy than the human brain. Employing AI in education also produces risks like technical expertise is needed and the cost of AI tool is very high in education. Even when AI plays a major role in all other technologies, risks are evolved equally and diminish the quality of human life.

Corresponding author: sathyabalaji33@gmail.com; sathyak2@srmist.edu.in

Ambrish Kumar Mishra, Shweta Anand, Narayan C. Debnath, Purvi Pokhariyal and Archana Patel (eds.) Artificial Intelligence for Risk Mitigation in the Financial Industry, (289–326) © 2024 Scrivener Publishing LLC

Keywords: Amalgamation, artificial intelligent techniques, smart home, medical industry, education, human life

12.1   Introduction

Artificial intelligence (AI) is rapidly permeating the medical industry, playing a significant role in various aspects such as managing medical care and supplies, as well as automating routine tasks within healthcare services. However, the development of intelligent systems to fulfill these responsibilities brings forth a range of challenges and risks. These include the potential for patient harm resulting from AI system malfunctions, the risk to patient privacy arising from data collection and AI interpretation, and other associated concerns. It is crucial to address these challenges to ensure the safe and ethical implementation of AI in healthcare. Figure 12.1 depicts the different types of risks in amalgamation of AI with other technologies.

The implementation of AI in healthcare requires investment in infrastructure, collaboration between regulatory bodies and healthcare providers, and the development of a medical discipline that prepares workers for evolving responsibilities.

This chapter also explores the influence of the financial sector on machine learning (ML) and artificial intelligence. It raises concerns about the potential for these technologies to exacerbate the digital divide

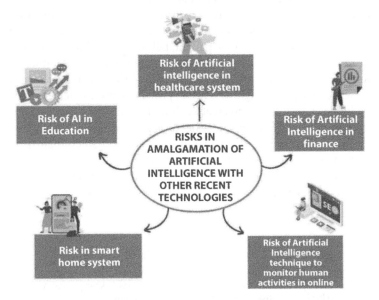

Figure 12.1 Different types of risks in amalgamation of AI with other technologies.

between developed and developing economies. However, it also highlights the advantages that high-tech advancements can bring in terms of fiscal growth and expertise. By embracing ML and AI in the financial sector, there is potential for increased efficiency, improved decision-making, and enhanced financial services. While acknowledging the need to address potential disparities, it is essential to recognize the opportunities that these technologies can offer in driving economic development and knowledge expansion.

This chapter examines the unusual risks that technology can pose to the stability and integrity of the financial structure, as well as the associated policy risks and potential managerial implications. By distilling and categorizing these risks, the discussion on the impact of technology in finance can be advanced. However, due to the ever-changing nature of technology and its applications in the financial sector, it remains difficult to fully comprehend its advantages and disadvantages. Given the uncertainty and potential for unforeseen pitfalls, it is essential for nations to strengthen prudential oversight. By reinforcing regulatory supervision and risk management practices, countries can better navigate the potential risks and ensure the stability of the financial system.

12.2   Risks of Artificial Intelligence in the Healthcare System

Specialists' expertise and performance can also be shared by AI to supplement providers who might not otherwise have it. Ophthalmology and radiology have gained significant attention as notable targets in the application of artificial intelligence primarily due to the extensive development of image analysis techniques. Various programs have been developed to utilize images of the human eye and enable diagnoses that would typically require the expertise of an ophthalmologist. These programs have made it possible for general practitioners, technicians, and even patients themselves to reach such conclusions. This democratization of diagnosis is particularly crucial, as specialists, especially highly skilled experts, are relatively scarce in comparison to the demand in many regions. The use of AI-powered programs in ophthalmology and radiology has the potential to bridge the gap between the limited number of specialists and the widespread need for diagnostic expertise in these fields. Figure 12.2 shows the roles of AI in the healthcare system.

Early detection of ailments

Help in treatment

Associated Care

Checking health through Wearable

Improve decision making

Expanded access to Medical Services

Giving a superior experience

End of Life Care

Figure 12.2 Roles of AI in the healthcare system.

12.2.1 Automating Drudgery in Medical Practice

AI has the potential to automate various computer tasks that currently consume a significant amount of time in medical practice. A considerable portion of providers' time is spent on handling electronic medical records, reading screens, and typing on keyboards [1]. However, AI systems have the capability to streamline this process by efficiently organizing the most relevant information from patient records and converting recordings of appointments and conversations into structured data. This automation has the potential to save providers valuable time, allowing them to dedicate more face-to-face interaction with patients. Moreover, it can enhance the overall quality of medical encounters by ensuring that providers have quick access to pertinent information, leading to more informed decision-making and improved patient care.

12.2.2 Managing Patients and Medical Resources

Finally, although less apparent to the general public, artificial intelligence can be leveraged to allocate resources and shape business strategies. AI systems have the capability to predict departments that may require additional temporary staff, recommend which patients would benefit the most from limited medical resources, and even identify practices that optimize revenue, albeit with some potential controversy.

12.2.3 Risks and Challenges

Artificial intelligence offers a range of potential advantages; however, it is important to acknowledge the presence of inherent risks and challenges associated with its use.

a) Injuries and Errors

The primary risk associated with artificial intelligence is the potential for errors in AI systems, leading to patient harm or other healthcare-related issues. For instance, if an AI system recommends the wrong medication, fails to detect a tumor on a radiological scan, or misallocates hospital beds based on inaccurate predictions of patient benefit, patients may suffer harm. It is worth noting that medical errors are already a significant factor in healthcare-related injuries, even without AI. However, AI errors may differ in two key ways. Firstly, injuries caused by software can have different implications for patients and healthcare providers compared to those caused by human error. Secondly, given the widespread adoption of AI systems, a single underlying issue in an AI system could potentially result in harm to a large number of patients, contrasting with the limited number of patients typically affected by an individual provider's error.

b) Data Availability

To train AI systems effectively, a wide array of data sources is necessary. These include pharmacy records, electronic health records, consumer-generated information, and insurance claims records like data of fitness tracker and history of purchasing. The integration of diverse data sets from these sources is essential for comprehensive and accurate training of AI systems in the field of healthcare. In any event, health information may often be harmful. The majority of the time, data are dispersed throughout several platforms. Patients frequently switch providers and insurance companies, which results in data being split between multiple systems and formats, in addition to the variety just mentioned. This fragmentation restricts the kinds of organizations that are able to develop effective healthcare AI, which also reduces the comprehensiveness of data sets, increases the cost of gathering data, and raises the risk of error.

c) Privacy Concerns

Privacy is a major concern in healthcare AI [2], as developers require large data sets that may involve sensitive patient information. Balancing data collection and privacy protection is essential. A few patients might be worried that this assortment might disregard their security, and claims have been documented in light of information dividing among enormous well-being frameworks and simulated intelligence designers [3]. AI could ensnare protection in another manner: Even though the algorithm never received that information, AI can still predict private patient information. AI in healthcare aims to achieve such objectives. For instance, an AI system could potentially detect Parkinson's disease based on a person's computer mouse tremors, even if the individual never disclosed such information. Patients may perceive this as a privacy infringement, particularly if the AI system's findings are accessible to third parties like banks or insurance companies.

d) Bias and Inequality

AI in healthcare introduces risks of bias and inequality. These systems can adopt biases present in their training data, leading to potential disparities in patient treatment. For instance, if AI is primarily trained on data from academic medical centers, it may lack knowledge and understanding of patient populations that are not typically represented in such settings. This can result in unequal treatment and limited effectiveness for patients outside of academic medical centers. Essentially, if discourse acknowledgment artificial intelligence frameworks are utilized to decipher experience notes, such computer-based intelligence might perform more terribly when the supplier is of a race or orientation underrepresented in preparing information [4].

AI in healthcare can perpetuate biases and inequalities if the training data reflect underlying systemic issues, even with accurate and representative data. This can lead to biased outcomes and decisions, further exacerbating disparities in healthcare. For instance, compared to white patients, African-American patients typically receive less pain medication [5]. Even though that decision reflects systemic bias rather than biological reality, an AI system that learns from health system records might learn to recommend lower doses of painkillers for African-American patients. AI systems involved in resource allocation have the potential to exacerbate inequality by disproportionately allocating fewer resources to patients deemed less desirable or less profitable by healthcare systems due to various unjustified reasons. This can further perpetuate disparities and contribute to inequitable access to healthcare.

e) Professional Realignment

Longer-term risks in the medical profession arise from the automation of tasks, leading to significant shifts in certain specialties such as radiology, where a substantial portion of their work is expected to be automated. This transformation can have implications for the roles and responsibilities of healthcare professionals in the future. Some academics are concerned that the widespread use of AI will eventually lead to a decline in human capacity and knowledge, making it harder for healthcare providers to spot and correct AI errors and advance medical knowledge [6].

f) The Nirvana Fallacy

One more risk needs to be mentioned. The field of healthcare could greatly benefit greatly from AI. The nirvana paradox places that issues emerge when policymakers and others contrast another choice with flawlessness, instead of business as usual. AI in healthcare faces challenges and risks. The current system has its own issues, as AI's inherent flaws pose a risk of perpetuating problematic situations.

12.3   Risks of Artificial Intelligence in Finance

The financial industry is undergoing transformation due to the capabilities of artificial intelligence and machine learning in processing vast volumes of environmental data. Improved capacity for economic, financial, and risk prediction is made possible by AI/ML; restructure the financial markets; increase compliance and risk management; fortify prudential oversight; also, furnish national saves money with new instruments to seek after their financial and full-scale prudential commands. However, there are more drawbacks than advantages when using AI in finance, as each is discussed in detail below. Figure 12.3 shows the role of AI in finance.

12.3.1   Forecasting

Computer-based intelligence/ML frameworks are utilized in the monetary area to estimate large-scale financial and monetary factors, fulfill client needs, give installment limit, and screen business conditions.

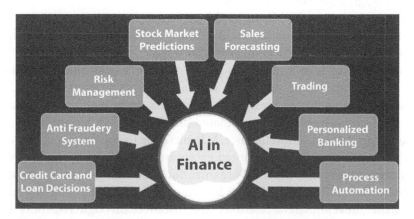

Figure 12.3 Role of AI in finance.

AI/ML models, in comparison to traditional statistical and econometric models, offer increased adaptability, the ability to uncover complex relationships between variables, and expand the range of tools used by institutions. Evidence suggests that ML techniques often outperform conventional regression-based approaches in terms of prediction accuracy and robustness [7].

The application of AI/ML in forecasting brings advantages, as it allows for the utilization of nontraditional data sources like social media, browsing history, and location data, enabling the discovery of new relationships between variables. However, there are also drawbacks associated with this approach. In a similar vein, unstructured data, such as text in emails, can be incorporated into the forecasting procedure by means of artificial intelligence's natural language processing (NLP). In any case, the utilization of forward-thinking information in monetary determining raises a few worries, including the overseeing lawful and administrative structure; privacy and ethical implications; and the quality of the data in terms of their relevance, accuracy, cleanliness, and potential for bias.

12.3.2   Investment and Banking Services

The investment management industry has experienced significant impact from recent advancements in AI/ML within the financial sector. Technology has long been utilized in trading, client services, and back-office operations to handle vast amounts of trading data and enable high-frequency trading. However, AI/ML and related technologies are now reshaping the industry by introducing new market participants, improved client interfaces, enhanced analysis and decision-making strategies, and cost reduction through automated processes.

The adoption of AI/ML in banking has been relatively slower compared to investment management. While the banking sector has historically been at the forefront of technological advancements with the introduction of ATMs, electronic card payments, and online banking, the implementation of AI/ML in banking has been comparatively less rapid. Be that as it may, classification and the exclusive idea of banking information have eased back simulated intelligence/ML reception. In any case, computer-based intelligence/ML entrance in the financial business has advanced as of late to a limited extent because of rising contest from monetary innovation (fintech) organizations (counting fintech loan specialists), yet additionally fueled by simulated intelligence/ML's ability to further develop client relations (for instance, through visit bots and simulated intelligence/ML-controlled versatile banking), item situation (for instance, through social and customized bits of knowledge examination), administrative center help, credit endorsing, and, significantly, cost reserve funds.

The adoption of AI/ML in investment and banking brings new challenges and risks. Timely and high-quality data are crucial for successful implementation. Data privacy and cybersecurity are paramount when handling sensitive information. AI/ML algorithms may uncover unknown correlations, making it difficult for stakeholders to understand the underlying causality, leading to challenges in explaining AI/ML-based financial decisions. Likewise, these models might perform ineffectively in case of major and unexpected developments in input information bringing about the breakdown of laid out relationships (for instance, in light of an emergency), possibly giving mistaken choices, with unfriendly results for monetary establishments or their clients.

12.3.3   Risk and Compliance Management

Simulated intelligence/ML progresses as of late are changing the extension and job of innovation in administrative consistence. Administrative innovation (RegTech) has expected more prominent significance because of the administrative fixing and rising consistence costs following the 2008 worldwide monetary emergency. Generally, innovation has been utilized to digitize consistence and detailing processes [8]. Recent strides in simulated intelligence and machine learning have revolutionized risk and reliability for executives. Leveraging extensive datasets in a progressive manner, these technologies automate decision-making processes, resulting in reduced costs and enhanced compliance quality. Costs have been reduced, and compliance quality has improved.

The adoption of AI/ML technology has the potential to accelerate the implementation of RegTech in the financial sector. According to a global survey, AI/ML is considered the most effective technology among RegTech firms [9]. The application of AI/ML in RegTech has expanded to various activities in banking, securities, insurance, and other financial services, including compliance with COVID-19 relief requirements, identity verification, anti-money laundering, fraud detection, risk management, stress testing, and reporting at both micro and macro levels.

Regulators have generally shown support for regulated financial institutions adopting RegTech. They have implemented plans to raise awareness, promote innovation, and enhance regulatory engagement in the RegTech ecosystem, as seen in the Hong Kong Special Administrative Region. Even in the absence of explicit strategies, authorities have backed RegTech adoption. For example, AI/ML systems with facial and voice recognition, as well as NLP capabilities, can play a significant role in facilitating digital banking license applications and streamlined customer onboarding processes, as observed in jurisdictions like Hong Kong and Malaysia.

12.3.4   Prudential Supervision

Although supervisors' judgment will ultimately guide decisions, AI and machine learning do have a place, particularly in data collection and analytics. Numerous Monetary Soundness Board part country specialists are as of now utilizing ML and NLP apparatuses in information examination, handling, approval, and plausibility [10]. With simulated intelligence, managers can draw further experiences from information and make more educated information-driven choices. The quality of supervision can be improved by AI's ability to spot patterns that human observers are unable to. By alerting supervisors to anomalies in real time, it can also improve supervision's agility [11]. Additionally, applications of supervisory technology (suptech) that make use of AI can offer a predictive analysis, which has the potential to raise the standard of supervision. Regardless of all its true capacity, simulated intelligence/ML is certainly not a silver projectile, and the viability of management will constantly especially rely upon human judgment and an association's gamble culture.

Currently, the analysis, reporting, and data management of misconduct comprise the majority of suptech use cases. A smaller percentage of cases involves virtual assistance, micro, macro, and market surveillance [12]. Workflow automation, structured and unstructured data collection and analysis, conduct risk profiling, and early warnings are all applications of AI in market conduct supervision. Market conduct authorities are interested in off-site surveillance, on-site inspection, and complaint handling [13].

Supervisory authorities are actively assessing the use of AI/ML systems in their risk-based supervision process. AI/ML technology can enhance risk analysis and forward-looking assessments in micro prudential supervision, allowing supervisors to focus on evaluating risks such as credit, liquidity, governance, and risk culture in financial institutions. Sectoral assessments can improve macro prudential supervision by identifying risks and trends specific to different sectors, enhancing overall financial stability. In the securities market, AI/ML systems are also used for market surveillance to detect collusive behavior and price manipulation—potential misconducts that can be particularly difficult to detect using traditional methods [14]. The COVID-19 pandemic has led to an increase in remote work, prompting authorities to utilize technology to enhance the effectiveness of remote supervision. After the pandemic, supervisors may rely more on off-site supervision engagements supported by AI/ML based on these experiences.

The utilization of computer-based intelligence/ML by administrative specialists accompanies difficulties and dangers that should be painstakingly thought of. The viability of artificial intelligence/ML-driven management will rely upon information normalization, quality, and fulfillment, which could be trying for specialists and directed organizations the same, especially while utilizing modern wellsprings of information, for example, online entertainment [15]. Lack of resources and skills may make it difficult for supervisory authorities to use AI/ML safely and effectively. The workforce pool could be extended to incorporate man-made intelligence/ML-trained professionals and information researchers. At long last, conveying simulated intelligence/ML frameworks gives bosses chances, incorporating those related with, protection, network safety, result reasonableness, and installed inclination.

12.3.5 Central Banking

While AI and machine learning have the potential to enhance central banks' operations and policymaking, many central banks have been cautious in adopting these technologies. AI and ML systems can support improved monetary and macro prudential policies, as well as provide deeper insights into economic and financial developments. They could also speed up crisis response, assist in predicting the development of systemic risks, and strengthen systemic risk monitoring. While there are anticipated benefits, the use of AI/ML for policymaking should be exercised with caution, relying on human judgment. Furthermore, AI/ML can provide central banks with improved internal control capabilities, including monitoring internal operations and optimizing resource allocation across functions.

Most of the technology needed to create these applications exists. Cultural, political, and legal factors, as well as a lack of sufficient capacity, are to blame for its slow adoption by central banks [16]. Nevertheless, AI/ML is being looked into by some central banks. In order to better inform policy decisions, central banks have conducted experiments and research aimed at increasing the capacity for near-term forecasting and monitoring market sentiment. A few national banks are likewise creating applications to work on inward cycles and administrative center capabilities (for instance, cash the executives).

Artificial intelligence/ML use in focal banking does not appear to raise huge worries for now; however, this could change with more extensive sending. When central banks utilize large nontraditional and unstructured data sets for policymaking, they may encounter data bias and potential errors due to unexpected shifts in the data. Lack of resources and skills to operate AI/ML and mitigate associated risks can further compound these concerns. Acquiring representative and high-quality data, as well as addressing data privacy and security issues, can pose additional challenges for central banks in adopting AI/ML.

12.3.6   Cybersecurity

The adoption of AI and machine learning introduces new and distinct cyber risks, expanding the scope of potential threats in the cybersecurity landscape. Notwithstanding customary digital dangers from human or programming disappointments, artificial intelligence/ML frameworks are helpless against novel dangers. These threats focus on manipulating data at some point during the AI/ML life cycle to take advantage of AI/ML algorithms' inherent weaknesses [17].

The manipulation of AI/ML systems can lead to poor decision-making and unauthorized extraction of information, posing a significant risk for financial sector organizations. Ongoing oversight is crucial to promptly detect and effectively manage such attacks, considering the complexity and potential impact of ML models. Notwithstanding commonplace network protection concerns, explicit digital dangers to computer-based intelligence/ML can extensively be gathered as:

- ▶ Data poisoning attacks seek to influence ML algorithms during the training phase by introducing specially crafted samples into the data set, posing a risk to the integrity and reliability of the algorithm. These assaults make the simulated intelligence inaccurately figure out how to group or perceive data. Trojan models, which conceal malicious actions and wait for special inputs to be activated, can also be created through data poisoning [18]. Data poisoning attacks, if executed with privileged access to model and training data, can be difficult to detect unless the malicious behavior disrupts routine diagnostic tests, highlighting the potential challenges in identifying such attacks on ML models.
- ▶ Attackers can manipulate data inputs through input attacks, deceiving AI systems during operations. By subtly altering images in ways imperceptible to human vision, attackers

can cause AI/ML image recognition systems to misclassify the images, showcasing the vulnerability of these systems to adversarial manipulation.

► Model extraction or model reversal attacks aim to retrieve training data or the model itself. Membership inference attacks, a variant of such attacks, aim to determine if a specific data instance was part of the training set. These attacks can be conducted as black box attacks, where attackers have limited access to the model. Model inversion attacks raise copyright and privacy concerns and are not explicitly addressed in current privacy protection laws like the General Data Protection Regulation of the European Union.

► Regulators in the financial sector are growing more concerned about the cybersecurity risks associated with AI/ML. These risks have the potential to undermine the integrity and trust in the financial industry. Faulty AI/ML systems could impact the sector's ability to accurately assess, price, and manage risks, leading to the accumulation of systemic risks. Moreover, attackers may target training data sets that contain personal and sensitive financial information.

The financial industry's regulatory cybersecurity requirements could be extended to include AI/ML-specific cyber threats. Suppliers and clients of simulated intelligence/ML applications in the monetary area ought to be expected to set up, as a component of their more extensive network safety structure, relieving procedures. These might include methods for protecting the privacy of models and data, robust security for training data feeds, and detection and reporting systems.

12.3.7   Data Privacy

The privacy implications of AI/ML are unique and require attention. While existing tools and legal frameworks address big data privacy concerns, new challenges arise from AI/ML models' ability to prevent data leakage and infer sensitive information. Robustness measures are being developed to protect sensitive data, but further work and updates to the legal and regulatory framework are needed to ensure enhanced privacy standards and compliance with anti-money laundering and counterterrorism requirements for AI/ML systems and data sources.

12.3.8   Impact on Financial Stability

The full impact of AI/ML systems on financial stability is still being assessed, but their increasing adoption in the financial sector is expected to bring about significant transformation. As featured above, on one hand, with painstakingly planned and tried calculations fulfilling an elevated degree of controls to restrict dangers and execution issues, simulated intelligence/ML frameworks might bring expanded efficiencies; better risk pricing, management, and assessment; increased compliance with regulations; and new instruments for prudential reconnaissance and implementation—all of which will contribute decidedly to monetary solidness. However, the inherent opacity of AI/ML systems, their susceptibility to manipulation, concerns regarding their robustness, and privacy issues pose unique risks. These factors have the potential to erode public confidence in the security and reliability of an AI/ML-driven financial system. Furthermore, the adoption of AI and machine learning could introduce new channels for the propagation of systemic risks.

- ► Given the specialized nature of AI/ML systems and the impact of network effects, AI/ML service providers have the potential to become systemically significant participants within the financial market infrastructure. This concentration of power raises concerns about the vulnerability of the financial system to single points of failure.
- ► The rise of third-party AI/ML algorithm providers in finance, alongside industry interconnectivity, may lead to more uniform risk assessments and credit decisions. This concentration of data and reliance on alternative data sources could amplify risks of herding behavior, potentially increasing systemic risks in the financial sector.
- ► The widespread use of AI and machine learning in credit underwriting and risk management processes could increase the procyclicality of financial conditions. The inherent nature of these processes to amplify and reinforce changes in the financial environment may be further automated and accelerated by AI/ML. However, the lack of explainability in AI/ML models may obscure the extent of this procyclicality.
- ► In the presence of a tail risk, incorrect risk assessment and response by ML algorithms could exacerbate and propagate the shock across the financial system, posing challenges for

an effective policy response. The speed and potential ampli-
fication of such shocks by ML algorithms may hinder the
ability to effectively mitigate the impact on the financial
system.

► There is a concern that economic policies or market strategies based on AI/ML models may be challenging to interpret
or predict, leading to increased asymmetric information in
the market and an uncertain impact on financial stability.
The difficulties in interpretation, sustainability of analytical
power, and prediction of these models could create additional uncertainties in the financial landscape.

► At long last, administrative holes could antagonistically
affect monetary steadiness assuming mechanical advances
dominate existing guidelines. Providers who may be outside
of the current regulatory framework are frequently in charge
of these advancements.

Regulatory responses to the rapid development of AI/ML vary across
jurisdictions. Some regulators, such as the Monetary Authority of Singapore
and De Nederlandsche Bank, have adopted comprehensive approaches
to address emerging issues. Others believe that existing regulations and
governance expectations are adequate. Common regulatory areas of focus
include AI/ML governance frameworks, risk management, internal controls, and improved oversight of models and data often through the implementation of new or updated regulations.

Addressing the challenges associated with AI/ML in the financial sector requires substantial regulatory and collaborative efforts. It is crucial to
prioritize the acquisition of technical skills and establish clear minimum
standards and guidelines for the industry. This will enable an effective
policy response and ensure that the necessary safeguards are in place to
mitigate risks and promote responsible and ethical use of AI/ML technol
ogies. Given the intrinsic interconnectivity of issues connected with the
sending of simulated intelligence/ML frameworks in the monetary area,
joint effort among monetary establishments, national banks, monetary
managers, and different partners is vital to stay away from duplication of
work and to assist with countering likely dangers. Many driving purviews
in the computer-based intelligence/ML area have depended on very much
expressed public artificial intelligence systems for advancing computer-
based intelligence/ML advancement while guaranteeing that administrative holes do not appear.

12.4   Common Risks of Artificial Intelligence Techniques

Man-made brainpower (artificial intelligence) strategies are for the most part used to tackle profoundly complex undertakings like handling normal language or arranging objects in pictures. Computer-based intelligence techniques do not just permit altogether more significant levels of mechanization to be accomplished; however, they additionally open up totally new fields of use [19]. The significance of artificial intelligence is continuously increasing due to the development of new applications and ongoing research successes. Figure 12.4 shows the various applications of AI in real life.

AI has the potential to revolutionize various industries and domains, offering advanced capabilities such as data analysis, pattern recognition, automation, and decision-making. As AI continues to advance, its impact on society, economy, and technology is becoming more prominent, shaping the way we live, work, and interact with technology. The rapidly expanding market for artificial intelligence will play an increasingly significant role in occupational safety in the coming years, driven by success in the fields of image recognition, natural language processing, and self-driving vehicles [20, 21].

However, secure and dependable artificial intelligence is required for human health and safety. This is due to the fact that, despite the new prospects for occupational safety and the rapid positive advancement of this technology, its increasing application will also result in new risks [22]. We are already seeing an increase in the number of accidents that occur in systems that employ artificial intelligence [23], and there have been numerous reports of fatal accidents caused by AI-related failures in automated vehicles [24, 25].

Existing safety standards are hardly applicable to AI systems because they do not take into account the technical peculiarities of these systems [26]. The development of software in the field of artificial intelligence poses unique challenges when it comes to risk reduction. Traditional measures used in software development, such as check and approval exercises, may be limited in their effectiveness due to the complexity and vast possibilities within the AI system's state space. Unlike conventional software, AI systems operate in a dynamic and complex environment, making it difficult to anticipate and plan for all potential scenarios. As a result, the traditional risk mitigation approaches need to be adapted and enhanced to address the specific challenges posed by AI development. These applications have to deal with a variety of biases [27], some of which are unique to AI systems and are not taken into account in the mandatory verification and validation activities of existing software safety standards.

Figure 12.4 depicts the applications of AI in real life. As a result, the creation of secure AI systems necessitates a thorough comprehension of the components of reliable artificial intelligence [28, 29], and risk management for AI-based systems must be carefully adapted to the emerging issues posed by this technology.

Assurance cases provide a structured framework for certifying the quality and reliability of AI applications, enhancing transparency and trust by documenting requirements, design rationale, testing results, and mitigation strategies. To meet a certain quality standard, these need to present arguments that can be evaluated and are organized [30 32]. However, these books fall short when it comes to a detailed breakdown of important requirements. We propose that the sources of risk for AI systems be used to define these criteria. These can then be used in the risk assessment to evaluate and analyze them to determine the best ways to reduce risk; this turns out to be essential.

Thus, it is crucial to identify these novel threats and investigate how computer based intelligence characteristics impact the risk management strategy of the executive, depending on the viability of the framework and its application environment. The majorities of AI-related international standards are still in the development stage and typically only address partial aspects like explainability [33] or controllability [34] or that they are not applicable to safety-related systems [35]. By their very nature, other

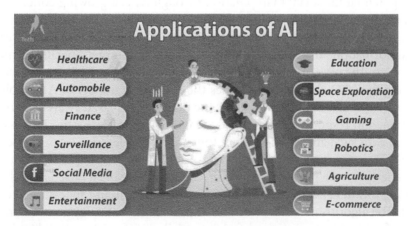

Figure 12.4 Applications of AI in real life.

legislative documents, such as the European Commission's Proposal for an Artificial Intelligence Act [36], only define generic requirements at a very high level from which relevant risk fields must first be derived.

Late methodologies for distinguishing and organizing explicit well-springs of chance for computer-based intelligence frameworks have proactively recognized a portion of these dangers [22]. However, assurance cases in the field of AI still have limitations. They often do not adequately address crucial aspects such as security and lack a comprehensive process model for holistic risk evaluation in the AI domain. Additionally, there is a need for a comprehensive classification of risk sources to establish corresponding guidelines for AI development. In a similar vein, they only provide a brief explanation of the risk sources, making it challenging to acquire a fundamental comprehension of the challenges they pose.

The impact of artificial intelligence extends beyond the tech industry and raises concerns in various areas. Job automation is one significant concern, as AI has the potential to replace human labor in certain tasks and industries. The spread of fake news is another pressing issue, as AI can be used to generate and disseminate misleading or false information at a large scale. Furthermore, there are concerns about the development of AI-powered weapons, which could lead to an arms race and raise ethical and security implications. Addressing these challenges requires careful consideration and proactive measures to ensure the responsible and beneficial use of AI technology.

12.4.1   Social Manipulation and AI Algorithms

The potential for social manipulation through AI is a growing concern in today's digital landscape. Politicians and other actors can leverage platforms and technologies, such as social media and AI-powered tools, to spread misinformation, manipulate public opinion, and target specific demographics. The case of Ferdinand Marcos, Jr., utilizing a TikTok troll army during the 2022 election exemplifies the real-world impact of AI-enabled social manipulation. This highlights the need for increased awareness, regulation, and responsible uses of AI technology to mitigate the risks associated with such abuses and ensure the integrity of democratic processes.

TikTok's AI algorithm plays a significant role in shaping users' content experience on the platform. However, concerns have been raised regarding the algorithm's effectiveness in filtering out harmful and inaccurate content. The algorithm's reliance on users' past media consumption to curate their feed has been criticized for potentially reinforcing echo chambers and amplifying misleading or dangerous media. These concerns highlight the importance of ensuring robust content moderation and implementing effective safeguards to protect users from potentially harmful or deceptive content on TikTok.

The rise of deep fake technology has significantly blurred the lines between reality and fiction, particularly in the realm of online media and news. With the ability to seamlessly manipulate images and videos, bad actors now have a powerful tool to disseminate false information and propagate propaganda. This has created a situation where distinguishing between accurate and false information becomes increasingly challenging, leading to a loss of trust in traditional forms of evidence. As public figure Ford mentioned, the inability to trust what we see and hear poses a significant problem, as it undermines the foundation of reliable information. Addressing the issue of deep fakes and developing effective methods to detect and counteract their impact are crucial to safeguarding the integrity of online media and ensuring public trust in information sources.

12.4.2   Social Surveillance with AI Technology

Ford is concentrating on the negative consequences that AI will have on privacy and security, along with the greater factual threat it poses. A perfect representation is China's utilization of facial recognition innovation in workplaces, schools, and different settings. Other than following an individual's developments, the Chinese government might have the option to assemble an adequate number of information to screen an individual's exercises, connections, and political perspectives.

Predictive policing algorithms in the United States, influenced by biased arrest rates, disproportionately target black communities, leading to over-policing. This raises concerns about the potential for AI to become an authoritarian weapon and questions whether democracies can prevent its misuse. Safeguards and oversight mechanisms are needed to ensure responsible and equitable deployment of AI in law enforcement.

According to Ford, "Authoritarian regimes use AI or are planning to use it." This raises the question of how much AI poses a threat to Western nations and democracies, as well as what limitations should be imposed on its use.

12.4.3   Bias in Artificial Intelligence Systems

Additionally, bias of AI in various forms is harmful. Olga Russakovsky, a professor of computer science at Princeton, highlighted to the New York Times that AI bias extends beyond gender and race. As AI is created by humans, who are inherently biased and influenced by data and algorithmic biases, the potential for bias in AI systems is significant and can amplify existing biases.

Russakovsky points out that those AI researchers primarily consist of men from specific racial and socioeconomic backgrounds, with limited representation of individuals with disabilities. This lack of diversity poses a challenge in addressing global issues effectively, as it hampers the ability to consider and understand the perspectives and experiences of a more heterogeneous population.

The restricted encounters of artificial intelligence makers might make sense of why discourse acknowledgment man-made intelligence frequently neglects to grasp specific accents and lingos, or why organizations neglect to acknowledge the results of a chatbot imitating a famous picture in mankind's set of experiences. Businesses and developers need to take extra care to escape reinforcing dominant prejudices and biases that put minority society people at risk.

12.4.4   Expanding Socioeconomic Inequality as a Result of AI

Through AI-powered recruiting, businesses may jeopardize their DEI initiatives if they fail to acknowledge the biases constructed into AI algorithms. AI's ability to measure candidates' traits through facial and voice analyses can perpetuate discriminatory hiring practices, despite claims of eliminating bias. This raises concerns about racial biases embedded in AI systems. Furthermore, AI-driven job loss has led to growing socioeconomic inequality, with blue-collar workers experiencing significant wage reductions, while white-collar workers largely remain unaffected or even receive higher wages. This demonstrates the class biases in the application of AI technology.

Deep claims that AI has expanded employment opportunities or broken down social barriers in some way are incomplete. It is essential to take into consideration the disparity that depends on race, class, and other classes. Contrarily, it will be more difficult to resolve how automation and AI benefit some people and groups at the expense of others.

12.4.5   Descending Goodwill and Ethics Because of AI

Pope Francis, along with other religious leaders, technologists, journalists, and political figures, has expressed concerns about the potential socioeconomic pitfalls of AI. In a 2019 Vatican meeting, Pope Francis emphasized the need for proper oversight and restraint in the development of AI to avoid negative consequences. He warned about the circulation of biased opinions and false information, highlighting the risk of regressing into a form of barbarism where the strongest dictates societal norms. The Pope stressed the importance of ensuring that technological innovation aligns with the common good and does not become an antagonist to humanity's well-being.

These concerns are further supported by the speedy growth of the ChatGPT, a conversational AI tool. Numerous clients have applied the innovation to escape composing tasks, compromising scholastic uprightness and innovativeness. OpenAI also exploited low-wage Kenyan laborers to carry out the work, despite efforts to make the tool less harmful.

Despite the warnings from influential voices, there is a fear that the pursuit of financial gain may lead us to push the boundaries of artificial intelligence without sufficient regard for the associated risks. The drive for profit can sometimes overshadow ethical considerations, underscoring the need for ethical frameworks and regulations to ensure responsible AI development and use.

"'The mindset is, 'In the event that we can make it happen, we ought to attempt it; Let's see what happens,' said Messina. 'We'll do a lot of it if we can make money from it.' However, this is not exclusive to technology. That has been going on for eternity."

12.4.6 Autonomous Weapons Powered by Artificial Intelligence

Technological advancements have been used to wage war, as is all too frequently the case. With regard to simulated intelligence, some are quick to take care of business before it is past the point of no return: In 2016, a group of over 30,000 researchers in AI and robotics expressed concerns about investing in AI-powered autonomous weapons. They warned that pursuing such development could lead to a global arms race and the widespread use of autonomous weapons, drawing a parallel between them and the prevalence of Kalashnikov rifles.

Aforementioned prediction has happened as expected as Deadly Independent Weapon Frameworks, which find and annihilate focuses all alone while submitting to not many guidelines. The proliferation of powerful and complex weapons has led some powerful nations to succumb to fears and engage in a technology cold war. In this context, the development and potential misuse of autonomous weapons raise significant concerns, particularly regarding the safety and well-being of civilians in conflict zones. Programmers have dominated different kinds of digital assaults, so it is not hard to envision a noxious entertainer penetrating independent weapons and impelling outright Armageddon.

In the event that political contentions and warmongering propensities are not held under control, man-made consciousness could turn out to be applied with the most terrible expectations.

12.4.7   Financial Implications of AI Algorithms

The integration of AI technology in routine financial and trading processes has gained significant traction in the financial sector. However, the reliance on algorithmic trading has been identified as a potential factor contributing to major financial crises. AI algorithms, while devoid of human judgment and emotions, often fail to consider contextual factors, market interconnectedness, and human trust and fear. These algorithms execute numerous trades rapidly, aiming to generate small profits within seconds. Auctioning off a great many exchanges could terrify financial backers into doing likewise, prompting unexpected accidents and outrageous market instability.

The Knight Capital Flash Crash and the 2010 Flash Crash exemplify the disruptive effects that can arise when trade-obsessed algorithms malfunction or engage in rapid and massive trading. These incidents underscore the importance of implementing effective risk management and oversight in algorithmic trading systems to safeguard market stability and investor interests, which does not imply that the financial industry does not benefit from AI. Truth be told, man-made intelligence calculations can assist financial backers with settling on more brilliant and more educated choices available. However, finance companies must ensure that they recognize their AI algorithms and how they produce results. Organizations ought to examine whether man-made intelligence boosts or brings down their certainty prior to acquainting the innovation with abstinence from stirring up fears among financial backers and making monetary bedlam.

12.5   Risks in Smart Home Systems

Smart home devices offer convenience and connectivity but come with security flaws that can pose risks to your data and property. These devices store a wealth of personal information that cybercriminals can exploit through hacking if proper security measures are not in place. Stolen data can be used for targeted attacks, such as tricking you into fraudulent transactions.

To mitigate these risks, avoid sharing sensitive financial information with smart devices and be cautious about connecting email clients, calendars, and other apps containing sensitive data to your devices. By taking these precautions, you can reduce the chances of falling victim to cybercrime in your smart home environment.

12.5.1   Identity Theft

In some cases, hackers may target a smart device company's database to gain access to the data of multiple users instead of individually breaching each user's device. This can result in massive data breaches where the personal information of numerous smart device users is compromised. If you become a victim of such a breach, it can lead to identity theft and significant disruptions in your life. To mitigate the risks, it is advisable to regularly monitor your credit report for any negative changes and minimize the personal information you share with smart devices. By taking these precautions, you can reduce the potential impact of a data breach on your personal and financial well-being. Various devices in a smart home system are shown in Figure 12.5.

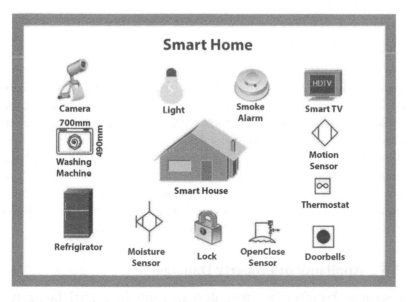

Figure 12.5 Various devices in a smart home system.

12.5.2   Password Exploitation

Securing smart home hubs with weak passwords poses significant security vulnerability, allowing clever hackers to tamper with the hub and other connected devices. This can lead to unsettling scenarios such as hackers remotely controlling lights or changing TV channels to frighten home-owners. To prevent virtual break-ins, it is crucial to use strong unique pass-words and implement two-factor authentication for all smart devices. By following these practices, you can enhance the security of your smart home and reduce the risk of unauthorized access and control by hackers.

12.5.3   Location Tracking

Smart home devices, which we rely on to safeguard our private data, can unintentionally compromise our trust by disclosing our location and enabling real-time tracking by hackers. For instance, vulnerable smart speakers can be tricked into revealing a user's precise location, including their street address, when a malicious link is clicked on a device connected to the same network. To protect your coordinates and maintain privacy, it is essential to be cautious of suspicious links and consider setting up a sep-arate network dedicated solely to smart home devices. By implementing these measures, you can reduce the risk of unauthorized location disclo-sure and enhance the security of your smart home environment.

12.5.4   Home Intrusions

While security devices like smart door locks and surveillance cameras are intended to enhance safety, the potential risk of remote device tampering outweighs the concern of physical break-ins. Undisclosed vulnerabilities in these devices can provide hackers with the ability to disable cameras, unlock doors, and gain unauthorized access to your property. To bolster protection against intruders, it is advisable to consider additional secu-rity measures such as installing security door braces and utilizing a reli-able security alarm system. By implementing these precautions, you can strengthen the physical security of your home and reduce the risk of unau-thorized access or tampering of smart security devices.

12.5.5   Appliance or Property Damage

The security breaches in smart devices controlling vital home func-tions, such as heating and cooling, can lead to severe consequences.

Hackers gaining access to these devices can cause system malfunctions or even start fires remotely. To mitigate these risks, it is crucial to select smart devices that allow you to lock the settings, making it harder for unauthorized individuals to tamper with them. By prioritizing secure devices, you can enhance the safety and protection of your home environment.

12.5.6   Unauthorized Recordings and Privacy Violations

Do you occasionally get the impression that someone is listening in on you? In the event that you own a savvy speaker, your anxiety is very much established. Not in the least do these computerized voice associates tune in on you ceaselessly while on; however, programmers can likewise take advantage of safety escape clauses to break into the speaker and issue their own orders or collect earlier accounts. To ensure your privacy, it is advisable to periodically delete stored accounts, avoid integrating security devices like cameras or door locks with smart speakers, and consider turning off your smart speakers when they are not in use. These measures can help safeguard your personal information and mitigate potential risks associated with smart home devices.

12.5.7   External Vulnerabilities

Many smart devices allow users to control various functions remotely through third-party mobile applications or smart home platforms. However, if someone gains unauthorized access to your phone, apps that lack secure authorization measures may allow them to impersonate you and manipulate your devices. Moreover, certain apps group multiple permissions together instead of requesting separate authorizations for each function, creating a potential loophole for hackers to remotely control aspects like locking and unlocking your front door. It is advisable to use trusted and authorized apps and platforms when managing your smart devices to minimize security risks.

12.5.8   Privacy Breaches and Data Exploitation

Sophisticated smart home hijackings can be stealthy, leaving no trace of evidence. As the data transmitted by smart devices such as printers and televisions are often unencrypted, malicious actors can access and manipulate the information collected by these devices. An intruder may, for example, replace the current video feed from your surveillance camera with manipulated footage. To enhance security, consider utilizing advanced network monitoring tools that can alert you to suspicious network activities or communications, helping to detect and mitigate potential smart home hijacking attempts.

12.5.9   Unsupported Software

Using outdated and vulnerable software on smart devices can significantly increase the risk of exploitation by cybercriminals. To enhance security, it is recommended to purchase smart devices from reputable brands that prioritize security measures. Additionally, ensure that your devices are configured to automatically update when new software versions are released. This approach ensures that your devices receive the latest security patches, closing known vulnerabilities and reducing the risk of malware or unauthorized access. By keeping your smart home up-to-date, you can maintain a smooth and secure environment for your devices and protect against potential security threats.

12.5.10   Hacking Through the Cloud

Sensitive data are transmitted and stored on Internet-accessible systems that are commonly referred to as "the cloud." However, tech companies sometimes use the term "cloud" to downplay the risks associated with unsecured storage and data transmission. Hackers are well aware of these vulnerabilities. Many cloud-based devices transmit data insecurely over the Internet, making them susceptible to cyberattacks. What is even more concerning is that some of these data transmissions are unnecessary and could be avoided with proper security measures. It is essential to be cautious when relying on cloud-based services and ensure that adequate security protocols are in place to protect sensitive information.

"Cloud gadgets can present security issues for property holders since information, like video information for cameras, are not encoded when sent over the web. In this manner, cloud equipment is an objective for digital interruptions," says Ruslan Vinahradau, chief of shrewd home innovation firm Zorachka, a major promoter of secure home frameworks. "In addition to encryption, homeowners should investigate internal storage technologies. Cybercriminals will have a harder time breaking into your home or data because of these features."

According to a 2019 survey by Pew, 54% of smart speaker owners (equivalent to 13% of all US adults) expressed concern about the collection of personal data by their devices. Additionally, 49% of respondents believed that it is unacceptable for manufacturers to share audio recordings with law enforcement. These findings highlight the growing apprehension among individuals regarding privacy and the potential misuse of personal information collected by smart speakers.

12.5.11   Batteries Drain Too Fast

For first-time smart homeowners, it is important to avoid relying solely on the "set it and forget it" feature of many smart devices. These devices require ongoing maintenance, especially when it comes to changing batteries. Wireless home technology devices such as security cameras, motion sensors, connected locks, lamps, thermostats, and speakers all need regular battery replacements to ensure uninterrupted functionality. It is advisable to have compatible backup batteries for frequently used devices to avoid situations like lack of light, malfunctioning thermostats or smoke detectors, or blacked-out security cameras. By staying proactive in battery maintenance, smart homeowners have an advantage in household management compared to nonusers who may inadvertently leave lights, appliances, or cooling systems on. According to McKinsey, 51% of nonusers accidentally left lights on, 41% left appliances on, and 35% unintentionally left the cooling system on.

12.5.12   The Hidden Risks of Granting Permissions

When using apps and devices, it is crucial to carefully consider the permissions they request, such as access to personal data, camera, microphone, and connected locks. While some apps may emphasize the importance of these permissions for customization, it can be challenging to fully assess the security risks without reading the detailed fine print. The complexity of smart systems introduces additional layers of complexity and potential vulnerabilities, such as the risk of a hacked app disabling connected locks or thermostats. Concerns about big tech companies acquiring personal data should also be acknowledged. Homeowners should reach out to manufacturers to inquire about options for opting out of data harvesting. While technology can simplify daily tasks, it is important to use common sense and judgment, as there may be obstacles or situations where technology could complicate rather than improve matters.

12.6   Risks of AI in Education

When it comes to being implemented in educational settings, the idea of artificial intelligence—which is still in its infancy as a technology—must also deal with a few obstacles and dangers. Before applying AI to a specific educational field, it is necessary to identify these obstacles. Choosing the right AI tool for specific tasks is crucial for optimal performance and outcomes. Because the geographical, social, political, and other considerations all play a role in determining which AI solution is most appropriate for the problem at hand. Those variables can influence the entire school system the greater part of time. For instance, every government in Sri Lanka has been accused of destroying the educational system as a result of its independence. Each time changes occur in government, there happens an adjustment of strategies of training with changes in school prospectus and different lessons, learning, and organization system.

Artificial intelligence, including models like GPT-3, is increasingly being adopted in classrooms worldwide to enhance educational experiences and instruction. Tools to help educators harness the potential of conversational AI are actively being developed by companies that specialize in education technology, such as Noodle Factory. While artificial intelligence could offer many invigorating conceivable outcomes, teachers should know about the expected dangers and moral contemplations that accompany this.

AI, such as GPT-3, offers valuable capabilities in generating human-like text and performing various language tasks in education. It can aid in summarizing course materials, personalizing lessons, providing feedback, and supporting tutoring. However, it is crucial to be aware of potential biases or inaccuracies that can arise from the data used to train these models. Platforms like Noodle Factory enable educators to repurpose their own content, reducing the risk of incorrect information in the knowledge base.

One of the main dangers is that students might misuse these tools or rely too much on them instead of learning how to think critically and solve problems on their own. Some schools and districts, such as New York City and Los Angeles, have chosen to ban ChatGPT from their networks due to concerns about biases and potential cheating. While this response is understandable, it might be more beneficial to regulate and control the use of these tools rather than a complete ban. Platforms like Noodle Factory's "Walter" provide a structured environment for using conversational AI tools powered by GPT-3, ensuring responsible and guided access to information for students. This approach aims to address concerns while still harnessing the benefits of AI in education.

Additionally, clients frequently express a concern that an increasing reliance on AI in education could result in a decrease in the workforce required to support education. To put it another way, the concern is that the use of powerful AI tools could eliminate the need for human teachers and result in the loss of employment opportunities for educators, particularly in lower-skilled positions. Given the ongoing deficiency of educators overall and the present status of computer-based intelligence, this worry is not grounded as a general rule. Could AI eventually replace teachers? The answer is "yes" if we are only thinking (hypothetically) about what might happen in the future. Be that as it may, assuming we are discussing the reasonable close term, the response is "no," and we ought to all embrace manners by which artificial intelligence can increase and help instructors or even somewhat lower-talented care staff.

The application of AI in education raises concerns about privacy, particularly regarding the collection and use of students' personal data. It is crucial to establish robust safeguards to protect student privacy when using these tools. Transparency is also vital, and teachers should be up front about the data collected and how it will be utilized. By prioritizing privacy and maintaining transparency, educators can address concerns and foster trust in the use of AI technology in education.

When utilizing AI in education, a number of ethical considerations must be taken into account. These incorporate the potential for these devices to screen or control understudy conduct and the need to guarantee that artificial intelligence is utilized mindfully and morally.

In general, simulated intelligence in schooling can alter our opinion on educating and learning. Educators have a responsibility to be mindful of the potential risks and ethical implications associated with the use of AI in education. By exercising caution and considering the broader impact on society, educators can ensure that AI technology is used for the benefit of all stakeholders, including students. It is crucial to prioritize the well-being and educational development of students while navigating the implementation of AI in an ethical and responsible manner.

12.6.1 Quality Over Quantity

Teachers gain expertise and improve their teaching skills over time through years of experience and repetition. However, AI-based tools, such as robots, rely on algorithms that are not influenced by the repetition of activities. Therefore, their effectiveness in the teaching process is not enhanced by experience. The unique qualities of human teachers, including their ability to adapt, empathize, and provide personalized instruction, make them indispensable in the educational system.

12.6.2   Stimulating Technology Addiction

Students have traditionally been required to open out-of-date textbooks and remove their tablets and smartphones from the classroom. With innovation executed inside each class, understudies would not have the option to consider their future lives without it. Growing technology addiction may result in a generation of adults lacking social adaptation skills. All of these will happen because AI can make people addicted to technology.

12.6.3   The High Cost of Delivery

The significant test with carrying out simulated intelligence in school training is arranging and planning the spending plan of schools. Forecasting a budget becomes extremely challenging most of the time. For instance, the potential power consumption calculation will increase if robot assistants are made available to all schools. Then, in order to recover expenses, nations would need to finance a substantial budget. Furthermore, another negative point with respect to this issue is that electrical power is definitely not an inexhaustible asset. To address this challenge, it is crucial to explore and understand the available AI-based learning tools and their potential benefits for students.

12.6.4   Unemployment

The potential unemployment of teachers due to the introduction of AI systems or robots in education is a significant concern, similar to past instances of technological disruption. This situation may lead to protests and movements, highlighting the importance of addressing the potential challenges of unemployment in the future.

12.6.5   Power Imbalance and Control

The risk of hackers accessing the system and broadcasting inappropriate content poses a significant challenge, hindering the timely and appropriate dissemination of information to teachers and students.

12.6.6   Reducing the Ability to Multitask

Integrating AI in education has the potential to provide greater assistance to humans, potentially reducing their reliance on their own capabilities. However, there is a concern that individuals may turn to machines not

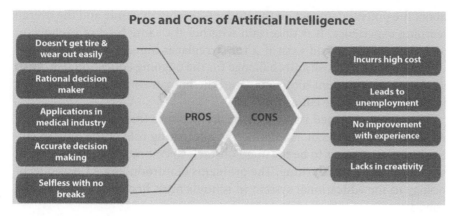

Figure 12.6 Pros and cons of artificial intelligence.

necessarily because they are more capable but because they lack the ability to perform certain tasks without them. This dynamic presents both advantages and disadvantages, as illustrated in Figure 12.6.

12.6.7   No Alternative Teaching Methods

Teachers may provide a few solutions to a particular issue. If a pupil is capable of using one strategy, the teacher will suggest a different one. It helps pupils' thoughts become more flexible. A robot will present a solution that is approved and correct but without any more variations.

12.6.8   Enlarge the Gap Between the Rich and the Poor

The requirement for students to have laptops or tablets for AI-based applications, such as e-content and bots, can create a financial barrier for some students. If the government assumes responsibility for providing technology to all students, it may create a divide between those who have access to such devices and those who do not. This presents an additional challenge in ensuring equitable access to educational opportunities.

12.6.9   Unclear Ability to Learn with a Virtual Assistant

Whether pupils will be interested in learning and driven to study when professors are not there for supervision is still an open question. Students may occasionally be motivated to prepare for class because they hope to impress a particular teacher. The introduction of AI in education raises questions about the potential impact on the student–teacher dynamic and the overall learning experience. It is uncertain whether the same level of excitement and engagement would exist if a robot replaces human interaction. This uncertainty poses a risk and challenge for the ongoing educational process, as maintaining student motivation and the human connection in learning is crucial for effective education.

The aforementioned issues may be divided into three categories: short, medium, and long term. Accepting the alternating role of the human factor, however, appears to be the main obstacle to embracing the most recent way of thinking and learning. The problems of introducing AI-based technology to the educational system in schools must first be recognized and solved.

12.6.10   Diminished Emotional Support and Mentorship

While smart devices can enhance the learning experience, it is important to maintain a balance and not rely on them as a complete replacement for human connection in education. Overreliance on robots for tasks like grading or tutoring may lead to errors in learning that could have a more negative impact than positive. It is crucial to consider the limitations of technology and ensure that human involvement and guidance remain integral to the educational process.

12.6.11   Loss of Information

When an AI system requires repairs or maintenance, there is a risk of data loss depending on the extent of the issue and the backup measures in place. It is crucial to have proper data backup and recovery systems to minimize the potential loss of data.

While there are undoubtedly more advantages than disadvantages to artificial intelligence, it is important to find a balance between human involvement and AI optimization. AI should not aim to replace teachers, but rather to assist and enhance their work in the classroom.

By combining a digital classroom with a school intranet, educators can provide students with more learning opportunities in a hybrid environment. Automation can be utilized to personalize responses, materials, and courses based on students' needs. Additionally, creating a social platform can facilitate communication between students, teachers, and parents, fostering a collaborative learning environment.

12.7   Conclusion

The chapter on Risks and Implications of Artificial Intelligence explores various aspects related to the integration of AI with other technologies and its potential risks in different domains. It highlights the importance of understanding and addressing these risks to ensure responsible and ethical deployment of AI systems.

Types of Risks in Amalgamation of AI With Other Technologies: This section discusses the risks that arise when AI is combined with other technologies, such as robotics, Internet of Things (IoT), and cloud computing. It explores the potential challenges of integrating AI into complex technological ecosystems and the need for careful consideration of security, privacy, and ethical concerns.

Common Risks of Artificial Intelligence Techniques: Here, the chapter delves into the general risks associated with AI techniques. It covers issues like bias and fairness in AI algorithms, potential discriminatory outcomes, and the importance of ensuring transparency and accountability in AI decision-making processes. It also highlights the ethical implications of using AI in sensitive areas, such as criminal justice and employment.

Risks of Artificial Intelligence in the Healthcare System: This section focuses on the risks and benefits of AI applications in healthcare. It examines the challenges of ensuring patient privacy and data security when using AI-driven medical devices and electronic health records. Additionally, it explores the ethical considerations surrounding AI's role in diagnostic accuracy, treatment recommendations, and patient outcomes.

Automating Drudgery in Medical Practice: Here, the chapter discusses how AI can automate repetitive tasks in medical practice, such as data entry and administrative duties. It explores the potential benefits of reducing physician burnout and increasing efficiency but also highlights concerns regarding overreliance on AI, potential errors, and the importance of maintaining a human-centered approach to healthcare.

Risks of Artificial Intelligence in Finance: This section examines the risks associated with AI applications in the financial sector. It discusses the challenges of ensuring the transparency and explainability of AI-driven algorithms in trading, risk assessment, and fraud detection. It also explores the potential impact of AI on job displacement and the need for regulatory frameworks to address these risks.

Risks of AI in Education: The chapter addresses the risks and implications of AI in educational settings. It explores issues such as data privacy and security when using AI-driven learning platforms. It also examines concerns related to algorithmic bias in educational assessments and the potential impact on educational equity. The chapter emphasizes the importance of ethical considerations and human oversight in AI-based educational technologies.

Risks in Smart Home Systems: This section focuses on the risks associated with AI-powered smart home systems. It discusses privacy concerns related to data collection and the potential vulnerabilities that can be exploited by malicious actors. It also explores the importance of securing these systems against unauthorized access and the need for user education and awareness.

The chapter concludes by emphasizing the significance of understanding and addressing the risks associated with AI integration. It highlights the need for interdisciplinary collaboration, ethical frameworks, and robust regulatory mechanisms to ensure responsible and beneficial deployment of AI technologies across various domains.

References

1. Block, L. *et al.*, In the wake of the 2003 and 2011 duty hours regulations, how do internal medicine interns spend their time? *J. Gen. Intern. Med.*, 28, 8, 1042–1047, 2013.
2. Nicholson Price II, W. and Glenn Cohen, I., Privacy in the age of medical big data. *Nat. Med.*, 25, 37–43, 2019.
3. Glenn Cohen, I. and Mello, M.M., Big data, big tech, and protecting patient privacy. *JAMA*, 322, 12, 1141–1142, 2019. https://jamanetwork.com/journals/jama/fullarticle/2748399
4. Bajorek, J.P., Voice recognition still has significant race and gender biases. *Harv. Bus. Rev.*, 10, 2019, 1–4, May 10, 2019. https://hbr.org/2019/05/voice-recognition-still-has-significant-race-and-gender-biases.
5. Goyal, M.K. *et al.*, Racial disparities in pain management of children with appendicitis in emergency departments. *JAMA Pediatr.*, 169, 11, 996–1002, 2015.
6. Froomkin, A.M. *et al.*, When AIs outperform doctors: The dangers of a tort-induced over-reliance on machine learning. *Ariz. L. Rev.*, 61, 33, 2019.
7. Bazarbash, M., *FinTech in Financial Inclusion: Machine Learning Applications in Assessing Credit Risk*, IMF Working Paper 19/109, International Monetary Fund, Washington, DC, 2019.
8. Arner, D., Barberis, J., Buckley, R., FinTech, RegTech, and the reconceptualization of financial regulation. *Northwest. J. Int. Law Bus.*, 37, 3, 371, 2017. https://scholarlycommons.law.northwestern.edu/njilb/vol37/iss3/2/.

9. Schizas, E., McKain, G., Zhang, B., Ganbold, A., Kumar, P., Hussain, H., Garvey, K.J. *et al.*, *The Global Regtech Industry: Benchmark Report*, Cambridge Centre for Alternative Finance, University of Cambridge, UK, 2019, https://www.jbs.cam.ac.uk/wp-content/uploads/2020/08/2019-12-ccaf-global-regtech-benchmarking-report.pdf.

10. Financial Stability Board (FSB), *The Use of Supervisory and Regulatory Technology by Authorities and Regulated Institutions: Market Developments and Financial Stability Implications*, Financial Stability Board, Basel, Switzerland, 2020, https://www.fsb.org/wp-content/uploads/P091020.pdf.

11. European Central Bank (ECB), Bringing artificial intelligence to banking supervision, 2019. https://www.bankingsupervision.europa.eu/press/publications/newsletter/2019/html/ssm.nl191113_4.en.html.

12. di Castri, S., Hohl, S., Kulenkampff, A., Prenio, J., The suptech generations, in: *FSI Insights on Policy Implementation*, Bank for International Settlements, Basel, 2019, https://www.bis.org/fsi/publ/insights19.pdf.

13. Avramović, P., Digital Transformation of Financial Regulators and the Emergence of Supervisory Technologies (SupTech): A Case Study of the UK Financial Conduct Authority. *SupTech Tools for Market Conduct Supervisors*, 2020.

14. Institute of International Finance (IIF), *Deploying Regtech against Financial Crime*, Report of the Regtech Working Group, IIF, Washington, DC, 2017, https://www.iif.com/portals/0/Files/private/32370132_aml_final_id.pdf.

15. Financial Stability Board (FSB), *The Use of Supervisory and Regulatory Technology by Authorities and Regulated Institutions: Market Developments and Financial Stability Implications*, Financial Stability Board, Basel, Switzerland, 2020, https://www.fsb.org/wp-content/uploads/P091020.pdf.

16. Danielsson, J., Macrae, R., Uthemann, A., Artificial intelligence as a central banker, VOX CEPR Policy Portal, March 6, 2020. https://voxeu.org/article/artificial-intelligence-central-banker.

17. Comiter, M., *Attacking Artificial Intelligence: AI's Security Vulnerability and What Policymakers Can Do About It*, Belfer Center for Science and International Affairs, Harvard Kennedy School, 2019, https://www.belfercenter.org/publication/AttackingAI.

18. Liu, K., Dolan-Gavitt, B., Garg, S., Fine-pruning: Defending against backdooring attacks on deep neural networks, in: *Research in Attacks, Intrusions, and Defenses*, M. Bailey, T. Holz, M. Stamatogiannakis, S. Ioannidis (Eds.), pp. 273–94, Springer, Cham, Switzerland, 2018.

19. Delponte, L., *European Artificial Intelligence Leadership, the Path for an Integrated Vision*, Policy Department for Economic, Scientific and Quality of Life Policies, European Parliament, Belgium, Brussels, 2018.

20. Charlier, R. and Kloppenburg, S., *Artificial intelligence in HR: A no-brainer*, PwC [(accessed on 10 October 2021)]. Available online: http://www.pwc.nl/nl/assets/documents/artificial-intelligence-in-hr-a-no-brainer.pdf.

21. Charlier, R. and Kloppenburg, S., Artifcial intelligence in HR: A no-brainer, PWC report, 2017. Accessed on 7 March 2023. Available online: https://www.pwc.co.uk/press-room/press-releases/AI-will-create-as-many-jobs-as-it-displaces-by-boosting-economic-growth.html.

22. Steimers, A. and Bömer, T., Sources of risk and design principles of trustworthy artificial intelligence, in: *Digital Human Modeling and Applications in Health, Safety, Ergonomics and Risk Management. AI, Product and Service. HCII 2021. Lecture Notes in Computer Science*, vol. 12778 Springer, Berlin/Heidelberg, Germany, pp. 239–251, 2021 [Google Scholar].

23. Steimers, A. and Schneider, M., Sources of risk of AI systems. *Int. J. Environ. Res. Public Health*, 19, 6, 3641, 2022.

24. Pietsch, B., 2 killed in driverless tesla car crash, officials say. *New York Times*, 2021. [(accessed on 10 January 2022)]. Available online: https://www.nytimes.com/2021/04/18/business/tesla-fatal-crash-texas.html.

25. Wakabayashi, D., Self-driving uber car kills pedestrian in Arizona. *New York Times*, 2018. [(accessed on 10 January 2022)]. Available online: https://www.nytimes.com/2018/03/19/technology/uber-driverless-fatality.html.

26. Salay, R. and Czarnecki, K., *Using Machine Learning Safely in Automotive Software: An Assessment and Adaption of Software Process Requirements in ISO 26262*, arXiv. 20181808.01614, 2018 [Google Scholar].

27. *Information Technology—Artificial Intelligence (AI)-Bias in AI Systems and AI Aided Decision Making*, International Electrotechnical Commission, International Organization for Standardization, Geneva, Switzerland, 2021.

28. *Information Technology—Artificial Intelligence-Overview of Trustworthiness in Artificial Intelligence*, International Electrotechnical Commission, International Organization for Standardization, Geneva, Switzerland, 2020.

29. European Commission, *Directorate-General for Communications Networks, Content and Technology, Ethics Guidelines for Trustworthy AI*, European Commission Publications Office, Brussels, Belgium, 2019.

30. Batarseh, F.A., Freeman, L., Huang, C.H., A survey on artificial intelligence assurance. *J. Big Data*, 8, 1–30, 2021.

31. Kläs, M., Adler, R., Jöckel, L., Groß, J., Reich, J., Using complementary risk acceptance criteria to structure assurance cases for safety-critical AI components. *Proceedings of the AISaftey 2021 at International Joint Conference on Artifcal Intelligence (IJCAI)*, Montreal, QC, Canada, August 19–26, 2021, [(accessed on 10 January 2022)]. Available online: http://ceur-ws.org/Vol-2916/paper_9.pdf.

32. Takeuchi, H., Akihara, S., Yamamoto, S., Deriving successful factors for practical AI system development projects using assurance case. *Joint Conference on Knowledge-Based Software Engineering*, Springer, Berlin/Heidelberg, Germany, pp. 22–32, 2018.

33. *Information Technology-Artificial Intelligence-Objectives and Approaches for Explainability of ML Models and AI Systems*, International Electrotechnical

Commission, International Organization for Standardization, Geneva, Switzerland, 2021.

34. *Information Technology-Artificial Intelligence-Controllability of Automated Artificial Intelligence Systems*, International Electrotechnical Commission, International Organization for Standardization, Geneva, Switzerland, 2021.

35. *Information Technology-Artificial Intelligence-Risk Management*, International Electrotechnical Commission, International Organization for Standardization, Geneva, Switzerland, 2021.

36. European Commission, *Proposal for a Regulation of the European Parliament and the Council: Laying Down Harmonised Rules on Artificial Intelligence (Artificial Intelligence Act) and Amending Certain Union Legislative Act*, European Commission Publications Office, Brussels, Belgium, 2021.

13

Exploring the Role of ChatGPT in the Law Enforcement and Banking Sectors

Shubham Pandey*, Archana Patel and Purvi Pokhariyal

National Forensic Sciences University, Gandhinagar, Gujarat, India

Abstract

This chapter explores the role of ChatGPT, a powerful artificial intelligence (AI) tool, in the law enforcement and banking sectors. ChatGPT has the potential to revolutionize these industries by offering a wide range of applications and benefits. In law enforcement, ChatGPT can assist in investigative analysis, risk assessment, virtual training, and crime prevention. In the banking sector, it can provide customer support, aid in fraud detection, assist with risk assessment and compliance, and offer personalized financial advice. However, the implementation of ChatGPT also raises concerns related to privacy, security, and the need for human oversight. Therefore, it is crucial to address these concerns and establish regulatory frameworks to govern the use of advanced technologies effectively. This chapter aims to provide legal and technical recommendations to regulate ChatGPT's usage and mitigate associated risks.

Keywords: Law enforcement, banking, artificial intelligence, ChatGPT

13.1 Introduction

Emerging technology is having a significant impact on many aspects of human activity. These technologies have impacted many sectors like communication and broadcasting where technology like social media, instant messaging, and video conferencing has revolutionized the way people communicate and stay connected. Healthcare where provisions

---

*Corresponding author: shubham.pandey@nfsu.ac.in

Ambrish Kumar Mishra, Shweta Anand, Narayan C. Debnath, Purvi Pokhariyal and Archana Patel (eds.) Artificial Intelligence for Risk Mitigation in the Financial Industry, (327–348) © 2024 Scrivener Publishing LLC

for telemedicine, artificial intelligence (AI)-powered diagnostics, and personalized medicine are transforming healthcare delivery and improving patient outcomes. Another sector is education where online learning, virtual classrooms, and educational technology are making education more accessible and personalized. More so, automation, AI, and the gig economy are changing the nature of work and the way people earn a living. These technologies have also impacted transportation; self-driving cars, drones, and hyperloop are revolutionizing the way people travel and goods are delivered. Entertainment where streaming services, virtual reality, and augmented reality are changing the way people consume and experience entertainment. Last but not the least is security where advanced technologies such as biometrics, blockchain, and cybersecurity are improving the security of individuals, organizations, and nations.

Recently, many emerging new technologies have come into existence, including OpenAI's latest technology, ChatGPT. ChatGPT has the potential to significantly impact the way we communicate; it may not necessarily be classified as a "disruptive technology" in the traditional sense. Disruptive technologies are typically defined as innovations that create new markets or fundamentally change existing ones by displacing established technologies or processes [1]. While ChatGPT may transform certain aspects of communication, it may not necessarily be seen as fundamentally changing existing markets or displacing established technologies in the same way that, for example, the introduction of smartphones disrupted the traditional cell phone industry. However, it is certainly a powerful new technology that has the potential to enable new applications and use cases in areas such as customer service, language translation, and content generation.

OpenAI and ChatGPT

OpenAI is a research organization dedicated to developing and promoting friendly AI that benefits humanity. OpenAI [2] is focused on creating and promoting AI technologies that are safe and have the potential to improve human life. OpenAI developed a conversational language model ChatGPT that was first released on June 2020. ChatGPT is a language model that uses a technique called transformer architecture, which was introduced in a 2017 paper by Google Brain [3]. It is based on the generative pre-trained transformer (GPT) architecture and is trained on a massive dataset of text data [4]. The transformer architecture uses self-attention mechanisms to process input text, allowing the model to effectively handle input of varying lengths and to weigh different parts of the input differently when making predictions. This allows the model to perform well on tasks such as language translation and text generation. Additionally, ChatGPT is fine-tuned on a large dataset of conversational text, which enables it to generate human-like responses to text prompts. ChatGPT can generate human-like text, making it useful for conversational AI applications like chatbots [5].

General Applications of ChatGPT: ChatGPT, as a language generation model, has made inroads in various human-oriented tasks and has completely automated many of them. This includes (a) **Text Generation:** ChatGPT can be used to generate human-like text on a given topic, making it useful for content creation, such as writing articles, stories, and poetry [6]. (b) **Language Translation:** ChatGPT can be fine-tuned for language translation tasks; it can translate text from one language to another [7]. (c) **Text Summarization:** ChatGPT can be used to summarize long documents or articles, making it useful for quickly getting the main points of a piece of text. (d) **Question Answering:** By fine-tuning the ChatGPT model, it can be used to answer questions based on a given context and provide relevant information. (e) **Conversational AI:** ChatGPT can be used to create chatbots, which can have natural conversations with users. It can be used to generate responses to user inputs, making the chatbot more engaging and human-like. (f) **Sentiment Analysis:** ChatGPT can be fine-tuned for sentiment analysis tasks; it can classify the text into positive, negative, and neutral [8]. (g) **Text Completion:** ChatGPT can be used to complete a given text prompt. (h) **Text Classification:** ChatGPT can be fine-tuned for text classification tasks; it can classify the text into different categories.

The rest of the chapter is organized as follows: Section 13.2 shows leveraging ChatGPT in the banking sector and law enforcement. Section 13.3 highlights the issues with regard to ChatGPT, and section 13.4 explains the regulations and nonlegal solutions to address crimes relating to ChatGPT. Section 13.5 shows the road map of ChatGPT and emerging technologies. Section 13.6 concludes the chapter.

13.2   Leveraging ChatGPT in Law Enforcement and the Banking Sector

Leveraging ChatGPT in the banking sector and law enforcement can offer various benefits, but it is essential to consider the ethical and security implications involved. This section explains the various applications and benefits of ChatGPT in the banking sector and law enforcement.

13.2.1   Banking Sector

In the dynamic landscape of the banking sector, technological advancements have played a significant role in shaping the industry's operations and customer experience. Among these advancements, ChatGPT, an AI-powered language model, has emerged as a transformative tool with immense potential. This section delves into the various applications and benefits of ChatGPT in the banking sector, highlighting its impact on customer service, fraud detection, risk assessment, and personalized financial advice.

a) **Enhancing Customer Service:** ChatGPT revolutionizes customer service in banking by offering personalized and efficient support. With its natural language processing capabilities, ChatGPT can understand and respond to customer inquiries promptly. Customers can obtain real-time assistance regarding account information, transaction history, and general banking inquiries. The availability of round-the-clock customer support improves accessibility and responsiveness, leading to higher customer satisfaction and loyalty.

b) **Empowering Fraud Detection:** One of the critical challenges in the banking sector is fraud detection. ChatGPT, with its ability to analyze large volumes of transactional data, can identify patterns indicative of fraudulent activities. By continuously monitoring transactions, ChatGPT can flag suspicious behavior, enabling banks to take proactive measures to prevent fraud. This not only safeguards the interests of customers but also helps protect the reputation and financial stability of banking institutions.

c) **Streamlining Risk Assessment and Compliance:** Effective risk assessment and compliance with regulatory requirements are crucial for banks. ChatGPT can assist in evaluating risks associated with loan applications, investment portfolios, and regulatory compliance. By analyzing customer profiles, financial data, and relevant information, ChatGPT provides valuable insights to support decision-making. This streamlines the risk assessment process, ensuring that banks make informed and compliant decisions while managing their operations effectively.

d) **Personalized Financial Advice:** ChatGPT offers personalized financial advice tailored to individual customers' needs and goals. By considering various factors such as income, expenses, risk tolerance, and investment preferences, ChatGPT can provide recommendations on budgeting, savings, investment strategies, and retirement planning. This level of tailored guidance empowers customers to make informed financial decisions and enhances their overall financial well-being.

While ChatGPT brings numerous advantages to the banking sector, it is essential to address certain considerations and challenges. Safeguarding customer data and privacy is of utmost importance. Banks must ensure robust security measures and adhere to data protection regulations to maintain the confidentiality and integrity of customer information. Moreover, human oversight remains crucial, especially for complex or sensitive matters, to prevent errors and mitigate potential biases in the AI-generated responses.

13.2.2   Law Enforcement

Law enforcement refers to the individuals and agencies responsible for maintaining law and order, investigating crimes, and enforcing laws in a particular jurisdiction. Law enforcement is generally responsible for, among other things,

a) **Generating reports**, which is an important aspect of law enforcement, as it helps to document incidents, investigations, and other important information. Reports can be used to communicate findings to other law enforcement officials, prosecutors, and other stakeholders.

b) **Transcribing and translating recorded conversations**, which are other key functions of law enforcement, especially in cases where evidence may be obtained through wiretaps or other surveillance methods. Accurate transcriptions and translations are important to ensure that evidence is properly interpreted and presented in court.

c) **Predictive policing**, which involves using data analysis and other techniques to identify areas where crime is likely to occur and taking proactive measures to prevent it. This approach has generated some controversy, as some people argue that it can lead to discriminatory or biased policing practices.

d) **Criminal profiling**, which is the process of using behavioral and psychological analysis to identify potential suspects in a criminal investigation. This technique is often used in cases where the perpetrator is unknown or where there is limited physical evidence.

e) **Generating legal documents**, which is another important part of law enforcement, as it involves preparing documents such as search warrants, arrest warrants, and other legal instruments that are necessary to carry out investigations and make arrests. These characteristics are essential to the effective functioning of law enforcement.

Manual approaches to law enforcement often involve a lot of paperwork, which can be time-consuming and prone to errors. In addition, manual approaches may involve a great deal of manual data entry, which can be slow and tedious. Manual approaches to law enforcement, therefore, have led to inefficiency and delays. However, with the immense potential of powerful new technologies like ChatGPT, it can be leveraged to assist law enforcement agencies in a variety of ways. **ChatGPT could be employed** for **generating reports** automatically and summarizing crime scenes, interviews, and surveillance footage. This could save time and resources for law enforcement agencies. It can also be used to **transcribe and translate** recorded conversations, which could be useful in investigations involving multiple languages. ChatGPT could be really successful in **predictive policing**, where it could be leveraged to analyze large amounts of data, such as crime statistics and social media posts, to predict where crimes are likely to occur, allowing law enforcement agencies to deploy resources more effectively. ChatGPT can successfully be employed in **criminal profiling**, where it can be used to analyze large amounts of data, such as crime reports, social media posts, and other digital footprints, to build profiles of potential suspects or criminal organizations. Lastly, it can assist law enforcement officers in **generating legal documents** such as warrants, indictments, and plea agreements, which could save time and resources for the legal system. Figure 13.1 shows the different applications of ChatGPT in the banking sector and law enforcement.

The increasing use of technology in law enforcement will help to address some of these issues. For example, digital systems for generating reports, transcribing and translating conversations, and generating legal documents can reduce the amount of time and effort required for these tasks.

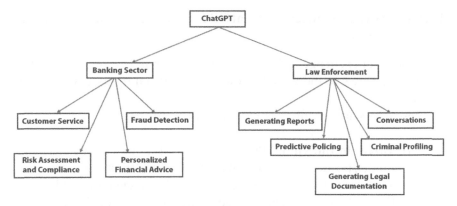

Figure 13.1 Applications of ChatGPT in the banking sector and law enforcement.

Additionally, digital tools for data analysis and predictive policing can help law enforcement agencies to make more informed decisions and allocate resources more efficiently. Furthermore, the use of technology in law enforcement can also improve the accuracy and completeness of data, reducing errors and inconsistencies that may arise with manual approaches. This can lead to more effective investigations and better outcomes for the justice system as a whole. While there may be challenges and concerns associated with the use of technology in law enforcement, overall, it has the potential to increase efficiency and reduce delays. As with any new tool, it is important to approach technology in law enforcement with careful consideration and planning to ensure that it is used in a responsible and effective manner.

13.3 Issues with Regard to ChatGPT

With every new technology, there is a plethora of challenges and opportunities. ChatGPT presents many such challenges. First is the challenge that is being posed by the architecture of ChatGPT that has inherent flaws and that poses a real threat to individual privacy, fundamental rights, and potential of bias. Second is the challenge with regard to the use of ChatGPT as a weapon in cyberspace to cause various cyber incidents like disinformation and fake news, manipulation of public opinion, cybercrimes including DDoS attacks, spread of malware, and the conduct of other types of cybercrimes [9].

13.3.1   Threats Caused by ChatGPT Architecture and Inherent Flaws

The first set of challenges is being posed by the architecture of ChatGPT's poses a real threat to individual privacy, fundamental rights, and potential of bias.

These issues are broadly classified into three threats:

a) **Threat to Individual Privacy:** ChatGPT, as an AI language model, poses a threat to individual privacy [10]. It is important to note that the data used to train language models like ChatGPT often include large amounts of personal information, such as text from social media and other sources, which could potentially lead to privacy concerns if the data are not properly secured or handled. Additionally, the use of language models like ChatGPT in applications or services that collect or store personal information could also raise privacy concerns. It is important for organizations and individuals to be aware of these potential risks and take steps to protect personal information.

b) **Affecting Rights:** ChatGPT, as a language model, inherently poses a threat to fundamental rights [11]. The use of language models like ChatGPT in systems and applications that make decisions affecting individuals' lives, such as hiring, lending, or justice, could potentially perpetuate or amplify existing biases and discriminatory practices. For example, if the training data used to develop ChatGPT reflect societal biases, the model may produce outputs that perpetuate those biases, leading to unfair or unjust decisions. It is important for organizations and individuals using AI systems like ChatGPT to be aware of the potential for bias and to take steps to address and mitigate it, such as using diverse and representative training data, monitoring and testing outputs for fairness and accountability, and following ethical and legal guidelines.

c) **Potential Bias:** The potential biases associated with ChatGPT, as with any AI language model, stem from the data used to train the model [12]. If the training data are biased in some way, the model may reproduce those biases in its outputs. For example, if the training data include a disproportionate representation of certain demographic groups or if they reflect historical or societal biases, the model may generate biased outputs that perpetuate or amplify those biases. Other potential sources of bias in language models include the choice of language used in the training data, the selection of certain topics or perspectives to be emphasized, and the presence of specific cultural references or beliefs. It is important for organizations and individuals using language models like ChatGPT to be aware of the potential for bias and to take steps to address and mitigate it. This may include using diverse and representative training data, monitoring and testing outputs for fairness and accountability, and following ethical and legal guidelines.

Mitigating Issues with Respect to ChatGPT Architecture

To mitigate privacy, fundamental rights, and potential bias [13] concerns with respect to ChatGPT, the following steps can be taken: (a) **Diverse and Representative Training Data:** Use a diverse and representative set of training data to help ensure that the model is less likely to perpetuate existing biases. This can include data from different demographic groups, perspectives, and cultures. (b) **Monitoring and Testing Outputs:** Regularly monitor and test the outputs of the model to identify and address any biases or unfair outcomes. This can include conducting regular audits, performing fairness testing, and evaluating the outputs of the model against ethical and legal standards. (c) **Transparent and Responsible Deployment:** Ensure that the deployment of ChatGPT and other AI systems is transparent, accountable, and responsible. This can include being transparent about the training data used, how the model works, and how its outputs are being used. (d) **Ethical and Legal Compliance:** Adhere to ethical and legal guidelines related to the use of AI, such as those related to privacy, fundamental rights, and due process. (e) **Human Oversight and Intervention:** Include human oversight and intervention in decision-making processes that rely on ChatGPT and other AI systems to help ensure that their outputs are aligned with ethical and legal standards and to address any potential biases or unfair outcomes. By taking these steps, law enforcement organizations and individuals can help ensure that the use of ChatGPT and other AI systems is responsible, ethical, and aligned with the values of fairness, justice, and the law of the land.

13.3.2   ChatGPT Used as a Weapon of Crime

ChatGPT itself is not capable of causing cybercrimes, as it is simply a language model that generates text based on input it receives. However, if it is used in an unethical or illegal manner, it could be involved in various cybercrimes, such as:

a) **Phishing Scams:** Phishing is a type of scam where criminals try to trick individuals into revealing sensitive information, such as passwords, credit card numbers, or bank account details. This is often done by sending emails or messages that appear to come from a trustworthy source, such as a bank, an online retailer, or a government agency. The messages may ask the recipient to click on a link that takes them to a fake website that looks like the real thing, where they are prompted to enter sensitive information. ChatGPT could be used to generate convincing messages that trick people into revealing sensitive information, such as passwords or credit card numbers [14]. Phishing scams are a common form of cybercrime and can have serious consequences, including identity theft and financial loss.

b) **Spreading Misinformation:** Misinformation refers to false or inaccurate information that is spread intentionally or unintentionally. In the digital age, misinformation can spread quickly through social media, messaging apps, and other online platforms. The spread of misinformation can have serious consequences, including misleading people, causing confusion, and even fueling violence and discrimination. Misinformation can also undermine public trust in institutions and organizations, as well as undermine the credibility of journalists and other sources of reliable information. ChatGPT could be used to generate false or misleading information [15], which could be used to spread propaganda or manipulate public opinion.

c) **Cyberbullying:** Cyberbullying refers to the use of technology, including the Internet and mobile devices, to harass, humiliate, or threaten someone. This type of bullying can take many forms, such as sending hurtful messages or spreading rumors online, creating fake social media accounts to harass someone, or posting embarrassing photos or videos without consent. Cyberbullying can have serious consequences, including causing emotional distress, damaging reputations, and even leading to self-harm or suicide. It can be especially damaging because it can reach a wide audience quickly and can be difficult to escape, since the Internet never forgets. ChatGPT could be used to generate hurtful or abusive messages, which could be used to harass or intimidate individuals [16].

d) **Distributed Denial of Service (DDoS):** DDoS attack is a type of cyberattack that aims to make a website or online service unavailable to users by overwhelming it with traffic from multiple sources. This is done by recruiting a large number of computers, known as "bots," to send a high volume of traffic to the target website or service, effectively swamping it and making it unavailable. DDoS attacks can have serious consequences, including causing financial losses for businesses and organizations, disrupting essential services, and damaging public trust in the Internet. DDoS attacks can also serve as a smoke screen for other types of cyberattacks, such as data breaches or malware infections. ChatGPT could potentially be employed to generate messages or content that encourages others to participate in a DDoS attack either knowingly or unknowingly. This could be considered illegal and unethical and could result in serious consequences both legally and in terms of harm to individuals and organizations.

e) **Malware and Ransomware Attacks:** A malware attack, also known as a malicious software attack, is a type of cyberattack that involves infecting a computer or network with harmful software, known as malware. The goal of a malware attack can vary but often includes stealing sensitive information, disrupting the operation of a system, or extorting money from victims. One type of malware is ransomware, which is a type of malware that encrypts a victim's files and demands payment in exchange for the decryption key. Ransomware attacks can have serious consequences, including causing significant financial losses, disrupting business operations, and exposing sensitive information. ChatGPT could potentially be used to write malware codes or generate malicious software, which could be used to infect a computer or network.

f) **Impersonation and Fake Identity:** Individuals or organizations can impersonate others using a language model like ChatGPT. This can involve creating fake social media accounts or websites, sending phishing emails or messages, or engaging in other forms of impersonation that are designed to trick people into revealing sensitive information or taking some other harmful action. Impersonation can have serious consequences, including damaging reputations, compromising sensitive information, and causing financial losses. It can also undermine trust in online platforms and communications and can be used to further other types of cybercrimes, such as spreading misinformation or conducting phishing scams.

g) **Violation of Bodily Privacy:** Bodily privacy is a fundamental right that is protected by the Constitution of India and other laws and regulations. It is possible for individuals or organizations to use language models like ChatGPT to violate bodily privacy. This could include using the model to generate false or malicious information about someone's personal health or medical history, to create fake profiles or websites that impersonate individuals and share intimate photos or videos without their consent, or to engage in other types of online harassment or exploitation that target someone's bodily privacy. The violation of bodily privacy can have serious consequences, including causing harm to individuals, damaging reputations, and undermining trust in online platforms and communications.

h) **Cyberterrorism:** Cyberterrorism refers to the use of the Internet, computer systems, and other forms of information technology to carry out acts of terrorism, such as disrupting critical infrastructure, spreading propaganda, or stealing sensitive information. This type of terrorism aims to cause widespread panic and destruction through technology, often with political or ideological motives. ChatGPT could be potentially employed by cybercriminals to initiate a DDoS or malware or ransomware attack on critical information infrastructure or to steal sensitive or confidential information.

i) **Cyber Fraud:** Cyber fraud refers to the use of technology, such as the Internet, computer systems, and other forms of information technology to deceive or defraud individuals or organizations, often for financial gain. This can take many forms, such as phishing scams, identity theft, credit card fraud, and other types of online scams. Cyber fraudsters use a variety of tactics to trick people into giving away sensitive information or money, such as fake websites, emails posing as trustworthy entities, and malicious software. ChatGPT could be used by cybercriminals to write malicious codes and scripts to perpetuate cybercrimes and dishonestly or fraudulently defraud individuals or organizations.

13.4 Regulations and Nonlegal Solutions to Address Crimes Relating to ChatGPT

This section focuses on legal regulations to address the misuse of ChatGPT and cyber awareness/cyber hygiene to combat the misuse of ChatGPT.

13.4.1 Legal Regulations to Address the Misuse of ChatGPT

There are currently no specific legal regulations specifically addressing the misuse of ChatGPT and other language generation models. However, there are several existing laws and regulations that could be applied to address potential misuses of the technology. Cybercrime laws, such as the Information Technology Act of 2000 (India) and the much-awaited Digital India Bill [17], can be used to prosecute individuals or organizations that use ChatGPT to conduct illegal activities such as spreading malware or launching DDoS attacks (Proving the Intent: If law enforcement were investigating the use of ChatGPT in a malicious activity, they would likely collect and analyze various forms of evidence. This might include network logs, chat transcripts, and other digital artifacts that could help to establish a timeline of events and identify the parties involved. They may also use forensic techniques to examine the devices used to carry out the attack and search for evidence of intent, such as the presence of malware or malicious scripts. Additionally, investigators might seek to interview the individuals involved or review their online activity, including social media profiles or forum posts, to understand their motivations and intentions. In some cases, it may be possible to establish a clear intent based on the available evidence, while in others, the evidence may be more circumstantial, requiring the prosecution to make a case based on a pattern of behavior or other indicators. Ultimately, proving intent would require a thorough investigation and evaluation of the available evidence, and the specific methods used would depend on the nature of the attack and the available resources. See further Philipp Hacker, Andreas Engle, and Marco Maurer, Regulating ChatGPT and Other Large Generative AI Models 2023).

At present, there are various provisions under the Information Technology Act, 2000, which can be interpreted to prosecute cyber offenders for crimes committed using ChatGPT. It is important to note that the IT Act, 2000, does not talk about ChatGPT or artificial intelligence, yet its provision might still be effective in combating against crimes committed using emerging technologies. A harmonious reading of the relevant provision of the IT Act, 2000, along with the Indian Penal Code, 1860, can be invoked to prosecute cybercriminals. Table 13.1 given below provides provisions for prosecuting cyber incidents caused using ChatGPT.

It is worth noting that most of these laws are regulations that are not specific to ChatGPT but rather apply to any technology that can be used for similar purposes. However, it is important for regulators to continuously monitor and update the laws and regulations to keep up with the rapid development of the technology.

Table 13.1 Identification/mapping of offences caused by ChatGPTs-IT Act, 2000, with Indian Penal Code, 1860 [18].

Sr. no.	Offences caused using ChatGPT	IT Sections	IPC Sections and Allied Laws
1	Identity Theft and Virtual Forgery (Video, Audio, Photo)	Sec. 66: Computer-Related Offences Sec. 66C: Punishment for Identity Theft	Sec. 420 IPC: Cheating and dishonestly inducing delivery of property and Sec. 468 IPC: Forgery for the purpose of cheating
2	Misinformation subverting and bringing hatred and disaffection against the Government of India (Sedition)	Sec. 66F: Cyber Terrorism The Information Technology (Intermediary Guidelines and Digital Media Ethics Code) Amendment Rules, 2022	Sec. 121 IPC: Waging war against the Government of India Sec. 124A IPC: Sedition

(Continued)

Table 13.1 Identification/mapping of offences caused by ChatGPTs-IT Act, 2000, with Indian Penal Code, 1860. (*Continued*)

Sr. no.	Offences caused using ChatGPT	IT Sections	IPC Sections and Allied Laws
3	Misinformation affecting public tranquility (Hate Speech and Online Defamation)	The Information Technology (Intermediary Guidelines and Digital Media Ethics Code) Amendment Rules, 2022	Sec. 153A IPC: Promoting enmity between different groups Sec. 153B IPC: Assertion prejudicial to national integration Sec. 499 IPC: Defamation
4	Digital Publications using ChatGPT: Corrupt Practices Affecting Elections	Sec. 66D: Punishment for Cheating by Personation by Computer Resource Sec. 66F: Cyber Terrorism	Sec. 417 IPC: Cheating Sec. 123 (3A), Sec. 123, Sec. 125 of Representation of Peoples Act, 1951: Corrupt practices affecting elections Social Media Platforms and Internet and Mobile Association of India (IAMAI), today presented a "Voluntary Code of Ethics for the General Election 2019
5	Violation of Bodily Privacy	Sec. 66E: Punishment for Violation of Privacy	Sec. 354C: Voyeurism Sec. 354D: Stalking
6	DDoS Attacks	Sec. 66: Computer-Related Offences	------
7	Malware and Ransomware Attacks	Sec. 66: Computer-Related Offences	Sec. 387: Extortion

13.4.2 Cyber Awareness/Cyber Hygiene to Combat the Misuse of ChatGPT

Cyber awareness or cyber hygiene refers to the practices and habits individuals and organizations implement to maintain secure and safe use of technology and protect against cyber threats. It includes simple steps such as using strong passwords, updating software and security measures, being cautious about opening emails or links from unknown sources, and backing up data. Good cyber hygiene helps prevent data breaches, identity theft, and other malicious activities in the online world.

To **protect oneself from phishing scams**, it is important to be cautious when receiving unexpected emails or messages, especially if they ask for personal information. Always verify the sender before clicking on any links or entering sensitive information, and be suspicious of emails or messages that contain typos or other signs of being fraudulent.

To **protect oneself from misinformation**, it is important to be a critical consumer of information and to verify the source and accuracy of the information before accepting it as true. This can involve checking multiple sources, looking for credible evidence to support claims, and being aware of potential biases or hidden agendas. Additionally, it is important to help prevent the spread of misinformation by not sharing unverified information and by encouraging others to do the same.

To **protect oneself or someone you know from cyberbullying**, it is important to be aware of the warning signs and to take steps to stop it. This can involve speaking up and telling someone you trust, such as a parent, teacher, or law enforcement, or blocking the person who is bullying you. It is also important to be kind and respectful online and to not engage in cyberbullying yourself.

To protect against DDoS attacks, organizations can implement measures such as having sufficient bandwidth and infrastructure to handle high volumes of traffic, using firewalls and intrusion detection systems to block malicious traffic, and having a plan in place for responding to and recovering from an attack. Additionally, individuals can protect themselves by keeping their devices and networks secure, avoiding clicking on suspicious links or downloading unknown files, and being aware of the signs of a DDoS attack.

To **protect against malware and ransomware attacks**, it is important to keep software and systems up-to-date, use strong passwords, avoid clicking on suspicious links or downloading unknown files, and regularly back up important data. Additionally, organizations can implement security measures such as firewalls, antivirus software, and network segmentation to limit the spread of malware and minimize the impact of an attack.

To **protect oneself from impersonation**, it is important to be aware of the signs of impersonation and to verify the identity of anyone you communicate with online. This can include checking for visual cues such as profile photos or verifying the email address of the sender, as well as being cautious when receiving requests for personal information or clicking on links in emails or messages. Additionally, it is important to report instances of impersonation to the appropriate authorities and to take steps to secure your online accounts and devices.

To **protect against the violation of bodily privacy**, it is important to be cautious about the information you share online and to be aware of the signs of online harassment and exploitation. This can include regularly reviewing privacy settings on social media accounts, avoiding clicking on suspicious links or downloading unknown files, and reporting any instances of online exploitation or harassment to the appropriate authorities. Additionally, organizations can implement measures to ensure that the privacy of their customers and users is protected, including by regularly monitoring systems for signs of malicious activity and implementing strong security controls to prevent unauthorized access to sensitive information.

13.5   Road Ahead for ChatGPT and Emerging Technologies

The rapid advancements in artificial intelligence and natural language processing have set the stage for transformative technologies like ChatGPT. Its future potential is vast and captivating, as it continues to evolve and refine its language generation capabilities. As ChatGPT progresses, it is expected to enhance its contextual understanding, enabling more precise and fitting responses in conversations. Additionally, its development will likely equip it with the ability to proficiently handle multiple languages, making it invaluable in a global and diverse context. As technology marches forward, ChatGPT's human-like interactions will become increasingly impressive, exhibiting an understanding of emotions, sarcasm, and other subtleties of human communication. As AI assumes a more significant role in critical decision-making domains such as healthcare and finance, the demand for explainable AI will grow, enabling models to justify their reasoning and conclusions. While the future trajectory of ChatGPT remains uncertain due to its ongoing evolution, it is anticipated to bring forth numerous benefits and opportunities for society in the years to come.

As an AI language model, ChatGPT relies on vast amounts of data from various sources, such as books, articles, websites, and online content, to generate responses. However, it is not always possible to provide an exhaustive list of sources for a specific response. In situations where AI technology like ChatGPT is utilized in critical decision-making that can have significant legal, ethical, or social consequences, promoting transparency and accountability is crucial. To address this, it is important to consider providing additional context and information regarding the sources used to generate information when ChatGPT is employed to provide such information. This could involve sharing links to relevant articles, studies, or resources that were utilized in generating the response, as well as details about the quality and reliability of those sources. By adopting this approach, users, including law enforcement agencies and banking industries, can evaluate the information provided by ChatGPT and make informed decisions based on reliable and trustworthy sources. Emphasizing transparency and accountability in the implementation of AI is essential for establishing trust and confidence in these technologies. It ensures their ethical, responsible, and unbiased use, especially when they have the potential to impact people's lives in a significant way.

Integrating ChatGPT and other emerging technologies into society requires careful consideration of their limitations and potential for misuse. To mitigate harm and misuse, it is crucial to prioritize ethical considerations and responsible usage of these models.

- Firstly, clear communication regarding the capabilities and limitations of the technology is essential. This helps prevent misunderstandings and misuse by setting realistic expectations and promoting informed use.
- Secondly, implementing protective measures such as content filtering, bias mitigation, and robust data privacy safeguards is crucial. These measures help prevent harm and ensure that the technology is not used to perpetuate biases or compromise personal information.
- Thirdly, promoting transparency in the development, deployment, and usage of language models fosters trust and accountability. Openly sharing information about the model's training data, limitations, and potential biases allows users to make informed judgments about the technology's outputs.

- Fourthly, incorporating ethical considerations in the design and development of language models is essential. This involves avoiding the perpetuation of harmful biases, ensuring data privacy, and proactively addressing potential risks and vulnerabilities.
- Lastly, regulating the use of emerging technologies is necessary to ensure ethical and responsible practices. Establishing standards for deployment, usage, and penalties for the misuse can help guide organizations and individuals in employing these technologies in an accountable and responsible manner.

By adhering to these principles and taking proactive measures, society can harness the benefits of emerging technologies while minimizing potential harm and ensuring their ethical and responsible integration.

13.6   Conclusion

The exploration of ChatGPT's role in the law enforcement and banking sectors has revealed its transformative potential and numerous opportunities for enhancing operational efficiency and customer experiences. ChatGPT stands at the forefront of transforming law enforcement and banking, redefining how information is processed, decisions are made, and services are delivered. Through a responsible and ethical approach, ChatGPT can truly become a driving force for positive change, enriching society's safety, financial well-being, and overall prosperity.

References

1. Flavin, M., *Disruptive Technology Enhanced Learning: The Use and Misuse of Digital Technologies in Higher Education*, Springer, Palgrave Macmillan, 2017.
2. Rahaman, M., Ahsan, M.M., Anjum, N., Rahman, M., Rahman, M.N., The AI race is on! Google's bard and open AI's ChatGPT head to head: An opinion article, 2023. Available at SSRN: https://ssrn.com/abstract=4351785 or http://dx.doi.org/10.2139/ssrn.4351785.
3. The Brain Team: Make machines intelligent. Improve people's lives, Google Research, 2017. https://research.google/teams/brain/. accessed 25th Jan 2023.

4. Kujur, R., What is ChatGPT? A video explaining ChatGPT, an advanced AI-powered ChatGPT that has taken the world by storm. *Hindu*, 23rd Jan 2023. https://www.thehindu.com/sci-tech/technology/watch-what-is-chatgpt/article66423376.ece accessed 18th March 2024.

5. Lund, B.D. and Wang, T., Chatting about ChatGPT: How may AI and GPT impact academia and libraries? *Libr. Hi Tech News.*, 2023. Accessed here at SSRN: https://ssrn.com/abstract=4333415 or http://dx.doi.org/10.2139/ssrn.4333415.

6. Haleem, A., Javaid, M., Singh, R.P., An era of ChatGPT as a significant futuristic support tool: A study on features, abilities, and challenges. *BenchCouncil Trans. Benchmarks, Standards Evaluations*, 6, 4, 100089, 2023.

7. Felten, E., Raj, M., Seamans, R., *How will Language Modelers like ChatGPT Affect Occupations and Industries?*. Cornell University, New York, 2023. arXiv preprint arXiv:2303.01157.

8. Paialunga, P., Hands-on sentiment analysis on hotels reviews using artificial intelligence and open AI's Chat GPT, with python. *Towards Data Sci.*, Dec. 14th, 2022. https://towardsdatascience.com/hands-on-sentiment-analysis-on-hotels-reviews-using-artificial-intelligence-and-open-ais-chatgpt-d1939850c79e accessed 18th March 2024.

9. Mijwil, M. and Aljanabi, M., Towards artificial intelligence-based cybersecurity: The practices and chat GPT generated ways to combat cybercrime. *IJCSM*, 4, 1, 65–70, 2023.

10. Hasal, M., Nowaková, J., Ahmed Saghair, K., Abdulla, H., Snášel, V., Ogiela, L., Chatbots: Security, privacy, data protection, and social aspects. *Concurr. Comput. Pract. Exp.*, 33, 19, e6426, 2021.

11. Asher-Shapiro, A. and Sherfinski, D., Analysis: Chatbots in US justice system raise bias, privacy concerns. *Reuters*, May 11th, 2022. https://www.reuters.com/legal/litigation/chatbots-us-justice-system-raise-bias-privacy-concerns-2022-05-10/#:~:text=Chatbots%20should%20not%20be%20relied,respond%20to%20a%20comment%20request accessed 18th March 2024.

12. Kasneci, E., Seßler, K., Küchemann, S., Bannert, M., Dementieva, D., Fischer, F., Kasneci, G., ChatGPT for good? On opportunities and challenges of large language models for education. *Learn. Individ. Differ.*, 103, 102274, 2023.

13. Zhuo, T.Y., Huang, Y., Chen, C., Xing, Z., *Exploring AI Ethics of Chatgpt: A Diagnostic Analysis*. Monash University, Australia, 2023. arXiv preprint arXiv:2301.12867.

14. Pernet, C., New phishing technique lures users with fake Chatbots. *Tech Republic*, May 23rd 2022. https://www.techrepublic.com/article/new-phishing-technique-chatbot/ accessed 18th March 2024.

15. van Dis, E.A., Bollen, J., Zuidema, W., van Rooij, R., Bockting, C.L., ChatGPT: five priorities for research. *Nature*, 614, 7947, 224–226, 2023.

16. Tlili, A., Shehata, B., Adarkwah, M.A., Bozkurt, A., Hickey, D.T., Huang, R., Agyemang, B., What if the devil is my guardian angel: ChatGPT as a case study of using chatbots in education. *Smart Learn. Environ.*, 10, 1, 15, 2023.

17. Lele, S., Digital India Act to be more principle-based: MoS IT Chandrashekhar. *Business Standard*, Jan. 19th 2023. https://www.business-standard.com/article/economy-policy/digital-india-act-to-be-less-prescriptive-more-principle-based-mos-it-123011901348_1.html accessed 18th March 2024.

18. Pandey S. and Patel A., Leveraging ChatGPT in Law Enforcement. Recent Advances in Computer Science and Communications, *Bentham Sci.*, 17, 2024.

Index

Printed and bound by CPI Group (UK) Ltd, Croydon, CR0 4YY

27/10/2024

14580132-0002